Mirror and Beacon

UNITED METHODIST CHURCH

HISTORY OF MISSION SERIES

Mirror and Beacon

The History of Mission of The Methodist Church, 1939–1968

Linda Gesling

GENERAL BOARD OF GLOBAL MINISTRIES
The United Methodist Church
New York, New York

Published by GBGM BOOKS
Copyright © 2005
The General Board of Global Ministries
The United Methodist Church
475 Riverside Drive
New York, New York 10115

Printed in the United States of America.

Library of Congress
Control Number 2003107309

ISBN 1-890569-69-0 cloth
ISBN 1-890569-75-5 paper

COVER PHOTOS *(clockwise from top left):*
Citrus workers protest, Texas; Bishop John Wesley Shungu,
Republic of the Congo; Japanese-American internment center,
Manzanar, California; returned Korea missionaries;
Hunting Horse being photographed by Toge Fujihira;
missionary Rose Thomas in Angola; *center;* Sara Estelle Haskin.

To my parents
who raised me in The Methodist Church

[Contents]

[Vignettes]

[Illustrations]

[Maps]

[Photographs]

[Foreword]

*M*ORE THAN FIFTY years have passed since a history of mission series was begun by The Methodist Church Board of Missions. Wade Crawford Barclay wrote *Early American Methodism, 1769–1844* as the first of what would become a four-volume series.

In that first volume, Barclay explained that the series was "designed to present a comprehensive, detailed, and accurate history of American Methodism in its character as a Christian missionary movement." He laid out the publishing program as including the content of volume one, early American Methodism, and then the mission histories of the three divisions of mainstream Methodism prior to 1939: the Methodist Episcopal Church (MEC), the so-called northern church; the Methodist Episcopal Church, South (MECS), the so-called southern church; and the Methodist Protestant Church (MPC).

By the time of the third volume, however, Barclay was apologetic: "The writing of this volume has required more time than was anticipated." The second volume had brought the history only up to 1844, and that only of the MEC. The third volume advanced the MEC history to 1895. A fourth volume, written by J. Tremayne Copplestone after Barclay's death, completed the MEC mission work, ending in 1939. With the publication of this volume in 1973, however, the project stopped. The four volumes had taken a quarter century and the Board of Missions had by then evolved into the Board of Global Ministries of a new denomination, The United Methodist Church (UMC). The Board decided the histories did not articulate an adequate vision of mission.

By the end of the twentieth century it seemed apparent to many that a continuation of the history of mission was needed. There were several reasons. The Women's Division almost alone in The UMC had continued to educate an important constituency about mission, supporting the National Council of Churches of Christ in its publication of annual mission resources and publishing many resources of its own. When the NCC found it could no longer continue publishing these books, the Women's Division led the General Board of Global Ministries to continue their publication. The Women's Division more than most was conscientious in publishing works about mission. Yet many in the rest of the denomination remained untouched by any serious study of mission, present or past.

A second large reason consisted of the bridges that had gone under the water since the conclusion of the Barclay/Copplestone series. The history of mission of The Methodist Church, in existence from 1939 to 1968, had never been written. The history of mission of the Evangelical United Brethren, in existence from 1946 to 1968, had never been written. Since these two merged to become The United Methodist Church, critical changes had occurred in the comprehension, strategy, and practice of mission in the newly united denomination. The very nature of the denominations had altered greatly in relation to the rest of the culture and in relation to the ecumenical movement. A need existed to write all these histories taking these changes into account. Furthermore, the MECS and MPC histories needed to be written and published.

A third reason lay in the religious and cultural changes that affected the way history is conceived and written. At the time Barclay began his series, women were almost totally absent from the official leadership of the mainline churches. African Americans, Hispanics, Asian Americans, and Native Americans were not well represented in that leadership. Bishops, officers of the major program boards like the Board of Missions of The Methodist Church, and other denominational officials consisted almost entirely of white men.

The need, then, was to develop a history of mission that did justice to the role of women, ethnic minorities in the United States, and also indigenous leaders in various countries. For most of the histories of mission previously published had ignored the leadership and contributions of indigenous leaders as well.

Finally, the field of history itself had changed. Chronicles of official events and even large-scale interpretations, or "metahistories," had given way to more detailed studies of local and culturally specific developments. "Thick description" was preferred to chronicles of facts and dates. Traditional histories are still being written, those that take a large field and attempt to provide an overriding image or concept for interpretation and those that relate personal histories. These efforts, while entertaining and even popular, eventually fail because of their biases, the inevitable inability of a single historian to know that large field, or simply because they ignore the diversity of the human race.

This series might seem to be attempting such large-scale interpretations. Writers were advised to provide an interpretive framework while avoiding the attempt to create "repositories of facts," to "provide readable narratives" that would be placed "within the context of culture/religion interaction." We were keenly aware of the dangers of attempting histories "from the center," as it were, rather than "from the periphery," that is, from the perspective of previously neglected people. We hoped, however, that by breaking the histories into periods of fairly brief epochs and by seeking diligently to give voice to the voiceless inasmuch as the historical record allowed, we could fill the vacuum left in mission history since the conclusion of the Barclay/Copplestone series.

We hoped even more that we could produce histories that might be actually read by United Methodists and others committed to mission. This may seem an even more dubious undertaking, since the advent of electronic media has threatened to abolish reading entirely. Yet the publication of books and magazines on the electronic media itself gives us some hope that reading may extend into the next generation.

The General Board of Global Ministries (GBGM), through grants provided by the office of the general secretary, initiated the "United Methodist History of Mission" in 1999. It was conceived as a way to accomplish four goals:

1. To complete the outlines of the history of mission of The Methodist Church and its predecessors as given in *The History of Methodist Missions* by Wade Crawford Barclay and J. Tremayne Copplestone.

2. To provide readable narratives or thematic treatments that can be used by both scholars and the general church membership.

3. To do justice to the contributions of women, ethnic minorities, and indigenous leaders to the history of mission.

4. To provide the basis for a video and other resources to be used in orienting GBGM staff and missionaries in our history.

This volume is one of a series that will consist of the following:

- the history of mission of the Methodist Protestant Church, 1830–1939
- the history of mission of the Methodist Episcopal Church, South, 1845–1939
- the history of mission of The Methodist Church, 1939–1968

- the history of mission of the Evangelical United Brethren, 1946–1968
- the history of mission of The United Methodist Church, 1968–2000
- reflections on Christian mission in the early decades of the third millennium of Christian history
- first-person accounts of presidents and directors of the United Methodist General Board of Global Ministries in undertaking significant mission initiatives from 1980 to 2002.

These histories are dedicated to past and present generations of Methodists, EUBs, and United Methodists who helped to fulfill the commitment "to reform the Continent and to spread scriptural Holiness over these lands." They are also offered in the hope that future generations will find in them not only information and interpretation of Christian mission but inspiration to continue that mission in the future. Although a reading of these histories will reveal failures as well as successes, contemporary Christians cannot but be grateful for the accomplishments of our foreparents in the faith. "We feebly struggle, they in glory shine."

Charles E. Cole, EDITOR

CHAPTER 1

Union, Organization, and Philosophy

*T*HE DENOMINATION KNOWN as The Methodist Church existed for twenty-nine years—from 1939 to 1968. The years of its beginning and ending were both arguably "watershed" years during the tumultuous twentieth century. To begin to understand the achievements, challenges, and even failures of the church is to examine the context in which ministry took place. In 1939, Germany was expanding its dominance over Europe. Japan's influence was increasing in Asia. A major independence movement was flourishing in India. International events often made their way into the headlines in the United States, but economic news continued to occupy the thoughts of most citizens, still in the throes of the longest depression in U.S. history. Change was in the air.

And in Kansas City, Missouri, on the 26th of April 1939, the Uniting Conference brought together 4,684,444 members from the Methodist Episcopal Church (MEC); 2,847,351 from the Methodist Episcopal Church, South (MECS); and 197,996 from the Methodist Protestant Church (MPC).[1] The merger was more of a family reunion than a creation of a new body. A century earlier all three had been part of the same body, only to split over the issues of slavery, the rights of laypeople, and concerns about power. The coming together was not a surprise, nor was it necessarily destined to be a big adjustment for either worshipers or most administrators. But the "family together" again did not mean that many of the issues that had divided it had been resolved. Nonetheless, the merger made The Methodist Church the largest Protestant denomination of its time.

The year 1968 opened with the U.S. involvement in Vietnam still white hot. Major battles abroad caused major battles at home over policy and commitment. President Lyndon Johnson, elected four years earlier by a huge margin, chose not to run for another term. Four days after his announcement to that effect, the Reverend Martin Luther King, Jr., was assassinated while preparing to defend the economic rights of sanitation workers in Memphis, Tennessee. Cities around the country erupted in violent reaction to the loss. In Prague, Czechoslovakians sought new political freedoms, only to have Soviet tanks roll in to crush the protests. Presidential candidate Robert Kennedy, heir to the family magic and mantle, was assassinated just as he claimed victory in the California primary in June. The year unfolded even more surprises. Determined to keep order in his city, Chicago Mayor Richard Daley authorized the use of force against demonstrators at the Democratic National Convention. The country watched in amazement as the police and National Guard troops clubbed and dragged protesters from the streets. Richard Nixon was elected president. And on Christmas Eve, three astronauts orbited the moon, sending back pictures of a blue-green world hanging in the vastness of space. For those who lived through it, 1968 was unforgettable.

In the middle of that year of endings and beginnings, a new church was born: The United Methodist Church. With its birth came the end of The Methodist Church and its twenty-nine years of ministry and mission.

In between the tumultuous years of 1939 and 1968 were twenty-nine years of war, economic recovery, racial tensions, gender rights struggles, and advances in technology. The wars ranged from worldwide to bitter and violent independence conflicts within countries. Borders and alliances changed. Economic recovery efforts absorbed attention in the U.S. and abroad. Women asked for more recognition of their work both within the church and in society in general. Evaluation of the racial segregation and discrimination affected laws, societal customs, and education both in the U.S. and in other places where The Methodist Church was active. The depth of these changes began to be reflected in the music that emerged toward the end of this era. Lines from the song "The Times They Are A-Changin'" represent the difficulties these fundamental changes presented as individuals and institutions tried to cope:

> Come gather 'round people
> Wherever you roam
> And admit that the waters
> Around you have grown
> And accept it that soon

> You'll be drenched to the bone.
> If your time to you
> Is worth savin'
> Then you better start swimmin'
> Or you'll sink like a stone
> For the times they are a-changin'.

The song goes on to name writers, politicians, and parents as being among those who are struggling to cope with all that is happening. "For he that gets hurt/will be he who has stalled" admonish the lyrics. The words are not about any one event but the culmination of accelerating and bewildering changes that were touching the entire society. The song ends with words evocative of Scripture:

> The line it is drawn
> The curse it is cast
> The slow one now
> Will later be fast
> As the present now
> Will later be past
> The order is
> Rapidly fadin'.
> And the first one now
> Will later be last
> For the times they are a-changin'.[2]

But mid-twentieth–century listeners found such predictions as uncomfortable as did the hearers of Jesus nearly two millennia previously. What did all the change mean? How were people to act when so many lines were shifting — political borders, values, gender roles? As the largest Protestant denomination in the U.S. during this era, The Methodist Church can be examined as a mirror of the dilemmas and difficulties in the society at large. The diversity of its members in age, class, race, and geography gave it a far greater range of experience than many other denominations that were more ethnic, more geographically diverse, or more confined to one strata of society. But as an institution, the denomination wanted also to be a beacon of hope, love, and justice, shedding light on a changing world. During this midcentury era, the church lived out both of these metaphors. Just as did those in the surrounding culture, so also the members and institutions of The Methodist Church struggled to keep up with societal developments in the understanding of racism and sexism, in deepening conversation in theology, in meeting both social and spiritual needs for people, and in responding to the needs and changes on a global scale. Many members were comfortable with the world as it was, wanting church time to be a retreat from the challenges of the changing world. At the same time, the denomination initiated programs and made statements to push for higher standards of economic and racial justice for all people, challenged accepted gender roles, and provided resources to examine developing theologies.

The story of these accomplishments and struggles took place in many arenas and forms. One significant piece of that story has recently been told by Alice G. Knotts in *Fellowship of Love: Methodist Women Changing American Racial Attitudes, 1920–1968*. Knotts's work adds depth and context to an earlier publication by Thelma Stevens entitled *Legacy for the Future*. Knott's description of the goals of the newly formed organization describe the objective as "a new social order, a world in which people would be treated fairly, where there would be no artificial barriers of race, and where people could live in peace."[3] Although this book focuses specifically on the race question and the way that women in the church approached it, it makes a major contribution to the study of the mission objectives of the church through this period. Much of the leadership for change in racial attitudes and practices came from the Woman's Division, part of the Board of Missions.

Herman Will has also chronicled the efforts of the church to be a beacon in another aspect of its ministry. His book, *A Will for Peace*, looks at peace efforts and actions in The United Methodist Church and its predecessors. Although concerned with a different agency of the church (the Board of Church and Society), it also attempts to assess the actions of the church, setting them against the broader canvas of society.

Other important work has been done on the Central Jurisdiction, including *Heritage and Hope* by Grant S. Shockley and *Methodism's Racial Dilemma* by James S. Thomas. These texts provide critical information about the way the formation of The Methodist Church included racial divide in its very structure.

Implicit in these studies of church bodies was and is a Wesleyan approach and theology that has permeated the denomination without becoming doctrine. The theology is based on an understanding of grace that is available to all. Wesley preached that God is always working in the hearts of humans, making them ready for further expansion and growth in love. Response to God's calling, repentance, and commitment, then, become part of the process of justification and sanctification that is the Christian life. Wesley's understanding of salvation was that of God's action and human response — the response of changed hearts and changed lives. This theology led first to a zeal to share the good news with everyone. Wesley's traveling ministry has been a major model for the way the church has understood the ordained ministry. It was duplicated first by traveling preachers in Great Britain and soon after by men in the colonies and the new country of the United States. Wesley found no limits to the area of ministry, claiming, "The world is my parish."

Theology also led to a method. The mission of all Christians was to continue to share this good news, which Wesley made into a call to spread scriptural holiness throughout the land. From its beginnings on the North American continent, the church was on the move, growing in number and in mission. No limits were placed on where it might go. While other denominations argued over how to define "home" missions or who should be in charge, Methodists were sending out preachers and adding circuits and even conferences as needed. To be sent to a new place, to travel and preach in different circumstances, to empower local people to take some responsibility for the worship life made the life of the traveling preacher different from that of congregational pastors, who settled down more quickly and relied on voluntary mission societies to spread the work of the church.[4] Mission was the very core of the way the church went about its work.

But eventually the church expanded enough in North America that it began to consider its mission to other parts of the world. The first Methodist missionaries to go abroad went to Liberia in 1832. At the time of the church's division in 1844, this remained the only mission work outside the continental U.S. In 1847, however, both the Northern and the Southern branches of the church entered China. Ten years later, missionaries from the Northern branch began to enter India, though the numbers were still quite small. China and India remained the two major foci of mission efforts for many years. Missionary societies coordinated the efforts of these men and their wives. In 1869, the first single women missionaries sent abroad by specifically Methodist societies sailed for India. To achieve this possibility, women had organized their own society and began raising their own funds. The story of these women of the MEC inspired women in the MPC and the MECS to form their own societies. Each created strong ministries of education, medicine, evangelism, and other work targeted especially to women and children. These separate efforts represent a significant development in Methodism. Division of the work by gender at the national level allowed women to move into positions of greater visibility and power, even though these positions were originally mostly unpaid.

The story of those efforts and all that followed quickly diverged along three paths. The classic work for the study of missionaries in the MEC is the *History of Methodist Missions*, by Wade Barclay and J. Tremayne Copplestone. The value of this work is its great attention to detail, its chronicling of the institutional dilemmas that accompanied the missionary task, and its inclusion of women.[5] More than forty years since its publication, this book remains the most complete record of names, dates, and events in the major fields of Methodist mission. In the preface, Barclay noted some of the same questions about missionaries that have motivated this present study. He asked about the identification of the church with Western culture and industrialization as well as the possibility of the church's achieving its ideal of creating the Kingdom of God on earth. He has a purpose for the church in his history, however. The painstaking inclusion of names and dates is part of a "means of bringing to the ministry and laity of the Church a measure of clearer realization of the tremendous scope and difficulty of the Christian missionary task, and a challenge to deeper consecration and greater effort toward its fulfillment."[6]

This current work shares the former half of that purpose, updating the church and the general public on the scope of the task, adding evaluation of the ways that Methodists fulfilled these goals. While it was appropriate for Barclay to see his work as a challenge to greater effort, the present work is only one source to be added to others to aid in understanding the past and in discerning future directions for both the church and society. It aims to become one study among many. Some stories will be told from denominational perspectives; others from the point of view of one country or another or one kind of mission ministry. Within this plurality of stories, The Methodist Church offers a very special kind of window for looking onto the era and assessing the influence of the church in it. By examining the responses of the Board of Missions to the varying conditions of country, circumstance, world events, and even personality, one begins to see how a single group of Christians with a particular goal faced the immense changes and challenges of the mid-twentieth century.

Approach of the Study

The increased record keeping as well as the scope of Methodist missions during the twentieth century means that one volume cannot do justice to names and places in the way Barclay was able to with his earlier studies. With this in mind, one can consider this current study as having several purposes. The form it takes is designed best to achieve several very different objectives.

At the most basic level, it remains important to have in essay form some of the names, dates, institutions, and places that were part of the mission of The Methodist Church during its existence. Lists and tables are arranged by quadrennium in the appendixes. Although these are also available in more expanded form in the specific journals and reports, their inclusion here carries forth the spirit of Barclay's work in naming names and allowing the scope of the work in terms of geography, personnel, and budget to be easily accessible. This information is presented with the belief that easy access to some basic facts will help church members and others continue to claim their history. Maps are included to illustrate further the extent of the endeavors.

A second purpose of the work is to follow the development of the church's own definition of its task, moving from a focus on missionaries and missions to mission. In part, this might be viewed as a reflection of the evolution of the words in society. Words like "missionary" had come to carry a heavy weight, in part because of the publication of books like James Michener's *Hawaii*, which, although fiction, became sources of information about the colonial power attitudes of the missionaries. Even the word "missions" still conjures up for some the slaveholder-like practices associated with stories of the mission to Native Americans. By examining the publications and public discussions, however, one can look for the ways that those closely associated with the endeavors — whether board members, staff, missionaries, or other church leaders — tried to identify the work as "mission," integrating this kind of work into the life of the church in a new way. This effort was not universally accepted or even thought necessary, but the changing terminology helps to identify the evolving spirit and theology that is unfolded in these chapters.

Three different uses of the word "mission" in the popular culture in the last third of this era add further meaning and symbolism to the way the work will be explored in this volume. First, when the U.S. began sending people into space, "mission control" was the nerve center of the endeavor. But by the time mission control seemed to have become an all-knowing center of the space program, The Methodist Church knew that no one place was mission control for it any longer. The board and staff gave direction, support, and leadership. Reports and discussions kept communication lines open. Increasingly, those in mission — on site — had to make significant decisions as crises developed. In addition, the concern with transferring power to the national or indigenous churches in principle decreased the control of the board. Mission control was a contested arena for the church — philosophically by some, in real situations by many others.

Another use of the word "mission" in popular culture appeared in the title of a weekly television drama: *Mission: Impossible.* During the Cold War era, such shows had no trouble creating traps, dilemmas, puzzles, and other dangers and difficulties for the protagonists, whose mission, always on the side of the good, seemed impossible. Helping them achieve their goals were clever items of technology that caught the imagination of the viewers as much as did the story itself. Missions were not impossible; good triumphed. The work of the missionaries proceeded without fancy gadgets but with the awareness that new technologies offered possibilities. Given limited resources, the church asked questions about practicality and, increasingly, about method as well. How could new technologies help make a greater impact? What is good development? Yet the underlying question for some in church and in the society at large was even more important: What is the mission now, and is it even possible?

Finally, yet another television show opened each week with a description of the five-year mission of the characters. Ironically, they were being asked to go where "no humans had gone before," to encounter new civilizations and situations in much the same way that the missionaries had originally done. Adventure had moved from the earth's surface to other worlds. Encounter with "the other" was still an event that needed more discussion and exploration.

Given the negativity that had become attached to "missions," though not to "mission," it is not surprising that such events no longer took place on earth. The problems of colonization, civilization, freedom, and

Methodist work among Native Americans concentrated on the Oklahoma Indian Conference, but congregations, community centers, and other ministries were carried on in the Four Corners area, North Carolina, Michigan, New York State, and other areas. *(Map courtesy of United Methodist Archives and History)*

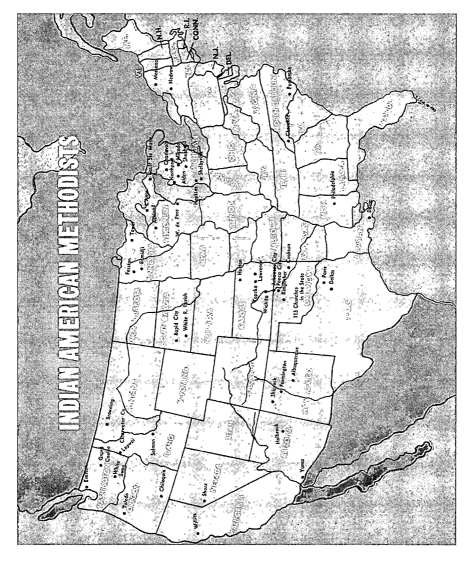

communication were too vexed to be seen as entertainment unless they were placed in a more inventive context. Meanwhile, in the name of Christianity and its spread, The Methodist Church continued to grapple with the meaning of colonization, civilization, freedom, and communication — *mission control, mission possible, mission explore*.

The main focus of this text, however, is to tell a story—a story of people and their institution, driven by a biblical commandment to spread the good news. The vision and its implementation were not new with the institution, nor were they particular to it. But several questions help to focus the telling of the story. How did the church and individuals articulate the theology and its outcome in the work done under the Board of Missions? How did the church respond to the challenges that interrupted the day-in, day-out plans for mission? The way people tried to live out the command and the vision for twenty-nine years is an exciting adventure.

Asia, Africa, North and South America, even parts of Europe — the Methodist mission took different forms in each place. To follow the particularities of each place is not the purpose of this volume, although each has its very own history. Rather, this work retrieves stories and circumstances that illuminate how the church did its work, how theology informed decisions, how outside events shaped development, how individuals contributed to a legacy. This history is representational rather than exhaustive, with the story organized around chronological themes, continuing the view of the church in the wider setting of society. Since race and gender were both contested issues within the church during this era, they are very much a part of the story.

Scattered throughout the book are short biographical sketches of persons who were associated with the work of the Board of Missions of The Methodist Church. The subjects of these vignettes are somewhat randomly chosen, but each represents the different kinds of persons who answered the call to mission, the form that different ministries took, and even the differing theology and experiences brought to mission and taken from it.

The mission of The Methodist Church was so comprehensive that the work of the Board of Missions often overlapped with the work of other agencies. Already books and articles have been written detailing many of the organizations and ministries, some of which are key to this story. Enough background on those stories is included here to give shape to the total picture, but since more detail is available in other sources, as noted, some of these areas will not receive the space and weight they might otherwise command.

Birth of the New Church

Creating the new church took much effort. A significant part of this endeavor was considering the program work of each of the merging churches, and more specifically how to structure the new institution to allow the functioning ministries to continue and grow. This was especially true for the mission activities of the three denominations. Coordinating the work the former churches had done within a structure new to all involved proved a challenge. Duplicate staff positions had to be combined and literature coordinated. Yet in many ways the mission work was an administrative challenge, and not a theological one. As early as the 1920s, the predecessor denominations had in their own ways begun a policy of nationalization of the ministries outside the U.S., establishing procedures and directions that would lead to autonomy for the churches begun by missionaries around the world. Plans for the future focused on how best to continue the work as already defined rather than whether to change it in any significant ways.

The new church created the Board of Missions and Church Extension to bring together mission work — "home" and "foreign," general and woman's — of all three denominations. With this legislation, nine different bodies came together to work as one. Anxiety about getting all the details in place in time was felt among both staff and board members. Paragraph 913 of the 1940 *Book of Discipline* listed all the agencies that were to be created to carry out the mission work of the church, not limiting the work to only those.

As agreed by the General Conference, the stated purpose of the agency was "to make the Lord Jesus Christ known to all peoples in all lands as their divine Savior, to persuade them to become his disciples, and to gather these disciples into Christian churches; to enlist them in the building of the Kingdom of God; to cooperate with these churches; to promote world Christian fellowship; and to bring to bear on all human life the spirit and principles of Christ."

This paragraph became the center from which all else flowed. It still provides a way to test the work of the board through those twenty-nine years. One can examine the ways in which the Methodists sought to tell about Jesus Christ and his salvific message, how they developed churches for and with the new followers, how they related to these churches, and how they defined the meaning of Christian life for themselves and anyone who would join them.

Having defined such a goal, it was necessary to establish a structure for its implementation. Administering the work were three divisions. The Division of Foreign Missions, in cooperation with the Department of Work in Foreign Fields of the Woman's Division, formulated plans and policies for administration of missions outside the U.S., particularly those relating to the areas and scope of the work, and made recommendations to the board for approval. An interdivision committee coordinated and correlated program for areas outside the U.S. This interdivision committee was important because most of the geographic areas of mission were served by personnel from both divisions. Missionary couples applied and served under the Division of Foreign Missions. Single women served in the Woman's Division.

The structure continued the practices of the three uniting churches that had developed historically in response to particular situations or needs. Mission work had been an area where women had managed to have significant and noticeable impact. Denied the opportunity to serve under the Missionary Society of the MEC, women had organized and funded their own structure in 1869. Similar organizations had been established in the MECS (1878) and the MPC (1879) as well. Working with men in many places around the world, missionary women often had far more autonomy and leadership opportunity than in either local churches or the denominational structure in the U.S. They were determined to keep that autonomy in the church, even at a time when women in other denominations were merging their missionary organizations with those of the men.

In the united church, mission within the U.S. and its territories (not including the Philippines) was coordinated by the Division of Home Missions and Church Extension. Its charge described work relating to the spiritual meaning of Methodism, as well administering donation aid, loans, and endowments for the work of church extension. Four departments divided the agencies and ministries: City Work (for populations of more than 10,000), Town and Country, Goodwill Industries, and Negro Work. At the time of the merger, three-quarters of the work was done through Goodwill Industries, which began in Boston in 1902. While the original aim of the organization was to provide work for the Irish immi-

Bishop Arthur J. Moore entered The Methodist Church from The Methodist Episcopal Church, South, was elected the first president of the Methodist Board of Missions, and became a well-known spokesman for the denomination's mission. *(Photo courtesy of United Methodist Archives and History)*

grants who experienced great discrimination, by 1939 the purpose was to provide for the religious, educational, social, and industrial welfare of the "handicapped and unfortunate." Not all branches were affiliated with The Methodist Church, but the department was established to coordinate all those that did. Over the years, a decreasing number remained affiliated with The Methodist Church.

The Woman's Division of Christian Service brought together work done in each church by several agencies. The resulting purpose was to "develop and maintain Christian work among women and children at home and abroad; to cultivate Christian family life; to enlist and organize the efforts of Christian women, young people, and children in behalf of native and foreign groups, needy childhood and community welfare; to assist in the promotion of a missionary spirit throughout the Church; to select, train, and maintain Christian workers; to cooperate with the local church in its responsibilities, and to seek fellowship with Christian women of this and other lands in establishing a Christian social order around the world."

The work of the Joint Division of Education and Cultivation was to give support to the total program through the preparation, publication, and circulation of books, literature, and periodicals. The division also promoted the development of a missionary spirit throughout the church through meetings, conventions, and means of spreading information.

The *Discipline* spelled out participation in the boards and agencies. Paragraph 940 set out the Executive Committee — nine from the Division on Foreign Missions, nine from Home Missions and Church Extension, and eighteen from the Woman's Division. This arrangement gave women a far more significant voice on this agency than in any other place in the new church. This fact set apart this agency for the entire life of The Methodist Church. In addition, special note was made that the board of the Woman's Division was to be composed of one-third youth representatives.

A key provision in Paragraph 1054 specified that Woman's Division funds were to be kept separate. Since the beginning of a Woman's Foreign Missionary Society in both the MEC and the MECS, the women had raised and expended their own monies in the mission work.[7] Although the new structure pulled together a variety of agencies, this separation of funds continued. This meant that funding for the divisions within the board came from different sources. The Woman's Division money was raised by local units and sent on to the national office, where it became part of that particular budget. The other divisions of the board were funded through the same apportionment system that funded all the other administrative outreach work of the General Conference. At a time when funding for women's organizations in other denominations was being merged with the funding for the general church, Methodists maintained the tradition of separate funding provided by different sources. This tradition of separate funding and its resulting effect on the power structure remained a constant theme of mission discussion throughout the entire twenty-nine years.

Missionary Theory and History

Decisions about missionary endeavors continued to follow the patterns that had evolved in the predecessor churches. Understanding the evolution of those ideas is aided by a number of recent publications that have clearly pointed out questions about culture, race, gender, and theology.

Some of the same cultural concerns named by Barclay were examined by William Hutchison in his book *Errand to the World*, published in 1987. This was an important addition to missionary research because the author laid out a framework that allowed room for understanding the variety of approaches taken by missionaries in encountering other cultures. He also gave space for the contributions of women. Hutchison's work could almost be characterized as a secular approach, in the sense that he looked at the U.S. character rather than the religious nature of the work of the missionary — contrasting developments in missionary thought and theory with themes in the society at large.

In this book, Hutchison uses arguments from H. Richard Niebuhr's *Christ and Culture* as a framework for examining the difficulties the missionaries faced. In general, missionaries represented their culture in ways that they celebrated rather than questioned. On the other hand, they also maintained a fairly critical view about the way U.S. culture did not live up to Christian ideals.[8] Hutchison pinpointed three areas of tension for the missionaries. One was the awareness of the sins of the sending culture. The model missionaries may have held up abroad in their evangelizing efforts was one they knew to be an ideal, not a reality. This distinction — understood by many missionaries — was missed by most people in the cultures they attempted to evangelize and continues to be missed by many historians.[9] A second tension was that some missionaries questioned the superiority of what they were offering in mission, either because of slavery (de Casas) or because the new culture had better qualities (Roger Williams). Finally, some questioned whether the message from the culture did indeed drown out the gospel.[10] All three of these tensions were present in the experiences of Methodist missionaries.

A further example from the "Christ and culture" tension is seen in the way that missionaries responded. Some focused on "Christ only" and were accused of ignoring the pain and suffering around them. Others began to respond to the great human need they saw, or they recognized the cultural imperialism of which they were a part and made a socially oriented witness. They could be criticized for promoting Western technology. The vast majority, who felt caught somewhere in the middle, went about their business only to be accused of insular thinking.[11]

What Hutchison set up in this analysis was a more complex understanding of both the missionaries and their task. The links he drew to the present were his way of reminding the reader that in studying this history we are not always looking back with enlightened eyes that now can see the most culturally sensitive way to do things. Rather, the tensions are inherent in Christian theology itself.

Another scholar who has given further insight into this tension is Lamin Sanneh. His 1989 work, *Translating the Message: The Missionary Impact on Culture*, provided an approach to the work of missionaries that focused on the way Christianity has always interacted with culture, an interaction that had effects in both directions. Using illustrations from his native continent of Africa, he countered the idea that Christian mission is by nature imperialistic. Instead, he emphasized the missionary nature of the faith as a strength that allowed continuing revelation of the ways that the religion had meaning in differing settings. The very fact that missionaries took the time to translate the Bible into other languages allowed understanding of the meaning of the faith to grow. In addition, the very use of other languages – contrasted, for example, with the importance of the Arabic version of the Koran – meant that Christianity continued to add symbols and meanings from other cultures.

Questioning the method and the meaning of missionary work has existed side by side with an attitude that would leave it unquestioned as a component of church life. One important early missionary to contribute to this reflection was Rufus Anderson, who was active and writing from the mid-1830s through the 1870s.[12] He believed that the proper pattern for missionaries was that they go in, proclaim the gospel and a new set of morals for society, and then leave. This theory was buttressed by his millennialism and his belief in the Holy Spirit and its work.[13] In other words, Anderson believed that the message was powerful enough that, once heard, listeners would be inspired to do the work themselves. Teaching should be done in the indigenous language, with as little intrusion of the missionaries' own culture as possible. Anderson, by virtue of his position with the American Baptist Board of Foreign Missions, had both an audience and credibility. He stands out in a study of missionary history and theory because his position, existing alongside traditions that made the work a subsidiary of a larger colonialism, was increasingly championed in the late-twentieth century as a more enlightened way to do mission. In giving significant attention to Anderson, Hutchison's work served to remind current historians of the ambiguities that have influenced North American missionaries to other lands since the beginning.

An important alternative view can be found in George E. Tinker's *Missionary Conquest*, which focuses on the gospel and Native American cul-

Eliza Bowman College, founded in 1900 in Cienfuegos, Cuba, served as one
of several secondary schools under the auspices of The Methodist Church.
Mission for Methodists often took the form of founding schools, colleges,
seminaries, hospitals, community centers, and other institutions. *(Photo
courtesy of United Methodist Archives and History)*

tural genocide. Although his examples center around the mission to Native Americans, he illustrates the ways in which paternalism often remained and remains even today a part of the approach. He is also critical
of the way that missionaries, in his terms, "usurp" some of the symbols of
the culture.[14] Such a study provides a counterpoint to Sanneh as well as a
way of evaluating the work from another point of view.

Dana Robert has documented the historiography of American Protestant missions in the last forty years in a 1994 article in the *International
Bulletin of Missionary Research*. This article is very comprehensive both in
the material it surveys and the analysis of the various approaches. She
notes that the pluralizing of missionary history owed its development to
the collapse of a consensus in understanding the meaning of "American."
No longer white, male, middle- to upper-class Protestant in definition, the
exploration of activities of those called American now included more mar-
ginalized religious groups as well as white women and men and women of
color.

Robert summarized the specific contribution that further research on missionary women can add both to feminist history and missionary history. In particular, she noted the need to account for women's piety as a factor affecting their actions directly rather than treating it as a cover for cultural imperialism. In general, feminist historians have not understood or given much credence to the faith dimension of the lives they have studied. What Robert pointed to is the need for histories that find ways to account for that part of the story. Her reminder is taken seriously in this work. The theological supports, though not mentioned as often as she mentioned them, are as much a part of the story as is the infrastructure of buildings and institutions.[15]

A number of recent publications look at missionary theory and history, taking into account the work of women, giving greater sensitivity to cultural issues. An important emerging source of evaluative materials comes from the "receiving cultures" themselves, where men and women, particularly in Asia and Africa, evaluate what difference Christianity has made, taking seriously the cultural imperialism and implications of the proselytizing activities.

Methodism and Vocation

Also taken into account in this study is the theological basis that both inspired and supported the work of missions and missionaries. Understanding this starting point provided both the backbone of belief for all missionaries encountered and sought to accomplish, as well as the necessary adaptability to incorporate change in their own lives and even to attempt to bring change to the church. Methodism reflected an emphasis on education for the development of the individual and a life of piety — "a living, energetic, all-conquering piety."[16]

Key to understanding Methodism is the way its founder, John Wesley, preached the gospel, emphasizing the aspects of grace mentioned earlier. In his understanding, Christians' response to the forgiving grace of God is shown by their works in the world. These works do not earn the grace but are a response to it. For Methodists, faith and action are inseparable in the Christian life. Admonitions and reminders are found within the *Discipline* that personal salvation has always involved Christian mission and service to the world. Wesley believed that salvation meant a heart habitually filled with the love of God and neighbor and having the mind of Christ.

Olin Stockwell was a missionary to China who initially believed the church could survive under the Communist government after the long civil war that ended in 1949. As a lifetime missionary, he typified the traditional missionary who traveled to a distant part of the world, learned the language and the culture of the people, and planned to spend his entire career in one country. *(Photo courtesy of United Methodist Archives and History)*

Within Methodism is the understanding of vocation, defined as an approach to life that takes seriously a call from God about one's life and its meaning. In taking seriously that call, one becomes responsible for how time is spent, whether or not it is in a job that earns wages, in a way compatible with Christian theology. Vocation is empowering in the sense that persons feel a purpose in their lives, that they are a part of a larger plan.

They are not just planning activity and work in a vacuum but are responding to a larger call. Books like *Spirituality and Social Responsibility*, edited by
Rosemary Keller, demonstrate the ways that taking vocation into account
can give further insight into the choices individuals of faith make in their
lives.[17] The essays in this book show that it is possible and fruitful to talk
about faith and accomplishment without lapsing into hagiography. All
Methodists were called to service and mission. What form that took was
very individual—sometimes ordained, sometimes lay, sometimes paid, often volunteer. In the tradition of Wesley, the ways Methodists live their
everyday lives became the outward manifestation of the depth of their
faithfulness. Telling stories of a variety of persons has been one of the
ways the church has passed on this legacy and expectation.

Methods for carrying out missionary tasks flow from theology, as
James S. Thomas illustrated. He contended that, within the Methodist
tradition, theology has always needed to be practical, and when it finds a
way it both produces and emerges from polity.[18]

Issues at Union

Most of the resources named above are carefully researched works, designed to answer scholarly questions. For this history, a number of works
will be studied that are considered to have been influential in explaining
or determining policy or in some other way making an impact on the
church and how it conducted its mission. These works give insight into
the thinking of the era, often setting out goals and analysis. Even more,
they provide an understanding of the measure that would then be used by
those with decision-making power to evaluate and develop further policy.
These published essays, sermons, or opinion pieces were often written
with the purpose of inspiring persons to action or influencing legislation
at various levels of the church's life. These are very different goals from
those of the academic pieces mentioned above.

John R. Mott, a Methodist layperson, is synonymous with international
missionary enterprise for the first half of the twentieth century. He com-
manded great respect and attention, giving his 1939 book *Methodists
United for Action* authority in its discussions of what the Methodists faced
as a new church. His assessments are helpful in recapturing the concerns
of the merger and the vision for mission.

Mott identified themes related to methods and goals early in the book.

Regarding method, he praised the way that the board continued to find ways to use small amounts of resources—both personnel and money—to achieve significant results. Targeting particular cities, using students to reach out to larger groups, and even choosing nations to be in leadership to others were methods that he felt had worked and would continue to work. These elements for successful mission recur from time to time throughout the Methodist story. But his comment on the ultimate goal was most telling. He further noted that Methodists were the ones who could play a leading role in the shift to an indigenous church. He was stating again and anew the understanding that Christian leadership from persons from the U.S. was temporary in its very nature in many places in the world.

Of major importance to Mott was his belief that *the goal of the missionaries was to work themselves out of a job.*[19] This was not something new, but a policy that the newly formed church would continue. How to make this reality was the challenge that faced the board, the missionaries, and the church leadership during the entire existence of The Methodist Church. How the church accomplished its task with limited resources and how it worked toward a goal of indigenization are themes continually addressed in the present work.

Frankness about the difficulties also came easily for Mott. He did not ignore the pitfalls of pride, whether they were personal, denominational, or spiritual. All three churches had fears as well as hopes about the merger and what it meant to efforts already in progress. In particular, the women of the churches were concerned about their work. Mott raised the issue himself, hoping that what had been organized for the new denomination would safeguard their efforts. He noted the tendency on the part of the men to ignore women in the setup and conduct of organizations. Even though women were a majority of the membership of the merging churches, only one woman served on the Committee on Interdenominational Relations of the new denomination; she was from the MECS. Only five of the twenty-five members of the Committee on Missions were women. So often in the life of the church, these issues and the accompanying use of numbers as proof came only from the women. Mott's call for inclusion throughout church life was a testament to what he had witnessed of the women's work through the years. His voice lent authority to the concerns that had been raised.

Out of these observations Mott held out two particular concerns. One was that women needed still to have connection with the "foreign" work, even though it was now part of the larger church structure. He believed that if it were lost, there would be nothing really to compensate for it. A second concern was the danger of shrinking income for mission. Other than the actual withdrawal of Christ, he felt no greater disaster could strike that part of the church's existence.[20] Both of these concerns were revisited by the board several times in the years to come. Setting the tone for the new church, Mott's book was a mix of positive outlook toward expansion; straightforward, realistic critique; and caution. Mott may not have gotten everything right in terms of predictions and concerns, but he managed to cover the themes that would characterize mission for the existence of The Methodist Church.

Stories of church union can be found in the writing of Frank Norwood, Thomas Frank, and Russell Richey. In the work of these thinkers, the intricacies of what had to be worked out are given little space in order to focus on the real compromise that both brought the denominations together and provided continuing controversy for a number of years—the Central Jurisdiction. Although its creation and its specific history are well covered in other materials, no history of The Methodist Church can be written without recognizing its existence as a compromise between the understood theology that motivated the church and that part of the U.S. culture that had continued to maintain a division in the worth of human beings based on race. Wesley's strong opposition to slavery did not survive the transatlantic journey for a segment of the Methodist population. Yet for others, the overt form of racism known as slavery seemed so completely incompatible with Methodism that they had to separate as a church. The end of slavery had not ended the deep divide—a divide that was also theological, but rarely treated as such. Lacing the theological or sociological debate about race, polity was used to express the differences among the three united denominations.

Briefly, the structure of the new church divided the country geographically into five different jurisdictions. Bishops presided over the annual conferences that made up each jurisdiction. Jurisdictions in and of themselves had no power but were an organizing tool for many of the ministries and missions of the church. In addition, they became a more manageable way for the church to organize some of its program functions. Although controversial, the jurisdictions gave the church new possibilities.[21] To bring together disparate views, however, the structure included a nongeographic Central Jurisdiction, to which belonged the African-American congregations of the denomination. The organization was clearly a compromise, designed to appease the MECS, which had already endured vociferous concerns from local congregations about the new church structure. Northern churches, however, which often had not directly confronted the racism in their own communities, were willing to accept the terms of the compromise. But it was not well received by the African-American members of the denomination, who voted overwhelmingly against it. A small but significant number of non-African-American delegates, from all three denominations, voted nay as well, but it was not enough to stop its creation. Race remained an issue for The Methodist Church during its entire existence. The Central Jurisdiction was a visible reminder that the church was not one, in a society that also was not one.

Jurisdictions became important beyond their part of the race issue. The creation of the jurisdictions themselves had little impact on the actual day-to-day functioning of most of the agencies of the Board of Missions and Church Extension. But they shifted the balance of power within the church in ways that no one anticipated. When The Methodist Church was created, it maintained a polity that decreed that only the General Conference acted for the whole church. In the four years between its meetings, various Methodist agencies could make statements in the name of their agencies, but the statements had force in a society that did not care much about making the distinction. As the new board began its work, it did so in ways that were very visible to both the church and society.

Communications

The primary vehicle for information about mission work, the magazine *World Outlook*, formerly published in Nashville, moved its offices to New York after the 1939 union. It began in the MECS in 1932, with one editor relating to the World Division and one to the Woman's Division. It was a source of information for both aspects of the mission work. Dorothy McConnell, daughter of Bishop Francis McConnell, was coeditor for nearly the entire period, ending her tenure in 1964 at the same time that *World Outlook* ceased to be the official publication of the Woman's Division. Henry Sprinkle was coeditor from 1952 to 1964.[22]

Serving as the primary publication for the Woman's Division was *The Methodist Woman*, first published in 1940 in Cincinnati. Through editorials, photos, stories, and even how-to articles, the magazine linked women at the local level with national and international programs and ideas.

While these two magazines were most often the sources for information and opinions, the *Christian Advocate*, the news magazine of the church, often carried timely commentary, editorials, and articles. Ralph Diffendorfer, head executive of the Board of Missions, maintained frequent correspondence with Roy L. Smith, the editor of the *Advocate*, coordinating the way that much of the information about the agency and its work was disseminated. Even though the *Advocate* was not an in-house publication of the board, it often served that purpose, sometimes providing a timelier forum for discussion than was possible in the less frequently published official mission publications.

Already the church was beginning to think about audiovisuals as a way of interpreting mission. The MEC had a slide-lecture office that became part of the new board. Harry Spencer, who had also worked for the MEC in its Board of Foreign Missions, became an assistant in the Joint Division of Education and Cultivation. Spencer went to Cuba about 1940 and took color slides that became the first slide-lecture used in The Methodist Church. Shortly afterward, an Audiovisual Education Department was created, and Spencer became head of it. The board began using filmstrips instead of slides about 1942. Color films could also be used, but most congregations did not have projectors, and the board was waiting for a propitious moment to begin using them.[23]

Building on its legacy of theology and polity, The Methodist Church had a history of work in the world, of carrying the gospel to new places, and of maintaining it through finances, placement of personnel, and creation of institutions. Personnel, methods, and organization had all been tested in their previous denominational forms. The future appeared bright. For The Methodist Church, a new chapter of mission could begin.

CHAPTER 2

The War Years

*C*OMING OUT OF the uniting conference with a racially divided structure, the church was nonetheless prepared to move ahead with its
mission seemingly uninterrupted. But within the first year, the new body
of Methodists was caught up in the upheaval of a world at war, and its first
order of business became a greater refining of the borders and dimensions
of its work. These borders were both political, as national interests shifted
and changed the way the world was defined, and administrative, as the
board and staff coped with challenges they had never faced before.

Church unification was celebrated in many countries but went nearly
unnoticed in places where one or another of the uniting church bodies had
been the only Methodist representative of the United States church. For
example, in his autobiography, written during the 1960s, Bishop Ralph
Dodge, working at the time in Angola, made no mention of the uniting of
the church or even the change in administrative structures; it had little
impact on his work from day to day. For others, the change was most noticeable in the symbolism of unity in working with persons from other
branches. In reviewing this era, Tracey K. Jones, Jr., reflected on his own
entry into mission work. He noted that he was one of only eight new missionaries The Methodist Church commissioned in 1940, its first year of
existence. Of further meaning to him, even at the time, was the fact that
Bishop Arthur J. Moore presided at the ceremony. Bishop Moore came
from the Methodist Episcopal Church, South (MECS), while Jones was
from the Methodist Episcopal Church (MEC), the Northern branch of
the church.

So while effort went into figuring out the details of personnel, offices,
and relationships, the work itself continued mostly unchanged. The Board
of Missions might even have had less duplication to sort through than

some of the other church structures. Comity agreements, where different Protestant bodies agreed to observe certain set boundaries for their mission work, meant that in many countries there was less overlap in geographic areas than in the U.S., where some relatively small communities had both Methodist Protestant Church (MPC) and MEC congregations or MEC and MECS congregations. In the Division of Home Missions and Church Extension, the geographic divisions, as well as differing types of work, meant that duplication presented little concern.

The "Report to the Board of Managers" of the first annual Meeting of the Board of Missions, submitted in November 1940 at Philadelphia, was reflective of the needs of the times. After an extensive discussion of the guiding principles for carrying on missions in tense areas of the world, the report noted the special difficulties for Christians in totalitarian states. Missionaries had been through difficulties before, but the challenges presented in Japan and Korea, as well as Eastern Europe, seemed new. Missionaries in these countries needed primary attention rather than organizational adjustments. Of the five areas listed as concerns, only one had to do with the union, that being the adjustment of the salary scales of the three different church bodies. The other four concerns listed — strengthening the plan of cooperation with affiliated autonomous churches, studying the status of missionaries in central conferences, looking at the various charters, and coping with the varying ways of holding annual conferences — were about the relationship of missionaries to the indigenous churches and ministries.[1] Thus The Methodist Church was born with a continually developing and changing relationship among the Christians and the church bodies existing in its places of mission.

This method of not only establishing worshiping bodies but also gathering in connection with one another was part of the very identity of Methodists; the "connexion" went back to John and Charles Wesley. As part of their policy and by their personal choice, missionaries participated in the local churches they established, working to increase the participation and eventually the leadership of the indigenous members. As the numbers of churches grew, they related to each other in annual conferences, where ordained missionaries usually had their membership, rather than in the conferences in the U.S. Once they were members, their appointments came through that conference. With unification, bishops themselves were assigned to specific annual conferences, a change that made them more regional than national. This arrangement helped the mission work because the work of the bishops outside the U.S. now became much more like that of the bishops within its borders.

For ordained clergy to be members in the conferences where they served was a mixed blessing. On the one hand, this membership often gave them an influence far out of proportion to their numbers. Because of their prior experiences, they often retained the most powerful positions in the conferences. Because annual conferences had begun so early in the church's mission work, however, they also provided a forum for decisions to be made with greater participation by all those concerned.[2] Listing these four items of relationship and leadership, the new church signaled both concern and a further commitment to eventual autonomy for churches in places where it was financing mission.

By defining the borders of its work in this way, however, the major concern of the board remained one of coordination rather than any change in direction of its ministry. Greater autonomy had long been the goal. The staff also did not change much, but personnel from the uniting churches found new positions.

Heading the board was Ralph Diffendorfer. Born a poor farm boy in Hayesville, Ohio, he had listened to and become thrilled by stories of David Livingstone. He attended first Ohio Wesleyan, then Drew University and Union Theological Seminary in New York. For more than twenty-five years he served as corresponding secretary of the Board of Foreign Missions for the MEC and then as a general secretary of the Board of Missions of The Methodist Church. By the time of unification he had already faced a number of unexpected challenges for mission work. Following the great growth and expansion that had culminated in the great ecumenical missionary conference in Edinburgh, Scotland, in 1910, missionary enterprises were battered by changes from within and without. The Great War had altered both attitudes and borders. Questions were raised about the nature of missions and its ties to colonial governments. Before many had time to assimilate these changes, the years of financial depression brought further disillusionment at home and abroad. Through it all, Diffendorfer brought energy and passion to his work. He had been a delegate to the International Missionary Council conferences of Jerusalem in 1928 and Madras in 1938. In addition, between 1924 and 1940, he visited every mission station except those in central Africa.[3] This experience made him the easy choice to serve as secretary for the unified board.

Several other staff people were instrumental in the transition for the

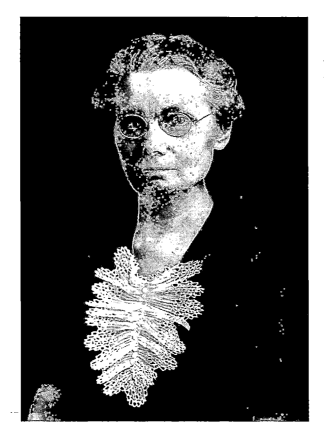

Sara Estelle Haskin.
*(Photo courtesy of United
Methodist Archives and
History)*

denomination. For example, Sara Estelle Haskin was an important leader
from the MECS who was influential in the unification process, though
she did not live long enough to be on staff. Another leader from the
MECS was Thelma Stevens. She served as staff of the Bureau of Christian
Social Relations on the Woman's Missionary Council, moving smoothly
into the new church structure as head of the staff of the Department of
Christian Social Relations of the Woman's Division.

But whether they were new to the work or just using new titles, the
newly formed board and its divisions had little opportunity to discover
their similarities and differences—personal or theological—or even to
think reflectively about the "good old days." Instead, by the time the divisions were having the first of their annual meetings and issuing their first
reports, they were coping with changes in both Asia and Europe.

In the Woman's Division, the report of Velma Maynor on Korea in the

Sara Estelle Haskin

When the Methodist Episcopal Church, South (MECS), began its foray into settlement work at the turn of the twentieth century, it asked Sara Estelle Haskin to take up the post in Dallas. With no equipment and no real pattern to follow, she plunged into the work and began a very successful ministry. Her goal was to be a neighbor to those around her in the neglected areas of the city where she settled. She started three settlement houses that provided much-needed services for the area. Afterward, she moved to Nashville, where she worked with Mrs. Sallie Hill, an African-American woman, to start another center to serve the neighborhood. Eventually, her success in such endeavors led her to a position as secretary of literature of the Woman's Missionary Council, located in Louisville. Biography was important to her, so she used many sketches of persons of faith in the literature she published.

With unification came a new position and title for her. She was elected editor of *World Outlook*. Reluctantly, for she dreaded the thought of living and working in New York, she went to the city to attend her first executive committee meeting and find a place to live. She accomplished both, giving a report full of hope for the new church at the committee meeting. After the meeting she drove with a friend to the hotel where she was staying. On the way, she was seized with pain and died shortly after she reached her hotel room.

The new church had barely begun life when hers ended, but eight years later, coworkers were still praising the vision she had brought to the union and the influence of her vision, which had persisted long after she died. Haskin was noted for her dedication to the Christianization of social relationships as well as the development of personal mystical relation of the soul to God. She was a crusader for race relations and gave leadership to considerations of labor laws and other concerns when these were issues being discussed by only a handful in the church. She was also remembered as a campaigner for the laity and clergy rights of women.

Her work increased the communication between women of the MEC and MECS churches long before they became officially one church. In this way, she was truly a founding spirit of the new denomination, even though her physical life was at its end.

Source: Material on Haskin in United Methodist History and Archives, Madison, New Jersey.

minutes of the first annual meeting noted the withdrawal of the missionaries there as well as nationalization in China. Behind this brief sentence was a complicated train of events and communications. The process illustrates the relationship of the board to its missionaries as well as the way unification affected personnel of the board serving outside the U.S.

Methodist Union in Korea

Koreans had joined in the celebrations of the newly formed church with their own service. On January 19, 1940, one hundred missionaries repeated the words of uniting in a service led by Bishop Moore. No Methodist Protestants had been serving in the country, but missionaries from the four sending agencies, two each from the Northern and Southern branches of the church, had been working together since 1930 in the form of The Association of Methodist Missionaries in Korea.[4] At the time of union, the 115 missionaries were almost equally divided: 12 men and their wives sent from the MEC Board of Foreign Missions, 13 men and their wives from the MECS Department of Foreign Missions, 36 women from the MEC Woman's Foreign Missionary Society, and 29 women from the MECS Woman's Missionary Council.

To facilitate the changes, Kristian and Maud Jensen, who had been missionaries in the country together since 1928, published a study booklet. They reminded the readers that women were equally represented with men on the division and on the board, as well as in running their own division. Addressing concerns that would be raised now that the women no longer had a completely independent agency, they also noted that these were "said to be the most liberal provisions for women made by any church."[5] Although Methodism in Korea was already an independent body, the missionaries felt seriously affected by the changes in their administrative ties. This publication from on-site personnel demonstrated the difference in perspective about the new structure, particularly from some of the women, from the more optimistic statements made publicly. Such concern about the voice of women was surely discussed in many places around the world, but it was not so apparent in printed materials.

Even more difficult was the pressure to collaborate from the Japanese occupiers during the war. The Methodist Theological Seminary in Seoul was closed and used by the Japanese to house soldiers. Its president, Fritz Hongkew Pyen, was imprisoned. After being released, he was elected

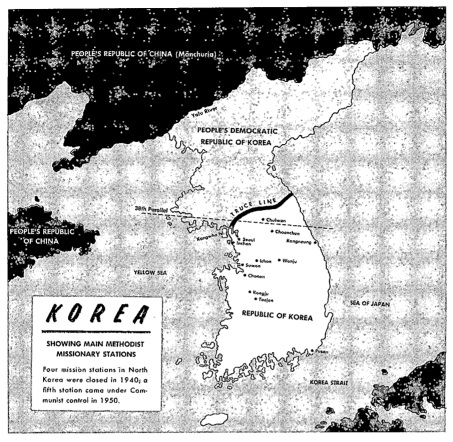

Although Methodists had a mission in the People's Democratic Republic of
Korea (North Korea) before the Second World War, its mission became entirely located in the Republic of Korea (South Korea) after the war. The truce
line shown here was the boundary between the two countries at the end of
the Korean War in 1953. Eventually the border became the 38th parallel.
(Map courtesy of United Methodist Archives and History)

bishop, but the police forced him to resign. At least one Methodist church,
also in Seoul, was converted to a Shinto shrine. Lew Hyung-ki, a Methodist religious education director, was tortured for four months in prison.
Since Bishop Ju Sam Ryang had been made custodian of Methodist property in Korea, he was harassed by the police.

Koreans had been divided on how to accommodate themselves to the
Japanese. Bishop Choon Chun-soo was accused of expelling dissidents
and selling church property. Hugh Cynn, who had been born in Korea

and educated in the U.S., was also accused of collaboration but defended himself and objected to "vengefulness" after the war.[6] These same complexities were mirrored in every country occupied by a foreign power during the Second World War.

A New Church in Japan

Methodist missionaries began work in Japan in 1873. As in many countries, they worked alongside Christians from many Protestant denominations as well as Roman Catholic priests and sisters. In the years preceding the war, both the personnel and the money sent to the Japan church greatly decreased, reflecting both the economic difficulties in the U.S. and the growing autonomy of the church.

Some areas of ministry, however, were particularly successful. In 1932 it was reported that Christian higher education institutions enrolled about 10,000 out of the 200,000 students in Japan. Laity as well as clergy were involved in student work. Kyosuke Mizuno, for example, head of the foreign section of the Imperial Household, presided over the opening of a new Wesley Foundation in Tokyo in 1940. David Yoshio Takahara, who had studied in the U.S., was secretary-director of Methodist student work in Japan. A disciple of missionary Thoburn T. Brumbaugh, Takahara received a master's in New Testament at Oberlin and seems to have considered becoming ordained, since he was "on trial" for orders in 1939. But he remained a layman.[7] Concern grew within the country as the armed forces expanded and conflict seemed inevitable. The Japan Conference elected the Rev. Dr. Yoshimune Abe bishop, believing that his leadership would be key in handling the crises ahead. Abe came from a highly ranked family at the court of a chieftain of the Tsugaru Clan. He had joined the church while in high school, winning a scholarship to Drew University in 1911. After graduate studies, he returned to Japan, joining the faculty at Aoyama Gakuin in Tokyo. In addition to pastoring a church, he became a national officer of the YMCA. His many connections made him a highly visible leader for the Methodists.

At the same time, many of the Christian groups were in dialogue about the possibility of some kind of unification. Pressure for this came especially from the Japanese government, which saw it as an easier way to watch and control the Christians. The government wanted churches to

Yoshimune Abe was the first Japanese elected a bishop of The Methodist Church in Japan before it became part of the united church, the Kyodan. Abe later became general secretary of the schools and colleges related to the Kyodan. *(Photo courtesy of United Methodist Archives and History)*

concentrate on "religion"; it was particularly suspicious of student groups like the Wesley Foundation, which not only was "foreign" but also encouraged students to think "dangerous thoughts" — that is, to think critically about social and political issues. Under then-current Japanese law, denominations with fewer than fifty churches and fewer than five thousand followers could not be recognized. Larger groups realized that they could help these Christians achieve legal status if they all banded together. Finally, when the leaders of the Salvation Army were accused of subversion, many of the Protestant groups joined in a mass meeting. The initial ecumenical interests and the growing pressures helped to push the groups into forming the *Nihol Kirisuto Kyodan*, or Kyodan, the Church of Christ in Japan. This entity comprised about 70 percent of the Protestant groups in Japan, functioning as a denomination with a moderator, a biennial assembly, and other institutional aspects. The Council of Cooperation in Japan linked the missionary boards and agencies of the various denominations with the Christians of the new organization in Japan.[8]

Brumbaugh addressed some of the concerns about the church for the Methodists. He noted that the conference itself was composed of all Japanese, not missionaries, making it a genuinely Japanese institution. He also addressed the formulation of essential statements about the church as perhaps not the way U.S. Methodists might state them but as characteristically Japanese. Comparing the united church to both the formation of a united church in Canada and the recent uniting of U.S. Methodist Christians, Brumbaugh painted a positive picture of the benefits of such a development. But he also addressed the reality that the union grew out of pressures from the government. Because of these political pressures, the U.S. Government limited the ways that U.S. churches could financially support the institutions and personnel in Japan, resulting in concerns about the survival of the church. The article concluded as it began with support for the united church. In addition, the accompanying blurb about Brumbaugh called him "one of Methodism's most trusted missionaries, with a record of many years' service in Japan. . . . His opinions are therefore entitled to the most careful consideration by our readers."[9]

This kind of discussion demonstrated the way that the Board of Missions gave leadership in the growing ecumenical awareness of The Methodist Church. To become part of a united church was not popular among all missionaries and certainly not popular among laypersons for whom denominational identity still had much meaning. The continuing interpretation of such a step fell primarily to the board executives, who needed to find a middle ground that supported the unified approach yet still allowed for fund raising for familiar names and institutions. Bishop Abe followed the meeting that gave birth to Kyodan with a specially called conference. There the Methodists voted to disband as a conference of the Japan Methodist Church, abolishing the office of bishop as well. Abe then began service as chair of the drafting commission for the new church.[10]

Coming of War

Because he was unable to attend General Conference, Abe issued an invitation to the board to send a delegation because it was "urgent to have a conference and advice from the 'home Church.'" The board was glad to receive such an invitation because the ever-changing politics in Japan meant more conversation was needed with the united church.[11] The board authorized Bishop James C. Baker, Bishop Moore, Sallie Lou McKinnon (formerly of the MECS), and Diffendorfer to make the trip. Their report included suggestions for immediate missionary strategy. The first concern was whether to evacuate the missionaries. One-third of the Protestants had already been evacuated, but most Roman Catholics remained. Seventy Methodists remained in Japan and seven in Korea. The U.S. Government continued its pressure for withdrawal as a precautionary measure. It cited the increasing evidence of Japan's determination to push out all foreign interests from the Far East and the seeming crisis near at hand, making the scene ripe for incident. In addition, some missionaries felt complete evacuation was advisable aside from the war situation because the nationals could work through adjustments without the embarrassment of foreign missionaries.

In the light of these concerns and in keeping with its policy, the board concluded that the welfare of the Christian movement should be the guiding principle. It further added that the missionaries needed their boards at home to make recommendations because the missionaries were too close to the situation for good judgment. In addition, they could not make the decision in the presence of Japanese colleagues, who might see the international situation differently. Because there would be less embarrassment all around if boards chose, the Methodist board chose to accept responsibility and recommended all women and children leave as soon as possible. It also suggested that others make arrangements to go before April 1 by taking care of personal items and arranging with colleagues to leave work with good will.[12]

In tandem with all the events that led to the uniting conference in Japan were missionary and board concerns about the growing military tensions and actions. By April, criticism of the actions reached such a pitch that at the *Christian Advocate*, Roy Smith planned his editorial of support for the board actions, sending a copy off to Diffendorfer for his comments and approval, offering to pay the expense of Diffendorfer's wiring his comments back. The editorial noted that the order for all missionaries to leave was without precedent, leaving the Christian movement in Japan without any U.S. Methodist leadership. At the same time, he reminded readers that the withdrawals were temporary and that everywhere in Japan people believed that war with the U.S. was inevitable. He assured readers that Japanese Christians were in agreement with the actions, that the missionaries were not regarded as deserters, and that their departure

The battleship USS *Arizona* belches smoke as it topples over into Pearl Harbor during the surprise attack by Japanese forces on December 7, 1941. This ship sank with more than 80 percent of its crew of 1,500, many of whom are still entombed in the ruins. The ruins have become a memorial in the National Park system. The attack on Pearl Harbor changed The Methodist Church mission drastically, not only because of military threats in Asia, but also because the church's inability to resist the imprisonment of Japanese Americans seemed to make the church merely reflective of its culture.
(AP/Wide World Photo, used with permission)

would not jeopardize future work. He wanted readers to recognize that the order was in response to a new challenge for mission boards, working in a place that seemed in great danger of soon going to war.[13]

When the editorial reached Brumbaugh, he was quick to respond to Smith, writing on board the NYK *Tatsuta* as he returned in July from Japan. In the letter, he first expressed his own feelings that the withdrawal was "the most deplorable blunder of modern missionary history," a phrase he borrowed from a *Christian Century* editorial. He preferred the actions of the mission boards of the Presbyterians and Congregationalists, who were monitoring the situation and asking their missionaries to be extra cautious but were not requiring withdrawal.

But his biggest objection was that Smith had said that the majority of Japanese Christians agreed. Brumbaugh pointed out that the report of Diffendorfer and Baker of their trip had not made that point and that actually there was no way to find out if it were true or not. Brumbaugh, in fact, believed just the opposite, writing, "I know that every Japanese Christian with whom I have had contact is confused and troubled as to the reasons for missionaries of the Cross leaving Japan at this time, and that literally hundreds of them have come to me within the past few weeks expressing the hope that I stay with them or that, if I must go, I tell American Christians what a mistake it is to think that Japan doesn't need or want the loving service of foreign missionaries in these times of crisis." The existence of the united church made no difference in the desire of the Japanese Christians to continue to work with missionaries from a variety of Christian churches. The letter concluded forcefully, asking Smith to change his opinion with this further knowledge of the facts and taking him to task for saying that criticism of the action usually came from persons who had no knowledge of the facts.

Smith sent the letter to Diffendorfer, asking his opinion and promising a copy of his own reply as soon as he had written it. Diffendorfer's reply opened, "You are a peach to send on the copy of Brumbaugh's letter." He suggested that they wait until Brumbaugh had been in the country a while and felt the anti-Japanese sentiment in the air. He also thanked him for "helping us through this unnecessary and difficult situation with Brumbaugh." Smith responded a week later with another letter to Diffendorfer, reporting on more correspondence and Brumbaugh's plans to meet with him. Brumbaugh's letter had raised concerns about the directions of the church and its commitment to missionary traditions. It brought to a head the differences in consideration of how the work was to continue through the unprecedented circumstances of war.

Ministries with students continued into the war, albeit with difficulties. "Japanese Christians were under pressure because of their associations with foreigners," one historian reported. "Although attendance [at a Wesley Student Center] decreased Christian students remained loyal and a program of study and social activities was maintained." Once financial support from outside Japan stopped coming in, work continued with sacrificial support from Japanese Christian leaders. U.S. missionaries who were unable to return home also contributed money. But as the war went on, "food became scarce and sanitation levels dropped." Takahara and his wife, Grace, had moved into the Wesley Student Center in Tokyo, but in

1943 the government tore down the dormitory and other buildings and the work ceased.[14]

Michi Kawai, the founder of Keisen Girls' School, a Christian school, reported that at the beginning of the war she had been subjected to pressure from the government because of her Christian faith. Her feelings about the impending conflict were expressed in a letter as early as 1937: "We Japanese must be more penitent, humbly kneeling before God with contrite hearts." In August 1941, she addressed a church audience in Kyoto. Afterward, she was detained and questioned for more than two hours. Among the questions asked her was, "'Why do Christians say 'My Lord' to Jesus Christ when this term should be used only to His majesty the Emperor?" The next day she was released after completing a form document. During the war she was tormented by the war's destruction but kept her sanity by gardening. She wrote: "The intelligentsia class of Japan had no heart, no enthusiasm to fight against Britain and America from the very outset of the war." Although she and others often had to find refuge in bomb shelters during air raids in Tokyo, the school lost only one student because of U.S. bombing. She described how Japanese women were drafted to serve as factory workers, laundresses for soldiers, and personal servants to military officers. Despite the war, she began a new project for the school, a horticultural college, which elicited more interrogation from government officials about the school's Christian identification. Despite pressure from the government, she insisted on her school's being called Christian. She received permission for the horticultural college only in the last year of the war.[15]

Destruction in the Philippines

The Philippines was occupied by Japan during the war. The "Protestant churches in the Philippines shared heavily in the general suffering and destruction. Eighty per cent of all Protestant church property was destroyed, congregations were scattered, many members and ministers were killed, and virtually all foreign missionaries were interned."[16] Despite these difficulties, the church in the Philippines continued to exist and to develop its leaders. José Labarrette Valencia, Sr., had studied in the U.S. and was a district superintendent during the war. He reported many encounters with Japanese soldiers, who were often looking for guerrillas who resisted them. A Japanese classmate he had known at Cornell College

Mary Johnston Hospital in Manila, the Philippines, was destroyed during the Second World War but rebuilt by the Woman's Division and the Division of Foreign Missions, with help from Presbyterians. It continues as an important center of health mission for the church. *(Photo courtesy of United Methodist Archives and History)*

was working as a banker in Manila. He and Valencia made contact, and he advised Valencia always to give the same answers to repeated questions by the soldiers, advice that Valencia followed in several incidents. In 1944, the Valencia family was caught in the crossfire during heavy fighting between the Japanese and Filipino guerrillas in the Cagayan Valley. José Valencia, Jr., narrowly missed being shot. The next day the Japanese captured Alejo Laudencia, one of the guerrillas, and tortured him to death. The Valencias cared for the Laudencia family afterward and stayed in the area. "We knelt down in prayer and committed to God our lives and those who stayed . . . asking that His will be done," the elder Valencia wrote. "The barrio was not invaded. The Japanese soldiers who were on their way to Bangag returned to their garrison in Solana. We felt that God had answered our prayer."

Another Filipino leader was Benjamin I. Guansing, who had studied at Union Theological Seminary in Manila and then in the U.S., returning to become a pastor. He had been elected secretary of the Philippines Conference, a central conference, in 1932.[17]

U.S. missionaries who remained in the Philippines spent the war in prison camps. In the camps they suffered the same lack of food and basic supplies as everyone else. The largest camp had been built to hold 650 people, but during the war, 3,400 were packed inside. Missionaries worked with others to grow crops, scrounge for and organize supplies, and even arrange for worship.[18]

Korea on the Approach of War

As in other Asian countries, conditions in Korea began to deteriorate rapidly. A. Gaylord Marsh, the general consul in Seoul, had begun advising U.S. citizens to leave in July. By mid-October 1940, many Koreans regarded the missionaries with great suspicion, treating them as outcasts. Often their presence caused trouble for Korean friends; projects and plans had to be abandoned. Yet, response from the U.S. missionaries to Marsh's concern was slow. No other governments were giving missionaries the advice to leave. Many of these men and women had been in Korea for a number of years. They did not like the idea of leaving, especially when they saw life becoming difficult. For some, this became a reminder of how much they were still needed. They wanted to stay with their life's work. Since missionaries often cooperated across international lines, sharing housing as well as ministry, U.S. citizens saw no reason to set themselves apart. In addition, for those who decided to make it, the trip back to the U.S. was itself a long one — travel to Pusan by train, then a ferry to Japan, and yet another train trip to Kobe, thirty-six to forty-eight hours of travel. But when the USS *Mariposa* began evacuations, the seriousness of the situation was much more apparent. U.S. Methodist missionaries rapidly joined missionaries from other denominations and other countries in deciding to leave. When Christmas 1940 arrived, more than 90 percent of the Christian missionaries had left the country.

While on board the *Mariposa*, several of the missionaries of the Woman's Division issued a careful report that chronicled the events leading to their departure. Its contents revealed a number of the difficulties they faced. Summarizing their reasons as the changed attitude of the Japanese government and the impossibility of Christian work in the event of war, they tried to explain the rapidly changing atmosphere in which they had to work. They noted the ways that the meanings of words were being changed and that the oath of allegiance was a closely watched component of all meetings. The document demonstrated the determination of the missionaries not to be compromised by the Japanese government. Noting that it is "tragic to leave" and "terrible to have to remain," the missionaries made their choice because of their position as guests of the government and because of their conviction that "though we be removed, the church of Christ remains and it is to further the interests of that church in the land of our adoption that we are returning to our homeland."[19] Even after most of the group had left, political incidents continued to bring home the growing danger of the situation. Dr. Sherwood Hall was arrested because of a large check he had written while in Peking trying to purchase drugs for the hospital. He was fined and released, but two Presbyterian missionaries were sentenced to ten months of hard labor. Another Presbyterian nurse was removed from a passenger ship and sent to jail.

The most noteworthy incident was the Day of Prayer case. In January 1941, a Presbyterian woman whose surname was Butts and Methodist missionary Ruth Moore supervised the translation and printing of the program for the annual prayer event that Christians worked on together. On the last day of February, the police confiscated all copies of the program and arrested the two women. After being questioned, they were released. Later, however, Butts was again arrested and confined for four weeks in a tiny cell.

Meanwhile, Moore and her husband, also a missionary, packed and prepared to leave. But during the process, their permits were pulled and departure delayed for no apparent reason. They found themselves waiting in an empty house, since their possessions had already been shipped, stored, or disposed of. Restrictions had been placed on currency and exchange, so when permission finally came for them to sail, they had to borrow money in order to purchase their tickets. Any remaining currency had to be left behind. They never saw their possessions again. The Moores were not alone in their difficulties. Some missionaries were required to sign a document as they left, promising that they would never return. Many lost possessions. Others had lived much of their adult lives in the country, so that "returning home" had mixed meanings.

The serious nature of the changes was reflected in a report from Diffendorfer and Bishop Baker, following their visit in January 1941,

Ruth and John Z. Moore, left, Methodist missionaries, were forced to leave Korea in 1941, leaving all their possessions behind. The disposal of property of evacuated missionaries became a concern because it implied that if left in storage, the missionaries would return. All of the missionaries were forced to leave Korea by the Japanese occupiers, however. Also shown in this 1936 photo are the Moore children, Betsy and James. *(Photo courtesy of United Methodist Archives and History)*

which they marked "Strictly Confidential—Not to be Quoted." Because of all that had happened, they were concerned at the outset about the arrangements and whether they could even visit with any Koreans. Even as they wrote that the results were different from what they expected, their words revealed the conditions they faced and now even accepted as almost routine by the missionaries and board members. "The only police and detective surveillance of which we were aware was that ordinarily experienced during the last ten years."[20] Despite the severe war economy already in evidence, the shortness of time, and the concerns for the safety of the Koreans, the two were able to see everyone they needed to visit and accomplished all the tasks on their list.

The "Japanizing" of Korea affected The Methodist Church as it did all segments of Korean society. The concern of the board was to fit into the changing political structure without compromising itself or the Korean church members. One major area of concern was the "Manifestoes" that had been issued the preceding autumn. Written under Japanese direction, one document opened: "It is both urgent and proper that we Christians should bring to reality the true spirit of our national polity and the underlying principle of Naisen Ittain (Japan Proper and Korea form one body), perform adequately our duties as people behind the gun, and conform to the new order, therefore, we, the General Board of the Korean Methodist Church, hereby take lead in deciding upon and putting into effect the following."[21] Among the provisions were an agreement that national polity and military training be taught in theological schools, an agreement for attendance at Shinto shrines, and an expression of support for the army.

This manifesto, similar to one the Presbyterians were made to accept, created serious division among the Korean Methodists, particularly with regard to attendance at the shrines. The government stated that this was a patriotic act, not a religious one. The church decided to accept this explanation. A further area of difficulty was the creedal statement of the manifesto. The government claimed it had not required such a statement. The board report included the explanation that it appeared to have been written by a small minority of the Korean Christians but that it was accepted at the October meeting, despite concerns raised by church leadership, including Bishop Abe. The statement read, "To make the Gospel (Christ's teaching and example) the basic substance of Christian education; to dissociate Jewish history and the pagan thoughts and usages that have crept in on the path of Western cultural progress; and to make clear exposition of the Gospel by the use of philosophies and traditions of Oriental saints."[22]

Because this statement was officially adopted with no debate, it was considered the legal position of the Methodists. Bishop Abe concluded that any union of the Japanese and Korean Methodists would take further consideration because of the statements of the document. Such theological divisions added to the difficulties of determining the future of the church under the growing war conditions.

Baker and Diffendorfer were able to make progress in other areas of concern, however. They reviewed the conditions under which the missionaries had evacuated, noting the role of the manifesto. Its adoption spurred some missionaries to make the decision to leave more easily because they wanted to protest visibly its provisions. While the personnel structure still presented ongoing difficulties that were not solved by the visit, the more immediate concerns about property were carefully addressed. One significant decision missionaries made was to establish holding bodies for the properties; in these missionaries still composed the majority of the membership, revealing the reluctance to move forward with empowering nationals in church structure. Koreans were also assigned to the committees, however, to help maintain the structures and make decisions in the absence of the missionaries. As the two bodies stated, "We believe that the Christian solution is to trust the Korean Christians."[23]

Although the report contained more details about committees and provisions, this statement was an affirming focus for this, the last visit in several years. Writing their report on board the USS *Taft*, the two reiterated the impossibility of predicting the days ahead as well as the already difficult conditions of the present for the Korean Methodists. They had done what they could.

All these difficulties were noted in the published board reports of the year but only in brief ways. The Woman's Division report commented in passing on the difference of interpretation of obeisance at the shrines between the Presbyterians, who saw it as idolatry, and the Methodists, who looked on it as an act of patriotism. But no further information was given to explain the references. The report also printed the cable that announced the departure of most of the missionaries who were becoming an embarrassment to their Korean friends.[24] The terse prose of the report gave little hint of the soul-searching that had accompanied the two important decisions. It served one significant purpose, however, by informing the larger church that all was under control when it came to its own missionaries.

With such information, when the whole board met, it sent a cable of support to Chinese leader Chiang Kai-shek and pledged increased efforts for civilian relief. The board also devoted meeting time to receive further reports about these concerns. Members discussed the growing possibility that Japan was creating an empire and that the police surveillance in Korea could further hinder Christian efforts.[25] Missionaries were advised to return to the U.S. In China, medical and educational work continued, but it was punctuated by air raids and other signs of the growing conflict.

China before the Deluge

Methodist mission work had established a large number of educational and medical institutions in China. Their names and stories are well known in the literature of the Woman's Division. Churches and other organizations of the division work were also integral to the mission. The first report to the board was full of positive news about the colleges and hospitals. At the same time, it noted the increasing air raids that were changing life for the missionaries. Questions were raised about the operation of the seminary in Nanking. Methodism had been in China for a long time. No one even considered that major change might lie ahead.

An example of how indigenous women were encouraged in the mission is Li Yu Kuei. Already a practicing Christian, she came to one of the Methodist hospitals to become a nurse. After completing her nursing education, she went to the Peking Union Medical College and took a public health course. Although she contracted tuberculosis, she went to Kiukiang, west of Shanghai, to work in the Methodist medical mission there. She taught health in day schools and was active in the church, "presenting Jesus Christ by her winsomeness." When her father died, she returned to Beijing to be near her mother. There she became head of public health nursing in the Methodist mission, overseeing several hundred women in the hospital, a bean milk station, a high school, a day school, and other institutions. Her becoming a leader fit perfectly with the goals of the Woman's Division.[26]

A leader of the Chinese church during this period was Z. T. Kaung, who served as pastor in Shanghai, Huchow, and Soochow. When he was pastor of Allen Memorial Church in Shanghai, where Madame Chiang was a member, he baptized Generalissimo Chiang Kai-shek. In 1941, Kuang was elected bishop and served the Beijing area. He seemed to have had a genius for canny delay and maneuvering. When the Chinese government implemented a policy of disallowing religious groups to operate in China if foreign personnel or funds were used, Kaung insisted he was the bishop and was in charge of the church. At the same time, he reassured missionaries, "No new law can break our fellowship in Christ." Kaung and the Christian church were forced to give up educational, medical, and social services; but Kaung continued an evangelistic ministry. Under the Japanese occupation, it was suggested that the Chinese church adopt a unified organization like the Kyodan in Japan. Kaung agreed but told the

Z. T. Kaung

Kaung was born in Shanghai to a wealthy family and enjoyed many luxuries during his upbringing. At the age of fourteen, he went to a school operated by the Methodist Episcopal Church, South, and was challenged by missionary Clara E. Steger to become a Christian. Realizing this new faith would require him to renounce many of his materialistic pleasures, he nevertheless decided to be baptized at age eighteen. At first his family rejected him, but later his mother and other members of his family also became Christians. After study- ing two years at the Anglo-Chinese College, established by the Methodist Epis- copal Church, South, he entered Soochow University, which had initiated a theological department. Other students dropped out, but Kaung persisted and received a B.D. His first appointment was as assistant pastor of Moore Memor- ial Church in Shanghai. He served other churches and was a district superin- tendent and a chaplain at Soochow University.

Kaung was elected bishop in 1941 and through skillful administration man- aged to keep the church going during the Second World War. After the war, the church again came under pressure from the Chinese Communist government. Kaung persevered, however, and remained at work until his death on August 23, 1958.

Sources: Ellen M. Studley, "Z. T. Kaung: Prince for God," *World Outlook* 38 (July 1948): 25–27; W. W. Reid, "Kaung, Z. T.," *Encyclopedia of World Methodism*, Nolan B. Harmon, gen. ed. with Albea Godbold and Louise L. Queen, 2 vols. (Nashville: United Methodist Publishing House, 1974), 1: 1314.

Japanese it would take as long as five years to make the change. A new constitution would have to be created. When the organization was finally approved, it was as a federation, not a union. Kaung also came under pres- sure to sell church property to the puppet government during the Second World War. Kaung made so many objections that the Japanese finally dropped the matter. And when the Japanese offered financial help, Kaung told them an indigenous church could not accept foreign aid. Whether in saying so he made a distinction between aid from an outside government and aid that the Methodist denomination had made is not clear. [27]

While monitoring the rapidly changing situation in Asia and making decisions about policy, members of the board and staff asked questions about the way the policy would be received among persons of Asian de- scent in the Christian movement in the U.S. They wanted to treat the

Z. T. Kaung.
(Photo courtesy of United
Methodist Archives and
History)

Japanese in the U.S. as they would like to have Americans treated in Japan.
But they knew that other difficulties might lie ahead. One test in the
churches of the U.S. was the attitude toward Japanese Americans. Anti-
Japan sentiment could create even greater problems for future work in
Japan. In addition, board and staff members were concerned about evacuated missionaries. They resolved to do what little they could, including
watching attitudes toward the Japanese, acknowledging U.S. share of guilt
in some of the difficulties, and especially asking for repeal of the Exclusion
Act, which denied Asian immigrants citizenship rights.

Christ and Politics in India

Farther south in Asia, the work in India continued to be one of the largest
concentrations of the board's personnel. Church-related institutions were
well established, many with a mix of U.S. missionaries and national leaders. In a 1932 article in the *Indian Witness*, Diffendorfer had written "Mission or Church?" to discuss the focus on the development of the church in

India, attempting to leave out the word "mission." This philosophy was translated into action with mixed success. Missionaries often continued to live in compounds, especially those centered in educational institutions or churches that had been long established in the cities. A letter from Lila Templin to Diffendorfer in January of 1939 described attending American dinners where not one Indian was present. She reported that when she and others arrived in India, they were told that their social life would be in the military club, where they would be "secluded from the problems of the world."[28]

Not all the missionaries were happy with these attitudes. Some of them were attracted to the work of E. Stanley Jones and the Christian *ashram* movement. Others followed with interest the way that Mahatma Gandhi was leading a nonviolent resistance to the British government. A number attended a conference in Lucknow, where they discussed the situation with British, Indian, and U.S. Christians. From this conference came a manifesto, followed by a four-page open letter to the viceroy, asking that the British respond to a call for a redemptive nationalism rather than an aggressive one. The letter was signed by Ralph Templin as president and J. N. Wilson as secretary.

The letter raised a furor among the missionaries, several of whom accused the signers of breaking the missionary pledge to do nothing contrary to the lawfully constituted government of the country of appointment. Indians were continuing to pressure the British for freedom, and the missionaries struggled to define their role. Paul Keene, the Templins, and the Reverend J. Holmes Smith signed a second manifesto, called "The Missionary Stand with Christ," in support. In it they declared that their stance was not against Great Britain if it really wanted a world order based on democracy. Further, they noted that the missionary pledge was being extended when it was used to criticize them because it forced missionaries to be progovernment rather than siding with the nonviolent nationalists. They considered themselves unaligned with anyone but only trying to speak from their conscience as ministers of Christ's church. The bishops in India requested that the board recall the missionaries. Smith and Keene left, but the Templins wanted to stay. They received another letter, specifying that they were to leave because they were ineffective missionaries. The Templins continued to push for clarity, wondering whether it was their political stance that made them ineffective. The bishops stood firm, and the Templins left India in 1940.[29]

Reaction to their removal was, predictably, mixed. Mrs. Arthur E. Harper, a missionary wife, wrote them to lament the edict, "We need you here." Students wrote asking what they could do as a protest. Ruth Robinson of the Woman's Division, serving in Lucknow, wrote that their stance had caused her to look more carefully at her own position and whether she was doing enough to live out the love she taught. She knew that it was easy to take a position because of the security it offered, rather than challenge the authorities. In her letter of support, she wrote, "May your courageous spirit light a flame in other hearts." In contrast Dorothy Pearson, a Canadian missionary, sent a letter full of criticism. She noted that not only was there not an intelligent thought in the manifesto but that Stanley Jones and all his followers should be expelled as well.[30]

In requesting withdrawal, however, the bishops were continuing the Methodist missionary tradition of noninterference. They were able to confine the question to one of government authority, partly because the Templins themselves made their stand as a conscience statement. Real official discussion about the place of the missionaries and the meaning of the gospel was avoided. Larger questions about independence for India were not addressed.

As the second-largest area of Methodist work after China, India had a large number of assigned missionaries from both divisions. Institutions were well established, continuing to play an important role in developing leadership not only for the Indian church, but also for all of Indian society. Schools and colleges, though supported more and more by the Indians themselves, still received significant amounts of financial and personnel support from the U.S. These close connections between the supporting churches and the work in India were reflected in the India reports for 1940, which remained similar to those from years past in their concentration on needs in particular situations. For example, once again the Division of Foreign Missions reported the need for greater literacy. Mrs. Otis Moore wrote of the ongoing needs of the fifty boarding schools run by the Woman's Division, the role of training women as they continued to move toward leadership in politics and other areas, and the need for continuing change.[31] Medical work was equally important. The women used the annual report to raise the issue of expanding one of their women's hospitals to serve everyone. The stories behind these reports were told in the magazines and mission materials the women used throughout the year.

Not everyone believed that this was where the emphasis belonged.

Brooks Howell
Archives 960

James E. McEldowney

James E. McEldowney represents the classical missionary story of the early twentieth century. At a student volunteer meeting in Detroit in 1927, he pledged to be a missionary. Stories of the needs of the people inspired him. He continued his education, thinking that he might be going to China when he finished. But by 1935, the Japanese were already there, and the Board of Foreign Missions of the Methodist Episcopal Church asked him to go to India. Before he went, he studied carefully what people were saying about missions, both pro and con. He believed that his job was to train Indians to be leaders in the church.

After three years of ministry in a city church, he moved to Jubbulpore, a large city in the middle of the country. He joined the faculty of Leonard Theological School, one of the primary training centers for clergy and church workers in the northern part of India. The school was built on the grounds of the estate of a former British official and formed its own community. Most of the faculty had homes on the school grounds, contributing to a feeling of community or large family. After two years, he took a furlough to finish his doctorate. When he finished, the Second World War was still raging, but he chose to return to India even though his wife and children had to stay behind.

As he worked among the Indians, McEldowney grew in appreciation of the lives of people of faith, whether Hindu, Christian, or Muslim. At the same time he was aware that many Christians were not living up to their ideals. He did not believe that his job was to go out into the streets and try to convince people to become Christian.

Instead, he drew on a particular Hindu method to develop a special kind of ministry in addition to his teaching. Hinduism used plays recounting the lives of gods and goddesses to teach. McEldowney began to write scripts of Christian stories to be used for telling the good news. He began to do a lot of photography and arranged to have the scripts made into films. He also worked with students to use flannel boards, taking them out into the villages to provide both entertainment and witness in the large rural area around Jubbulpore.

Working in India presented challenges. In addition to the unreliable availability of electricity and telephones, people often had to make do with a more limited range of materials and supplies. Yet one of the things that impressed him most about the Indian people was their ability to take what they had and make something beautiful. McEldowney had his own experiences of making do. Scenery for the films was made of papier-mâché. One day he and his associates worked on a wall, leaving it partially finished when they went home for the night. The next morning they returned to find that termites had already eaten half of it. Eventually they learned that adding sulphur oxide to the paste kept the termites from devouring their work.

Looking back over his life, McEldowney felt great satisfaction in the lives that he touched. He was part of the transitional time for missionaries. When he started, mission work was the outreach of the church, and missionaries were really needed. By the time he was done, missionaries knew that their efforts and gifts were best directed to the development of indigenous leaders.

Sources: James E. McEldowney, *The Making of a Missionary: The Story of My Life* (Bradenton, Fla.: Printing Professionals, 1993); interview with McEldowney by Ben Houston, January 13, 2001.

Frank Laubach championed the cause of literacy through his books *Toward a Literate World* and *India Shall Be Literate*. The movement that developed focused on practical forms of education at the primary and secondary levels, taught in the vernacular. Laubach criticized the emphasis of most of the missionary schools because he believed there was still not enough attention to the poor and the masses. Methodist institutions most often benefitted middle- and upper-class families.[32] In addition, for all the glowing reports and impressive-sounding numbers, they were a small force in a populous and large land. He predicted that as the Indian government assumed more control of education, the institutions the Methodists supported, in which English was used for instruction, were likely to have diminishing government support and, therefore, importance.

Indigenous Leaders in Africa

At the first meeting for the women, Sallie Lou McKinnon reported not just on China, but on all the work in Africa. Because of comity arrangements, the U.S. Methodist work was concentrated in a few areas of sub-Saharan Africa—Angola, Belgian Congo, Southern Rhodesia, and Portuguese East Africa. MacKinnon's report introduced a theme that remained with the board and its work. She called for concern "not for the primitive church in Africa nor for the suffering church in China, but for the somewhat complacent church in the U.S."[33] The work of the Woman's Division was not about affecting the lives of people in other places but was to change lives everywhere.

John Wesley Shungu of the Republic of the Congo typified the way mission education prepared indigenous leaders for responsibility. Shungu was educated in mission schools, became an ordained pastor by the 1940s, and was elected a bishop in 1964. *(Photo courtesy of United Methodist Archives and History)*

Slowly leadership was being trained in Africa. Escrivâo Anglaze Zunguze had studied at mission schools in Mozambique and went to Old Umtali Biblical Institute in what was then Southern Rhodesia from 1939 to 1941. His singing skills undoubtedly helped him as a pastor, and he was ordained an elder in 1950.[34] John Wesley Shungu was educated at Tunda Methodist School and Wembo Nyama Bible School in the Belgian Congo. He was a local preacher for a while, went to Old Umtali Theological School, and began the process leading to ordination in 1942. He served pastorates and also taught the Bible at Wembo Nyama Bible School and Lodja Bible School.[35] Ngandjolo Mose was perhaps more typical. He was also educated at Methodist mission schools in the Belgian Congo but became an indigenous pastor who did evangelism and also supervised other pastors. Traveling by bicycle, he went from village to village, helping the white missionaries. Indigenous pastors were very effective in converting other Africans.

Evangelism was not confined to pastors, however. Mama Jundu had been cured of illness in a mission hospital in the Congo, became a Christian, and returned to her village and extolled the virtues of Jesus. Like Mose, she also went from village to village doing evangelism.[36]

Joseph Boayue's story illustrates how a young person could move from a non-Christian background to one of leadership in the church. Boayue was born in central Liberia, a descendant of a Mano chieftain. His parents believed in God, but their beliefs differed from that of Christians. They sent him to the Methodist mission school at Ganta when he was eleven. There he learned English, and, as Boayue wrote, "Through education, these missionaries elevate youths from the villages to the position where they can serve their people and their nation as Christian citizens." From the mission school, he went to the Booker Washington Institute at Kakata. The school was a cooperative effort of Methodists and others. Boayue received a certificate as a blacksmith from the institute, then went to the College of West Africa in Monrovia, another Methodist school. While he was there, Bishop Willis J. King of the Central Jurisdiction noticed his work. The bishop and missionaries recommended Boayue as a Crusade Scholar, which enabled him to go to Iowa State A & M. "Then I will return to Liberia as an engineer and builder for The Methodist Church," he wrote.[37]

Europe at War

News from Europe also reflected the shifting forces and powers. Of the two former MECS affiliated churches in Russia, only one reported in. Belgian church buildings were damaged, the status of the Italian churches was precarious, and no word at all was received from the Balkans.

In Poland, representatives of only five of the thirteen congregations attended annual conference, though work continued in spite of the Third Reich. Konstanty Najder, a superintendent, kept the Methodist Polish Church alive during the war, without any contact with the outside church. U.S. missionaries Ruth Lawrence, Gaither P. Warfield, Edmund Chambers, and T. J. Gamble were imprisoned.[38]

Warfield and his Polish wife, Hania, later wrote about their experiences in *Call Us to Witness*. Gaither had been in Warsaw when the Germans came, but managed to flee on a bicycle, traveling with a group of church

J. W. Ernst Sommer was head of the Methodist seminary in Germany during the Second World War and astutely protected it (and its single student) from Nazi intrusion. *(Photo courtesy of United Methodist Archives and History)*

members and young preachers. They went east, sleeping and eating by the roadside, flattening their bodies to the ground when the German bombers flew overhead. Eventually they met the Russian army and were taken prisoner. After two weeks in the camp, the Warfields were included in a prisoner exchange with the Germans. Warfield was released in November 1939 because of illness and returned home to Warsaw. In the months that followed, he organized the Americans living in Warsaw to care for stranded citizens. The Gestapo arrested him in December 1941 and put him in a political prison. Eventually the Swiss helped with a prisoner exchange, and he was able to return to the U.S.[39]

Congregations in Bohemia and Moravia reported despite surveillance by the secret police and the scarcity of food they continued to worship. Vaclav Vancura, superintendent and treasurer of the Methodist Church in Czechoslovakia, was also isolated. Because he proclaimed, "One is your Master, even Christ," the Gestapo arrested him and beat him. Several members of his family were executed by the Germans. Nevertheless, Vancura became part of the underground. The pastor of the Central Methodist Church in Prague, Ladisla Schneider, was imprisoned and when he was released, he weighed only eighty-two pounds. Joseph Kocourek was another Methodist pastor who became part of the underground.[40]

Pastor W. K. Glaeser, an Austrian who before the war had gone to Spa Carlsbad in the Sudetenland to serve a German-speaking congregation, was expelled at the outbreak of the war. He was assigned to a church in Linz, Austria, but was almost at once imprisoned. "Ten months in prison," he wrote, "this has been the hardest time in all my life. I suffered from starvation and undernourishment and lost nearly half of my weight." Nevertheless, in a manner reminiscent of Dietrich Bonhoeffer, Glaeser became the unofficial pastor of other prisoners. "I had an opportunity to talk to them about the Gospel," he wrote. When he became ill and had to enter the prison hospital, "There also I had the chance to preach and to pray." And like the apostle Paul, Glaeser reflected a triumphant faith: "Sometimes it was like a miracle to me: living in the poorest conditions, suffering from hunger and need, I often felt like a happy and rich man."[41]

Of great concern to the board was the report of the Latvian treasurer who had fled his country when the Baltic states were incorporated into Soviet Russia. He sent word of the desperate plight of the people, many of whom were of German descent.[42]

Work of the Woman's Division in Europe was much more modest, with only three missionaries on staff—one in Poland and two in Bulgaria. Elizabeth Lee reported that communications became infrequent.[43] The Methodist Committee on Overseas Relief reported on assisting with the rescue of pastors in Norway. Many Scandinavian Methodists worked in mission sites in both Asia and Africa. The report was clear that "no funds are in slightest peril of getting into the hands of the aggressor."[44]

Not all mission areas faced these crises. In Latin America, the Woman's Division, through its ninety on-site missionaries, continued its work with eighteen schools and eight social centers. The women had taken to heart President Franklin Delano Roosevelt's statement that while it might be "more dramatic to fight with ships and planes and naval bases, the really important task, in this hemisphere as elsewhere, lies in the realm of the mind and the spirit."[45] The church structures continued to grow and develop in Latin America. With the Disciples of Christ, the board developed a union seminary in Buenos Aires. Methodists in Brazil united their seminaries into one in São Paulo. When visiting the area, Ralph Felton gave special leadership in developing these programs.[46] While the 1940 report focused on education efforts, it also acknowledged the rural nature of the church in México and called for study of the land reform efforts in that country.

The report concluded with directions for future missionary policy. Heading these were both concern for the welfare of the younger churches and the ever-increasing responsibility taken by the indigenous leadership. In addition, the board urged keeping channels of fellowship open despite nationalism, the need for adjustment in the geographic fields, and the emphasis on different forms of work from what some might have been accustomed to. Working with the leadership, the board urged greater emphasis on united planning and administration, naming such areas as literature distribution, curricula for training schools, and financial development. Finally, the board pledged to rekindle a sense of mission in the U.S. church and to find opportunities for youth.[47]

Principles for Mission

At the same time the board was looking to publish a new missionary manual, it was also working to develop principles for carrying on missions in the changing political situations. These included sympathy for persons in belligerent countries, work goals of reconciliation and relief of suffering, and policies regarding evacuation notices. The principles specified that women and children would return to the U.S. and that only those missionaries who wished to stay would do so. All missionaries were reminded to avoid unnecessary risks, to remember to stay neutral, and to keep personal safety more important than concerns about property.[48]

Work in the U.S.

While the signs of war and upheaval were growing increasingly ominous, work in the U.S. was still affected by the lingering economic forces of the Great Depression. A symposium in October of 1940 evaluated the most urgent challenges of missions in the U.S. for the new denomination. Dr. Charles Schaeffer reminded people of the need to supply a vivid consciousness of the reality of God; Bishop U. V. W. Darlington called the church to establish congregations in urban and rural waste places; Bishops E. L. Waldorf and Hoyt M. Dobbs reiterated the need for maintaining morale; and John R. Mott identified the need to augment leadership,

In the 1940s, the lingering economic forces of the Great Depression meant that many small churches were no longer economically able to support themselves. When the church sent rural workers like Elizabeth Thompson and Ann McKenzie to rural areas, the congregations were unfamiliar with the concept of such missionaries and at first did not know how to respond to them. By the 1960s, however, the church had established ministries in the places shown on this map. *(Map courtesy of United Methodist Archives and History)*

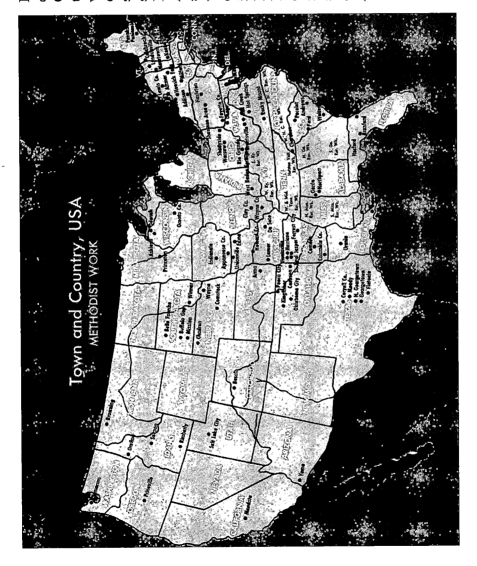

Town and Country, USA
METHODIST WORK

especially among laypeople.[49] Shifting populations were changing the composition of both urban and rural churches. Metropolitan areas were growing, but not inner cities; many small churches were no longer economically able to support themselves. Looking for new directions, participants suggested group ministry plans that would pool resources and personnel, providing help with home ownership to those in need and developing local church education projects.

One example of how the church sought to minister to relocated wartime workers and military personnel was a ministry in Hunter's Point, San Francisco. Families had moved there from all over the country to work in military industries. San Francisco was also the home for military personnel who were stationed there to protect the U.S.

Members of The Methodist Church visited families in their homes, developed a childcare center, enrolled children in Sunday school, organized a unit of the Woman's Society of Christian Service (WSCS), held a vacation Bible school, and had Wednesday night prayer meetings. The connection between this ministry in 1945 and the delegates meeting in San Francisco to organize the United Nations was made by an anonymous author: "While world security is being built by the great United Nations Conference in San Francisco not many miles from Hunter's Point, the church does its part in building for family security. The two tasks are not dissimilar."[50]

Not everything went smoothly with the transition to the new structure. Elizabeth Thompson told the story of her appointment as a rural church worker, the first one to be appointed without a particular institutional assignment. When she arrived in north Alabama, the district officers did not know what to do with her. Remembering that the district secretary had held office for twenty-five years, they sent her on to Huntsville, sure that the secretary, who lived there, would feel honored to have a rural worker.

Mrs. E., the district secretary, was taken aback, having no idea what to do with Thompson either. But she gave her a room for the night and assured her that the next day all would be settled at a meeting where many of the conference officers and staff were gathering. Eager to hear of her assignment, Thompson rose early the next morning and dressed carefully in a simple black dress (reminiscent of the deaconess costume) with white collar and cuffs—but with a red petticoat underneath for courage. "I felt like a show horse being trotted out for inspection," she wrote many years later.

The red petticoat may have boosted her courage, but it did not seem to be making a difference in the life of the church. One after another the ministers of the conference found reasons *not* to have this woman help them in their church. Lunchtime came and went. Talk turned to winding up all business for the day so that everyone could return home. And still Thompson had no place to be in ministry. Finally, the district superintendent noted the one minister in attendance who came from the former Northern branch of Methodism (there had been a few Methodist Episcopal churches that far south). Even though with the unifying conference the church was now all one and the same, he had no standing within the conference to refuse anything that might be asked. His church seemed the perfect placement for a woman.

Thompson traveled to Woodville the next day by train. Church members were puzzled about her coming: "We aren't as bad off as some of the other churches," they told her. Their pastor kept the secret that no one else had wanted her when he introduced her to the congregation. "Here is Miss Thompson. She is some kind of woman preacher, I think. Let's hear what she has to say for herself."

The year in Woodville was a frustrating one, since Thompson often spent time explaining her presence and work. But the women of the conference quickly recognized her worth, and soon she was able to find more fruitful fields in which to work.

A few hundred miles away, another community worker, Martha Almon, was organizing in rural Tennessee. Every Saturday night she drove along winding gravel roads through the mountains to the community of Genesis, which had no churches. When she arrived she would share the books and pamphlets she kept in her trunk with any of the young people who showed up for the meeting. Then she would unload the Cokesbury worship hymnals and set up the folding organ. The young people would help her light the Coleman lanterns and hang them from hooks around the one-room schoolhouse where they gathered. After a rousing hymn-sing, Almon would give a devotional.

One rainy evening, only four people came. They decided to go home early because of the wet conditions. But just as they were singing the last hymn, a family of five came in the door. They had walked a mile and a half to get to the meeting. Almon decided that she would give the devotional after all, ending with the usual prayer and invitation to accept Christ. Then everyone went home.

Ann McKenzie

Ann McKenzie's entry into ministry matches that of many women who chose to become deaconesses in The Methodist Church. When she heard about women doing church work, nothing was said about ordination—women could not be full members of annual conferences at that time, and no one mentioned mission work; the focus was on being assistants to others in ministry. But she heard the call and answered it, attending Scarritt and becoming a commissioned deaconess in 1948.

Her first position as a rural worker was with an elderly country preacher who served small churches. She was the only such worker in her conference, so she had no colleagues with whom to discuss her experiences. After the preacher retired, she moved to a new assignment—seven churches on the other side of the conference. Her pay was low, as it was for most deaconesses, but she often was invited to Sunday dinner along with the preacher. Her days were varied. One day a parishioner invited her to bring her laundry along; together the two tackled the chores of washday. As they were hanging out the clothes, they discussed some of the issues before them, particularly the need for Sunday school rooms. They decided to approach one of the women in the church who had some land to see if they could use it for the Lord's Acre program.

Under this program, farmers could devote part of their crop (an acre or more) to God, sell the harvest, and give the proceeds to the church. Informally they talked with various people in the church about what they could donate to help the project. As McKenzie tells it, women talked to their husbands, who then thought it was all their own idea and helped do the work. They grew cotton, selling enough to be able to make the money they needed for the Sunday school rooms. Word got around about this project, and other churches tried the idea, achieving success as well.

(Continued on next page.)

The next Saturday as she came over the last hill to the schoolhouse, she could see it blazing with light. Horses and mules were hitched outside near a parked truck. People were milling around both outside and inside the church. As she got out of her car, a man came to greet her, asking, "Are you Miss Marthy?"

As they walked into the building, she learned that he was the county representative for the area. He announced to her and the crowd that his grandson had been converted the week before, and they were gathering in thanks. The meeting was the beginning of successful efforts for commu-

(Ann McKenzie, continued from preceding page)

She spent six years at that assignment, with the help of a US-2 (a volunteer spending two years in mission in the U.S.) the last two years. Then she moved on to Wayne County, Tennessee. One of her new churches had never had a vacation Bible school. So she nominated three men to run it. After she explained to them what they were supposed to do, they went around and visited all the families, so that one hundred children participated in this first-ever program in the community.

McKenzie's work with rural churches continued throughout her years of ministry. She claimed she got to know the power company very well because she paid many a bill for poor parishioners. But not all were poor. She took youth on trips to Methodist mission projects where they slept on the floor, cooking their own meals. Her stories and work typify that of many rural workers—day-in, day-out identification with people and their needs, willingness to take on a variety of responsibilities and tasks, and creativity in facing all sorts of situations and problems.

Source: Interview with McKenzie, January 17, 2001, by Melynn Glusman.

nity worker Almon to work with the people of her area for a better life. Years later she reflected that she had nearly closed the small meeting without the devotional and final prayer. Never again did she judge success or failure in terms of numbers.

Measurement in numbers of converts was not restricted to those who worked in faraway lands. Rural workers in particular found that they often had to interpret their work for the larger church, whose members did not understand. The rural workers knew that they were in a ministry and mission that produced in its own way and time, but they still faced the report writing and interpretation that were essential for continued mission.

Adjustments to the new structure for "home" mission were not limited to the rural settings. One example was the Methodist Girls' Club in Minnesota, a home for single young women in the middle of St. Paul. The home itself was an example of the mission projects that were designed to meet particular needs in particular places. Similar to the Esther Halls run by the Division of Home Missions and Church Extension in many areas of the country, the Girls' Club provided a safe place for young women who had come to the city for jobs. Families—and the young women themselves—felt safer in the carefully monitored environment.

One supporter believed so strongly in the mission that she left a

Police used tear gas to disperse a crowd gathered on a main street in Detroit in an effort to halt rioting on June 21, 1943. The riots resulted from white unhappiness that blacks were moving into a new housing project. The occurrence of these riots along with the "zoot suit" riots in Los Angeles the same year embarrassed the country at a time when it was ostensibly fighting for freedom in Europe and the Pacific. *(AP/Wide World photo used with permission)*

substantial legacy to help fund the ministry. This money from the Emma Norton Fund gave the Minnesota women a feeling of security for both the present and the future regarding this ministry. But the national changes in the church gave them pause. They "feared that in the new huge structure of the Woman's Society their small project . . . would be changed or even abolished."[51] The women did not transfer the property or the fund to the Woman's Division. Instead, they organized themselves into "Trustees of the Continuing Corporation of the Woman's Home Missionary Society of the Minnesota Conference of the Methodist Church" and continued to administer the fund, originally donated by Emma Norton, and operate the residence for young women and its activities with only token responsibility by the Woman's Society.[52] The solution to its organizational standing sought by the women was a reflection of that individual nature rather than distrust of the new church hierarchy. Women of Minnesota continued to support the work just as they would have had it been under the national division. In fact, during the war, the residence was home to five young Japanese-American women from relocation camps.

Race was a major factor in the structure of the new church. Within the Division of Home Missions and Extension, the Department of Negro Work was a visible sign of awareness of race issues. In its initial report, the department called for the church to be aware of discrimination in labor and the armed forces. It proposed better training for ministry, work on both city and rural life issues, and the need for better understanding between the races.[53]

The situation of African Americans in the U.S. during the Second World War was complicated. Many African Americans had joined the armed forces, but units were still segregated. And in 1943, riots occurred in Detroit that worried the nation's leaders. The Ku Klux Klan and other segregationist groups were active in the area. When African Americans were about to move into the Sojourner Truth Federal Housing project, whites tried to stop them, and the riots began. Twenty-five African Americans were killed, along with nine whites; nineteen of the former and none of the latter were killed by the police. Three-fourths of the 1,900 people arrested were African American. The 1944 General Conference asked that African Americans be given full citizenship rights.

Public authorities were confused about the conditions under which federal troops could be requested, although eventually a presidential proclamation was issued, and military police and an infantry division were called into action. But because of the confusion, Attorney General Francis Biddle made several speeches in 1943 and 1944 about racial tensions among the military. He suggested some of the reasons for the tensions, including the poor treatment of and inferior housing for African Americans. He also spoke of the "contradiction between our profession of faith in democracy and our acts."

Charles Hamilton Houston, a distinguished African-American law professor at Howard University, complained about the Navy's barring African-American women from the WAVES (Women Accepted for Voluntary Emergency Service) and the treatment of African-American military personnel when they were trained in the South. He pointed out that some of the German prisoners of war were treated better than African Americans. "Meanwhile," he wrote, "enemy propaganda is carrying the stories of racial dissension in the United States to all corners of the earth, and the colored peoples of Asia, Africa and India are getting an eyeful of how white Americans act abroad."[54]

Hispanic Work

In the 1940s, most of the Spanish-speaking mission work of The Methodist Church was concentrated in the Southwest and Southern California. Although some work had been done with Cuban immigrants in Tampa and Ybor City, Florida, the vast majority of Hispanic Methodists lived in Texas and westward.

The Latino American Provisional Conference had some forty churches and 3,000 members, located in Southern California and Arizona. La Trinidad Methodist Church in Los Angeles had 500 or more members in the early 1940s.[55] At least two congregations in the Southern California–Arizona Annual Conference also included some Latinos: Plaza Methodist Church and The Church of All Nations, near the Plaza in Los Angeles. The latter congregation had been served by G. Bromley Oxnam in the 1920s. The conference had also created a Spanish American Institute under the leadership of Vernon McCombs, a former missionary to South America. The institute sought to train young Latino boys in farming, crafts, and industrial skills. McCombs established a Plaza Community Center to help Latino men and women obtain the skills for employment. It had a medical clinic, a welfare department, and various clubs. Similar was the Hollenbeck Center in East Los Angeles, which provided recreational and educational opportunities for Latinos from age six to twenty-five.[56]

The people served by these churches were almost all immigrants from México or were descended from Mexican immigrants. They were working-class people who helped to build the famous interurban rail lines in Southern California and were its most frequent riders. Mexican Americans were highly regarded as tile workers and cement finishers, not incidental occupations in a city that had styled itself as "Spanish" in the 1920s and 1930s and had built enormous numbers of houses in a style reminiscent of that culture.[57]

Mexican Americans were segregated in schools, housing, and other arenas in Southern California.[58] The Southern California–Arizona Conference seems to have been slow in arousing its members to the destructiveness of this segregation. At the 1942 annual conference, resolutions were presented on the problems of African Americans and Japanese Americans, at that time not yet restricted to internment camps. No mention was made of the problems of Hispanics. In 1943, however, the conference went on record as saying, "Our large Spanish speaking minority has long presented a high responsibility and rich opportunity for the Protestant Church." The statement went on to speak of social and economic conditions creating racial tensions, especially "a situation in which industrial farmers can capitalize on prejudice against these people as they have in turn against Hindus, Chinese, Filipinos and Japanese." The conclusion was that bilingual churches be developed.[59]

The conference's action may have been a reaction to the famous "zoot suit" riots that took place in Los Angeles in June 1943. Young Mexican Americans adopted a flamboyant costume of loose-fitting trousers and pointed shoes, set off by ducktail haircuts. When several sailors got into a fight with some of the zoot-suiters, hundreds of soldiers and sailors invaded the barrio and downtown Los Angeles. Street fights went on for several nights. The violence spilled over into attacks on African Americans and Filipinos. The assaults stopped only when the Mexican government objected, and the U.S. State Department pressured the commanding officers of U.S. military bases to place Los Angeles off limits.[60]

There were no riots in Texas and New Mexico, where the Southwest Mexican Conference stretched from northern Texas to the state's southernmost tip at Brownsville and west to El Paso and Albuquerque, New Mexico. In 1939, the conference had 6,364 members and slightly more in church school. The conference changed its name to the Río Grande Conference in 1948.[61] It had three significant institutions: Holding Institute in Laredo, Texas, which began as a girls' school with close ties to México; Lydia Patterson Institute in El Paso, a secondary school with departments in English and theology; and Harwood Girls' School in Albuquerque. All of these, as well as the conference itself, were supported by the denomination. In addition, the conference created a "WhoSoEver" community center in San Antonio, Texas, with a program of education, spirituality, and health care.[62]

Southwest Hispanics were especially interested in México and Latin America, publishing news of Methodist churches in their conference paper. They were loyal to their own denomination, however, and supported conference-wide programs like the Crusade for Christ. Their support for the crusade fitted naturally into their own emphasis on evangelism. Charts were published showing that Methodists enrolled 11 percent of the population in Sunday schools—meaning that the rest of the population offered potential recruits. Pastors were commended for their evangelistic zeal and winning of new members. A report on a Methodist Conference on Christian Education was quoted approvingly, citing the Great Commission and saying that the goal of the denomination was to win 1.2 million souls to Christ and church membership through the church school. An article in the conference paper asked, "Can Mexico Be Totally Evangelized in Thirty More Years?"[63] The evangelistic efforts of the conference had results. By 1950, membership had doubled and was almost ten thousand in fifty-five churches.[64]

Although they had modest incomes, these Methodists contributed to the Crusade for Christ as well as World Service. For example, the Rev-

Lydia Patterson Institute in El Paso, a secondary school with departments in English and theology, became one of the premier educational institutions of The Methodist Church in its efforts to serve a growing Hispanic constituency. The school continues as an institution of The United Methodist Church. *(Photo courtesy of United Methodist Archives and History)*

erend Eduardo Luján led his church in McAllen, Texas, to contribute $300 to the crusade, and another pastor, the Reverend Librado Castillo, sent $700 from his church. When the Advance was created, Río Grande members supported it.[65]

The clergy members of the conference in the 1940s sometimes were Mexican immigrants. Such was the Reverend Manuel C. Galindo, who was a colorful character born in México and became a soldier in the army of Don Porfirio Díaz, ending his military career as a major. After being converted to Methodism, he left México for the U.S. to escape the difficulties of the 1913 revolution.[66] He served churches in Arizona, then went east and served as a pastor in several places in Texas and New Mexico. His somewhat conservative disposition can be deduced from a story told by another pastor who knew him. He was "always punctual in the extreme," the pastor wrote. "On one occasion he drove me to Hayden, Arizona, and we came to the railroad station five hours before the train arrived. 'But brother [I said], we're five hours early.' To which the brother replied, 'I have never been late in my life in order to catch a train.'"[67]

This conservative style expressed a theology typical of the upwardly mobile and also the disciplines that reflected such a theology. Southwestern Hispanics emphasized their own heartfelt faith and, although passionate, were also devoted to hard work, temperance, and sobriety. Reflecting their awareness that Protestants in México and South America felt repressed by Roman Catholics, they affirmed the need for civil liberties. Along with other Protestants in the 1940s, they objected when President Harry S. Truman tried to name an ambassador to the Vatican. They also noted that Japanese Americans and African Americans suffered from discrimination and took careful note of progress of those groups toward civil liberties.[68] But their preference for maintaining a low profile inhibited them from making any public protests. Their eagerness to model better relations between Hispanics and Anglos was shown in their pointing to the success of the Río Grande City church, which merged Anglo and Hispanic congregations under the leadership of the Reverend Pablo O. Calderon.[69]

This willingness to work with Anglos also expressed itself in church relations. Its bishop from 1939 until 1960, A. Frank Smith, an Anglo, was also chair of the National Division for much of his tenure, and his influence no doubt led to the increase of support from the National Division, both in clergy salaries and in the construction of buildings. Since the

Lydia Patterson Institute could not provide enough education for ministerial students to become qualified for ordination, the Board of Missions
supported the creation of a ministry to Spanish-speaking students at
Perkins School of Theology in 1946.[70]

A member of the Río Grande Conference who helped to build ties to
Perkins was Alfredo Náñez, who was the first Hispanic in the conference
to receive a seminary degree. He had been converted under the ministry
of the legendary Frank Onderdonk. He served as a pastor in several Texas
cities and became the executive secretary of Christian education for the
conference, where he served for twenty-one years. He was the author of
numerous articles in the conference paper, *El Heraldo Cristiano*, and his
history of the conference became a major resources for scholars.[71]

African Americans in Mission

African Americans in The Methodist Church were concerned with their
segregated status in the denomination from the beginning. They took
every opportunity to raise questions about the issue of equality and also
tried to raise the consciousness of the church about segregation in U.S.
society. These efforts meant that Methodist African Americans were concerned with mission within the U.S., and they served in community centers, settlement houses, rural ministries, and work camps.

Lillian Warrick, for example, served as the first African-American field
secretary for the WSCS from 1940 to 1943, leading workshops for both
male pastors and laywomen and teaching in schools of Christian mission.
She was followed by Vivienne Gray and Theressa Hoover.[72]

African Americans had a history of serving in missions outside the
U.S. Martha Drummer and Susan Collins had served in Angola early in
the twentieth century. Their service was part of an effort by many U.S.
denominations, white as well as African American, to recruit African-
American missionaries. Unfortunately, the tide of racial prejudice in the
U.S. after 1900 led the white denominations to discourage their enlist-
ment, and in some cases mission boards actually withdrew African Americans from service. The turning point may have come in 1942, when a
Church Conference on African Affairs was held at Otterbein College, a
United Brethren school in Westville, Ohio. The conference participants
proposed that a larger role be given to African Americans, both as missionaries and as members of mission boards.[73]

Vivienne Gray, center, along with her husband Ulysses, was among the first African-American missionaries sent by The Methodist Church to serve outside the U.S. The Grays went to Liberia in 1948 and served many years. About the same time, Thomas and Jennie Harris, also African Americans, were sent to Sarawak, Malaysia. *(Photo courtesy of United Methodist Archives and History)*

Both African Americans and others seemed to assume that the natural place for African Americans to serve was Africa. Indeed, the Central Jurisdiction bishops regularly called for more African Americans to offer themselves for service, and the place they often specified was Liberia: "Our first responsibility as a Jurisdiction is to Liberia," said Bishop R. N. Brooks in the Central Jurisdiction Episcopal Address in 1948.[74] These pleas were answered when Ulysses and Vivienne Gray went to Liberia.

Ulysses Gray had spent two years at Wiley College in Texas and then earned degrees from Clark College and Gammon Theological Seminary, both in Atlanta. He also spent a semester at Cornell University, in New York, which had a highly respected agricultural school. He and Vivienne met at Gammon, and they were sent as missionaries to Gbarnga, Liberia, in 1948. She worked with Liberian women in the church, and he taught agricultural methods, introducing new breeds of poultry, new methods of growing rice, and new varieties of fruits and vegetables. He also organized boys' clubs, and several of the young men under his tutelage went to Booker T. Washington Institute in Liberia. He led Liberians in economic development, including showing them ways to grow rubber, coffee, and cocoa trees. In addition to his work in agriculture, Ulysses was a pastor and district superintendent to forty-nine stations. "A well-fed nation is a happy nation," he said. "A happy nation is easy to teach. My primary purpose is to teach Christ and his way."[75]

Perhaps even more noteworthy, however, was the assignment of Thomas and Jennie Harris, also African Americans, to Sarawak, Malaysia, in 1948. They demonstrated that African Americans could serve in places other than Africa. The Harrises went to a mission and agricultural training center in Borneo, where they operated a school, a community center, an agricultural experiment station, and a training center for the Sea Dyaks, also called Ibans. He taught agricultural methods, and she taught boys using a phonetic system she developed, based on the Laubach method.[76]

As for the evil of segregation, the leaders of the Central Jurisdiction had to walk a narrow line between their own objections to this injustice and their loyalty to the church. When Peter Berger, a young Austrian student at Wittenberg College in Ohio, sent a questionnaire to African-American bishops inquiring about the policies of The Methodist Church on segregation, the published answer denied that there was complete segregation in the denomination: "There are many individual Negroes belonging to white churches in Methodism, and in some cases white persons belong to Negro churches." The efforts being made to end discrimination were also described, including the work of Thelma Stevens of the Woman's Division and other Southerners.[77] African Americans continued to call attention to the problems of separatism, although they also noted its advantages — mainly that it allowed them to have representation on the boards of the church and to be heard in the Council of Bishops.

Like Hispanics, African Americans supported church programs like the Crusade for Christ. Bishop Brooks of the New Orleans area of the Central Jurisdiction proudly reported that his area was the first in the denomination to fulfill its asking for the crusade.[78] The Central Jurisdiction churches also supported the overall mission program of the denomination through World Service.

Native Americans: Education and Growth

The largest concentration of Native Americans in the early years of The Methodist Church lay in the Indian Mission of Oklahoma. At union it had 3,294 members in thirty charges. Members came from many peoples:

When Toge Fujihira photographed Hunting Horse in the 1950s, the event symbolized the enduring dignity of two peoples deprived of their rights. Hunting Horse was a Kiowa in Oklahoma who had served U.S. military troops in the nineteenth century. He lived to be more than 100 years old and was an active member of the Oklahoma Indian Mission Conference. Fujihira was among Japanese Americans interned during the Second World War. He became the official photographer of the Methodist Board of Missions and before his death in 1973 succeeded in presenting the face of mission to the church in thousands of photographs. *(Photo courtesy of United Methodist Archives and History)*

Choctaw, Chickasaw, Creek, Seminole, Euchee, Kiowa, and Comanche. The mission had originally been organized by the Methodist Episcopal Church, South. One of its bishops, A. Frank Smith, continued as the episcopal leader of the mission; after him, beginning in 1944, his brother, Angie Smith, presided. Although the Smiths were admired for their forcefulness, they continued to appoint whites as superintendents. This paternalistic practice did not go unnoticed by Native Americans, who understandably felt they were more capable of administering their own affairs. Angie Smith, however, was willing to appoint Native Americans to white churches.

Among the prominent Native American leaders were Delos Knowles Lonewolf, who was probably the first Kiowa to be licensed to preach; Johnson Wilson Bobb and his wife, Mae, who served in the economically depressed southeastern area of the state among the Choctaws and the Chickasaws; and Mrs. D. B. Childers, who was director of Christian education in the Creek District, in central Oklahoma, for eighteen years. Another laywoman who bridged the MECS – Methodist era was Lena Benson Tiger, who organized the Woman's Missionary Society and was its president until 1940. At that time, the mission had forty societies with a membership of 623.

Despite the paternalism, Methodists seemed more interested in developing indigenous leadership than did other denominations. After criticism that Methodists were encroaching on areas served by other denominations, missionary Don J. Kliningsmith wrote that the real issue was "the Methodist use of native pastors and leaders rather than white ones." Methodists encouraged Native Americans to gain an education to enable them to become full members of the conference, and many studied at colleges and universities, not always receiving degrees but gaining an education nevertheless.[79]

The Woman's Division supported the Navajo Methodist Mission School in Farmington, New Mexico, as well. Besides a 100-acre farm and a health center, the mission had a school that by the late 1940s had some 170 students from elementary through high school. It was related to two community centers several miles from the school. Vina Todacheene, herself a Navajo, was one of the missionaries at the Heurfano Community Center in 1949. Some graduates of the school went on to attain higher education.[80]

In the 1940s, the 400,000 Native Americans in the U.S. were concentrated in Oklahoma (70,000), Alaska (32,000), and seventy-eight reservations (200,000). The remaining 100,000 were scattered among towns and cities across the country. During the Second World War, some 18,000 served in the military and another 45,000 worked in defense industries. Although these numbers seem small, they indicate that Native Americans were becoming acculturated, sometimes to their detriment. Methodists had work not only in Oklahoma and New Mexico but also among the Lumbees in North Carolina; a collection of small tribes in Mendocino County, California; the Winnebago, Sioux, Omaha, and Ponca in Iowa;

the Ottawa, Potawatomie, and Ojibway in Michigan; and Chippewas in Minnesota. Alaskan missionaries served among indigenous peoples there as well.[81]

Communication and Education

As it brought together men and women into one board, The Methodist Church planned *World Outlook* as the official publication. Its sixty-four pages were to be divided equally between the Woman's Division and the Division of Foreign Missions. Dorothy McConnell was not alone when she raised concerns about this format. She likened the division to the doorflap on a *zenana* that held others at a distance.[82] By labeling a whole section as Woman's Work, the magazine risked marginalizing women's contributions. The final decision was to continue *Woman's Home Missions*, a magazine of the Methodist Episcopal Church, as *Methodist Woman*.[83]

World Outlook had a key role within the new church. Through its pages readers could discover new information and descriptions about the ministries in places where their own church—whether MEC, MECS, or MPC—had not had active mission. As always, McConnell noted, *World Outlook* was not just a report of missionary projects, but of missionaries.[84] All of these means of communication were related to efforts at mission education. The church had a system that on paper called for education to flow from the national agencies through the conferences and into the local churches. These efforts were sometimes successful, but their limits were illustrated by a report that Karl Quimby, sent by the Board of Missions in New York, filed after visiting several states in the West.

Quimby met with district superintendents and other clergy, theological students, and local churches in Colorado, Arizona, Utah, and California. The conference churches, Quimby felt, were interested in mission but needed more cultivation: "The people were interested but not informed." Quimby called Utah "a mission conference." He concluded that more mission cultivation was needed. "Our preachers are not informed, they are not pioneering in this direction, and their people are merely following along." More cultivation, he concluded, "is a titanic task, but it can be done. It ought to be done. It must be done!" Despite his concern, The Methodist Church found that its very size and complexity presented large obstacles to developing mission support in the local churches.[85]

Ralph Diffendorfer

Diffendorfer claimed that as a Sunday school student he was inspired with such a passion for mission by British missionary David Livingstone that it lasted his whole life. But his mother claimed that his personality had elements of P. T. Barnum in it as well. The passion and the leadership became apparent early, and after his education he began to work for the Board of Foreign Missions of the Methodist Episcopal Church.

He moved into leadership just when the Interchurch World Movement in 1924 was failing, leaving a host of financial difficulties. Diffendorfer's abilities allowed him to gain stature and prestige among his colleagues. Bishop Francis McConnell marveled at his active mind, commenting wryly, "He's got more ideas than any other fellow I ever knew, and most of them aren't of any account. But once in a while he gets a hold of one of them that we accept, and it is worth more than any of the others."

W. W. Reid evaluated his tenure as covering some of the most difficult times for "foreign" missions. The excitement was over, the money was scarce, and support was diminishing. Worldwide depression followed by war put unending strain on the creativity and resources of the leadership. Such circumstances made Diffendorfer's tenure and accomplishments all the more impressive.

While Diffendorfer could be brusque, insistent, and even thoughtless of the feelings of others, he was also remembered for his honesty, his ability to listen to others, and even his willingness for his staff to differ from him. Openness to other ideas meant that he was able to change his mind if necessary, measuring his decisions not by popularity or expediency but by what he discerned to be the will of God. Frank Cartwright praised him as well for his willingness to help colleagues who needed to "get out of a mess." On holidays Diffendorfer invited students or even lonely bishops who were in town to share in his home and hospitality.

Like many of the leaders of his generation, Diffendorfer was influenced by Gordon Parker Bowne and Edgar S. Brightman and the school of Boston personalism. Diffendorfer believed that Christ was relevant for the whole person as well as for every person. This belief helped lead his passion for Christian service to projects that were interfaith and interracial. When the Second World War ended, he emphasized that relief of human need should have first place in all plans, with reconstruction of property second.

Following his retirement in December 1949, Diffendorfer served as executive for the Japan International University Foundation, living out his commitment to education in yet another way. His tenure lasted until 1951, when he died suddenly from a heart attack.

Sources: W. W. Reid, remarks at funeral of Ralph Diffendorfer, typescript in the Diffendorfer files, and letters of Diffendorfer, both in United Methodist Archives and History.

Ralph Diffendorfer.
*(Photo courtesy of United
Methodist Archives and
History)*

Effects of War on Policy

Within a few short months the board had faced more changes from without than from within its own newly formed structure. Events in the world
continued to unfold. With all that the board had already faced, the actual
declaration of war made more official and visible the altered conditions in
which it had to work.

By 1941, upheaval in many parts of the world was seriously affecting the
ability of those in Methodist mission to stay in touch with one another.
The second annual meetings of both the Division of Foreign Missions
and the Woman's Division were far more absorbed with details of a daily
changing world scene than with any minutiae from the effects of the
church union. Regarding Europe, no communications at all arrived from
Norway, Denmark, or Hungary. Although the Germany Central Conference continued to meet, the district superintendent, his wife, and Ruth

Lawrence of the Woman's Division were not permitted to leave Poland to attend.[86] Other places were also affected. Women were advised either to leave or not to enter Liberia and Central Congo at all.

But the biggest effects continued to be in Asia. Reports were written to explain the withdrawal from Korea in more detail. Finally making the decision at the board level relieved individuals of having to explain what would have been very difficult personal decisions. Instead, since all women had left by the end of 1940 and the last five men only two months later, the staff and board had to make new kinds of personnel assignments.[87] The board assisted the newly returned missionaries in making decisions about their employment for the immediate future. This support established a pattern that was needed often during the war years. Once war-related decisions were made that changed assignments, personnel were redeployed to other countries or relocated to particular ministries in the U.S. Meanwhile, the board continued to assure the general church that the Koreans and indigenous Methodists in other countries were able to carry on with leadership and to continue the development of the church.

After Pearl Harbor, of course, the board was faced with emergencies. Properties in Korea were transferred to the Korean church. Communications with the churches in the Philippines were cut off, and no one had any idea what had happened to family and friends stationed there. Finally, in 1943, a Red Cross telegram arrived asking the board to inform the families that all was well. Some missionaries in Malaysia who had left to attend a conference in Singapore never returned to their homes. Tyler Thompson had chosen to remain on Sumatra. When no communications were received, the board began to suspect that he might be interned, which they later found to be true. In China, the number of missionaries decreased from 189 in 1937 to 127 in 1941. When the Japanese came to Foochow, conditions changed even more. The theological seminary in Nanking continued to operate, but in other places in China, seminary and college faculties were confined. In response to this news, the executive secretary called for an increase in missionaries to Free China, the unoccupied area where missionaries could still operate. When possible, those from the occupied sections were reassigned. At the same time, the board continued to plan for a time when the country would be open to missionaries again. Because so many of the women missionaries were near retirement age, the report called for the Woman's Division to seek out the "choicest young women" and train them. Such a statement was not made without awareness of the present dangers. Written in November 1941, the report concluded with the belief that Christianity in China was strong enough for the challenges of war.[88]

By the following year, the annual report carried much more detailed information about the institutions in each conference of China. For example, in the North China Conference, most of the schools and hospitals were closed or taken over by the government. Only one hospital in Peking remained open. All missionaries left the Central China Conference and occupied portions of Kiangsi Conference, which included Nanking. Some of these had spent time interned before they were permitted to leave. In some places, Chinese Christians continued to carry on the work, but in others, no activity was allowed.[89]

To those who remained in Japan, the board sent a telegram: "Board unanimously orders farewell," meaning that all were to leave. Because of work done previously, the board felt assured that a church presence would remain even with all the missionaries gone. Removing personnel was seen as an official recognition from the board that the presence of foreigners was a liability to Japanese Christians and that the church would continue to develop without foreigners. Returning missionaries met with Dr. John Cobb in San Francisco to evaluate their experiences and plan for the future. Gradually they received assignments for further work in the U.S.

Dislocations and Other Tragedies

From the point of view of the two branches of mission that ordinarily had workers in Japan, the war brought real change. The Japanese people were still the recipients of mission work, but it was primarily within the borders of the U.S. or, in some cases, in other countries where Japanese had emigrated. The missionaries who had served faithfully in Japan were deployed in a variety of ways in the U.S. and abroad during the war years, but they did not let those in the church forget the connection they still felt with the people of Japan. Through its literature, for example, the mission board communicated relationship and concern for the many parts of the church, still reflecting the point of view that developed in those who took seriously Wesley's dictum, "The world is my parish." The Woman's Division published a booklet in 1942 called *Workers Together with God,* by Bertha Starkey. In the foreword, Starkey wrote of a beautiful fan she received from Christian women in Japan, including its accompanying words: "We are workers together with God, There is not West or East in Christ, Love Japan Methodist Women to American Methodist Sisters." Then she went on to give her assurance that these women were still carrying on the work: "War may destroy buildings but it cannot destroy the Christian influences of these personalities." In the booklet were pictures of women and the stories of their lives and work. Such a booklet provided an alternative to the sentiment that allowed the internment of U.S. citizens of Japanese descent and found expression in all sorts of anti-Japanese cartoons, literature, and epithets. Mission work was the grounding of a different worldview — one that saw beyond the present world situation and tried to create a different way of looking at human beings. Such a worldview was harder to maintain during a time when the predominant culture encouraged the vilification of whole groups of people.

Christians within Japan faced an even harder struggle. Kiichi Kanzaki had been a dean at Kwansei Gakuin, the Methodist school for men, located between Kobe and Osaka. In 1941, he became president. Japanese militarists urged him to remove Christian principles from the school's constitution and give the buildings to the government. Kanzaki refused. Then the government proposed that the school become a regulated institution, which would mean that its graduates would have a much higher standing for university entrance. Regulation meant, however, that the government would then determine the curriculum and that religious instruction would be prohibited. Kanzaki again refused, and his decision was protested by parents and students who saw benefits in the changed status.

Kanzaki's friends suggested that he resign as president. He said, though, "I would not resign. For two reasons. First, Kwansei Gakuin must remain a Christian school. Second, if I resigned it would have meant that we admitted disloyalty to the country. . . . I refused to have anyone dictate to me what patriotism and loyalty were." Because so many of the students had been mobilized for the war, many of the buildings were vacant. Kanzaki had to compromise, and the Japanese navy took half of the campus for its use.[90]

The situation in India was affected both by the war and by the independence movement. Bishops in India asked for power in making decisions about the missionaries' going home. A commission granted them the power they requested but suggested that missionaries remain there, in spite of the advice of U.S. consuls, who suggested that the missionaries return home.[91] Instead, the missionaries added another element to their mission: ministry to U.S. troops in India.

Not all of the concerns were about the war. At the beginning of his 1942 report, the executive secretary reiterated the long-term goals of the church as nationalization of the ministries, reminding everyone that the basic plan was always to give nationals equal ecclesiastical status, despite the early predominance in the leadership structure of missionaries. At the same time, the decreasing numbers of missionaries in many places in the world was noted as "disturbing." When the three churches merged, they brought together a force 2,389 strong. Three years later, the number stood at almost exactly half—1,291—and that included persons not actually abroad because of the war. Achieving a strong indigenous church had been the priority for a number of years, but not all places had managed to develop the kind of self-support that might be demanded by the war conditions.

After the Japanese attack on Pearl Harbor, hysteria led to the imprisonment of 70,000 Japanese Americans. Representative of widespread fears of the Japanese was the comment of the general who carried out President Franklin Roosevelt's Executive Order 9066: "A Jap's a Jap." A Hearst newspaper columnist wrote: "I am for immediate removal of every Japanese on the West Coast to a point deep in the interior. I don't mean a nice part of the interior either. Herd 'em up, pack 'em off and give them the inside room in the badlands. Let 'em be pinched, hurt, hungry and dead up against it." California Attorney General Earl Warren argued for the internment.[92] Beginning in 1942, their possessions, including their homes, were taken away, and they were sent to eight centers located in several Western states and Arkansas. Methodists in the Southern California–Arizona Conference stated, "We do not join in a wholesale suspicion of disloyalty on the part of the Japanese of any generation. We deeply regret that the citizenship rights of many have been violated. We urge our church people to join in a positive movement to protect these persons from threats of permanent loss of civil and economic rights." Toward the end of the war, the conference asked for their release: "We hold that the time has arrived for the removal, by the War Department, of 'the unprecedented, quasi-martial law, suspending a small minority's Constitutional rights of personal liberty and freedom of action.'"[93]

The 1944 General Conference also asked for the restoration of full rights to Japanese Americans, linking this step with a request for full rights of citizenship for African Americans as well.[94] Criticism of the

The Manzanar War Relocation Center in California, shown in 1943, was one of many internment prisons established during the Second World War for Japanese Americans. The sparse surroundings expressed the intended isolation by the government. *(Ansel Adams photograph courtesy of Library of Congress)*

government's policy came from the Protestant magazines *Christian Century* and *Christianity and Crisis* as well as from the Federal Council of Churches. Everett W. Thompson, a former Methodist missionary to Japan, went to the Minidoka Relocation Center in southern Idaho, along with a Baptist minister, a Catholic priest, and several Japanese Christian clergy. They held church services and Sunday school classes for the internees. Thompson organized visits from Idaho youth to the camps to take groceries to the prisoners. The Federal Council of Churches sent Christmas gifts. The Reverend Toro Masumoto, a Reformed Church in America pastor who was interned for eleven months, remarked on this and other signs of sympathy from Americans, "We know that the spirit of Christ lives on despite hatred and strife."[95]

Ironically, many Japanese Americans became casualties when they answered the call of their government to serve in the armed forces in 1943. Some 1,300 of them were part of the 100th Infantry Battalion of the U.S. Army. One thousand Japanese Americans serving in the U.S. military were killed or wounded. One of those soldiers was Lt. Kei Tanahashi, who served in the 442nd Combat Team. He was killed in action in Italy on July 4, 1944, while his parents were imprisoned in the Heart Mountain Relocation Center in Wyoming.[96]

The Woman's Division joined other Christian women's organizations in issuing a statement of protest against the relocation. The statement affirmed the contribution of Japanese Americans and deplored their financial and personal losses. This joint statement went even further. It announced that the reassigned personnel would continue to work with the Japanese Provisional Annual Conference, providing important links with Caucasian groups. Looking ahead, the women called for the Christianizing of attitudes toward racial minorities, stating, "We must work for the removal of all traces of racial discrimination in the treatment of our fellow Americans."[97]

Internment of the Japanese in the U.S. gave the board new challenges and opportunities. Some missionaries were used as translators during the hearings before internment decisions. The board staff also served as interpreters of the events, noting that racial prejudice, economic pressures, local politics, public hysteria, and military necessity had preceded the decision.[98] In addition, missionaries helped to inventory the properties of those who were interned, to provide storage spaces for personal effects, and to arrange travel and other services. After the internment centers were established, the work was transferred to the Division of Home Missions.

As the war dragged on, some missionary personnel were again relocated, and other decisions were made as new information was received. In India, not only was there no widespread dislocation, but also many projects were able to continue despite rising prices, the presence of refugees, and other disruptions from a world at war. At Leonard Theological School, where several denominations worked together in training persons for ministry in India, classes continued despite the war. Many of these were taught by missionaries. Throughout India, most of the education endeavors were able to continue during the war years. Only one was taken over by the military.[99] Hospitals stayed open, and the publishing house continued its stream of literature, including the periodical *Woman's Friend*. The 1941 board meeting authorized a Medical Council that helped bring together medical work in the different divisions. Despite the continuation of ministries, the missionaries also faced difficulties. The government rationed gas and censored mail.

Africa news was limited because of the irregularity of the mail. Sarah King, returning from Rhodesia (now Zimbabwe), traveled on a ship that was torpedoed by the Germans. Her lifeboat capsized, and she spent another forty-eight hours on a second lifeboat before finally being rescued. But she was the exception for the missionaries to Africa. Other reports told of building projects that managed to continue, as well as the ever-present need for more personnel.[100]

The uniting of the church gave the women opportunity to evaluate missions in a variety of ways. They looked at some of the specific geographic areas to evaluate and plan for the future. One example of such a report was a discussion of the West China mission, which was originally under the MEC.[101] The report contained some of what was later seen as condescending language that occasionally characterized the interpretive work of the missionaries. But it also contained helpful information about the conditions, giving the U.S. readers a glimpse of the reality of the missionary task. Most of the churches were in cities or larger market towns, but the Woman's Division staff looked to the possibility of more evangelistic activity in rural areas, where 85 percent of the people lived. Author Mabel Ruth Nowlin also wrote of the work in the schools, which included a union seminary, a women's college, high schools, and a school of midwifery. She referred to the changes brought about by refugees pouring in, by living in a nation at war, and in particular by working in a place that had been bombed many times. The article illustrated the breadth of the women's work at the time as well as their willingness to continue to look ahead and plan for the future, even as current events were disruptive and destructive.

Work in China was significantly affected by Pearl Harbor. In the months that followed, nearly all "enemy nationals" from the Japanese-occupied areas had been relocated to one of the larger cities near the coast. The largest number of these were sent to Shanghai. Once relocated within these cities, however, they were allowed to come and go freely. Those who already had work in these locations continued it. But with war in the air and conditions tenuous, missionaries tried to be as inconspicuous as possible while they went about their work. By the following September, enemy nationals were also required to wear armbands and were forbidden entry into some public places. Staying inconspicuous became much more difficult. Because financial accounts were frozen, funds for expenses were obtained from personal bank accounts, if possible, and from selling personal effects — a practice also forbidden when the armbands were imposed. With each passing day, the lives of the missionaries were becoming more and more constricted. The missionaries were also subject to arrest and even detention by the Japanese authorities, who were looking for more sources of information.

Another immediate concern was accessibility of funds, since both the Japanese and the American authorities froze bank accounts. Personal bank accounts were soon depleted, and sale of personal effects could only raise so much money. By mid-1943, the staff had worked out ways to get money to the missionaries, however. But just getting the actual funds to them was only part of the problem. The inflation and continual rise in the cost of living meant that missionaries had trouble finding money for all their needs. Even though the Chinese government added a 50 percent bonus rate to the exchange, representatives of the agencies had to meet again and again to find other ways to meet the shortfall, since the money they had available bought only one-seventh of the goods it had in 1937.

Glenn Fuller in Chungking cabled the board, not just about the increasing dollar needs, but also with the suggestion that missionaries be withdrawn for the duration of the war. When they received this suggestion, the staffs of the Division of Foreign Missions and the Woman's Division cabled the China mission personnel with authorization for furloughs or India vacations as well as increased per diem expense allowances, hoping that this would provide more options or at least some relief for the struggling workers.

Just as all these arrangements were being made, general internment began. The remaining missionaries were given notice of the dates when they were expected to appear, bringing with them a bed, bedding, a chair, two trunks, and two suitcases. The camps to which they were sent were under the charge of Japanese civilian authorities, although they were guarded by military personnel. Within these camps, the internees had responsibility for administration, running them according to rules imposed by the Japanese. The board worked hard for an exchange of personnel, and most of the internees were allowed to leave on the S.S. *Gripsholm* in September 1943. Soon after their arrival in New York, the missionaries were able to report on the conditions they had left behind. Nearly all the property had been seized by the Japanese; some of it was locked up, but many buildings were looted or occupied. Some schools and hospitals continued under Japanese leadership; others were closed. Since many church buildings were no longer accessible, congregations began to meet in homes or other places they could find. The one bright spot in all the reports was that the policy of nationalization had already begun, so in many cases as the missionaries left, Chinese leaders could move smoothly into authority.

Even during the war the concern remained that the church stay out of any situations involving the internal politics of the countries in which they were in mission. The missionary pledge was an agreement that missionaries were guests and would do nothing against the lawfully constituted government of the country to which they were appointed. Because of this, missionaries had long kept distance from internal developments, but they had also on occasion drawn links between Christian response and some public positions.

Throughout the war, reports from India had focused on tensions in that country. But the kind of personal portraits that often characterized mission materials did not focus on the freedom struggles between the Indians and the British government. The legacy of the older missionaries, many of whom had sided with or been close to the British, still remained.

As the war continued, Methodist bishops in India faced more challenges within their own institution. Personnel from Korea and Japan arrived. U.S. consuls put pressure on the churches for the missionaries to return to the U.S. Troops from the U.S. were stationed in the country, providing both another place for ministry and a distraction from the internal concerns. As the churches moved to some form of union, the bishops began to work out agreements with the U.S. church so that their salary support would remain the same, even though they would not be directly under U.S. church institutions.

The Woman's Division reports were similar in their focus on organizational questions rather than the internal politics and freedom struggles. In 1942 the reports raised concerns about travel from the unavailability of gas. Rising prices meant that the boarding schools were having to reduce their numbers. A substantial gift helped to reduce the worrisome debt at Lucknow Christian College. Despite the war, mission work continued in many of the same forms, albeit under more difficult conditions than before.

War Years in Africa

As the war dragged on, the staff continued to look to the future in all parts of the world. To facilitate the planning, they convened a conference in Cincinnati to explore "Christian Education of the Methodist Church in the Belgian Congo" in 1943. The Methodist presence was significant—fifty-four missionaries with an average age of forty-four. Nineteen married couples, fourteen single women, and two single men shared the work. Thirty-three of these were in educational work, sixteen were pastors, and four were doctors. All of the missionaries were white.

On the agenda of the conference was discussion of the meaning of cultural heritage and what exactly the missionaries were asking Africans to change when they became Christian. Charles Iglehart reminded the group that any cultural heritage contains values that must be protected. Participants named a list of African values: religion as part of the totality of life, persons rather than things as being of primary value, belonging, emotional approach to reality (knowing that emotions as much as intellect reveal reality), and the religious significance of the soil. They raised the questions, "Are we as a Church—the Methodist Church—committed to the preservation of these values, and the utilization of them in our Christian education? If not, should we not be?"[102]

As they discussed this list and their main question, the participants estimated that about half of the missionaries appreciated the values and took them into account in their ministry, a quarter found them of little use, and another quarter were neutral but probably did not refer to them or take them into account very often.

Such conferences and reports demonstrate the attempts to become more sensitive, creating a better climate for evangelization. But despite the insights and possibilities, reports made during wartime did not receive the publicity or attention that they might have garnered. Evidence that such a conference made a significant difference is hard to find.

Outside the Conflict: México, Latin America, and the Caribbean

Although the attention of the U.S. was fixed on the war, the Methodist Church of México continued its evangelistic and educational efforts. The church, which had been organized as an autonomous body out of missions from the former MEC and MECS, had a strong and educated leadership.

Juan Nicanor Pascoe had served as its first bishop when the church was created in 1930.[103] Sixto Ávila became the second bishop in 1938 and, after ending his term in 1942, served as a district superintendent.[104]

The church emphasized both education and evangelism as it struggled

México, a part of North America, is shown as part of Latin America in this 1964 map. The Methodist Church of México became autonomous in 1930 but The Methodist Church in the U.S. continued to send missionaries there. During the Second World War, the Cuban government supported the Allies, making for a friendly relationship between Cuba and the United States. Mission work during the war continued throughout South America, and the Methodist churches in Uruguay, Argentina, and Chile began to send missionaries of their own to other countries in South America. *(Map courtesy of United Methodist Archives and History)*

with its minority status in a Roman Catholic country. The church grew from nearly 15,000 members in 1938 to more than 19,000 by 1943.[105] It still cooperated with U.S. missionaries but also cultivated its own leadership. Bishop Eleazar Guerra, who was elected in 1938 and re-elected in 1942, had been educated partly at Wesleyan College in San Antonio, Texas. He was unusual in having served pastorates in both the U.S. and México.[106] Among his highly qualified pastors was Luis Areyzaga Balcázar, who as a young man had been interested in commercial aviation. Areyzaga organized a youth group known as The Sowers, and it became the channel through which other young men entered the ministry, including the founder of the Salvation Army in México. Manuel Flores was a graduate of the Methodist Institute of Puebla, where he was converted. He had also been in business before entering the ministry. He studied at Scarritt College in the U.S. and founded a publication, *Youth Vanguard*, which was helped by his talent in design and painting. Raúl Ruíz López, another pastor, was also an artist, a musician, and a designer, who had studied at an engineering school. Eduardo Zapata was a veteran cleric, having served as a pastor in Panamá and Costa Rica with the MEC. His son, Rolando, also entered the ministry and became a district superintendent.[107]

Women also served in leadership positions in the Methodist Church of México. María W. De Frausto had been married to a Methodist pastor and after his death worked as a deaconess. She spent a year at Scarritt College and returned to work in the Nursing School at Palmore College, a Methodist school. (The nursing school itself was accredited by the Mexican higher education system, and its graduates served in hospitals all over the country.) Bishop Guerra's sister, Elódia, had studied in the U.S., at Holding Institute, and then at Roberts College, a Methodist school in Saltillo, México. Like her brother, she worked in churches in both México and Texas, her ministry being evangelism. Gertrudis Reyes was another woman who studied at Roberts College; she entered social work in Coahuila State. Concepción Peréz was also a social worker and worked in a federal penitentiary, where she converted an infamous prisoner, "Pug-nosed Barnabas."[108]

The church also emphasized its work with laity and in 1943 held a congress at Saltillo at which both U.S. and Mexican Methodist leaders spoke, including E. Stanley Jones. From this congress came the impetus for organizing a general board at the general assembly of laity in 1946.

Geneveo A. Ríos, one of the most active lay leaders, became its executive secretary.[109]

North Americans may have been preoccupied with the war, but in Latin America the work of mission continued. Pedro Zóttele, a Chilean, had studied at the University of Chicago Divinity School and Boston University and returned to Chile to serve as pastor. He served both the First Methodist and Second Methodist churches in Santiago beginning in 1931 and continuing until 1962. He was involved in both Christian education and social action for the Chile Annual Conference, a mission conference.[110]

In 1944, Union Theological Seminary in Buenos Aires, Argentina, sent several of its students for field work into Bolivia, then a developing arena for Methodist mission: Magda Peñaranda, daughter of a Bolivian pastor to the Aymara in La Paz; Cleto Zembrano, who had already served among the Aymara in the Altoplano; Alberto Merúbia, who organized the second Methodist church among whites in Bolivia; and Adelita Gattinoni, who served in the Methodist mission school in Cochabamba with the support of the Confederation of Methodist Women in Latin America.

The next year, Margarita Camino, an Argentine lay worker, also went to Cochabamba to teach. José Míguez went to Cochabamba to teach Christian ethics and education. He also served in the local church there. Mortimer Arias, a Uruguayan whose early plan was to become a medical missionary, went to La Paz.[111] The government of Cuba supported the U.S. in its war efforts, and in 1941 the annual conference observed a "Sacrifice Week," in which it raised $500 for Christians suffering in Europe. Methodists in Cuba continued their educational and evangelical work during the war, dedicating a Commercial Department at Candler College in Havana in 1941 and opening a dispensary at Mayarí in 1943. The head physician at the dispensary was Dr. Eduardo Catá, who had studied at both the college and the seminary level in the U.S. The church in Cuba, like the Mexican church, also had an educated leadership. The president of the Woman's Society of Christian Service in the 1940s was Dr. Luisa García de González. She studied at Methodist Buena Vista School and then received a doctorate at Havana University. She married Dr. Justo González of Santiago de las Vegas. She, her husband, and missionary Emily Eulalia Cook founded Alfalit, a literacy program that spread throughout Latin America.

In 1947, the church ordained its first woman as a local deacon: Petronila

Carballido de Reyes Monzón. Four other women who had been serving as missionaries and supply pastors in rural areas were also ordained: Frances Marie Gaby, Fannie Lorraine Buck, Sara Estrella Fernández, and Cook.

Not all Cubans came into the leadership of the church through formal education, however. Augustín Nodal had been a cigar-maker and by his own account worldly and an enemy of religion. He felt called into the ministry, however, after watching Manuel Deuloféu, pastor of his church at San Juan de los Yeras, in action. Deuloféu disregarded all criticisms; he died after a courageous struggle with a chronic illness. Nodal was asked by his former employer to return but finally decided for the ministry and went on to become pastor, district superintendent, and supporter of health ministries. Even in retirement, he continued to be an evangelist.

It would be misleading to say that U.S. missionaries did not have an important role in the Cuban church during the 1940s. Carl D. Stewart was a district superintendent. Clara Chalmers was principal and dean of Irene Toland School. Sterling Neblett was executive secretary of the Board of Education. Cuba was still a mission conference of the church, and bishops Paul Kern and Costen J. Harrell were among those who presided over annual conferences. In 1941, two missionaries of the Woman's Division, Ruth Diggs and Barbara Bailey, were transferred to Cuba from Korea. Mary Lou White had been sent from China to Cuba, and when she left, Elizabeth Earnest replaced her. Duvon C. Corbitt and his wife both taught in the high school part of Candler College. He studied Cuban life and history, and the Corbitts traveled extensively through Cuba, often by horseback, and interpreted Cuba to North Americans through magazine articles. Cubans and U.S. missionaries seem to have cooperated well.[112]

As a legacy from its previous missionary history, Cuban Protestants had the opportunity to go to more than a hundred elementary and secondary schools. The Methodist schools included Candler and Buena Vista colleges in Havana, Irene Toland College in Matanzas, Elisa Bowman College in Cienfuegos, and Pinson College in Camagüey. These "colleges" were often actually for secondary and even elementary students. The students were mainly from middle-income families.

Because most Cubans lived in rural areas, The Methodist Church established a Committee on Rural Work in 1940. Dr. Frank Laubach, the famous advocate of "each one teach one" in literacy, visited Cuba in 1943 to lend impetus to the literacy work in rural areas. Rural centers were opened in Omaja in Oriente Province; Báuganos, also in Oriente; Santa Rosa, in

Matanzas Province; and Herradura in Pinas del Río Province. The U.S. Board of Missions also opened an Agricultural and Industrial School in 1945. Students worked on the farm and in the school and were given financial assistance.

The WSCS provided property on which an interdenominational Evangelical Theological Seminary was established in 1946. Methodists, Presbyterians, and Episcopalians cooperated.[113] Challenges to the church during the war years came from every side. Supplies were limited, mission sites were occupied, and personnel were disbursed and even imprisoned. A private memo to Diffendorfer from Charles Iglehart even lamented that reports had to be padded in order to provide enough material for their usual length and content.

At the 1943 Foreign Missions Conference, leaders from The Methodist Church joined others in looking ahead. Diffendorfer spoke, outlining what he saw ahead. He called on the church to continue concern for human welfare, to plan for relief and reconstruction, to overhaul medical policies, to participate in a literacy movement, and to work with those in the social sciences to gain deeper understanding of the forces at work in the world.

By 1944 Diffendorfer was raising even more concern for the populations dislocated by the war. At the same time, he anticipated that even more students associated with Christian mission in their own countries would soon be seeking further education in the U.S. He encouraged the board to include this opportunity to educate the products of mission in its plans for the future. As board personnel and missionaries coped with the day-to-day challenges of the world at war, Diffendorfer's leadership helped to anticipate what lay ahead in the tasks of rebuilding and reaching out when the conflict ended. Peace would give The Methodist Church even greater opportunities for service and mission.

CHAPTER 3

Recovery — Creation of a New Order

*T*HE ENORMOUS ENERGY that characterized the American spirit was alive in many parts of the world in the years following the war. The United States was part of the recovery efforts on all three continents in which the war was fought, sending support with programs, supplies, and personnel. Mirroring those efforts were the Methodists, working at home and abroad with new energy and vision. Bishop G. Bromley Oxnam had worked during the war to publicize his vision for the new world order, with the result that many Methodists approached the challenges with an eager attitude that was both international and ecumenical. They were prepared for what was to come.

New activity in the factories, in agriculture, and in other sectors of the economy that had helped to end the Great Depression did not stop with the signing of the peace. Instead, manufacturers joyfully began to turn out domestic products that were marketed for the modern home and that built supplies of many items that had been depleted during the war years. Employment opportunities seemed plentiful.

Preparations made during the war eased the transition for the Board of Missions in its administration and policies as actual fighting ceased and societies began to readjust. To help the church connect with the task ahead, Ralph Diffendorfer, head of the board, laid out the situation and the philosophy that governed the mission approach — the Crusade for Christ — once the war had ended. The "priorities" were fairly comprehensive: relief and reconstruction, evangelism, the church school, stewardship, and world order. Some of the ministries involved aid to Christians of other denominations who were still suffering on account of the war. Although Diffendorfer and others were heavily involved in the ecumenical ventures of the Federal Council of Churches, this effort represented even broader cooperation, opening channels of communication with Orthodox and Roman Catholic Christians.[1]

Diffendorfer named priorities that remained central to the work of the division for years to come. "Out from the compounds into new areas of service" was a call to the missionaries to continue the outreach work that had been interrupted by the war. With the use of picturesque nouns and verbs, he tried to reverse thinking that focused on institutions as centers into which money and resources were flowing. Instead, he called on the church to see the institutions as sources of that flow of work, energy, and resources. He grounded his ideas in a pioneer spirit that was not so much about geography as about new ideas, new methods, and greater varieties of people to be reached. In addition, he highlighted the Kyodan in Japan, the cooperative work of many U.S. denominations, as part of the pioneer spirit present in the mission work.

As an integral part of the postwar effort, he also addressed race relations. This was one of the key ways that those involved in international mission work were able to provide the church with a much-needed measure of some its own practices within the U.S. "It is becoming increasingly embarrassing to missionaries abroad, preaching the universal sonship of Christian believers in one loving Father, to have the horrible practices of intolerant America scrutinized by amazed and inquiring new converts." Later in the address, Diffendorfer returned to this theme, hammering home the importance of this concept in the mission field and in the church. Stressing the urgency, he even reminded his audience that in some parts of the world, persons suspected with growing conviction that the Soviet Union was more realistic in its approach to minorities than was the U.S. The work of missionaries abroad was compromised by the inequities of the culture they represented. They needed efforts from the church at home in the area of race relations to match their own work abroad.

At the same time, Diffendorfer and others were aware that the U.S. culture in which many of the missionaries had been reared meant that many of them carried attitudes about race and culture that affected and even compromised their work abroad. All candidates had to answer questions about their racial attitudes and their assessment of the abilities of various groups of people to handle the work. This examination was not supposed to be about merely appearing to get along. The policy of the church was to continue not only to develop indigenous leadership but also to transfer power to that leadership as it developed. Missionaries increasingly served not just alongside indigenous people, but under them as well. The vision for the postwar period was to help this happen in *all* the countries where the missionaries were involved.

A related issue was the incorporation of African-American Christians into the missionary work. Although some had served in Liberia, few Methodist missions had ever had any missionaries of color. Greater racial inclusivity was an immediate goal, but Diffendorfer also looked to a day when African Americans would be sent, not just to Africa because of their race, but to whatever mission assignments best matched their talents and gifts.

Another new direction that Diffendorfer put before the church was the concern for economic justice. Before the war, the International Missionary Council had met in Madras, India, and emphasized the understanding that the economic life of the church was a spiritual problem. Diffendorfer agreed, saying, "We believe that a Gospel for the poor which has no concern with the cause and cure of poverty is an emasculated Gospel." Just as he addressed race relations as a systemic problem, so also he expanded the understanding of poverty as not just individual habits and choices but as incapable of meaningful change without change in the social order. While this statement provided many avenues for possible efforts, Diffendorfer pointed to one that came up again: the disparity between the missionaries and the indigenous people with whom they worked. On the one hand, missionary salaries remained low. But on the other hand, their standard of life and security still often contrasted greatly with their coworkers and "often brought the Gospel message into disrepute."

As the board looked ahead to rebuilding and expanding, its policy on indigenization was important. While John Mott had voiced this as a major concern at the time of the church's union, the war had brought immediacy to issues of safety and recovery rather than to those of a change in policy. At the same time, in some places, power had actually been transferred to the indigenous people during the war. Determining equitable policy for areas that had had very different war experiences was going to be a continuing challenge.

High ideals were also accompanied by cold facts. Even without thinking about economic disparities among workers, the costs of doing business in many of the countries was rising. World Service funds were not rising enough to keep up with increasing costs. Economics was to become an ongoing problem.

Diffendorfer's address was important because it pulled together themes that shaped the thinking of the board for a number of years. Its reprinting meant that many more persons were aware of it than the usual few who read or heard board reports. Finally, it represented for the public the board's evaluation of the various places around the world in which they were in ministry.

Rebuilding Europe

Estimates from war damage in Europe were high for the churches, as for all of society. Methodist losses alone were estimated at seven and a half million dollars. Shortages of both personnel and supplies slowed the rebuilding efforts.

Joseph Barták, the Czech pastor who had been imprisoned in a German concentration camp at the beginning of the war, returned to Prague to find that Methodism had somehow survived the war. The headquarters building in Prague, an eight-story structure that housed offices, a chapel, bookstores, and living quarters for the missionaries, had been destroyed and several churches damaged. Bishop Paul Garber found food and medical shortages. Clothes were also needed. Garber saw one box of supplies arrive from Arkansas and requested the Methodist Committee for Overseas Relief (MCOR) to provide further supplies.[2] Although Czechoslovakia enjoyed a brief interlude of freedom, Communist totalitarianism soon closed in. Methodists, under Barták's leadership, persisted in remaining a faith community into the early 1950s.[3]

Garber found that Methodism "has become the leading Protestant group in modern Poland." The reason why, he thought, was that Methodism had built on firm theological foundations that emphasized Jesus Christ and evangelism. Just as important, "we have worked with the native Polish people. . . ." Polish Methodists in the postwar period worked ecumenically with Lutherans, Baptists, Evangelicals, and Unitarians. One big need in the late 1940s was financial aid for pastors.[4]

The Methodist Church in Italy survived the war and in 1946 merged with the British Methodist mission. The church related to the British Methodist Conference until 1962, when it became autonomous.[5]

One Balkan church that managed to rebuild itself after the war was the Methodist Church of Bulgaria. Although the populace was predomi-

Deaconesses in Nuremberg helped to remove rubble in the aftermath of severe bombing by the Allied forces during the Second World War. The immediate problem for the churches in Europe after the war was not only relief
work but the rebuilding of morale of a depressed and discouraged people.
Deaconesses, an important and large part of the German Methodist movement, were instrumental in this spiritual recovery. *(Photo courtesy of United
Methodist Archives and History)*

nantly Greek Orthodox, Bulgarians had a friendly attitude toward Methodists and other Protestants because of the common suffering of the
country. Bulgaria was not heavily bombed during the war, although the
bombing of Sofia did damage the Methodist church and the adjoining
Methodist offices. The Crusade for Christ provided postwar funds for
reconstruction. The larger problem was that Bulgaria allied itself with
the Axis powers, and many Methodist pastors had been educated at the
seminary in Frankfurt during the Third Reich. After the war, this identification with Nazi Germany became an embarrassment, and the Methodist superintendent was forced to leave. His successor, Yanko N. Ivanoff,
re-established relations with the Bulgarian government. Also helping the
situation was the survival of the Methodist School for Girls at Lovetch,
where U.S. missionaries Mellony Turner and Ruth Carhart remained

The Sommers

J. W. Ernst Sommer was born to a German Wesleyan minister father and British mother in Germany. He went to Kingswood, Cambridge University, and the university at Lausanne for his education. He taught in London and married a Briton, Beatrice Dibben. From 1907 to 1912, he was a missionary in Turkey. On his return to Germany, he became dean of a missionary training college, then professor of Old Testament and Ethics at Frankfurt Methodist Theological Seminary. He became president in 1936 and was elected bishop by the Germany Central Conference in 1946. During the war, he refused to release rooms for the use of the National Socialist Party, saying that he needed them for the student body, which consisted of a single Bulgarian student, Zdrako Beslov. While serving as president of the seminary, he continued to pastor a circuit.

He was responsible for coordinating relief work in Germany after the Second World War. He wrote graphically about the damage incurred by the church during the war, both the destruction of buildings and the physical and spiritual demoralization of humans. His attitude remained positive and hopeful. He emphasized the possibilities for evangelism and the church's witness in numbers and influence. He also led the church to maintain relations with those under Communist domination in the East. The church built houses near Lubeck for refugees from East Germany. He also worked with Martin Niemöller in the Co-operative Fellowship of Christian Churches in Germany, a Protestant organization. Sommer died in 1952.

His son, C. Ernst Sommer, was born in 1911 in Turkey. He received his education in Germany and served in the German army in France and North Africa during the Second World War. He became professor of Christian education and church history at the Frankfurt Methodist Theological Seminary in 1950 and its dean in 1953. He was active in religious educational circles in Germany and wrote extensively on the Bible and church history as well as serving as a member of the Methodist General Conferences of 1964, 1966, and 1968. He was elected bishop by the Germany Central Conference in 1968, becoming the first bishop elected by a central conference of the new United Methodist Church. He died November 7, 1981.

Sources: J. W. E. Sommer, "The Church in Germany," *World Outlook* 38 (January 1948): 15–16; J. W. E. Sommer, "One Hundred Years of Methodism in Germany," *World Outlook* 40 (April 1950): 11–12; Ernst Scholz, "Sommer, C. Ernst," and Nolan B. Harmon, "Sommer, J. W. Ernst," *Encyclopedia of World Methodism*, 2: 2196–2197.

until 1942, when the school was placed under government control. When a revolution cast off the German ties in 1944, Turner received permission to re-open the school. By 1948 it had become the only U.S. school in Bulgaria and had an enrollment of two hundred fifty.[6]

The Methodist Church in Germany struggled to restore itself after a devastating war. Although German Methodists did not seem exuberant in their support of National Socialism, "there was no real criticism of the country's nationalist politics in World War II and of the Nazi regime," wrote Bishop Walter Klaiber in later years.[7] Still, German Methodists suffered greatly from the war and struggled heroically to restore their church afterward. Bishop J. W. E. Sommer wrote in 1948: "Terrible is the general religious and moral collapse brought about by the national social-istic rule and war. . . . Eighty percent of our children are undernourished, thousands upon thousands of our people crowded together in unspeakable dens, in cellars and ruins." He reported that one-third of Methodist build-ings had been destroyed, and "many of our young ministers and lay work-ers were killed or are still prisoners of war, many others are so debilitated that they are breaking down." Sommer yet retained Christian hope, and two years later was able to report that with the help of U.S. churches, in-cluding relief through the Crusade for Christ, many buildings were being restored. The Hennepin Avenue Methodist Church in Minneapolis pro-vided direct aid, as did the Indiana Area, then under the supervision of Bishop Richard C. Raines. The German church had always had a large deaconess force, and in 1950 Sommer reported that the number was grow-ing. Some 1,200 deaconesses were serving in forty-eight hospitals and homes, an amazing number in a church with a membership of sixty thou-sand. The German Methodist Church also participated in the *Evangelische Kirchentag*, an assembly of laity who became a force for spiritual renewal in Germany in the postwar years.[8]

But as grim as were the material analyses of Europe, so bright appeared possibilities in other fields of the mission work.

Gains in Africa: West and South

Changes in Africa heralded a coming era of greater participation and in-dependence. During the months that immediately followed the war there was encouraging news from many quarters. When the numbers were re-leased for the quadrennium, Africa conferences showed strong gains.

Southern Rhodesia (now Zimbabwe) led the way with a 140 percent membership increase, followed closely by Angola (124 percent), and Central Congo (114 percent). By contrast, the 70 percent increase in Rhodesia and the 53 percent in Southern Congo looked almost modest. The missionary force had not increased during those years. Many missionaries had deferred their furloughs, accepting extended terms of service instead. Missionaries to this area of the world had to master European as well as African languages. Only Liberia trailed with a mere 10 percent membership increase. Other ministries were growing there, however.

In Liberia, The Methodist Church organized a Home Missionary Society of the annual conference to aid further in moving work inland from the coastal centers. Crusade for Christ scholarships to central African students enabled four of them to go to college in South Africa. Perhaps the most exciting single event was the July 1946 meeting in the Belgian Congo. Nearly two hundred delegates attended the West Central Africa Regional Conference on Christian Work in order to plan for the postwar era. It was the first conference in central Africa in which African delegates were accorded the same status as Western delegates. At the same time, the first postwar report noted developments in the Southern Congo, where the increasing urbanization was breaking down tribal and rural customs and habits. Concern about patterns of lowered standards of morality was mixed with pride of achievement in the way that denominations were able to welcome and integrate new members as they moved across former comity lines. The church was facing new challenges as industrialization and westernization became more widespread.

Gaspar de Almeida, an Angolan, wrote a thoughtful article during this period about the way an African Christian adapts the gospel to an African context. Almeida had studied at a Presbyterian seminary in Portugal under a Crusade for Christ scholarship and returned to Dondo, Angola, to serve as pastor. "My work program is to adapt the teachings of Jesus to my people," he wrote, explaining:

> In Africa there is much that is similar to the spiritual, social, and political situation of Jesus' day. The masses are ready to accept a message of salvation. For this reason, having as a norm the adaptation of the teachings of Jesus, to give to man abundant life, the churches ought to feel more and more the responsibility to practice the teachings of Jesus in building a new world in which the kingdom of God will reign. As pastor, my first privilege and duty is to preach the gospel of our Lord Jesus

Christ to the people. . . . Besides the many complicated problems . . .
that I meet . . . there are others that deserve special attention: to encourage our members to have orderly villages with modest but clean
houses (this means well-built and whitewashed); to inspire our members,
above all, to have a devoted love to work, to raise animals, and to lose
the false idea that poverty is the primary condition for admission into
the kingdom of God.[9]

Contrast in North Africa

Most missionaries had the experience of working in countries where they
were part of a religious minority. But those who went to Algeria had their
own unique challenges. The board considered the country very carefully
at the end of the war, giving more serious than usual consideration to
whether any mission work at all should continue. Much of the work was
being done through institutions or with the French Protestants, a religious minority themselves. Working with missionaries from a number of
countries, those sent by both the Division of Foreign Missions and the
Woman's Division did much institutional and social work.

Executive secretaries Sallie Lou McKinnon of the Woman's Division
and Raymond L. Archer of the Division of Foreign Missions traveled to
Algeria in 1945 for a more detailed and in-depth assessment of missions. They listened to the stories of the effects of the war. For example,
the Woman's Division ran a girls' home in Constantine. When General
Dwight Eisenhower decided he wanted to use the home for his headquarters, he gave the missionaries two days' notice to vacate it. They were unable to find any trucks, so they had to hire Algerian workmen to carry the
loads on their backs or push donkey carts. Supporting the war effort had
made the missionaries particularly resourceful and adaptive. Even after
the war ended, the French government continued to occupy many of these
buildings.

The end of the war did not bring an end to the difficulties. Food was so
scarce that the touring secretaries had to stay with the military rather than
the missionaries. The missionaries spent as much as half their time just
getting enough food for each day. They found it impossible to get clothing. The government restricted the purchase of milk for consumption
only to children between six months and three years of age. The women,
in particular, found these restrictions very limiting in their work. With so

few missionaries assigned to their area, they decided not to try and work out a detailed plan for the future but to come to some general agreements. They knew that any plans they made must take into account the limited resources and not spread the efforts too thinly.

As they assessed the future, they looked around for possibilities that would advance the work. One realistic possibility appeared to be among the Kabyles, converts to Islam from Christianity. In a land so predominantly Muslim, they seemed the best hope. As they visited with the missionaries, the secretaries began to develop a list of concerns to raise with the board. They were aware of the long years of work with fairly large appropriations and no visible results. They saw the way that work had been reduced as a result of falling income from the church. Between retirements and the failure to get new recruits, staffing was at an all-time low. The Division of Foreign Missions had assigned only two families, while just four women served for the Woman's Division. The smaller staff size undermined morale among all who were there. In addition, the missionaries had not been able to develop many indigenous leaders. The church that was organized and functioning was primarily for the Europeans who were in the area.

But there were special ministries the visitors were eager to see. They viewed with interest the baseball mission that C. Guy Kelly had organized in Tunis nearly twenty-five years before. The teams were named after professional teams in the U.S. As an extra incentive, some even communicated with a professional team and its stars. More than eight hundred young people—all Muslim—took part in the baseball leagues that Kelly set up. Bible instruction was part of the outing. The secretaries liked this innovation and the numbers of young people that participated each year. Such activity was attractive not only for the ministry it established, but also because it was easily portrayed to supporters in the U.S. The Division of Foreign Missions always had to be aware of raising its funds through its lists of extra supporters. Giving to a baseball ministry was a clear and easily understood request and one that continued to generate funds. Less clear about the mission was how its success was to be measured or understood.

The secretaries asked if there was a place for Methodist mission in North Africa. It was not a question often asked, since by this time many missions had been operating for a long time. The question was rarely "if"; more often it was "how much and how many." This was a key moment in

Sue Robinson was one of several Methodist missionaries in North Africa who struggled with the question of Christian mission in a predominantly Muslim country. The church provided social services but had few converts. Any emphasis on evangelism, however, led to the Muslims' saying the church was not interested in them for their own sake. This question, never answered, remains open in Christian-Muslim relations today. *(Photo courtesy of United Methodist Archives and History)*

the life of the board and its divisions. "Foreign" missions were generally closed only because of war. At the same time, there were so many needs, so many places to invest the limited resources. The board would need good reasons for the choice suggested by the secretaries. McKinnon and Archer discussed the work they had seen, the ministry being done, and decided they were ready to answer a well-thought-out yes to their own question. They believed that the gospel was still needed in the region and that Christians could make a witness to the Muslims. The Methodists were the only Protestants doing work among the Muslims. They had been there for nearly forty years, building up a large reservoir of good will. No one could suspect them of having any kind of political motivation.

The secretaries had another reason. They believed that The Methodist Church needed a mission exclusively to Muslim people as an enrichment for its own role in world mission. They knew the depth of Methodist indifference to and ignorance of the Muslim world, an indifference paralleled by the rest of society. Their report from the area was heavily detailed with comments about each individual mission site. Among their recommendations was one for the continuation of the work, with a program designed especially for the Muslims. They recognized that the French Protestants were capable of looking after their own people. Instead, they suggested the selling of some land, relocating some of the missions, and opening of some new ones, especially an evangelistic center. They urged that the two divisions cooperate equally at each of the sites. They further urged that some of the missionaries who had left during the war return as soon as possible.

The report was a satisfying and positive outcome for the trip. After the excitement of seeing the progress in sub-Saharan African, the two had been worried about what they would find in the north. Their enthusiasm had been lagging. The outcome felt much more positive than they had thought possible.

This was not the last examination. Nevertheless, these careful conclusions allowed the board to proceed with assignments, having established a manageable context for the work. It also sent a message that the end of the war did not mean return without question to prewar policies and support.

One way to evaluate these policies is through the lens of individual lives, including how young people entered into the ranks of the church. One of the graduates of the girls' home at Constantine was Akilla Zaida, a former Muslim. She was commissioned as an indigenous worker at the North Africa Annual Conference of 1949. She had studied in French schools in Algeria and at Scarritt College on a Crusade for Christ scholarship. She returned from the U.S. to teach at a Methodist school. Solomon Boukechem came from a former Muslim family and was elected president of the Methodist Youth Fellowship of North Africa, then won the highest scholastic honors at a French school in Tunis. He planned to enter the ministry as a pastor or missionary. And when the Oslo Youth Conference met in 1948, a young Methodist from Tunisia, Allika Belyfa, represented Protestants. (Norwegian Methodists, along with Swiss and Polish Methodists, also had missions in North Africa.) He was a local preacher, and his brother, Amor Belyfa, was a delegate to the annual conference.[10]

Latin America and the Caribbean: Ecumenism and Conflict

Reports from Latin America detailed development in institutions in many of the countries. Methodists were continuing their work in schools and

Pedro Zóttele, a Chilean who had studied in the U.S., became a bishop in 1962. He supervised the area that included Costa Rica, Panamá, Perú, and Chile. He organized the Chilean church when it became autonomous in 1969. *(Photo courtesy of United Methodist Archives and History)*

social service agencies as well as their work for Methodist churches as alternatives to the predominance of the Roman Catholic Church. The report from Brazil raised a policy question, however, that was a reminder of the evolving relationships for the board. The General Conference of The Methodist Church of Brazil, an autonomous conference, elected three bishops at its February meeting. Two of the bishops, Cesar Dacorso, Jr., and Isaias Sucacas, were entirely supported by the Brazilian church, but the third was the Reverend Cyrus Bassett Dawsey, who had spent thirty-four years in Brazil, primarily in the frontier areas, helping to develop new churches. Even as a district superintendent he received his salary from the Division of Foreign Missions, and the plan was to continue that support despite his election to the episcopacy. Although an indigenous church was the goal, conferences and the board continued to make decisions on a case-by-case basis.

Latin American Methodists believed in an ecumenical approach, and during the 1950s some of their leaders began to surface in ecumenical circles. Sante Uberto Barbieri, who had gone to the Methodist seminary in Porto Alegre, Brazil, and had served churches there, went in 1939 to Buenos Aires, Argentina, where he was both a pastor and a teacher at Union Seminary. In 1949, he was elected bishop and was assigned to the

Río de la Plata region, which included Argentina, Uruguay, and Bolivia. He went to the World Council of Churches Assembly in Evanston, Illinois, in 1954 and became one of its presidents.[11]

Argentine Methodists continued to support the church's mission in Bolivia, sending Dr. and Mrs. Pablo Monti to work in health ministries there; on the *altiplano*, 90 percent of the population had tuberculosis. Also supporting the Bolivian work were students from Crandon, the Methodist woman's school in Montevideo, Uruguay. A group went to La Paz in the mid-1950s and then rode in a truck to Ancoraimes, where they saw the work among the Aymaras. Sixteen schools had been established in villages in that area by Methodists. The students collected funds for the health work, and several became interested in returning to Bolivia as teachers.[12]

In the Caribbean, Efraim Alphonse was identified by the board in New York as someone who could develop the mission in that region. Alphonse had received his early education in Jamaica under the British Methodist Church. Teaching school in Panamá, he learned tribal dialects, developed a written form of them, and wrote a grammar book. He translated parts of the Bible into indigenous languages for the American Bible Society and also composed hymns in those languages. From 1950 to 1954, the mission board called on him to serve as a traveling evangelist in Honduras, Nicaragua, Costa Rica, Barbados, Trinidad, and the Bahamas.[13] Alphonse's ministry showed that it was possible to go back and forth between branches of Methodism. As an indigenous leader, he showed how effective one can be not only with one's own people, but also in mission to other indigenous people. He quoted his mentor, the Reverend M. C. Surgeon, a British Methodist, as having seen a drunken Guaymi upon arrival in Panamá. When Surgeon asked who the man was, a local leader told him, "They can't be civilized." Surgeon replied, "We are not here to civilize. We are here to evangelize."

Alphonse did not take this dictum literally, however. In a confrontation with President Juan Demosthenes Arosemana of Panamá, he asked the president to provide schools for the indigenous people. Although Arosemana angrily refused at first, since his government was engaged in a civil conflict with other indigenous peoples at the time, Alphonse persisted, and the president finally relented. In a touching follow-up, Alphonse reported that the first Panamanian to be baptized in the region, Joshua Troutman, became the first principal of the school near Alphonse's church.[14]

In Cuba, Methodist work continued to emphasize the importance of

Efraim Alphonse

Alphonse was born in the Province of Bocas del Toro, Panamá, in 1896. His father was a fisherman from Martinique and his French undoubtedly influenced young Efraim to appreciate languages. He completed his elementary and secondary education at Calabar College in Jamaica, then returned to Panamá to teach the Guaymi (also called Valiente). He taught himself the Gauymi language, transliterated it, and wrote a grammar, which the Smithsonian Institute of Ethnology published. Later he translated several books of the Bible for the American Bible Society into Guaymi, and with the help of his wife, Philibert Hyacinth, published a hymnbook in Guaymi. She was a musician and arranged music and set it to words.

He received more education in Jamaica, this time in theology, then returned to his ministry. The Methodist Church asked him to serve as a traveling evangelist to several Central American and Caribbean countries, which he did from 1950 to 1954. His mentor was M. C. Surgeon, a British Methodist missionary, and Alphonse went to England twice on deputations. Eventually he became chair of the Central American area of British Methodism. He was a participant in the formation of the autonomous Methodist Church of the Caribbean and the Americas in 1967. He received the highest honor of the Panmanian government in 1963, the Orden de Vasco Nuñez de Balboa. In retirement he taught at the Methodist Theological Seminary in Costa Rica. Two of his sons served as missionaries in the U.S. Methodist family: Ivan, who was an educational missionary in Zaire, and Alford, a missionary to Jamaica and a staff member of the General Board of Global Ministries in New York. Efraim Alphonse died in 1995.

Sources: Marion F. Woods, "Alphonse, Efraim (Ephraim) Juan," *Encyclopedia of World Methodism* (Nashville: United Methodist Publishing House, 1972), 1: 96–97; Adelaide Jones Alphonse, ed., *Autobiography of the Rev. Dr. Ephraim John Alphonse* (Panamá City, Panamá: Imprenta Universitaria, 1994), pp. 22–23, 108–112; "Biography of Rev. Dr. Ephraim S. Alphonse," two-page mimeographed document provided by Alford Alphonse, Miramar, Fla. The "S." is for Simeon, Alphonse's other middle name.

missionaries, and Methodists lagged behind other denominations in developing indigenous leadership. The Evangelical Theological Seminary in Matanzas organized a Rural Work Committee in 1957 under Methodist missionary Eulalia Cook, continuing to develop the rural ministries begun a decade before. Methodists in Cuba were affected by political currents.

Fulgencio Batista y Zaldivar had become dictator of Cuba, with the blessings of the U.S. Government, in 1954. But the year before, Fidel Castro
had led an attack on the Moncada army barracks in Oriente Province. This
action was the beginning of a civil war that led eventually to Castro's becoming the leader of Cuba in 1959. Methodists, like many others, including Roman Catholics, at first welcomed some of the reforms brought about
by Castro, since Batista's regime had been a police state. But as Castro's
administration became more oppressive, some Methodists joined the wave
of emigrants out of Cuba in the early 1960s. The churches and schools that
Methodists had built remained, but it became more and more difficult to
live openly as a Christian.[15]

Eleazar Guerra Olivares

Guerra was born in Reynosa, México, and studied in the U.S. His ordination in
the U.S. was in the Methodist Episcopal Church, South. He became a district
superintendent of the Methodist Church of México and was elected the third
bishop of the church in 1938. Although bishops served only a four-year term,
he was re-elected in 1942, 1946, and 1950. He then served as secretary of
evangelism and was elected to a final term of the episcopacy in 1958.

He addressed the first General Conference of The Methodist Church and
emphasized the continuing connection between autonomous churches like the
one in México and the rest of Methodism: "It is true that an autonomous
church has been created in our country. . . . But we want to take part in this
forward movement that this Church has taken, when all forces of Methodism
are united for better service." Guerra spoke at several General Conferences of
The Methodist Church and in 1944 gave a comprehensive report on the growth
of church membership, the strengthening of institutions, and the good relationships with U.S. missionaries. He again affirmed the need of both the U.S.
and the Mexican churches to work together and said the church in México was
also engaged in ecumenical work with other Protestant denominations. Guerra
died on September 14, 1970.

Sources: Vicente Mendoza, ed., *Libro Conmemorativo de las Bodas de Diamante de
la Iglesia Metodista de México, 1873–1948* (n.p.: Imprenta Nueva Educación, 1948),
p. 89; *Journal of the First General Conference of The Methodist Church,* ed. Lud H.
Estes (Nashville: Methodist Publishing House, 1940), pp. 728–729; *Daily Proceedings,* 1944 General Conference, The Methodist Church, p. 61; W. W. Reid,
"Guerra Olivares, Eleazar," *Encyclopedia of World Methodism,* 1: 1047–1048.

Eleazar Guerra.
*(Photo courtesy of
United Methodist
Archives and History)*

Puerto Rico experienced no revolution in the 1950s, but some 41,000 of its citizens emigrated to the East Coast of the U.S. during the decade. Eighty-five percent of them settled in New York. This move led to a new mission to Puerto Ricans on the part of the U.S. church. One Puerto Rican who was strategically located to help meet this new need was Gildo Sanchez, a Methodist student at Union Theological Seminary in New York, who served a Spanish-speaking congregation at Grace Methodist Church as a student pastor. He eventually returned to Puerto Rico and, in 1957, was serving as pastor of First Methodist Church in Ponce, which had a membership of only 320 but also had 800 preparatory members and 719 in church school.[16]

Puerto Rico was a provisional annual conference. It had many small churches with one-room buildings, and growth in church membership led the conference superintendent, Dr. Tomás Rico Soltero, to ask the denomination for more help in church construction. Rico, the first conference superintendent in Puerto Rico, knew the problems well because he had once pastored the church in Hatillo without salary because of economic conditions. The conference also needed help in recruiting and paying clergy. It had a shortage of clergy, and one reason was the very low salaries, according to Rico. The Advance raised some funds to help meet both these needs.[17]

México: Intention and Improvisation

The work of the Methodist Church of México continued to blend indigenous leadership with assistance from the U.S. church. Eleazar Guerra's term as bishop ended in 1954, and he then became secretary of evangelism for the church in México. In 1958, he was again elected bishop for another four-year term.[18]

One of the missionaries from the Woman's Division serving in México was Mamie Baird, whose work could be characterized as a combination of pastor, doctor, and farmer. She worked in and near Cortazar, a town of 13,000 in Querétaro Province, north of México City. Besides distributing food, Baird acted as visiting nurse. She often helped families with internal conflicts. When the government held a literacy campaign, she organized classes in villages of the indigenous people, the Otomí. She advised villagers on caring for diseased poultry and distributed hybrid corn and fruit tree saplings for planting. She also opened a social center with programs for children and classes for adults in reading, cooking, and sewing. She was greatly relieved when Rubén Casales and his wife arrived to serve the local church. Thus Baird illustrated the age-old saying of missionaries that whatever one trained for, experience in mission was one of improvisation.[19]

Korea after the War

As elsewhere after the war, missionaries were eager to return to Korea. They had not forgotten the people, the culture, or the conditions. During the years of war, many had suffered from afar with their colleagues and friends. They were eager to return to the land and people they loved, to the work to which they were called. They knew they had valuable skills that could help them be part of the recovery.

One such person was Charles Sauer.[20] He wanted missionaries to be in partnership with government officials. He wrote, "It was also hard to realize that American Army officials in Korea would not be anxious to bring them [missionaries] back at once on special ships if necessary." Indeed, the U.S. Army was responsible for the speed and conditions under which some of the early returnees found their way. General John Hodge over-heard George Zur Williams talking with some laborers and arranged for Williams to become an interpreter on his own staff. Williams's parents, who had gone to India during the war, were invited by the army to return so that the Reverend Frank E. C. Williams could act as agricultural ad-viser. In December, 1945, the general cabled the U.S. State Department to request the return of ten missionaries. Dr. B. W. Billings was the first to arrive. Three more came in the summer, followed by four in November. Dr. Henry Appenzeller returned in February with the economic mission and was soon broadcasting on the radio in Korean. But no more mission-aries were allowed to enter the country until the following June. Since all passports depended on General Hodge, it was he rather than the board who made decisions about the speed and timing of the returns. This pol-icy made work much more difficult for the staff in New York. For Hodge, the missionaries were only one part of a much larger group being gathered to rebuild the infrastructure. Although the board understood this attitude, it continued its focus on rebuilding the churches and re-establishing mis-sion connections and institutions.

Since for many years the Japanese had held posts in banking, trans-portation, and police, advising Korean replacements was of prime impor-tance in rebuilding. The U.S. Army took over hotels, office buildings, and department stores as it tried to accommodate the advisers. Even the homes of the missionaries were often used by the army and related per-sonnel. As with so many of the buildings in Korea during the war, the houses suffered from lack of repair and upkeep. By 1946 even hardware and plumbing were gone. As the soldiers tried to use the structures, they developed their own innovations—toilets on the front porch, earthen stoves in the rooms. Although this occupation of the buildings certainly had its drawbacks for the missionaries, it did mean that some repairs were begun, although often in lieu of rent.

Conditions were difficult in many ways. Services such as mail delivery and even limited money exchanges were provided through the military. Fuel was scarce. Transportation was often difficult; lack of coal meant that trains could not run as often. Trains even sat for hours at stations as work-ers tried to find enough coal for them to finish their journeys.

The after-war economic inflation also made life difficult. Ten yen bills were tied into bundles of one hundred in order to keep counting simple. The official exchange rate for U.S. dollars did not take this into account as much as was needed, leaving the missionaries with little buying power for their funds—funds that were allocated by formulas figured out in New York. With limited funds, board and room costs seemed exorbitant. Thus during the first year, missionaries depended on the army for food and lodging, even at times having the use of some discarded jeeps.

When Maud and Kristian Jensen returned to Korea in October 1946, they found not only the country itself rundown, but also the people looking tired and worn. An apple cost the equivalent of two weeks' salary, while a pair of shoes cost what one might make in a whole year. Hard times or no, the Koreans were glad to have the missionaries back among them. Inchon District prepared a reception for them that was attended by more than 150 church leaders.[21] But the army was not always a willing partner in the missionaries' efforts to re-establish themselves. According to Sauer, the missionaries complained that housing the army considered as adequate for men did not meet the standards necessary for women. The army did not want to have to think about providing this higher standard. Sauer does not say that the women demanded it. He was ambivalent, noting that while it was fortunate that the women uplifted the standard of living, he could see why the army did not welcome them. In many cases, men and women had worked collegially on projects, leading the men to a greater appreciation of the women's abilities. Yet Sauer's lukewarm attitude represented men whose ideas about gender relationships and women's supposedly more limited abilities often reflected that of the larger society.

Finally by May 1947, enough of the details were in place so that two more men, four wives of missionaries, and seven single women were able to return, doubling the size of the community. Physical conditions began to improve, but organization remained difficult. No one was designated with any authority. The treasurer of the Korean Methodist Church took a government job, so he was not around very often to work with others who were full time in the church. Inflation concerns, property questions, and other organizational difficulties added to the strain on the missionaries. No one had the authority to make appointments, so most people tried to take up where they had left off six years before. Lines of accountability and authority were blurred. Because there was so much to be done, missionaries and church leaders could not wait to get all the details and job descriptions sorted out before they plunged into the work at hand. But occasionally the blurring created problems.

For example, although the seminary had been closed in 1940, it was granted a charter as a college in 1946. The board allocated funds, and students enrolled. The Reverend Kang Tau Heui at Methodist headquarters insisted that the seminary was under the jurisdiction of the Korean church. Mission personnel did not agree. They reported the situation to Frank Cartwright, secretary of the Board of Missions for eastern and southern Asia, but voted to make no change until a planned visit from the board. A visiting delegation from the board could not clarify it either. Board staff member T. T. Brumbaugh and Laura Jean Brooks, vice president for foreign work in the Woman's Division, who came to consult, were new to the problems. Margaret Billingsley was not around when the missionaries were forced to leave and did not know the details of what had been done. Trying to reach some understanding, a committee of missionaries began to consult with the Koreans. But it was really a committee without much authority. Before they left, the board representatives notified Bishop Ju Sam Ryang and Chairman Heui that they did not want the school reopened until agreement had been reached. They also stated that no funds would be available from the board after November 1. While some people at the Methodist headquarters were pleased, the general reaction was bitter. Ryang reiterated that the seminary was needed and that he would sacrifice his home for it if necessary. He and several others issued a statement saying that they would keep the seminary open with or without missionary cooperation. This determination helped the missionaries to overcome their concerns about procedure. Since their deepest concern was always the development of future ministers, they gave their support. Within six weeks, the seminary had begun to make repairs on its buildings. The late date meant, however, that many things could not be completed before winter came in earnest. Many of the North Korean students spent the winter in icy conditions; a naked light bulb under the covers was the only source of heat in some rooms. The following year, Dr. H. J. Lew was installed as president, and the mission cooperated fully with the seminary and its further development as a training site.

Woman's Division: Continued Service

Just as Diffendorfer's reprinted address became an important publication noting the evaluation and goals of mission, so also the quadrennial document *The Golden Cord* helped the Woman's Division publicize its efforts and accomplishments in the postwar years.

The booklet opened with numbers — numbers that give a picture of the way that the Woman's Division built upon a network of local groups for both study and fund raising. For example, the division represented the work of 27,000 local units of the Woman's Society of Christian Service (WSCS) with a total membership of 1,377,000 (out of approximately four million women members of the church). Two-thirds of these societies had fewer than fifty members. In addition there were 3,701 Wesleyan Service Guilds with 80,765 members, out of an estimated 1,333,000 church women who worked outside the home. These members contributed a little more than $15.5 million of appropriations to the Woman's Division during the quadrennium, as well as sending more than a million dollars as gifts for the Week of Prayer. Two hundred and twenty-five missionaries and deaconesses served the division in ministries in the U.S. and abroad.

The Woman's Division educated women about mission through materials designed for use in the churches. These materials were introduced at schools and training sessions around the country. Nearly ten thousand women attended these schools, with nearly half a million women doing some kind of study in classes in their local churches. Although these percentages were not high, and certainly not as high as the Woman's Division wanted, they represented a significant amount of education that was not available to women in many other venues. Woman's Division materials gave serious consideration to theology, to politics, and to social understanding as well as to the cultivation of spiritual life. The steady stream of materials that poured out provided women with up-to-date information from around the world. Issues of *World Outlook* told of mission projects and gave ideas for local programs, serving as interpreters to local churches and the active women in them. Methodist women had no excuse for being ill informed.

By 1948, the division was ready to move beyond its postwar mode, which had included much rebuilding and reassessment. The fresh look turned to mission was tempered with personnel needs. Despite some good recruitment efforts, the total numbers in service were down as a result of retirements, death, and changes in career plans. The women put out a call for teachers as well as workers in religious education and social and medical fields. They sought women with college degrees who were willing to get further training and to face unfamiliar settings and challenges.

Leading the organization in 1948 was newly elected president Laura Jean Brooks, who had served previously as the secretary of finance and as

Laura Jean Brooks, an Iowan who taught languages at Methodist-related Cornell College, was elected president of the Woman's Division in 1948. She became an active spokesperson and leader of Methodist women during the 1950s and in 1954 was elected to the Central Committee of the World Council of Churches. *(Photo courtesy of United Methodist Archives and History)*

a vice president for foreign work. She traveled to New York meetings and foreign mission sites from her home in Mt. Vernon, Iowa, where she had been teaching Latin, German, and English at Methodist-related Cornell College. She gave up teaching in order to take on the volunteer responsibilities of the position. During her tenure as president she also was named to the Central Committee of the World Council of Churches (WCC) in 1954. She was one of six women on the ninety-member committee and went on to other committee work for the WCC. Other officers of the WSCS as well as women in her own church credited Laura Jean Brooks with being an inspiration for the ways that women could get involved. Her leadership enlarged the horizons of Methodist women and inspired them to a new understanding of ecumenical responsibility.[22]

Within the Department of Work in Home Fields, an array of institutions and individuals carried on a variety of service efforts. The educational work was housed in the Bureau of Educational Institutions. Its staff of 474 maintained thirty-three different educational centers, serving more

Community centers established by Methodist women across the U.S. became important urban institutions, serving the poor, including immigrant and racial/ethnic minority populations. Most of these centers continue today. *(Map courtesy of United Methodist Archives and History)*

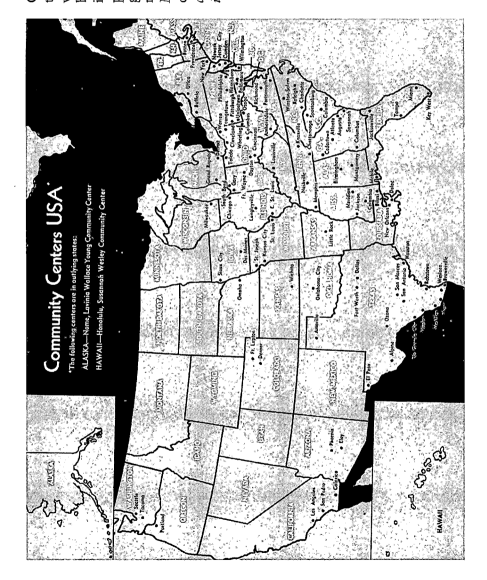

Community Centers USA

The following centers are in outlying states:

ALASKA—Nome, Lavinia Wallace Young Community Center

HAWAII—Honolulu, Susannah Wesley Community Center

than 6,000 students. Nine of the schools were administered cooperatively with other organizations. Many of the schools had a special focus for their clientele, including eleven that were African American, three that were Mexican or Spanish, and one that was Native American. Two were training schools for Christian workers.

Each year the division included special stories or reports that highlighted the work and its meaning in some of these places. Occasionally these reports revealed an attitude reflective of the culture of the time but a little in conflict with that of the national office. For example, highlighting the ministry at Holding Institute in Laredo, Texas, the report told of the baptisms of ten students during religious emphasis week, with eleven joining The Methodist Church, some of whom were Roman Catholic. Anti-Catholic sentiment was still common at the local level at this time. Yet the board had long been confronting questions about the focus of its work for conversions.

The vast majority of the institutions were not only active in the Southeastern part of the country, but also had been started by women of the Methodist Episcopal Church, South (MECS). In general, when the institutions were discussed in any of the meetings or reports, it was because the women wanted to highlight some new development or important ministry. Anecdotes kept the network of agencies and schools personal for their women supporters. In addition, the end of the war gave the women the opportunity at long last to conclude the business of some of the property concerns remaining from the time of the merger.

The Bureau of Urban Work also had a large number of projects in the Southeast. By 1948 it had ninety-seven projects and employed about three hundred workers. Some of the work was modeled after the settlement projects of the turn of the century, a model that was examined for its relevance to the postwar era. Others looked at the variety of projects and concluded that this aspect of the church's ministry was just beginning. Reports continued to focus on individual projects; the work was generated locally with persons then making appeals to the national office for help. Those appeals arrived almost daily.

Town and country workers were also primarily in the Southeast and the lower Midwest. Even more specifically, they tended to be in rural areas rather than towns. Nearly every report from the bureau emphasized the difficulty of characterizing and categorizing the work. While missions reports made good use of stories, anecdotes, and word pictures, they also emphasized numbers and measurable successes as much as possible. The annual explanation of the variety and remoteness of town and country ministries probably helped to remove expectations of detailed statistics from the minds of the readers. In addition, this work often involved ecumenical ventures, making quantifying it less meaningful for denominational concerns. Its inclusion demonstrated the broad spectrum of the church's mission and ministry.

Social welfare and medical work were geographically much more widespread than that which fell into the urban or town and country categories. Homes for girls, residences for young women starting careers in cities, and rest homes for deaconesses and missionaries all fit into this category. The homes for the retired workers from the division were filled and had long waiting lists. The residences for young women varied from city to city but even included one in San Francisco for young Chinese women. The women chose the location of a home in Los Angeles specifically to attract young African-American women but found that it soon had a racially diverse set of residents. The women knew that in some cases questions would be asked about how the homes related to the church's mission. To help prove that these places were carrying out the church's values, the 1948 report even listed the amount of money the young women in one residence had raised for charity. Twenty-nine of these residences for young women were operated by the bureau.

Social welfare programs paralleled efforts made by the missionaries in a number of locations around the world. But while the missionaries outside the U.S. sometimes went to great lengths to describe exactly why, given the culture of the women, such homes filled an important role in their lives, little background was given in this report. Presumably the readers knew why young women in the cities of the U.S. would need the protection provided by such a secure place of residence.

Among the medical work projects, the women sponsored five hospitals. Two were located in Alaska, along with a tuberculosis sanatorium. Another was in El Paso, Texas, which ministered to the large Mexican and Mexican-American populations. Another hospital was operated in Washington, D.C., and the fifth was primarily for African Americans and specialized in children in Jacksonville, Florida.

Methodist deaconesses were located in every state except Nevada, Idaho, and North Dakota. "Home" missionaries were located in most states, with few in the northern Midwest and the West. The 1948 report did not tell anecdotes or stories about the work. Instead it invited women to apply for service. The numbers, when one studied them, told their own story of need. In a postwar world with what seemed to be many opportunities for women, the division was faced with a recruitment problem.

If the women had chosen to do so in 1948, they could have written of the great contributions made by the deaconesses in the past. They had a proud legacy on which to build, even when the numbers appeared low. Instead, deaconesses shared space in the report with workers in a variety of categories.

But if the numbers were somehow low, the women's work in other areas was not lagging. The Department of Christian Social Relations and Local Church Activities had only eight years of history, but it was already exerting influence. Dorothy McConnell, coeditor of *World Outlook*, did not hesitate to put a little social commentary into her report. Suddenly, in the midst of reading about homes for girls and other institutional successes, the reader was confronted with reflections on the New Deal. McConnell reminded her readers that not long before, the idea of helping people when they were out of work seemed like a radical idea. But most had now come to accept it.

Even more telling was her comment about war talk. She reminded the women that even during the war, the church was busy working on plans for the peace, to be ready when it came. She wrote, "Today—with war talk thrown about almost irresponsibly—it is amazing to reread what we were saying in the midst of a shooting war. Surely we sounded, as a people, far more pacifist than we do now."

McConnell's evaluation of the past quadrennium was equally interesting. She believed that one of the important changes was the development of local programs, ones not necessarily "sent down" but developed out of the interests of the local groups and the needs of the community. The division was recognizing the power at the local level. Nothing, however, could quite match the results of one particular monthly program developed at the national level of the WSCS. Soon after it had been given in churches throughout the country, the National Committee on Child Labor actually had to hire extra secretarial help to deal with all the requests for information that came in from Methodists.

McConnell's story of this one particular campaign is a good reminder of the system of study and action that the women employed month after month, year after year. It may not have been as effective as the women dreamed it could be if adopted by all women in all churches, but it had a significant impact. WSCS members had opportunities for learning and service with issues and places that mattered on a continuing basis. Through participation in a local unit, women were continually confronted with the people and needs of the world.

While McConnell could point to these and other stories of the impact of the Woman's Division on legislation and policy, she knew that one of the most important tasks the women were undertaking was the improving of race relations.

The Central Jurisdiction was the glaring reminder in the new church that all was not resolved when it came to the race issues that had originally divided the different parts of Methodism. But as the still newly united Woman's Division began its work after the war, it could tell a much more positive story about its past, its present, and its future. One method of telling the story was through the booklet *Adventure in Building Brotherhood (Methodist Women and Race)*, written by Betty Jane Thompson in 1946. The pamphlet provided important history of the Woman's Home Missionary Society, noting that almost from the beginning racial concerns encompassed more than black and white issues. The Woman's Missionary Society of the Pacific Coast grew out of the need and desire to be in ministry to Chinese women. The booklet made exciting reading for those who wanted to focus on the leadership and work that the women had already begun. With stories about Belle Harris Bennett and others, Thompson illustrated that the concern for race relations was a legacy brought to the new church by all the uniting bodies.[23] Pictures and an attractive layout made for a booklet that many women were likely to pick up and read.

Concerns about race within the Woman's Division went beyond inspirational stories from the past. The pamphlet detailed numbers as a way to raise awareness of the scope of racial relations, information that was not easily available to the women through other sources. The inclusivity of the list of "America's Minorities" is significant. It read:

13,000,000 Negro Americans
5,000,000 Jewish Americans
3,500,000 Mexican or Spanish-speaking Americans
400,000 American Indians
125,000 Japanese Americans
75,000 Chinese Americans

72,000 Alaskan Americans

45,000 Filipino Americans.

The information did not stop with the numbers. The centerfold of the pamphlet listed the centers of work for the Woman's Division by categories. French and Italian people were listed along with the others. The lists ranged from community centers to schools and colleges to retirement homes. And among all the institutions—many with long histories for the women—was the item "scholarships for women, Gammon Theological Seminary, Atlanta, Georgia." Training for the future was part of the work as well.

Yet another item of interest in the booklet was a small box that noted: "Traveling almost constantly among the Central Jurisdiction societies is one full-time Negro worker from the Woman's Division. Employed by the Board of Missions and Church Extension as secretaries and assistants are fifteen Negroes, eight Japanese Americans, two Jews, and one American Indian." While later generations would take church agencies to task for glass ceilings, the board, especially the Woman's Division, talked about the issue as soon as the war was over.

This concern was also apparent in the discussions about a meeting place that had characterized early reports. Quoting from the Fourth Annual Report, the booklet noted, "The jurisdictional organization of our church tacitly accepts the principles of segregation. Methodist women have an obligation to stimulate within the church an increasing awareness of the contradiction between our Christian ideals and our plan of organization."[24] Holding to the ideals was a struggle. Many places in the U.S. still did not allow housing for persons of color. Participation in ecumenical events became a difficult decision if the events were held in locations not open to all persons. Local groups were urged not only to adopt these policies, but also to continue to monitor events arising from racial tensions.[25]

Passages from the recently released statement of the Federal Council of Churches were also scattered throughout the booklet. These quotes reminded women that segregation was still a reality in most church-affiliated hospitals and that it was especially apparent in Sunday morning worship. Thompson reminded her readers that in the past the church had successfully incorporated various language groups. A map showing pictorially a large number of different ethnic groups as "Makers of the U.S.A." illustrated her point. Without prescribing uniform solutions, the booklet served to remind the women of a heritage of "adventurous dreamers," of progress, and finally of the work to be done to have a more inclusive church that could witness to and serve a racially diverse world. With only a few changes, the booklet could have been a useful tool for many years in the division's struggle to bring great racial justice to U.S. society as a whole.

Although the merger of the church had combined the various groups of mission work into one board, for many people, missions still meant "foreign" missions. And for some of the women who worked tirelessly for their local units, this was a well-known, personal relationship with one or more of the twenty-one sites the division maintained in countries outside the U.S. Returning missionaries had fostered the deeper relationship by visiting and speaking when on furlough. Gifts from the local groups went to New York with the understanding that special projects the women had heard about would benefit. Missionaries continued to write letters that highlighted changes to buildings and increases in numbers.

The 1948 report was designed to give a more detailed view of the work in all the locations. In addition, it served to remind the women and men of the church what they had done in the past and what was still possible. As the report introduced the various areas of service, it laid out for the readers—without naming it as such—the policy of the division, indeed of the board, in its work. The report noted a past filled with substantial achievements despite the small numbers that had been deployed throughout the years. It gave praise to the new and developing churches, some of which had carried on in the war years without the missionaries there for extra support. But it also spelled out the key philosophy: "As we go forward with them, it is to work by their side as sisters, helping them to train Christian leaders who in turn will train and evangelize their own people." This statement and variations of it permeated the literature of the work of the whole board. But how deeply it was understood by local churches, and even by some of the local churchwomen who worked so tirelessly to raise the money, is questionable.

The ability to institute the policy of shared leadership varied from place to place. In India, the women had already reached the point where 50 percent of the administrative positions were held by women from India. In addition, the Woman's Division worked with local churches in many of the countries to help establish their own woman's societies at the local and conference levels. These societies chose their own local projects and contributed to missionary efforts in other countries as well. The pattern was not new; from the beginning missionary women had established local units wherever they went. But the push for more support in indigenous churches was increasing.

Personnel and policy were only part of the picture. With the war recovery work well at hand, the division began to look at its buildings and organizations. In some places it planned for new buildings or additions. Both the aging of buildings—many as much as half a century or more old—and crowding contributed to the need for this development. Many buildings had gone many years without needed repairs. In other places, the programs and classes had been so successful that rooms were being used for twice the number of people they had been intended to hold. The women were also concerned about equipment needs. Even as they tried to turn more and more of the work over to the younger churches, they still felt a tremendous responsibility. In each area, they tried to balance the needs that U.S. dollars could help with so easily with the desire to encourage local development. Older missionaries, some of whom had considerable power in the hospitals and schools they had been serving, did not always follow the direction from New York to turn over responsibility to the indigenous people.

Buildings were not being planned in a vacuum. The women explored ways to work with other denominations in hospital and even educational work. An example of this cooperation was the work in Burma. Practically all the Methodist property in Burma was damaged during the war; some of it was completely destroyed. Yet by the time the U.S. missionaries were able to return, they found that the trained Burmese and Chinese women had already reopened coeducational middle and high schools in several of the cities. These schools were supported primarily by fees paid by the students. The women were also able to begin reopening primary schools, although this process was slowed by the needs for books and materials that could not be easily obtained. By May 1947, the missionaries had opened yet another school: the Union Christian High School. Both the Woman's Division and the Division of Foreign Missions cooperated in this endeavor, joining two Baptist boards as well. U.S. and British Methodists cooperated in establishing yet another high school. These examples from just one country begin to indicate the variety of configurations in which the missionaries worked. In addition, Burmese men continued to be trained for ministry, and women served as Bible women, calling on families, organizing Sunday schools, and even visiting the sick.

Similar joint efforts helped to rebuild the Mary Johnston Hospital in the Philippines. After its total destruction during the war, the Woman's Division and Division of Foreign Missions cooperated with the Presbyterians to rent rooms and re-establish the Mary Johnston Clinic and Health Center.

India: Mission in Maturity

The end of the war meant that independence could again become the major focus in the area where The Methodist Church had the largest number of missionaries: India. The board continued its educational endeavors by publishing an informational booklet in 1945, *Methodism and India*, by W. W. Reid. Reid was a trained journalist working for the Board of Missions in its Department of News Service. He used his skills to tackle a difficult area of interpretation. The book first summarized the economic and political conditions that were important factors in discussion of India's immediate future. Underlying this, Reid seemed to have another objective in addition to this recital of facts and conditions. In a country where Methodists had been working for almost a century, only a small fraction of the population was Christian, let alone Methodist. In the light of these results after the years of major investment of money, resources, and personnel, he needed to give reasons for continuing the efforts.

In a short section, he gave credit to the missionaries who inspired and even trained many of the contemporary freedom leaders. Since the difficult conditions in India were well known, he stressed the importance of contributing food for both body and soul as part of the message Christianity could continue to bring. Finally, he noted the more than three hundred missionaries as well as the Indian laypeople and clergy serving in the churches and institutions of The Methodist Church. He summed up future plans with goals laid out by Diffendorfer: providing greater leadership, strengthening institutions, working on rural reconstruction, engaging in city problems, and supporting church union.

The brochure featured a centerfold of the map of India with main centers of Methodist work indicated. In contrast to Africa and China, where nineteenth-century comity agreements kept Methodist work confined to particular areas, India's map was well marked with Methodist missions. Historically, comity broke down much earlier on the subcontinent, leading to a larger field of ministry.[26] Some of that ministry was also portrayed in the photographs through the booklet, several buildings, students at a seminary, a reading lesson, and a village scene. But for all the information and numbers it contained, the brochure was subdued in style, a contrast to many other materials produced at the time. As India entered a new phase in its political life, the mission work in which the U.S. was most active was defined primarily in terms of institutions. At the same time, U.S. bishops continued to serve in Indian conferences, and U.S. missionaries pastored many congregations.

The very longevity of the church's efforts led to this situation. The pioneering work of the Christians, with Methodists prominent among them, in providing schooling for women had led to a number of fine institutions that had national recognition and reputation. For a long time the Christian colleges and schools had been a major force in offering educational opportunities to persons who might not have had them otherwise — men as well as women. By midcentury these schools represented only a fraction of the educational possibilities in the country. Medical facilities as well were matched by the development of many institutions in India's superstructure. Methodists in India were able to locate able women leaders from other Christian churches. Sarah Chakko, a Syrian Orthodox woman from south India, went to a Hindu high school and to a government college for women in Madras. She then taught for six years at Isabella Thoburn College in Lucknow and studied in the U.S. Her primary field was the history of India, but she also taught economics, political science, and physical education. After becoming head of Isabella Thoburn, in 1951 she was elected one of six presidents of the World Council of Churches, the only layperson to be elected. Her work ended abruptly in 1954 when she died suddenly after playing in a staff basketball game. She was only forty-eight.

Chakko was concerned not only with the status of women but also with the meaning of being a Christian in the twentieth century. Although she did not think secularism was dominant in India, she was prescient in seeing that India's traditional religions were being revived. "We have today in India," she wrote in 1949, "a combination of nationalism and a revival of the cultural element of the old faiths." Echoing what some leading Protestant theologians had said about the rise of fascism, she wrote,

Sarah Chakko, a Syrian Orthodox Christian, became president of Methodist-related Isabella Thoburn College in India. She was elected one of six presidents of the World Council of Churches in 1951, the only layperson to be elected. Chakko presciently raised questions about how Christians can witness to Jesus Christ in a pluralistic society. *(Photo courtesy of United Methodist Archives and History)*

"Nationalism in India today has many of the characteristics of a religious cult." Because of the passion in India for the new state, particularly on the part of youth, "educational and other institutions maintained by religious bodies are looked upon with suspicion, because they are considered to be working against the forces of unification."

In the midst of the religious pluralism of India, in which Jesus was sometimes blended with Buddha and Mahatma Gandhi, Chakko believed Christians had to witness to their peculiar faith: "I believe therefore that the biggest function of those who bear Christian witness in India is to bring home to the people the uniqueness of Christ, who came to reveal God to man [*sic*] and served as the means of our redemption." The churches, she believed, had accomplished significant things in India: "They have proclaimed the love and care of God for the individual and society through the gift of educational opportunities, medical relief, social emancipation for the downtrodden peoples, by a new status given to women." Nevertheless, Indians had hard questions for the church, asking "in what way has the Christian message re-created society?" She thought Indians were horrified by Christian societies in the West and that the Christian church as a redeemed community was "not particularly attractive."

Indians were also asking what the Holy Spirit could do for the individual. It was not enough, she wrote, to say that Jesus Christ is the answer. Because Indians look at Christians and find "us no different—in our daily life and actions at least—from the many who have not accepted Christ." For these reasons, Chakko believed the church needed to make a united witness, to provide its support for India and other countries through ecumenical channels, and that "Indians themselves should bear the responsibility for the witness to their own people."[27]

Carrying out another of Chakko's challenges, that of involving more laypeople in Christian witness, Dr. Jaya Luke combined her professional training as a physician with the work of Christian ministry. Coming from the family of a Methodist clergyman, Luke went to Vellore Medical College in Madras and also studied in the U.S. Returning to Sironcha, she supervised a twenty-six-bed hospital and six dispensaries in surrounding villages. She served as a women's representative on a local governmental board. Asked about how she had the strength to accomplish all these tasks, she said, "I am a Christian, and my strength comes from the Eternal Father."[28]

Punlick John studied at Methodist Bidar School in Mysore Province in southeast India. But he was not a good student and left after the fifth grade. He became a tailor's apprentice, bought himself a sewing machine, and married Rathni, who had also gone to Birdar School. They moved to a village where there were no Christians. "There, like Paul, he sewed for a living; but his main job was to witness for Christ." His wife opened a day school, and the couple also taught in an adult night school. The two Christians started a congregation and requested that a Methodist missionary, David Seamands, baptize the entire village. After Seamands baptized more than 300 people, Punlick returned a few months later, and another village of 250 persons was baptized. Bishop Paul Martin came for a visit and baptized another village of 117 people.[29]

As the Templins had discovered earlier, the institutional church was concerned to stay out of any political situation. The missionary pledge was taken seriously, and with only a very few exceptions, missionaries had long kept distance from internal developments that they deemed political. It was a fine line for some, because they had also drawn links between Christian response and some public, and therefore political, positions on issues. When Indian independence came, however, The Methodist Church joined in the celebration by issuing its own pledge of loyalty during the Bombay Annual Conference in November 1947. Quoting Romans 13:1 — that the "powers that be are ordained of God" — Methodists expressed joy and satisfaction at independence and agreed during the difficult days ahead to work for peace and cooperation.

China between Wars

One of the first missionaries to enter postwar China was Tracey K. Jones. The board had assigned him to study Chinese in California during the war; therefore, he was ready to travel as soon as the opening came. A few months after he arrived in China, his wife and small daughter were able to join him, coming by armed troopship. His wife had been raised in China and was quite willing to go as soon as the board gave the word, despite the uncertainties of the postwar conditions. In her eagerness to return, she was even willing to ignore the lack of railings on the ship, a concern for a parent with a small child.

In later reflection, Jones gave the board great credit for preparing him for difficult circumstances. He arrived already with a respect for Chinese culture and an awareness of the social changes that were inevitable. Even so, he found that because of heavy fighting, he and his family were forced to leave Canton eight different times.

His assignment in China was simply the overwhelming task of recovery. This meant trying to reopen hospitals; to administer relief goods, especially in places of great poverty; to start schools; to find out what buildings had been closed; and finally to assess what could be done to improve conditions. In addition, he worked with the Chinese ministers, many of whom were still recovering from the shock of the years of war. The church also wanted to start a theological school as soon as possible. All of this he did, working both with and under the Chinese leaders who had survived the war. At the same time, he found that the job took lots of personal motivation, since there were not always established authorities and certainly no established routines. "We had to make it up as we went along," he reported later.

Communication with the board in New York was by cable. Since it took a week for the cables to go back and forth, the missionaries were not dependent on New York to tell them what to do. It became more of a partnership between the staff and the missionaries, with each having to trust the other and especially trust the local leadership. Jones and other missionaries shared the challenge and struggle of the many changes, anticipating a happy outcome to their work. They looked forward to the days of greater growth and autonomy for China's church.

The biggest problems were not administrative, but the day-to-day challenges of living in a society trying to recover from one war, just as its own civil war was heating up. "Inflation was the biggest problem," Jones said. Travel, too, was fraught with problems; buses were crowded and did not always run on schedule because of the war. Bicycles often proved the best way to get between churches and institutions.

Postwar work in China, as in other places, was an attempt to build on the goals articulated by Diffendorfer, goals that focused on the development of autonomous leadership. Two of the four bishops were Chinese — Bishops Kaung and Chen Wen Yuan; the two from the U.S., Ralph Ward and Carleton Lacy, were both experienced in the Chinese culture. All the heads of hospitals were Chinese, which was noteworthy since half of all hospital beds in postwar China were in Christian hospitals. The top leadership in the church was also Chinese. Many of the national leaders had received more training than had the missionaries with whom they worked. Even if they were so inclined, missionaries in China found it difficult to feel superior to the people.

One of the concerns of the Christian work had always been examining the role of women in society. Early women's work had pointed out the injustice of female foot binding and early marriage. When it came to women's work, the missionaries set a high standard, since not only were those with the Woman's Division especially trained for their appointments, but also the board required that all missionary wives receive college training before approval. In their work, the Christian institutions had tried to match this standard for Chinese women as well, making training for women a high priority throughout the century.

Horace Dewey and his wife had first gone to China before the war. He actually spent part of the war interned there. After his release in December 1943, he returned to New York for reassignment by the board. Like many missionaries, he took the first opportunity to return to his prewar work, arriving back in China in 1946. He soon realized that he was once again in a war zone, this time with a civil war raging all around him. His letters home from Changli in northern China detailed the situation for

Bishop Chen Wen Yuan, who had served in the Chungking area since 1941, disappeared after the Communist rise to power in 1949, and his final where-abouts were unknown for years. He appar-ently was under house arrest and not permit-ted to participate in church activities. An important early indige-nous leader among Chinese Methodists, he died in 1968. *(Photo courtesy of United Meth-odist Archives and History)*

his readers, explaining the activities of the Chinese Communists who had worked so hard during the war to oppose the Japanese and were fighting to control the country. Cities along the railway lines remained open to the Americans who were siding with the Nationalist forces of Chiang Kai-shek, but only eleven of the fifty-five churches previously open to Dewey for his preaching were now accessible. At the same time, pastors and leaders from the churches were still able to visit him, telling him sto-ries of the needs and of their struggles. The mission was the only one on a 320-mile stretch of railway; no missionaries were in the interior of China any longer. In 1949, there were 100,000 Methodists in China, 500 of whom were pastors and 350 who were missionaries.

Bishop Chen Wen Yuan, who had served in the Chungking area since 1941, disappeared, and his final whereabouts were unknown for years. Ap-parently he had been imprisoned, perhaps under house arrest. He was known to have served as a translator of English and German documents for the Communist government. His fate was similar to that of many Christians of China at that time.[30] Letters from Dewey and others reflect the strong anti-Communist rhetoric of the era. They tell of living with a guerrilla campaign that was set in motion by an outside invasion and continued under the deteriorating conditions of the postwar era. Missionaries to China had already been through a lot leading up to the Second World War, and like many of the people they lived with in the cities and towns, they believed that the present troubles were only one more thing to endure, but one that would soon be over.

Dewey informed friends as well as the board in June 1947 of the invasion of the compound by Communist forces. As was the case in many of the Chinese mission locations, the church had its own compound surrounded by a high wall. In the compound were four residences, the church, a hospital, and three schools (serving about five hundred students). These enclaves concerned some of the board and staff because they separated the missionaries from the rest of society, but they represented business as usual in most places of Methodist mission. When the soldiers came, the first group entered the compound, greeting the missionaries with the news that they had come to rescue the poor people from the capitalist Chinese government. The soldiers did not touch any of the people's possessions or the buildings. But the next group to enter began to loot the buildings of anything that seemed valuable. Later that night, yet another group came, setting fire to the house where the Deweys had lived for eighteen years. Nearly 20,000 soldiers had entered the area, creating chaos as well as destruction. For those who were violently affected, like the Deweys, the emotional responses took many forms. Besides the pain of loss of material possessions, there was constant uncertainty about safety. Several times those in the compound were threatened by the soldiers, who told them to follow orders or they would be shot. At one point during the looting, Dewey and others had to escape through a window out of the house in which they were hiding, then climb over a wall out of view of the looters. The material losses were great as well. When they returned to China, many of the missionaries had carried more supplies than usual, knowing that they could not obtain food, medicines, and other materials easily after the war. To lose these provisions, which they had hoped would last many months, just as inflation was growing worse, was a severe blow to their spirits and a real concern for the days ahead.

The Deweys relocated to Peking (Beijing), where Carol taught music. Horace continued to return to war-damaged areas to supervise the relief work. They continued to feel the effects of the postwar economy and the difficult civil war. To deal with the increasing toll of inflation, they had to carry suitcases of money just to pay for some items.

The Deweys' letters home communicated to their readers the brutality of the civil war, expressing deep concern about the godless Communism represented by the coming regime. Their physical descriptions of the suffering and violence were helpful to many in the U.S. who knew little about what was happening. But their analysis was not shared by all the missionaries. A somewhat more philosophical response came from E. Pearce Hayes in a letter he sent to "homeland friends" in 1949. He reminded them that many Americans who preferred to think of themselves as the "common man" were by Asian standards millionaires. Since under the new regime all persons were to receive the same wage and were to give of their talents equally, the problem for Christians became how to take Christ into the new society. In a section entitled "What America Has not Understood," he wrote: "Some of my finest Chinese friends will admit the humanitarian service to mankind that has come from America, but still their total reaction is 'yes — but.' What do they mean? It is growing upon me more and more that what they mean is just this, that no matter how much good you may do with what you have, you have no right to have it while most of the world is starving and has so little." He suggested that Americans needed to share their abundance far more than was being done — a sharing that was about responding to the missionary needs but that reached far beyond to an understanding of economic justice.

Joining Hayes in presenting a view different from the usual anti-Communist analysis was Olin Stockwell, who believed that Christianity could carry on despite the changes. He noted the support of the U.S. for the government on Formosa (Taiwan), anti-Communist rhetoric broadcast daily on U.S. radio, and the statements of Secretary of State Dean Acheson, all of which would lead any government to be highly suspicious of those aliens in their midst. He found remarkable not the pressures on the missionaries but the fact that, for the most part, the missionaries experienced relative security, despite the many ways their government was aiding and abetting one side in the conflict.

This more positive response to what was happening around them was echoed by Creighton and Frances Lacy in their reports. They mentioned in June 1950 their concern that special gifts to China projects had fallen off, even as they continued to be needed. They saw themselves as part of China's future.

Taken as a group, these missionaries present a complex picture of work being done in China. The challenges for the board were how to continue to place personnel and resources in an area that seemed not just unstable but counter to all the U.S. stood for. The missionaries themselves faced the challenge of making sense of the events happening around them and finding an interpretation that gave continued meaning to their work. The Lacys were offered a move to Manila but chose to stay in China, believing that Christian work remained there. The old ways had ended. But moving to new ones was not easily accomplished when chaos and war still surrounded their daily lives.

In the light of these reports and letters, Frank Cartwright issued a memorandum late in 1949. At that time the medical work was not yet affected by the political changes, but schools were. While they were able to remain open, enrollment was small, leading to a number of financial problems. In addition, teachers were required to attend indoctrination classes led by the Chinese Communists. Many of the missionaries believed that private education was only a few years away from being eliminated altogether. Planning for the future became increasingly difficult.

Churches continued to operate with fairly normal schedules and large attendance. But an air of uncertainty hung heavy around the Christians and their work. While one new church had been built since the political liberation, its construction was viewed as an exception rather than a harbinger of changes to come.

Their work at war relief remained a question for the missionaries. For a while people had believed that they would have to discontinue the efforts, but to their surprise, the government appeared to encourage the work. Missionaries were reassured that after the uncertainties of the financial institutions in the postwar years, money was again being received and converted promptly. Providing relief was easier with access to funds, giving a place where the church felt it could make a real difference in Chinese lives.

Cartwright used material from another denomination, which he did not name, to make a series of points about the new regime. These are similar to the information summarized in individual missionary letters. A number of the ideas ran counter to the view of the Communist government that was current in U.S. circles, however. The positive change he was able to see included the attack on graft and corruption by the new regime; the concern for the common people; the opposition to colonialism, aggression, imperialism, and warmongering; the emphasis on economic planning to benefit all people; and the enthusiasm for the new movement. Running counter to this were concerns about the restriction of civil liberties, trends toward a police state, close alliance with the Soviet Union, thought control, Marxist-Leninist ideology, and persecution in certain provinces. The ability to see these positives as well as the negatives in a dangerous and politically charged situation demonstrates the insights their experiences gave the missionaries into changes that could benefit the people with whom they had worked. Not all Chinese missionaries agreed with Cartwright. But he was not alone in his analysis.

The China experience was one of many places where voice was given to an alternative view. Getting beyond the borders of the U.S. often altered the way that missionaries saw the world. Most of the time such attitudes were expressed as a response to a particular situation rather than establishing a pattern that challenged popular U.S. political and economic beliefs. This particularist focus kept missionaries from straying into the political sphere, a place they knew they did not want to be.

Japan—"Worth Redeeming"

Before the war ended, the board began to evaluate the form its work would take as soon as missionaries could return to Japan. Charles Iglehart, professor of missions at Union Theological Seminary, published an article in the *Duke Divinity School Bulletin* that named the challenges the church should face. At the same time, he wrote a paper for the Division of Foreign Missions that spelled out the reasons the church would want to re-establish its work. Such early preparation for the work ahead is a tacit reminder of the still prevalent atmosphere of anti-Japanese sentiment. His opening words, "Japan is worth redeeming," reminded his audience that this might be a controversial position for some.

John Cobb, Sr., was the first of the missionaries to return to Japan. He reported a brief period during which many denominations seemed eager to resume their individual identities following the war. Within a few months, however, most were strongly supporting the Kyodan once again.[31]

Charles Germany's story of his entry into the mission field in postwar Japan illuminates the spirit of opportunity as well as the process of the board at the time. Germany, a fourth-generation Methodist minister, saw the possibilities of the wider parish of the world both through the Crusade Scholars he met while at Drew Theological Seminary and through his participation in the Student Volunteer Movement. He visited with Mel

Williams, then the secretary of mission personnel. Germany was accepted by the Division of Foreign Missions, began to make plans to go to China, and even became engaged.

When the war ended, General Douglas MacArthur, the U.S. commander in Japan, issued an invitation to the churches to send missionaries back to Japan. The board approached Germany and asked if he would consider changing fields for his work. He married his fiancée, Julie, and they went to California for a year of language study. On completion of their study at the language institute, they received traveling orders and were among the first new missionaries to enter Japan after the end of the war. While they did not know what to expect, they found an openness to people from the U.S. that surprised them very much. They discovered a conviction among many of the people with whom they worked that the war had been the wrong path, and its ending had given a sense of release and freedom to pursue new opportunities. The air seemed full of possibility despite the difficulties of postwar recovery. They opened their home in Kobe and found that the students flocked to the English Bible classes. The days were exciting and filled with satisfying work.

Because the military was still in charge during this period, the missionary boards needed to work together to make a joint approach in reestablishing their work. The original joint group was called the Commission of Six and was followed by the formation of the Council of Cooperation. These groups were able to lay the groundwork for the return of the missionaries and to perform many tasks essential to the relief work so necessary in the war-torn and war-tired society. The Council of Cooperation functioned to manage all the cooperative matters among the Church of Christ in Japan, the Japan Christian Association, and the Interboard Committee, which some saw as the U.S. counterpart to the council. The Interboard Committee had a carefully designed membership that reflected the participation of the U.S. denominations. Methodists constituted about one-sixth of the Protestant missionaries. With the original number of members at thirteen, the Woman's Division and the Division of Foreign Missions each sent a representative to the board. The Interboard Committee had complex tasks because it carried responsibility for financial, organizational, and personnel-related matters. This work was primarily administered through committees. For example, one committee of the board was established to be responsible for the maintenance of the missionaries.

The provisions for missionary relationships were carefully spelled out.

These included the possibility that missionaries would have joint membership in the united church as well as in their U.S. denomination. The manual stated that each was expected to associate with the joint organization, "expressing the same loyalty he would give to the denominational body." Strictures against participation in politics were also made clear in the manual. Study of the manual reveals some of the intricacies involved in the ecumenical structure. For example, in the U.S., The Methodist Church recruited missionaries for Japan in the same way it did for other countries, trained them along with other Methodist missionaries, and paid them on the Methodist missionary scale. But when they arrived in Japan, they worked structurally with missionaries who were paid on a different scale, trained by a different organization, and possibly even recruited with a different philosophy. The cost of living in postwar Japan was a further factor, as boards coped differently with the inflation as well as the effects of the destruction of the war.

The Interboard Committee again gave leadership in ecumenical efforts to deal with the property. The Methodist Church became the holding body for the many schools and social centers in the country. In addition, although Methodists owned housing, they were asked to participate in sharing that housing with other denominations on an as-needed basis. These areas and others were all hammered out for the Interboard Committee agreement. They represented a significant step in ecumenical work and a challenge for the division in the U.S., which had to be aware of differing conditions for its Japan missionaries.

At the same time, Christians in Japan remained a relatively small number, totaling fewer than half a million believers. The united church itself had fewer than 150,000 members. Yet Methodists and others supported a significant number of schools, hospitals, and other major institutions within the country.

The atom bombs the U.S. dropped on Hiroshima and Nagasaki in 1945 killed many Japanese Christians and destroyed many church institutions. At the Jo Gakuin girl's school in Hiroshima, 350 students and eighteen teachers were killed on August 6. The buildings were totally destroyed. The Chinzei Gakuin Methodist Boys' School in Nagasaki was heavily damaged by the second bomb that fell on August 9, although the Kwassui Jo Gakuin, the girls' school, was spared. The Foreign Missions Conference of North America in the Orient estimated that half the facilities for Christian work in Japan had been "destroyed or seriously damaged." These facilities included churches, schools, and social work centers. Besides those Christians killed outright, some were also exposed to radiation and were doomed to die a slow death. Others were discouraged and disabled.[32]

The way the Woman's Division worked to develop indigenous leadership in these institutions can be shown through the experiences of Japanese women. Yoshiko Ueda had been a Buddhist until she went to Eiwa Girls' High School in Sapporo. She became interested in social work and went to Nagoya, where she joined other women working in a factory. "When I worked in the factories," she said, "I was sure that evangelism was the only way to save the people; so I became an evangelist, appointed solely to Kumano Church. Eiwa gave the start of my life and Kumano Church established its foundations." Ueda's husband was also a Christian and supported her active life in the congregation and her service as representative of Christian churches in the Federation of Women's Associations. She was appointed by the national government to be supervisor of working women and minors in Hokkaido in northern Japan. She became the first president of the Japan Association of College Alumnae.

Hamako Hirose was in a country village school near Hiroshima when Nannie B. Gaines, principal of the Methodist girls' school there, met her. Gaines recognized Hirose's potential and persuaded her to go the school. At the time Hirose had never heard of Christianity. Upon the completion of high school she went to college in Hiroshima for three years. Following that she studied in the U.S., including a period at Scarritt. She returned to Japan to teach religious education at Lambuth Training School for Christian workers in Osaka. Eventually she became president of the school and, later, president of Seiwa Joshi Gakuin, a women's school. She was also ordained.

Yoshi Tokunaga went to Kwassui Girls' College in Nagasaki, then studied at Boston University. She returned to Japan to be principal of the Methodist school in Fukuoka. Although the school buildings were bombed and burned during the Second World War, Tokunaga remained there.[33]

Much leadership also came out of the schools and student movement. Many leaders studied in the United States. Takeshi Muto, for example, was graduated from the theological department of Aoyama Gakuin and then went to Northwestern University. Back in Japan, he taught and was a pastor and the editor of *Christian Newspaper* (*Kirisutokyo Shimpo*). After serving as president of Kwassui Girls' College, he was elected moderator of the

Michi Kawai

Kawai was born the daughter of a Shinto priest in a small village near Kyoto. She became a Christian through the influence of an uncle, going first to a Methodist school at age ten and then as a teenager to a Presbyterian school in Hokkaido, where she mastered English. Japanese friends arranged for her to receive a scholarship to Bryn Mawr. She returned to Japan to teach in a school established by Ume Tsuda, one of the famous seven women who first went to the U.S. in 1871. In 1905, an American friend persuaded her to help in bringing the YWCA to Japan, for which she became one of several secretaries and the first Japanese secretary. On another visit to the West Coast, she saw the possibility of the YWCA in Japan preparing Japanese people who were going to emigrate to the United States. She also met many influential foreigners in her YWCA work, such as John R. Mott and John D. Rockefeller.

Kawai had a gift for appreciating other cultures and learning from them. In her encounters with foreigners, she invariably found something to affirm. For instance, she wrote: "When we first meet Americans, they seem to us to entertain themselves by talking to each other without listening to what is said; but, later, when our reserve has melted away, we can enjoy the American custom of spending a social hour together in the exchange of news and ideas." She also had a prudent side, such as when she reported with approval that an American friend "came to consider it a favor to rich people to enable them to find worthy causes to help with their money."

She dreamed of beginning her own girls' school, a dream that became a reality in 1929. She converted her home in Tokyo into Keisen Jogaku-en school. The school opened with nine girls aged twelve and thirteen. The school was remarkable in being an indigenous Japanese Christian institution. By the time of her death, the school had almost two thousand students and consisted of a junior high, a senior high, and a junior college. She died on February 1, 1953.

Sources: Kawai, *My Lantern* (Tokyo: Kyo Bun Kwan, 1939), pp. 13–193 passim; John W. Krummel, *Letters from Japan, 1956–1997* (Kearney, Neb.: Morris Publishing, 1999), pp. 141–142.

Michi Kawai.
(Photo courtesy of United Methodist Archives and History)

Kyodan in 1954 and served until 1958.[34] Masa Nakayama was graduated from Kwassui, went to Ohio Wesleyan, and returned to Japan to teach. She soon became interested in politics, however, and after the war was elected to the lower house of the Diet. She served as Japanese representative to the UN and the U.S. State Department in Washington, D.C., in 1951.[35]

Michi Kawai, who received her undergraduate degree from Bryn Mawr, founded the Keisen Girls' School in Tokyo in 1929 and became principal, thus creating an indigenous Japanese Christian school and one that was not a mission school. She named it Keisen Jogaku-en, which in Japanese means "a fountain of blessings girls learning garden."[36]

Other pastors, teachers, and leaders followed a similar pattern of study at Christian schools in Japan followed by studying in the United States. Some Japanese pastors and teachers who studied at Christian schools in Japan remained there.[37]

Birth of the Advance

Wanting to build on the success of the Crusade for Christ, the 1948 General Conference adopted a new four-year plan. The "Quadrennial Plan for Christ and His Church" included both preaching and teaching to advance the church and enrich Christians and a ministry of relief for the worldwide Advance for Christ and His Church. Within this latter goal was the recommendation to increase World Service apportionments by another third *plus* a recommendation to set up a special fund for additional individual and group giving. Advance Special projects were written up individually so that givers had specific information about the recipients. In addition, Advance money was designed to go directly to the projects, bypassing the administrative costs of the New York offices. The Woman's Division set up Advance Specials as well; projects in both the U.S. and outside were part of the plan. The goal for the Crusade was $25 million, and Methodists gave $27 million.[38]

Advance Specials quickly gained their own identity, moving from the Quadrennial Plan into an important place in the funding structure of many of the church's mission projects. In the first year, the Methodist Committee on Overseas Relief sent food, clothing, and medicine to thirty-two countries (including countries in Africa and South America, as well as war-torn Europe and Asia). Missionaries helped with the distribution and organization. Much of the rebuilding was funded through the Advance rather than the World Service or Woman's Division budgets. In part this was because the specific nature of assigning gifts allowed the funding to be revised more quickly on a yearly basis. Projects could be added and given prominence in a timely fashion.

Evaluation of the Advance from The Methodist Church's perspective was a way to see real accomplishment and development in the church's mission work. The success of the plan obscured the small voice of concern from indigenous people in many places in the world. Because projects could potentially be funded for large amounts from this extra giving, the eloquence of the furloughed missionary, or the extra "oomph" in the way it was portrayed in the literature, could make the difference between plenty of money or next to none. At its inception, however, many were pleased with the success of the Advance in getting resources from people who had them to people who needed them.

In 1948, when the church had amassed $27 million for the Crusade for

Christ, surpassing its goal of $25 million, it decided to continue the effort. The Council of Secretaries, which comprised the heads of general agencies, decided to produce a film to promote the crusade. *We've a Story to Tell* was co-produced by several boards, including the Board of Missions. It was probably the first general church film ever produced and raised the question of whether Methodist Church boards should not be cooperating in producing such audiovisuals in the future.[39]

Crusade Scholars were a significant part of the Crusade for Christ. Originally conceived in 1944 as part of the Crusade for Christ, the program was a joint project of the Board of Missions and the Methodist Board of Education. These two boards, including the Woman's Division, collaborated in administering the program. Its purpose was to provide education for students from outside the U.S., especially those from countries damaged during the Second World War. The emphasis fell on graduate and professional studies, although some allowance was made for those at the undergraduate level. The assumption was that students would spend two or three years studying in the U.S. and then return to their own countries.

This program was to prove spectacularly successful during the next decades and undergirded the church's determination to empower indigenous Christians. Some three hundred had entered the U.S. for study by 1948. These students included more people from China than any other country but also included all the major continents and Polynesia.[40]

Korea at War Again

As the missionaries continued to return to Korea, they were faced with decisions about resuming more and more of their previous work. Of particular concern was the reopening of the Songdo station, since it was near the 38th parallel, the line that divided the north from the south in the new alignment of Asia. Persons in opposition to reopening cited the constant danger to be faced by those who would have to live there. Again, a deputation from the U.S. visited the various missions stations, evaluated the situation, and quietly gave its approval. Charles Sauer was one person who felt he had more information than the visiting delegations. He did not voice his opposition in a way that showed up in any official reports, but he was very much against it. He did not think the delegation had really been in a position to know what was best. He wrote about this decision, saying it was "to their later regret. With no authority vested in the mission or-ganization, the delegation from America had made its second mistake."[41]

Identifying and locating possessions after the war was one of many problems the returning missionaries and their colleagues in the Korean church faced. Bishop Ju Sam Ryang had kept track of all the properties of the church during the war. In 1948, he presented all the records back to the mission, receiving high commendation from the missionaries. They knew that what he had accomplished was difficult, indeed, under the war conditions. But missionaries who had lost personal items from their homes in Pyenyong, Heiju, Chulwon, Wonsan, and Yeng Byan never saw them again. Personnel in other locations also reported many items miss-ing. Occasionally, missionaries would see one of their possessions for sale in some shop and buy it for the stated price, primarily for the sake of past memories and sentiment rather than because they needed it any longer.

Leadership for the church and its projects continued to be an issue. Sauer voiced one point of view, asking for strong leadership, criticizing the board, whose policy was to have no official organization for the mis-sionaries, since they were to take part in the life of the Korean church. In response, T. T. Brumbaugh suggested that they might organize for community among the missionaries. But the board only recognized deci-sions that were made by a duly constituted body of missionaries and na-tionals. "Board executives were living in a dream world where missionaries were fellow workers under the leadership of a national bishop. The at-tempt to force the Korea situation into this mold did untold injustice to many national leaders." Again these comments from Sauer serve to counter the stated policy about the way that indigenous churches would be in power with missionaries as their colleagues. Sauer represented mis-sionaries who believed that the board executives who were making deci-sions were out of touch with the local situation. This group was also more comfortable with the older model of mission, which allowed missionaries much more independence in their work.

The lines of conflict over decisions were not always between missionar-ies and indigenous peoples; sometimes there was conflict among the mis-sionaries themselves. In addition, Sauer's conflicts were with the Division of Foreign Missions specifically, although touring delegations always rep-resented both divisions. Once the government allowed the return of the women, he did not focus much on the Woman's Division and its work in his critiques.

The strength of the workforce compounded difficulties with leader-

Thoburn T. Brumbaugh, who had been a missionary to Japan, became area secretary for Asia in the Methodist Board of Missions. He was deeply involved in the way Methodists responded to the Kyodan in Japan, the evacuation and eventual return of missionaries before and after the Korean war, and the civil war in China. Although a traditionalist, his greatest concern always seemed to be the Christian church as such, apart from political developments. (*Photo courtesy of United Methodist Archives and History*)

ship. Between 1946 and 1950, twenty-three new missionaries arrived, but only ten stayed beyond the first term. The board, through each division, grappled with the problems, seeing them in the larger context of societal changes that followed the war. The board was not so surprised at the personnel difficulties and dynamics surrounding them. By contrast, long-term missionaries saw only that newer missionaries were fewer in number and seemingly less committed than were prewar veterans. With so much disruption of long-established patterns in missionary roles and duties, the job description was becoming more contested than it had been before.

Indigenous leadership remained a problem, as well. Educated and experienced Koreans could find many jobs helping the country in its recovery, and these jobs paid more than the church could. In a report in November 1950, Brumbaugh reported that he found the loss of Christian leadership in the church more serious than the destruction of property.[42]

Some of the best-trained leaders responded to the invitation by the

U.S. military to help solve government problems. Others had been forced out of the church by Japanese pressure and were no longer available. Many city churches had closed because of persecution. In the rural areas, however, it had been a little easier to keep some of the churches open. Lay leadership training before the war had borne fruit. But lack of Christian literature and a shortage of paper made progress slow. The American Bible Society was able to provide a few thousand Korean Bibles, but that was the primary source of materials for the missionaries and Koreans to use in rebuilding. Mission schools were crowded; frictions and tensions among some of the Christian people also slowed recovery and work.[43]

Missionaries in Korea had barely been able to begin the rebuilding process when war came again, this time along the 38th parallel. In June 1950, Margaret Billingsley reported that at the time the conflict had begun there were three hundred Christian missionaries in Korea, two-thirds of them Protestant. As the situation worsened, one-third returned to the U.S., one-third were appointed to posts in Japan, and the final third were living elsewhere.[44] The report also listed Korean "friends" who were either safe in Seoul, who had been arrested and not heard from, or who were known to have been killed. Cryptic notes referred to some who had escaped through the sewers. In addition, careful notes were sent back about the state of the buildings — some bombed and burned, others occupied by the military and damaged, a few empty with only minimal damage. Ewha High School, for example, was completely destroyed, but Ewha College had only minor damage to its building. Even with some bright spots, the list was formidable. Until the way was opened for supplies to be sent, however, the board issued requests for cash only.

In that June, tragedy struck the Methodist mission in Korea. Kristian Jensen was awakened on Sunday, June 25, 1950, by the sound of artillery as tanks approached the house where he was staying, located less than a mile from the 38th parallel. The fighting had begun, and during the night the line had already pushed past where Jensen was staying. The hospital, by then behind enemy lines, treated wounded and dying soldiers from both sides. Jensen went to check on the three women missionaries who were also serving at the site. Although their mission house was shot full of holes, the women had been able to find hiding places and remain safe. In the group were Helen Rosser, Nellie Dyer, and Bertha A. Smith. Dyer was an experienced missionary who had been in the Philippines during the Second World War. In addition to Jensen, the men included the Reverend

Lawrence Zellers and Dr. Ernst Kisch. Dr. Kisch was an Austrian citizen who had been imprisoned in Dachau. He had escaped to China, where he joined the Methodist mission as a physician. When the Communist invasion forced the mission out of China, the board reassigned him to Korea. He had come to Songdo only three weeks before to take charge of the hospital. The wives of both Jensen and Zellers were in Seoul.

All that day tanks and artillery rumbled past, until finally, on June 29, the missionaries were called down to military headquarters. The interrogation went on all night. In the early morning, they were led straight to a "dungeon-like building" filled with wounded, bleeding, and dying Koreans. The group recognized some of the prisoners as leaders from the churches. Even more people were thrown into prison over the next day. Only the dead were removed. Finally the missionaries were taken in a truck to Pyengyang, divested of any personal articles, and placed into yet another prison. While there they endured the sounds and explosions of tons of bombs from the forces fighting under the United Nations. The sounds were terrifying, causing the group to believe the building would collapse, but it held firm. Four days later, they were piled onto another truck, this time with a group of foreigners who had been gathered from all parts of South Korea. They were herded into a small abandoned schoolhouse outside the city and kept there for two months. Many times the guards stole their meager rations, leaving them near starvation.

When the UN forces drew near, they were forced to move again. For the next month they were always on the move, often hiding during the day as the ground around them shook under the heavy bombing. The group of prisoners had also grown much larger, with nearly eight hundred American GIs added to their number. The travel through the countryside was not without its inspiring moments. When the guards were not looking, the villagers would show pictures of their pastors or congregations to the missionaries. They made an effort to prepare tasty meals for the prisoners despite the meagerness of the supplies they were forced to share. Jensen found himself strengthened by these encounters.[45]

The difficult times were not yet over. The group moved farther and farther to the north in what came to be called a death march. Because many of the group were so weakened by the poor food and dire living conditions they had endured for nearly six months, they moved much more slowly than their captors liked. Instead of the shelters their guards had hoped to reach, they often slept in open fields and had no food at the end of the grueling days. Some mornings they left behind group members who had frozen to death overnight. More than one hundred members of the group died during the hundred-mile march. Even more died during the winter, spent high in the cold mountains.

After the first year, the civilians were separated from the GIs. Jensen noted the differences in reaction to the incarceration between the two groups. Most of the GIs were very young and had been in Japan and Korea for only a short time before their capture. Their unfamiliarity with the food, language, and customs meant that they suffered much more than did the missionaries. During the first year, a much larger percentage of the military members died than did the missionaries and civilians, but those who made it past the first year began to adjust and cope with the rigors of the physical deprivation. On the other hand, while the missionaries had more internal resources with which to handle the adversity, they often did not have the physical resources of youth and good health to make as easy a recovery. One such person was Kisch, who, worn out from the adversity of earlier years, was not able to withstand the devastating conditions. He died at the end of the first year.

As the second year began, conditions eased, allowing the prisoners time to be alone rather than always crowded into small spaces. They searched for wood on the mountainsides, taking the time to be alone with God. They also had more freedom with which to worship, both together and alone. These experiences increased the inner resources that were critical to their survival. Jensen commented, "There were times when I was almost afraid that, released and again sent back to the free world, I might lose that sense of God's nearness."[46]

Meanwhile, the board was continuing to assess the ongoing conditions in Korea. Brumbaugh reported after a fall 1952 visit that rehabilitation and relief would continue to be the focus of most of the work in Korea for some time to come. One could not expect normal church or Sunday school life under the conditions that had left most of central Korea in ruins.[47] The third year brought slightly better conditions. A few more items of warm clothing were available as well as slightly better food. But increasingly good health also meant that the prisoners had more energy for interactions with one another. Occasionally tempers flared and arguments erupted from the enforced intimacy. The missionaries again had to draw on their inner resources to cope with the difficulties of their imprisonment.

Then came the day when a truck arrived, and all the British prisoners were loaded on and taken to places unannounced and unknown. The French left a week later. Finally, one day in April 1953, the Americans were ordered to pack all their things. Their time to leave had come. To their surprise, after a stay in Pyengyang, they were taken to the train station for a long trip by train across Manchuria to Russia; the Soviet government had asked for and obtained their release. Only when they reached Moscow were they turned over to the surprised U.S. ambassador and other authorities.

Their families had known for only a few days about the release. For three years they had had no news at all. The board joyously released the news as the group returned home to their families and friends. With the help of the Joint Section of Education and Cultivation, follow-up literature was quickly printed, telling the story of the imprisonment and the role of faith in their survival. Central to the piece was the panel entitled

These Methodist missionaries arrived in New York May 13, 1953, after being imprisoned by North Korea Communists. Shown from front to rear are Nellie Dyer (waving hand), Kristian Jensen, Helen Rosser, Bertha Smith, and Lawrence A. Zellers. Others are not identified. (*Don Collinson photo courtesy of United Methodist Archives and History*)

"Their Hearts Are Still in Korea." It reminded readers that money sent to World Service, the Advance, and the WSCS would "help send them back, if they are strong enough to go" as well as support other missionaries. Another panel concluded, "The story has not ended. You are writing the next chapter." Through these materials the board hoped to make links that would go beyond the telling of an inspiring story, a story of bravery beyond faith issues that might easily be embraced by the secular community.

Despite the war, the Korean Methodist Church (KMC) continued to add members. As soon as the war was over, it began sending missionaries to other countries. The Women's Mission Society in the KMC supported education for the Aymaras in Bolivia as well as for Korean students in Borneo.[48] While the war raged, Methodist schools, like Ewha, became refugee institutions in Pusan, the beachhead to which UN troops had retreated. Louise (Young Shin) Yim, president of Central Women's College, another Methodist school, also was found there, along with her faculty and students. Yim had served as Minister of Commerce and Industry in the first administration of President Syng Man Rhee of South Korea.[49]

Discouragement and Hope

The war-torn lands of Asia were not the only places where the board was active in the postwar years. New missionaries were trained for Africa and sent off with a few belongings to work in agricultural, educational, and social service, as well as continuing to work in evangelism. The end of the war meant more resources for such places as well. The church participated in efforts to rebuild in Europe as well as to expand ministries in Latin America.

The years following the war, with their own endings and beginnings for countries where Methodists were active and for programs in which Methodists believed, were a time of advance and development despite the pain and occasional discouragement. The loss of China was a tremendous blow, but it was not enough to dampen the energies that were pushing to improve society in the U.S. and abroad. Now that buildings had been repaired, personnel was trained and in place, and the U.S. economy was functioning well, the days ahead seemed bright.

CHAPTER 4

Mission at Midcentury

*P*OLITICAL RHETORIC, television programs, and paintings by Norman Rockwell enhance the common picture of the 1950s in the United States as stable and prosperous. Some churches added education wings to house the growing number of Sunday school classes and family activities; others helped to start new branches in the growing suburbs. Trained personnel were often in short supply. But while the growing prosperity at home contributed to a feeling of stability and optimism for the Methodist Board of Missions and the church in general, the U.S. society also developed an increasing underside of restlessness and change.

On the one hand, the success of the relief efforts that had followed the war now allowed the missionaries to move ahead with program planning and development in many places throughout the world. But on the other hand, postwar changes in China, India, and the Middle East were only the most visible evidence of the beginning of ferment for freedom in many colonized parts of the world. Korea was the first of the hottest and most visible of the battlefields on which the conflict between Communism and capitalism would be waged.

The Second World War had torn the fabric of U.S. society. Not all women who had flocked to the factories when their nation called went home at the end of the war. As they began to assume more visibility in society, women in the church, whose role was discussed every four years at General Conference, were harder to restrain within traditional lines. Race relations also became an ever-larger concern. The freedom rides in the years that followed the war had helped to awaken the awareness — for some that change was needed; for others that change was possible.

Within The Methodist Church, political ideology, gender, and race all played strong roles in the decisions and directions for the decade. Just as small but significant groups were contesting those things at home, so also some of the younger, newer missionaries brought voices of change to the work abroad. Race, gender, and politics played a part for these missionaries, not because of a particular ideology, but because missionaries had to struggle to find ways in their assignments to put their training into practice. This training had raised their sensitivity to other ways of doing things, to different cultures. It pushed them to question relationships with indigenous Christians and the churches in countries outside the U.S., mirroring what was happening in the political sphere. Hidden by so much evidence of growth and stability in both the U.S. and the rest of the world were seeds of change. Dwight Eisenhower's election to the presidency in 1952 brought reassurance to many. The popular general symbolized the victory of U.S. efforts in the past as well as their continuation. Americans were bursting with optimism.

Racism in the U.S.

When the U.S. Supreme Court declared in 1954 that school segregation was unconstitutional, certain groups within The Methodist Church began to reflect this cultural change and also to try to bring to it resources from the perspective of Christian faith. African Americans drew on both the ideals of democracy and their faith to strike a hopeful note: "America is now approaching a higher level in race relations because of what she basically is committed to. At heart, it is what America is that constitutes both her glory and her opportunity. We are, or claim to be, Christian. It is from this source that our light must come," wrote James S. Thomas, an African-American executive of the Methodist Board of Education. It was still possible to avoid open conflict: "Let us continue to seek every reasonable approach to co-operation between the races."[1] The fate of the Central Jurisdiction became clear at the General Conference of 1956, which set in motion the machinery that would eventually bring its dissolution. The conference adopted a proposed Amendment IX to the church constitution, which allowed African-American conferences to transfer into white annual conferences. The amendment had to be approved by the annual conferences.[2] At the same time, some African Americans in the church were wary of what the abolition of the jurisdiction would mean. The Central Jurisdiction had given African Americans certain advantages they did not previously have: "These are principally representation, church-wise, on all boards and commissions and the right of self-determination in selection of episcopal leadership." African Americans needed to continue to seek empowerment. The evil to be overcome was segregation. And it would be possible to eliminate the jurisdiction and still have segregation.[3]

All over the church, strains began to appear as protests erupted throughout the 1950s. In 1955, Martin Luther King, Jr., began protests in Montgomery, Alabama, after the now-famous refusal of Rosa Parks to move to segregated seating on a bus. In 1957, the National Guard was called out to protect African Americans entering Central High School in Little Rock, Arkansas. African Americans joined a white church in Chicago without violence, but the white pastor, who refused to exclude them, was forced out of his parsonage.[4] In Knoxville, Tennessee, segregationists harassed a Methodist pastor, Fred R. Witt, who was chair of the citizenship committee of the ministerial association. The association had asked education officials to comply with the Supreme Court decision. Many others besides Methodists were persecuted, of course, and sometimes clergy who objected to desegregation were forced to leave their conferences.[5]

Some of the developments were positive. In Atlanta, Dow Kirkpatrick, a Methodist pastor, and nineteen other Methodist clergy urged that citizens obey the law, preserve the schools, and give first-class citizenship to African Americans. The New York Conference declared it would accept an African-American bishop. Charles Golden, an African American, became director of the Division of National Missions in the Board of Missions in 1956. The same year, layman J. Ernest Wilkins became the first African American to be elected president of the Judicial Council of The Methodist Church. Ethel Watkins became the first African American appointed to a national staff position in the Woman's Division (Theressa Hoover, another African American, was already serving as a field worker, following Lillian Warrick and Vivienne Gray). In 1955, five African Americans were graduated from Perkins School of Theology, one of eight Methodist theological schools to have accepted African-American students. Dan Towler, an African American who had been the fullback for the Los Angeles Rams, became the pastor of interracial Lincoln Avenue Methodist Church in Pasadena, California. Willa Player was the first African-American woman to serve as president of a four-year college when she became president of Methodist-related Bennett College in Greensboro, North Carolina, in 1955.[6]

Charles Franklin Golden

Born August 24, 1912, in Holly Springs, Mississippi, Golden received degrees from Clark College and Gammon Theological Seminary, both in Atlanta. He was ordained an elder in the Methodist Episcopal Church (MEC) in 1938. He served several congregations in the South before becoming professor in the Department of Religion and Philosophy at Philander Smith College in 1938. He served as a chaplain in the U.S. Army from 1942 to 1946. After serving as director of field service in the Department of Negro Work of the Board of Missions from 1947 to 1952, he became the first African American named to the staff of the Board of Missions. He was associate secretary and later director in the Division of National Missions, where he served until 1960. He was a member of the General Conference Commission to Study the Jurisdictional System from 1956 to 1960, when he was elected bishop in the Central Jurisdiction. He presided over the Nashville-Birmingham Area 1960–1968 and in The United Methodist Church served the San Francisco Area 1968–1972 and the Los Angeles Area 1972–1980.

Just before the 1964 General Conference, Golden went with white Bishop James K. Mathews to worship at Galloway Methodist Church in Jackson, Mississippi. They were turned away, and their rejection was reported in the national news media. After the 1966 conference adopted an omnibus resolution proposing specific steps for merger of black and white conferences, the three annual conferences over which Golden presided failed to give approval. Golden emphasized through his articulation of issues and his episcopal leadership that Methodist African Americans would not settle for anything less than full and complete integration. Golden was noted as a forceful and even authoritarian bishop, but he was respected as fair and a person of integrity. He died in 1984.

Sources: Nolan B. Harmon, "Golden, Charles Franklin," *Encyclopedia of World Methodism*, 1: 1014; Peter C. Murray, "The Racial Crisis in The Methodist Church," *Methodist History* 26 (October 1987): 3–14; Charles F. Golden, "The Nature and Purpose of Christian Missions," *Central Christian Advocate* 133 (June 1, 1950): 5–6; communication from Mark Shenise, United Methodist Archives and History, March 31, 2004.

The church also began recruiting more African Americans as missionaries, among them Dr. William A. Brown, who went to Angola and later to Liberia, and Barbara Patterson, who also went to Liberia. Several African Americans went to India, among them Pearl Bellinger of Indianapolis, who went to Bangalore; James M. Lawson, Jr., from Uniontown,

Pennsylvania, who went to Nagpur; and Julius Scott of Houston, who went to Deccan. A few African Americans went as missionaries to Latin America, including Janet Evans to Lima, Perú; and Emmett and Henrietta Steele to Brazil.[7]

Other African Americans had served in the U.S. for many years. Isabelle R. Jones had served at the Allen School in Asheville, North Carolina, from 1906 to 1949. Florence Daniels began serving in Detroit in 1922. Lucille Holliday had served at the Mother's Memorial Center in Cincinnati since 1923. Willa Stewart served at the Friendship Home in Cincinnati from 1924 to 1954. Josephine Beckwith began serving in 1942 on a pilgrimage that took her to several cities, including Philadelphia and Oklahoma City. Merna Mae Parker and Aline Sykes went to Tennessee. Amanda Pleasant and Betty Harris went to Fort Worth.[8] Some of these women were deaconesses, some were "home missionaries," and some were short-term missionaries. The Reverend George W. Carter, a Crusade Scholar, became superintendent of Browning Home and Mather Academy in Camden, South Carolina.[9]

Native Americans: Laity and New Ministries

The Navajo Methodist Mission School in Farmington, New Mexico, and the Oklahoma Indian Missionary Conference continued as two permanent institutions for Native Americans. Although their numbers were small in the denomination, Native American churches illustrated how adept they were at incorporating laity into the life of the church. One example was Hazzel Botone, a Kiowa in Oklahoma. She was the daughter of Chief Lone Wolf, a prominent Native American leader in the Methodist Episcopal Church, South, in the nineteenth century. She was raised as a Christian, but she married a non-Christian, Mathew. Hazzel became active in the Woman's Society of Christian Service (WSCS) and was director of the district children's work. She organized the teacher-training school and went to several WSCS assemblies. Mathew, who had been participating in peyote ceremonies, was eventually impressed with his wife's faith. "I never fought my husband," she said. "I knew that some day he would decide for the right way of worship." Sure enough, Mathew "saw many truths that I had missed before," as he put it, and became a Christian, then a minister. Together he and Hazzel were said to have made more conversions among other Native Americans than had any other Methodists in Oklahoma.[10]

Guy Quetone, a Kiowa pastor in the Oklahoma Indian Mission Conference,
is shown in the center of this gathering during an annual conference in the
1940s. *(Photo courtesy of United Methodist Archives and History)*

In New Mexico, the Reverend Robert W. Brooks, chaplain of the
Navajo Methodist Mission School in Farmington, went to Shiprock in
1957 and organized a Methodist church with the graduates of the school
living in that historic community. Bennie and Edna Gibson, Choctaws,
and Stella Lee and Carl Tohdacheeny, Navajos, were among the stewards
of the new church. The congregation slowly grew through the 1960s. Beginning in 1967, the church moved from a non-Navajo to a predominantly
Navajo leadership. The Reverend Fred W. Yazzie was the first Navajo to
become an ordained Methodist clergy.

From this effort grew the Four Corners Native American Ministry,
with Navajo congregations in four states: Utah, Colorado, and Arizona,
besides New Mexico. The ministry was served by missionaries from the
Methodist Board of Missions. It developed a classical mission outlook, one
in which indigenous converts cherished their new identity as Christians
and in doing so rejected much of their indigenous tradition. This issue had
arisen earlier in Oklahoma and eventually generated a serious debate
among Native Americans in the U.S. Some Native Americans felt that

what was called a "Christian" faith was heavily tainted by European and U.S. cultural thought and its adoption would turn Native American Christians into followers of the "white man's religion." Those at Four Corners felt, however, that their new faith gave them a new perspective that was freeing and empowering.[11]

Name Changes

Reflecting this new era were other changes at home. The 1952 General Conference changed the name of the agency to the Board of Missions, dropping "and Church Extension" from the title. To develop further this new understanding of the terminology, the work was divided among the renamed divisions — World and National, with Woman's remaining the same — and the Joint Section (formerly division) of Education and Cultivation.

The church was entering the fourth quadrennium of successful efforts with a combined board. Once again an Interdivision Committee on Foreign Work was established to consider the work that came from the field committees of conferences outside the United States. The purpose of the field committees was to coordinate the work of the World and Woman's divisions. The *Book of Discipline* also stated that "in each foreign mission field of the Board, each Annual Conference and Provisional Annual Conference shall have a Field committee with resident bishop, mission superintendent, and equal number of missionaries from the Division of World Missions and the Woman's Division, chosen by the missionaries, and national men and women elected by the Annual Conference."[12] Central conferences had their own executive boards that submitted estimates of the funding they needed; the board had to approve these requests for funds. This provision reflected the continuing efforts to work with the indigenous churches. In many countries, these churches had grown much stronger just in the years since the end of the war. Pressure came from the churches to the board for increased power and responsibility. The board, however, retained most of its financial power.

As more and more of these annual conferences outside the U.S. became larger and stronger institutionally, they trained an increasing number of their own pastors and provided a larger amount of their own funding. The work for the missionaries gradually changed so that in many places the bulk of the missionary group filled positions in particular institutions. For example, in 1953 the board supported 350 schools; more than forty colleges and training schools; twenty-three theological seminaries; 160 medical institutions, including clinics, training schools, and hospitals; and more than one hundred urban and rural centers. Some of these were in countries with relatively small membership in The Methodist Church itself, but as institutions serving a wider population, they provided the church with ways to touch thousands of lives.

Within the Division of National Missions were the sections of National Missions and of Church Extension. The latter was to assist in building whatever facilities were needed by local churches. The Section of National Missions was further split into the departments of City Work, Town and Country Work, Goodwill Industries, Negro Work, Spanish-speaking and Indian Work in the Southwest, and Research and Surveys. Most of these were similar to the organization of 1939. Some were fairly large with ties to many projects that had had strong local ties as well. Others were more limited in scope.

The Woman's Division still split its work into three departments: Work in Foreign Fields, Work in Home Fields, and Christian Social Relations and Local-Church Activities. Changes in title did not have much effect on many of its ongoing programs. In particular, the Department of Christian Social Relations continued its work on race.

Origin of Charter on Race

Pauli Murray, a young woman from North Carolina, worked for two years to compile data on *States' Laws on Race and Color*, published by the Woman's Division. Its 800 pages brought together in one place evidence of the extent of discrimination throughout the U.S. The division hoped to use the information as it evaluated its own institutions and practices, noting the role of both law and custom. In the year that followed, the women used this and other research to develop a Charter of Racial Policies. It was written on the wall for the January 1952 division meeting. After discussion, the group voted unanimously to adopt it.

The charter had two sections. The first was titled "We Believe" and listed six points, including the sacredness of every individual and the belief that the church, and the Woman's Division as an agency, needed to demonstrate the principles through its organization and program. Following were a list of policies in which the division pledged to make assignments and hires without regard to race. Other provisions were the assurance that the division would take into account the needs of various racial groups in its program work and the integration of all groups into the life and work of the church. Jurisdictions and conferences received reminders to work across racial lines and to keep concerns about accessibility in their decision making. The charter also named local societies and guilds as needing to increase their emphasis on working together with all racial groups. Finally, the charter asked that the conference and jurisdictional societies carefully study the charter and vote on its early ratification.

Leaders in the organization took this to heart and worked for ratification by the Woman's Assembly, scheduled for May 1954 in Milwaukee. As conference presidents signed in, they were asked whether their conference had studied the charter and if they had ratified it. Nearly three-fourths of the conferences had, as well as had five of the six jurisdictions. While the women met, the nation also was forced to think more seriously about racial policies, because the Supreme Court handed down the *Brown* v. *Board of Education* decision, calling for desegregation of public schools.

The charter did not change churches overnight. The Fifteenth Annual Report noted, "The implementation of the Charter *in practice* is moving slowly but with progressive determination." As concerned individuals struggled to find ways to make it a reality, the charter continued to function as a reminder that the church still had much to do to model the Kingdom of God for all of society. Its adoption was the women's way of saying that they were very serious about confronting the disparities that Murray's research had highlighted.

The women continued to prod the church on racial issues at the 1956 General Conference. Their petition requested that the process of transferring Central Jurisdiction churches to the jurisdiction in which they were located geographically take place "without necessary obstructions in the process," a reference to the criteria placed on the process in 1952. The Woman's Division did not get the kind of enforcement they wanted for the action, but they made their point.

Indeed, churches did understand the point, and some were quick to take the women to task. An example of the response from such churches is that which came from Thornton Methodist Church (location unspecified in the documents).[13] The choice of wording indicates the deep differences in attitudes about race that had permeated theology in the denomination. The church wrote, "We believe that it is high time that we, as true Christians, who love and cherish the religious heritage that our forefathers

fought, bled and died to preserve, rise up and take whatever steps necessary to safeguard this heritage and to guard against any further breakdown
of religious beliefs as we now know them and to strengthen our faith and
love for Methodism in its truest sense." The petition called for an end to
all integration efforts. The division in the church, even with the Central
Jurisdiction as a compromise, remained deep. The work of the Woman's
Division, the Methodist Federation for Social Action, and other parts of
the denomination was difficult and always contested. In its public denial,
Thornton Church did not represent the majority of churches in the denomination, but it was willing to express publicly what a significant number of them quietly felt.

Woman's Division: Deaconesses and Institutions

The war had both obscured changing patterns and, with its end, contributed to them. In city and country, church and home, as the pressures
of postwar recovery receded, the women evaluated their mission and their
methods.

One area where these changes for women became more and more a
pattern that the church could not ignore lay in the appeal of deaconesses.
Married and single women were making different choices about employment and their relationship to the church. Deaconesses had made a place
for themselves in the lives of many churches. As news of their contributions spread, more churches requested such an addition to their staffs. In
1954, for example, thirty-eight new requests were added to a list of ninety
that remained unfilled. The talented women who answered the call to
service and commissioning only increased the desire of many agencies and
churches for more. But women were marrying or finding higher-paid and
increasing opportunities in service professions outside the church. Agencies that carried "deaconess" in their name sometimes had none on their
staff.[14] In her annual report, Mary Lou Barnwell lamented that "it takes a
heap o' recruiting in the church to get a candidate." Eleven women were
commissioned in that year after having received training at either the National College in Kansas City or Scarritt College in Nashville.

Even with fewer deaconesses than they wished, the Woman's Division
continued to support an array of institutions. The Bureau of Educational
Institutions maintained oversight for junior colleges and colleges, primarily in the South.

Under the Bureau of Social Welfare and Medical Work were children's homes, homes for retired workers, and thirty-one residence halls for young business women, located in many cities throughout the country. These residence homes gave a special service to young women, many of whom were new to the city, giving them a safe place to live, a community, and either cafeterias or a communal kitchen in which to prepare meals. As a first stop in the move away from home, they gave the women much for their money, including a library, a laundry room, a television room, a spacious yard, and a place in which to entertain guests. Beyond that, residents reported on intangibles. "Habits which I have formed while living at Esther Hall, such as eating nutritious food at regular meals, coming in at the designated hour, showing consideration for others and worshiping God, not only at church on Sunday, but every day throughout the week, will doubtless stay with me as long as I live . . . it has meant a pattern of Christian living which I can follow the rest of my life."[15]

These residence halls took on special personality depending on their location. The Esther Halls in Utah were sought out not only by Methodists but also by other young Protestant women. All were looking for a faith community with which they were familiar while living in an area where the religious practice seemed very different. In San Francisco, Gum Moon (Golden Portal) Hall was a special refuge for young Asians and Asian Americans. The residents there spent some of their free time assisting at local churches or in other community activities. The medical work of the women ranged from hospitals to clinics in both rural and very crowded urban areas. Several facilities in Alaska provided much-needed services to the Seward Peninsula.

Within the Bureau of Town and Country work were a large number of community and educational institutions, many designed to meet the very particular needs of a certain geographical or ethnic area. The Woman's Division supported thirteen facilities that were designed for the needs of Native Americans. Some of these evolved in their service as the needs changed. For example, in Houma, Louisiana, the women had maintained a school for the children of Native American shrimp fishers. In 1955, when the local school board at last built a building and agreed to accept its educational responsibilities for these children, the women adjusted their own ministry. While they no longer were needed to provide the primary educational offerings, they turned their school into a community center that could provide classes and training for the adults of the area, who were also ignored by other social service agencies. This adaptability was a theme for much of the work in the U.S.

The largest number of projects administered by the bureau was in rural areas. These were often not institutions but individuals sent to an area where needs were great and resources often few. The projects were often small and so individual that each year the women tried to feature some in the annual reports. For example, reports from the Arkansas-Oklahoma rural work of 1954 came from Dorothy M. Kelley. She told of efforts for interracial opportunities that included a highly successful Easter sunrise service, the country ministerial alliance, and a special worship service when a staff member from the Woman's Division came. With such limited but important efforts, the decentralized system of rural workers was able to make a difference in many ways and places. In that year as well, work in coal-mining communities, with unstable employment and poverty, was another focus of the Woman's Division.

A counterpart of the activities in the rural areas was found in the Bureau of Urban Work. The settlement houses of earlier decades evolved into community centers, which the women continued to staff and run. Clubs, crafts, games and sports, and even music and ballet were offered in many of the centers. In explaining the work, Mabel Garrett Wagner wrote, "Back of this program activity in all centers is a deep Christian purpose to help people grow and develop in harmony with God's plan and purpose."[16]

Although rural workers were often more visibly attached to a church, workers in the city might have their strongest institutional identity with one of these centers. In many cases, the governing board represented a partnership among community leaders, the assigned staff, and other representatives in accomplishing these aims. Some of these centers managed to maintain a fairly high profile with their work, but others became more centered in the community than in the institution of the church.

The outward symbols of society were captured by Norman Rockwell in paintings of families gathered around the well-spread table, but the realities for many families were much less ordered. To read the literature from the Woman's Division and the reports of the work of U.S. missions of the board is to be reminded of juvenile delinquency, loneliness for persons of many different age groups, and continuing racial disharmony, not just for black and white Americans, but for Asians and Latinos as well.

Mabel Garret Wagner reported on urban work for the year ending in

Ethel Watkins became a staff member of the Woman's Division in 1956, the first African-American woman to serve on the national staff of the Board of Missions. *(Photo courtesy of United Methodist Archives and History)*

1955. She described challenges that included petty thievery, vandalism, and drug addiction. Methodist women focused their efforts on prevention, believing that involvement in clubs and other activities would provide an alternative to life on the streets. One focus of their efforts during these years was the Marcy Center on Newberry Avenue in Chicago. This project was located in a continually changing neighborhood in which the only constants were poverty and crime. Workers in the center sponsored clubs in their efforts to refocus the energies of the young people around them. In the mid-1950s, these clubs served more than 150 teenagers. But within the reports is still the trace of concern about what measures will be used for success. "Should the value of the program be measured by the youth who come or by the change in lives?" is asked in the report, which also quoted comments from the youth who were served.[17] Centers such as this could be busy and thriving at all times; yet, workers knew that what they did was only a small effort for the huge problems around them. Wagner concluded that signs of success must be left in God's hands, with the knowledge that it might be only after ten or twenty years that one could truly know how many peoples' lives had been turned around.

One community house in Fort Worth targeted leadership programs to the Spanish-speaking youth of the neighborhood. In Little Rock, Arkansas, Aldersgate Camp was established immediately following the Second World War to bring together black and white youth for leadership training. By the time Little Rock schools were making national news because troops had to be called in to help with school integration, Methodists had already conducted training for eight years, moving in 1954 to more permanent buildings. The efforts were small but were clearly needed. An Oklahoma City program — considered biracial because it served Mexican and Italian children — learned to expand even its understanding of integration when African-American children began to move to the neighborhood.

Growth was not just a matter of adding to or changing the names on the lists of what groups were included. In Ohio, one of the organizations supported by the division decided that just being integrated was not enough. It began to question what other changes it needed to make in program and design to meet its increasingly multicultural community.[18]

As always, interpreters for the mission projects had to answer the same questions over and over. One was: "Is religion taught?" Making the distinction between the work of the local church and the place and work of the community center remained a challenge. The mission studies of the Woman's Division and materials in *World Outlook* helped lead those closest to home to a deeper understanding of the varied goals of church-supported projects, but this understanding was not always widely shared.

Just as the urban work seemed to be increasing, other parts of the "home" mission work were changing. During the war, women had served in ministry near the defense plants. By the middle of the 1950s, most of these ministries had been phased out, leaving only four of the community workers in defense areas. By contrast, twenty-five worked in mission churches and four in Native American mission fields. Eighty-eight of the community centers were in urban areas, thirty-one in towns and villages. Reflecting the distribution of the work prior to the 1939 union, the women continued with seventy-four rural church and community projects.

Telling the Mission Story

With a seeming stability following the need for much rebuilding, the Woman's Division was able to print a variety of booklets and pamphlets to illustrate what was happening in many parts of the world. These ranged from pictorial booklets about Burma or Spanish-speaking Americans to a carefully produced publication entitled *Want a Real Job?* The division hoped this resource, which illustrated the work of deaconesses, would attract many new educated young women to the field. Program pieces for the studies were produced every year. The women continued to feature an area of the world as well as some social concerns, in addition to the Bible studies produced each year for local units. *The Methodist Woman* continued through the period as a major source of information and inspiration for the Woman's Division. With *World Outlook*, the editors began to experiment in 1954 with integrating the work of the two parts of the board. Rather than the previous format with all the women's work at the back, they presented the materials by geographical area with a unified story of what was happening. This presentation helped to give a clearer picture of the broad range of work that was being accomplished.

The entire denomination began using radio, television, and audiovisuals to communicate with the rest of the U.S. public. The 1952 General Conference created a Radio and Film Commission, which in 1956 became the Television, Radio and Film Commission (TRAFCO). As its name suggests, it produced programs for radio and television and also produced audiovisuals — records, slide sets, filmstrips, and films. This media work was coordinated with the National Council of the Churches of Christ in the U.S.A., which was then producing television programs that were broadcast over major networks. The Board of Missions participated in these ventures through its Joint Section of Education and Cultivation. Two other church units were closely related to these media efforts: the Commission on Promotion and Cultivation, which promoted the Advance, and the Commission on Public Relations and Methodist Information, which prepared news releases for the public and other, church readers.

The denomination also had a number of periodicals — so many that a perennial question was how to coordinate them. These included *Christian Advocate*, *Concern* (a social action publication), *Together*, *motive* (for college students), *Methodist Layman*, *Music Ministry*, and *The Methodist Story*.

The Board of Missions participated in these efforts by sending its staff to interagency meetings for coordination. But the board in the 1950s also regularly sent writers and photographers all over the world to report on mission. They would often spend weeks in an area, gathering information

Dorothy McConnell with Henry C. Sprinkle. *(Photo courtesy of United Methodist Archives and History)*

and learning about the particular area of mission they were covering. Thus their reports were firsthand and were made with real understanding of situations. Photography in the 1950s had probably more impact than television, then in its infancy. Board magazines were larger then; they imitated the size of the mass media magazines, such as *Life, Collier's,* and *Look.* The board magazines were able to use this large format effectively for photo essays and other features. Of course, the photographs sometimes prompted the use of slide shows and filmstrips that became efficient ways of meeting the needs of local churches. Congregations often wanted "programs" on mission, and although the visit of a missionary was considered the best means of communication, the infrequency of such visits meant that a slide show or filmstrip was the best alternative. The Board of Missions produced a plethora of these audiovisuals as ways for local churches to interpret mission. For instance, in 1956 the board produced a 16mm color film, *India—Crucible of Freedom*, and sound filmstrips on Alaska, Southeast Asia, Methodist women globally, Korea, Hawaii, Malaya, Burma, Pakistan, Costa Rica, and urban missions. A thirty-minute color movie, *Reply to Reality*, was produced to recruit missionaries. Many of these audiovisuals were used by missionaries, staff, and others who visited annual conferences, districts, and local churches to interpret mission to the denomination.[19]

Africa: Apartheid and Independence

Methodists joined in ecumenical efforts both in the mission lands and in the U.S. to give shape to mission work as it emerged and changed midcentury. One such conference, to focus on the joint mission efforts in Africa, took place at Wittenberg College in Ohio in 1952. More than three hundred people gathered, including fifty Methodists. Besides church people, both Roman Catholic and Protestant, government officials from some of the colonial powers attended. People from seventeen African countries joined as well.

The conference represented growth along a spectrum. In the past, most decisions were made by the missionary churches. At this conference, Africans were still a minority, but with increased participation opportunities, they were making their presence felt.

In his role as board secretary, Ralph Dodge traveled back to the same continent where he had been in ministry, Africa. His observations and reports were an important contribution to continuing policy development as situations changed. Reporting on South Africa in 1953, Dodge brought back critical information about the political changes that had taken place since the end of the war. Afrikaaners had re-established themselves as the dominant political power with a victory in 1948. Soon after, new laws were passed that served to separate the various racial groups. Black Africans, numbering eight million and a majority in the country, were denied rights of ownership and occupation and even rights to travel freely. The two-and-a-half million whites, while needing the labor of the majority, curtailed opportunities for free speech and collective bargaining. Also suffering from many restrictions were the one million "colored" persons (mixed race) and the 300,000 persons of Asian descent.

Dodge painted a stark picture of the situation that had been created. At

Ralph Dodge

Born on a farm in Iowa in 1907, Dodge grew up anticipating the life of a farmer. But a series of incidents, including nearly being electrocuted while working in a grain elevator, forced him to think about life and death and God's call. With the help of the district superintendent, he chose to study at Taylor University in Upland, Indiana. To raise money for the first term, he sold a team of horses and some machinery. His mother went along to keep house. There he met Eunice Davis while attending services at the local Methodist church. Several years later, they were married. Following seminary graduation, the Dodges answered the need for ministers in North Dakota and moved to Moho, a small town near the Canadian border. But the young couple had already determined that they wanted to take the Word into all the world and filled out forms for missionary service. When the time came to be interviewed, however, they were disconcerted to hear the first question, "Are you certain that the motivation for going to Africa is not to get away from the cold winters of North Dakota?"

When the Dodges went to Angola for the Methodist Episcopal Church in 1936, they found that the work of missionaries already put them in tension with the Portuguese colonial government. Naturally, the government was most interested in maintaining its power and felt threatened by the education the missionaries were bringing to Angolans. From the beginning, the Dodges conducted a ministry that respected the people with whom they worked, responding to concerns and needs. When young missionary Dodge was asked to visit places in more rural Angola, he inquired about how he should travel. Older missionaries told him to take all the provisions he needed. But local people said they were willing to host him on his visit, so he decided to accept this hospitality, even though it was not the custom. In following this method, Dodge put himself at odds with older, more established missionaries; but he opened up better lines of communication with the African people. It set the pattern for ministry for the rest of his life.

In his autobiography, Dodge credits these decisions partly to the time in which he entered Africa and the mission field. But his leadership in advancing the indigenization of the African church was more than just a matter of timing. When faced with decisions, he made them personal. If he wanted education for his own children, then he wanted it for Africans as well. He did not favor separation by races, nor did he support separation of religion completely from society. His efforts were never aimed at directly undercutting the civil authorities in the countries where he worked, but they were always about preparation for ministry and church leadership. If the byproducts of this approach were considered threatening by the government, this was not reason enough for him to stop.

Sources: Interview with Ralph Dodge by Ben Houston, January 29, 2001; Dodge autobiography, *The Revolutionary Bishop Who Saw God at Work in Africa* (n.p., no date).

Ralph Dodge.
*(Photo courtesy of
United Methodist
Archives and History)*

the same time, he held out hope that through a racial partnership, the
trend could be reversed. He named three barriers: the possibility that the
standard of living for whites might go down, the decision of the Dutch
Reformed Church to give moral support to apartheid, and fear that the
majority might try to dominate the minority.

Although The Methodist Church did not have missionaries in South
Africa, Dodge's report provided early important information for the
board. The pattern that was emerging in South Africa was one the church
had to respond to for many years to come.

Algeria provided a different kind of challenge. Since the evaluations
immediately after the war, the board had been continually aware of the
challenges posed by the Muslim society. Now Algeria was joining other
colonial nations in its ferment for independence. Dodge described it in
terms of a world movement, even though he thought that the local authorities were not viewing it that way. In any case, he reminded the board
that the fact that non-European Algerians being better off than their
forefathers did not carry any weight with a people who wanted political

change. In addition, the contrast between the wealthy and the poor was evident. These conditions, both economic and political, were of far more import than religious differences.

But while the upheavals in Algeria were not of as great a concern to the board, Algeria as a mission continued to be the focus of attention and discussion. For the Woman's Division, the challenge in Algeria was one of trying to sustain the personnel and buildings of the work it had undertaken. Although the division had to end its work in Algiers, it worked with the women in Switzerland and was able to help support a French school teacher who took up the work in Kabylia.

As early as 1945, W. W. Reid had reminded missionaries that their challenge was to help Africans prepare for new life. This new life took shape religiously, as Christianity grew in many of the countries; socially, as customs evolved and changed with more contact as well as pressure to deal with the racism in South Africa; and politically, as countries sought to release the bonds of colonialism.

By midcentury, the long years of such faithful work, particularly in parts of sub-Saharan Africa, were bearing fruit. For example, the Woman's Division work in Quessua, Angola, had started in 1899 with a girls' school, a hospital, a nurse training school, and a kindergarten. In 1952, nearly three-fourths of Africans (fifteen of twenty-two) who were teaching in the girls' school were graduates.[20] At the same time that Ruth Lawrence filed her reports celebrating these gains, she noted numbers of places where the Woman's Division was unable to keep the staffing levels it had previously enjoyed. The same societal trends that affected the number of deaconesses that could be recruited for "home" mission work were cutting into the recruits for "foreign" missions as well.

Yet Africans were beginning to take responsibility for their own work. In 1958, African Christian leaders gathered at Ibada, Nigeria, to form the All Africa Conference of Churches. Its first general secretary was D. G. S. M'Timkulu of South Africa. Methodists were among the many member churches who would grow immensely during the rest of the century.[21]

Empowerment in Asia

The church in China continued to thrive, despite the loss of Western missionaries. The disappearance of Bishop Chen illustrated the veil of secrecy that kept the rest of the Christian world from knowing what was actually happening in China. And Christians were having difficulty, not only because of oppression from the Chinese government, but also because of their linkage to systems that were considered exploitative:

> In many parts of the world the Christian Church does not stand like a rock over against the Communists' attack. It is accused. It is called into question by the power of Communist success. And this accusation takes a moral form. As the leaders of the churches in China went to the Communist government to ask what the conditions of religious liberty would be, they were met first of all with the question, "Are you prepared to liberate yourselves from imperialism in your inner attitudes and the structure of your churches?"
>
> The charge had force for these [missionaries]. They knew that the churches of China were in fact still deeply dependent on foreign finance and leadership. But they knew more deeply that a spirit of dependence was widespread in the churches and hindered Christians from developing a truly Chinese approach to theology, church organization, and even politics.[22]

This accusation would become more common in other countries as former colonies became independent. Christians were put on the defensive about their alliance with Western powers.

In March 1956, Eugene Smith, a board staff member, attended an ecumenical conference in Prapat, Sumatra, in Indonesia. Calling the conference a product of the Asian revolution, Smith's report revealed some of the tensions and concerns that were developing in the relationships and work with Asia churches. It was understandable that nations in Asia had significant differences with each other. Some Western Christians were concerned, however, that Asian insistence on making the conference thoroughly Asian would also make it too exclusive, leading to "a new color bar in reverse." The steering committee members were all Asian, and even the seating arrangements reflected the concern with staying focused on delegates from the countries concerned. Most Westerners were considered consultants only and had no vote. Smith noted that the most helpful thing that Westerners did in the early days of the conference was to keep silent.

The cautions that he detailed in his report were shared by many missionary-sending churches, not just the Methodists. While most had given lip service to the need to be in partnership with the younger churches, few

Eugene Smith and wife Idalene Gulledge and daughters LuAnn (left) and
Rosemary. As a Board of Missions staff member, Eugene Smith traveled
widely throughout Asia in the 1950s and was one of the first to recognize that
for Christianity to move forward in Asia, leadership must come from Asians
themselves. *(Photo courtesy of United Methodist Archives and History)*

concrete changes had been made. As the Asian churches banded together,
their unity across denominational lines made many of the sending nations
uncomfortable. Smith made clear the importance of their action. One
suggestion at the conference was that no Western boards should consider
requests from their churches unless the request had been passed by the
council of churches in that country. Working together across these kinds
of denominational lines was much more comfortable for Asians.

For Smith the experience went even deeper than the words that were
said in the meetings. He described traveling to a small village for a service
of worship. He had traveled much in many parts of the world. He was
quite accustomed to being the center of attention. But in this village, the
eyes of the children were not on the Westerners among them but on

the Asians from other countries. He noticed, too, that the opinions of the Westerners did not carry as much weight as he had expected them to. More than ever, he realized that for Christianity to move forward in Asia, the leadership must come from the Asians themselves.

Already this kind of indigenous development was taking place. The principal of the Methodist Girls' School in Klang, Malaya, in the early 1950s was Sarah Arumugam, an ethnic Indian. She herself had been educated at a Methodist boarding school in Penang. Having been orphaned at the age of five, she became intensely Christian. On graduation from high school, she help start the Methodist Girls' School. Through the Epworth League, the Methodist youth organization before 1939, she met and married a Ceylonese man, G. S. Arumugam, whose father was a Methodist pastor. After their marriage, Sarah continued to work as a teacher, and her husband became principal of an Anglo-Chinese school. During the Second World War, the family was reduced to poverty, and the Japanese threatened to take their home. But with the end of the war, the girls' school was revived and by 1953 had nine hundred students. Sarah's comment was, "I owe everything to Christianity. The Methodist mission gave me an education, and in the work of the church I met my husband. God has certainly blessed me!"[23]

Another example of work in a secular arena was Wembley Alexandra Saw Beng Goh of Singapore. Her father was a prominent Methodist layman who was the mayor of Penang in the 1950s. Mrs. Goh went to St. George's School in Penang and then received a social science degree from the London School of Economics. She also became a lawyer in London, then returned to Singapore and was a lawyer in a private firm. She became magistrate of the juvenile court and assistant director of the Legal Aid Bureau in Singapore in 1958. She often had to deal with children of broken marriages, including runaway adolescents. Other young people were arrested for theft, trespassing, and gang activity. Goh would place them under probation or in approved schools. Her experience made her consider the importance of religion in family life: "So many of the problems are the result of the recognition of polygamous unions," she said. "When such 'marriages' break up for one reason or another, the children are left on their own. The parents cannot be bothered. . . . Every child should grow up with some moral teaching. This moral teaching is found in religion, not only in the Christian religion but in the others, too."[24]

Rebuilding in Korea

Among the Methodist Koreans who led both the church and the country during and after the Korean War was Helen Kim. She had become president of Ewha College in 1939 and led it through the Second World War. During the Korean War, the college was forced to relocate near Pusan under refugee conditions. But afterward the college returned and resumed its place as a major institution of higher education for women in South Korea.[25]

The return of the missionaries who had been prisoners of war also marked the end of the worst fighting of the conflict, and the two sides began to settle into the lines drawn around the 38th parallel. The board sent another travel delegation to begin to make recommendations for continuation of the work. The delegation first attended a June 1954 conference at Taichun Beach. Adelaide E. Wegner represented the Woman's Division, joining Korea secretaries Margaret Billingsley and T. T. Brumbaugh; Bishop Frederick Buckley Newell, representing the Methodist Committee on Overseas Relief (MCOR); Charles Adams, lay member of the board; and Eugene Smith, board staff member.

In his report, Smith wrote glowingly of the conference. He noted the Korean leadership and the high level of participation, schedule of worship and work, and fellowship. More important was the method of discernment in decision making. The MCOR, the Woman's Division, and the Division of World Missions were not considered to be the starting points, and thus separate entities, but as resources for a Korean church. Actions included further church construction, continued relief activities, and specific recommendations on questions regarding educational institutions.[26]

Other parts of the report were not so positive. Smith noted the challenges of divisions among the Korean people. For example, regionalism went very deep. Parents had been known to forbid the wedding of their child to someone from another part of the country. Leaders from churches in the north were generally better educated and organized than those in the south. Leaders from the north were now refugees but were more aggressive and progressive than those in the south and wanted to assume leadership. These divisions were visible not just within Methodism but among the Presbyterians as well. Competition between the two Protestant denominations also affected the work.[27]

Smith's report continued with careful words. He attributed the difficulties to a long tradition of leadership tyranny from both within and without. Further, the floods of refugees and the unstable political situation continued to make education—a priority for the mission work—difficult. The leadership shortage noted after the Second World War continued to be a problem as well. All these concerns were carefully worded in his report, in which he attempted to stay positive and affirming, yet still based in the realities of the difficulties.

Brumbaugh had also spelled out the conditions for the missionaries. On the one hand, they were trying to work with a church that had been independent for many years. But on the other, the church in Korea was tragically deprived of leadership. At one point, twenty of its leaders were ordered to meet for a conference with Communists and were never heard from again. Among these were Bishop Yu Soon Kim and twelve other Methodist pastors. Church members heard how the bishop's family had watched him being taken away. Mrs. Kim hid the children, keeping them safe as the invaders stole food from their home. In the days that followed, she was forced to sell their possessions and move many times. Her story was only one of many. Missionaries agonized with retired workers who found that their savings were worthless. The board established categories of support for Korea: funds for relief and rehabilitation, continued support of missionaries, reimbursement for lost personal effects, funds for work while in Japan, funds for provision of residences, funds for board appropriations, and Advance Specials.

One of the workers to enter Korea to help with these efforts was Edward Poitras. Poitras had signed on as a K-3 (Korean-3, meaning a commitment to serve in Korea for three years), believing that he would be going to a country at war, willing to help with the wartime work. Instead, he became part of the recovery. Despite the realistic and helpful training he received, he found his assigned responsibilities to be a dramatic initiation into the life of a missionary. Much had been destroyed; children wandered the streets. He began by spending his time unpacking relief items that had been shipped, sorting bales of clothing and other items. Soon, however, he was assigned to teach English at the seminary, the first foreigner to teach there in quite some time.

As a short-term, single missionary, Poitras was assigned a room with one of the missionary families. The families all lived in the compound in Seoul, which also had the school and church. A guard watched the entrance. Each day Poitras would walk across to teach his classes, carrying

Helen Kim

Born in Inchon, Korea, in 1899, Helen Kim went to a mission school for girls and was graduated from Ewha College, the school for girls and women founded by the Methodist Episcopal Church. She was unusual in that she was a woman who received an education in a culture in which many females remained illiterate. She received a degree with Phi Beta Kappa honors from Ohio Wesleyan University in 1924 and a master's degree from Boston University. Returning to Ewha, she became its dean in 1926.

Always articulate with original ideas, Kim suggested that Methodist women in mission countries should form themselves into an organization that would relate to the U.S. church. This idea later became a reality through the World Federation of Methodist Women. She went to the International Missionary Council meeting in Jerusalem in 1928 and argued for a role for young Christians, an idea that was also taken seriously and implemented later by ecumenical bodies. She achieved another milestone in 1932 when she became the first Korean woman to receive a Ph.D. from Columbia University.

She became president of Ewha just before the Second World War, and despite the difficulties of Japanese occupation, led Ewha from a college to university status. The school was again placed under duress during the Korean War, when it had to evacuate its Seoul campus and relocate under refugee conditions in Pusan. Nevertheless, the school returned to Seoul after the war and continued to grow. It had a student body of 8,000 in the 1950s.

Kim served her government as public information officer, as ambassador to the United Nations, and as ambassador at large. She was also a leader in the Korean YWCA, the Korean Red Cross, and the National Christian Teachers' Association. She continued to participate in ecumenical bodies, including the International Missionary Council and the World Council of Churches. Although she retired as Ewha president in 1961, she immediately became chair of a commission on evangelism for the Korea Methodist Church. She went to Chung-ju, where a U.S. company had built a large chemical and fertilizer plant, and established an outreach to the workers there. "I feel most content after visiting non-Christian homes for my mission," she said. She died in Seoul on February 10, 1970.

Sources: Charles A. Sauer, "Kim, Helen," *Encyclopedia of World Methodism*, 1: 1335; Dorothy McConnell, "Helen Kim," *World Outlook* 44 (June 1954): 39–40; William Clark, "Korea's Helen Kim," *World Outlook* 50 (August 1960): 29–30.

Helen Kim.
*(Photo courtesy of
United Methodist
Archives and History)*

the lunch packed by his hostess. He found it confining and announced to the missionaries that he wished to have a room with a Korean family. The other missionaries turned down his request. Not discouraged, he wrote to Area Secretary Brumbaugh. When Brumbaugh visited a month later, he gave Poitras permission to find other housing on the condition that he would meet with a missionary family for one meal each day. The fear that missionaries would "go native" ran very deep.

Poitras found other sources of conflict with the older missionaries. Rather than take advantage of the cars at the missionaries' disposal, he would ride the public buses. Missionary colleagues warned him this was dangerous; he might contract tuberculosis. But he found other ways to get to know the culture as well. Every weekend he would take students from the seminary out into the countryside for evangelistic work. Not only were these efforts successful, but they gave Poitras a chance to get to know the culture, the people, and the language.[28]

Gender Relationships: Korean Example

The compound in Seoul was fairly typical of the Methodist establish-
ments in a number of places in the world. World and Woman's divisions
had institutions and housing for their personnel in a fairly small area.
While it created convenience, community, and in some cases safety, it also
set the missionaries apart from the members of the churches with whom
they worked. In addition, inside the walls there were differences between
the two divisions — differences in style, in expectation, and in support.

The Woman's Division maintained an impressive but restricted list of
projects. It funded programs for women and children, with a major focus
on education and development. Over the years it had built an impressive
array of institutions, which it continued to support through buildings and
personnel. Evangelism and other more open-ended programs were rarely
included on its list of projects. Although the women of the division had
many ideas about ways to expand their ministries, they pushed ahead only
when the money was in hand for the proposed project. It was a style that
worked well. The women of the church gained the reputation for solid
work — smooth administration and successful funding.

By contrast, the World Division had a broader agenda. It worked with
indigenous churches, sometimes supplying personnel or supplementing
evangelistic efforts. Willingness to try new approaches or ideas meant that
the World Division sometimes moved ahead with a particular idea or
project without all the funding in place. The difference in style led to a
difference in perception and expectation: "The women have the money."[29]

Gender played a role in differences of expectation. The historic origins
as separate institutions remained in the structure. Persons sent by the
Woman's Division who married had to reapply in the World Division if
they wanted to continue serving outside the United States. Wives of missionaries had many kinds of assignments, but this was usually by their
choice or by decisions made at the site. Since in the eyes of many in the
Woman's Division they were not there by the same sort of calling as were
the single women, married women were not always viewed as missionaries.
In truth, some of the wives shared this opinion; but others resented what
they considered a lack of respect. When committees were formed or assignments made, they felt unrepresented. Rarely was this difference
openly addressed. Public reports, even within the board, give little hint of

such attitudes. Differences were "in the family," a term that did not include even the wider church.

One area of difference that occasionally made its way into discussion was that of compensation. Salaries were low, but some resented the single women's freedom from supporting dependents with their compensation, as married couples did. On the other hand, the board paid housing costs and education, including college expenses, making a significant difference for some of the families. Housing was separate as well, though both divisions often had buildings in the compound. The Woman's Division, in an effort to care for the holistic well-being of the women, insisted that all residences have pianos — and provided the funds for them. Pianos were not mandated in the World Division.

But both divisions were facing challenges from their new personnel during these years. The training the young missionaries received focused on living and working with the people, on letting go of power so that a new generation of indigenous leaders would be in control of the churches. This approach often clashed with the attitudes of missionaries who had been working for many years. They found it hard to let go of their decision-making power, sure that chaos would ensue without the tight controls they had held. Younger missionaries sometimes found it hard to hang on to the ideals they had brought with them. The comfort of the compound was appealing in cultures where the food, smells, colors, temperatures, and sounds were so different from their own. There was enough tension in the assignment without adding it to the community from which they needed support and encouragement. The newcomers found it easy to give in to the authority and "greater experience" of the older missionaries. Goals set out by Diffendorfer and Smith in reports in New York proved difficult to implement.

The style of living had historic roots. But the reasons why that change was difficult went very deep. Most missionaries had been raised not just with a Western civilization perspective but with the value judgment that this perspective was superior to all others.[30] On the one hand, many missionaries came to a deep appreciation of other cultures and values. But while a smaller number of the missionaries valued other cultures as equals to the West, most remained true to a lifetime of teaching in which their own ways were presented as not just different, but superior. This sense of superiority was communicated by the predominant use of Western symbols, music, and style of worship and education. Further, missionaries reinforced it in small ways every day by the choices they made in food, clothing, child rearing, and other day-to-day activities.

The issues for missionary wives in Korea were mirrored in most of the placements throughout the world. The board required the wives to have a college degree, although one in six did not. This was not a uniform statistic; half of the missionary wives in Africa lacked a college degree, but only one in eight in Latin America and Asia did not fulfill the requirement. Wives were part of the missionary assignment, but the board did not always make clear what was expected. The women were often torn between their roles as wife and mother and the many possibilities for service as missionaries.

Demands on missionary wives paralleled those for clergy wives in the United States. In many places the home was also the center of activity and needed to be open to a variety of people. Privacy was considered a luxury. Salaries were also low, but most found that they not only had basic needs, but often were better off than many families around them, including missionaries from Europe. By 1960 most U.S. missionaries had refrigerators and three-quarters had washing machines.

These items sometimes created dilemmas for missionaries who were trying to lessen the distance between themselves and the nationals with whom they worked. They were concerned, for example, that their homes were larger and better, often because the missionary residences had been built as part of a compound. This was most true in Africa, where for every missionary who lived on a standard comparable to nationals, four had something better; less true in Asia, where the ratio was three to one; and least true in Latin America, where only half the missionaries had better homes than their national counterparts. Home size remained a concern because many saw the greater size as symbolic of imperialism, power, and detachment. When it came to labor-saving appliances, and even when it came to employment of servants, most made choices that allowed them greater time and opportunity for missionary work.[31]

Japan: Social Analysis and Theology

Despite modest growth in membership, the Kyodan expanded during this period by adding more than two hundred new buildings and opening several rural and youth evangelism centers. There were more than three hundred Kyodan churches in the early 1950s. Members also spent four years working on a Confession of Faith that would be satisfactory to all. Methodists were very involved in the Student Christian Fellowship (SCF); nearly all of its funds came from the Methodist Board of Missions, and the SCF directors during the 1950s were all Methodists. Some of the student work involved social service. In the Ueno section of Tokyo, many children were left homeless after the war. Students created a Social Service Center that fed the children and led them in a form of Christian education.[32]

Elizabeth Clarke, missionary to Japan, analyzed many of the challenges in 1953. Among the problems she noted were the re-emergence of Buddhism and Shintoism, the growing evangelical movements that did not cooperate with the Kyodan, and the need for a social reawakening within the church so that members, often comfortable secluding themselves from the society in which they were a small minority, would be more public in their activities. At the same time, she celebrated certain accomplishments: that over half of the church buildings had already been replaced and nearly all the schools and educational centers were already rebuilt. Of more concern was re-establishing the scattered congregations, developing the leadership, and replacing the educational materials.

Especially helpful under these circumstances were the J-3s, who lived and worked with the Japanese youth. Recruited to serve for three years, they brought enthusiasm and energy into the missionary force.

Clarke's work was not the only evaluating done by the board. Eugene Smith visited Japan in 1954 and wrote an analysis of his findings, though not for publication. While the board and its missionaries made good use of the publications available to them for both education of the church members and promotion of the missionary works, they also wrote many much more explicit papers that detailed the difficulties of the mission settings. Smith's paper spelled out the political options he considered to be as important for Japan as was the economic dilemma it faced in recovery. Because rearmament was still not an option, he dealt quite forthrightly with the attitudes about the presence of U.S. military forces as well as nuclear testing and its perceived threat to both the environment and the military balance in the world. Some, particularly the young, had lost their early enthusiasm for the occupation forces. "The continued presence of foreign troops in Japan and the blatantly immoral conditions around the military bases also contributed to disillusionment with the 'Christian' U.S.A."[33]

Although the political analysis in the paper was shared by some in the church, the theological analysis was even harder to communicate. For example, correctly noting the heavy influence of European thought on much of the theology in areas of mission work, he also stated, "It is distinctly Japanese. The prevailing theological climate of Japan is one in which most Americans would be acutely uncomfortable."[34]

In addition, Smith noted the tradition of academic scholarship that meant many of the clergy were more preachers than pastors and more lecturers than preachers. While one might argue that this could lead to a more informed congregation, he was concerned about the lack of life in the Word being preached. These comments directly followed concerns about the flood of evangelical missionaries from various denominational groups in the U.S. that came to Japan as soon as possible after the war. Because they did not join the Kyodan, their presence created a feeling of disunity in the Christian work. Smith noted the ways that the role of authority in Japanese life was transferred to the pastor, who was expected to preside at all meetings and whose word was law, rather than one who delegated authority.

The report went on to name some of the real barriers the missionaries were facing. Publications to highlight the work for the church did not hint at the barriers that Smith named. In addition to noting the European emphasis in seminary training for the pastors, he named frustrations that are "more intense in Japan than in any other field." Missionaries experienced great difficulty with the Japanese language, few ever learning to read a Japanese newspaper or act as an interpreter. In the rural areas, missionaries found it especially difficult to gain a level of acceptance that allowed them to go about the evangelistic work they desired. At the same time, Smith noted that because the missionaries did not have authority in Japan in the way they did in other places, they were also more appreciated. Nevertheless, a gap appeared between the Japanese and Western missionaries: "There are some Japanese ministers who will not cooperate with missionaries and who think that it is impossible or at least very difficult for missionaries to lead young people to Christian faith, because of the handicap in the language and the lack of understanding of traditional Japanese culture."[35]

Methodists supported a number of significant schools in Japan. But the shortage of Christian teachers and the demand for funds in many places meant that decisions were constantly being made about distribution. Fol-

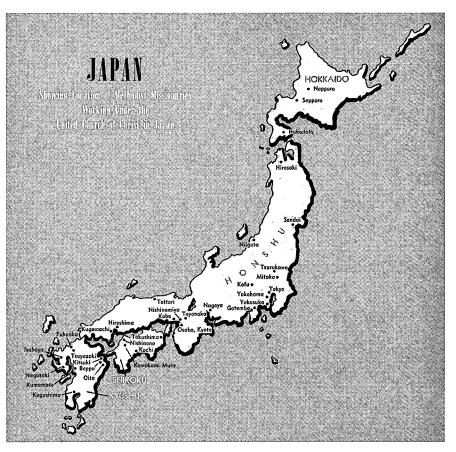

Methodist missions in Japan covered the country, as this 1965 map shows.
The mission emphasized higher education and student work, which meant
many of the clergy were more preachers than pastors and more lecturers
than preachers. *(Map courtesy of United Methodist Archives and History)*

lowing his visit, Smith wrote the president of Kwansei Gakuin, a school
of nearly 8,000 students in Nishinomiya. In his letter, he addressed the
composition of the faculty with its decreasing percentage of Christians.
Since the faculty participated in choosing deans and leaders, he was concerned that the number of Christians would continue to decrease, thus
decreasing the Christian character of the school. Smith warned the president that "my own support for the financial askings for Kwansei Gakuin
will be influenced by these expectations of its future."[36] More evangelical
institutions would receive first consideration. While Methodist support

for education continued strong, in the face of stretched resources, Christian emphasis played a big role.

The nature of mission work continued to challenge the Methodists. Woman's Division notes on training from this period emphasize that the differences between the Japanese and Americans did not mean that one group was not as good as the other, counseling against saying, "We do it this way in America."

Emphasizing this fact even more clearly was Charles Germany's presentation to the 1958 Division of World Missions staff retreat. His presentation came from years of experience in Japan, starting when he was one of the first new missionaries to go to Japan after the war. He reminded the staff that in the years following the war, the Japanese church had been dominated by a theology that tended to deny culture, defining Christian responsibility as purity of faith and witness within the church. This approach helped Christians to develop a clear identity, but it did not allow the full flowering of the faith. In his years of teaching at Tokyo Union Seminary, Germany encouraged Japanese theologians to participate in the worldwide task of developing theology as well as expanding their own understanding by including social concern.[37]

When they first went to Japan, Charles and Julie Germany asked the same questions that many postwar missionaries had asked: How did one make a Christian witness and not violate the culture of others? With less than 1 percent of the population being Christian, what were the best ways to have influence? They saw the work of God demonstrated in many ways and through many people and wanted to have persons of faith talk not with dogma against dogma but with doxology against doxology. For several years they lived in a village where their children could attend the local school and they could live in a Japanese home. Charles developed the ability to preach in Japanese and worked with the local ministers, providing supportive fellowship. Both of the Germanys appreciated the Kyodan and the united approach to ministry. Assignments were made under the authority of the Council of Churches, who sent requests to the Interboard Committee for Christian Work in Japan (composed of boards from the sending denominations). Under its direction they moved to Tokyo, where they could continue their educational work as well as their work with churches. Later, when Charles was asked to join the Methodist staff overseeing the Asian work, the couple consulted with the Japanese church leaders, wanting to make the best decision for the life of the church.

Changing Roles of Missionaries in India

In the years that followed Indian independence, U.S. missionaries to India experienced change in their roles. In 1955, Harold N. Brewster, M.D., who was a member of the staff and its medical secretary, visited the country as part of his evaluations for the board. He noted both the relative stability of the democratic system the Indians had chosen for themselves and the increasing hostility toward missionaries, who were seen as leftovers from the colonial period. Getting rid of foreigners in the government should be matched, went the popular refrain, by getting rid of them in the church. Naming this as one of the problems did not signify that many of the Christians themselves wanted the missionaries to go, but it did indicate the climate that existed. Brewster raised questions that he thought needed to be answered by all concerned. He wondered whether the church should do a new study of the situation, if perhaps it might be time to leave.

Within the Indian church, leaders discussed these questions. Some had experienced problems from other Indians who thought that all Christianity should be tossed aside. Those in charge of some of the educational and medical institutions of the church had to sort out the meanings of the new laws that had been passed by the now independent government. If Methodists had at one time played a significant role in education, especially of women, they now had to rethink their role as the state took responsibility for the schools. Indian Christians told the board that they would continue to welcome missionaries, but that they expected personnel who were well grounded in Christian experience and who did not expect to be put into roles of leadership.[38] Through this midcentury period, the number of missionaries gradually began to decrease, somewhat more slowly because several of the missionaries of China relocated to India. At the same time, the Indian church did accept more responsibility for training its leaders and running its institutions.

Discussion of these changes also appeared in U.S. mission publications. In the July 1959 issue of *Methodist Woman*, Lucile Colony raised the question, "Are missionaries needed in India?" Stories of India had long been prominent in the women's publications. But these stories were balanced by reports in newspapers about the Indian government and its independence from Western influence. Visas were sometimes hard to obtain for U.S. missionaries. Colony answered her question by assuring readers that missionaries were still needed and would always be welcome but that they also

José Labarrette Valencia. *(Photo courtesy of United Methodist Archives and History)*

had to prove they would not replace Indian workers. The evolution in many agencies meant that indigenous leaders now filled many positions, but the process remained sometimes slow and even painful.

Leadership in the Philippines

Bishop José Valencia had initiated a dialogue with the United Church of Christ in the Philippines in 1948 regarding comity. Early in the century, various denominations agreed to carry out mission in designated areas. When the united church was formed in 1948, Methodists declined to join. The united church seemed to abrogate the comity agreements, however. Methodists remained a member of the Federation of Christian Churches and carried out their comity agreement through it. Over a long, disputatious period, the two bodies finally agreed that each would have the right to establish congregations anywhere in the country but with the understanding that the heads of churches, "before opening up

José Labarrette Valencia

Born in Tagudin, Ilocos Sur Province, in 1898, Valencia grew up as a Roman Catholic, although he became acquainted with Protestants through the United Brethren mission near his home. He came from a family involved in the Filipino struggle for independence. His uncle was a guerrilla in the conflict with the U.S. after the Spanish-American War and was executed by the Americans. Nevertheless, Valencia determined to learn English and even joined the U.S. Navy. This military service brought him to the U.S., where he completed his high school education and entered Cornell College in Iowa, a Methodist school. Here as throughout his life, Valencia worked his way through school. While at Cornell, he became a Methodist through the influence of Enjie Tsukasaki, a former Shintoist from Japan. After a stint at Garrett Biblical Institute, he decided to enter the ministry. He entered Drew Theological Seminary and received a B.D. in 1929.

He returned to the Philippines and entered the pastoral ministry in the northwest part of the country, near his birthplace. He married and as a pastor received very low pay in his early churches. His biography relates journeys like those of a veritable Saint Paul: He walked, rode horses and carabao (a type of domesticated water buffalo), traversed flooding rivers on rickety ferries, and endured typhoons as he went from village to village. Although his theology was conservative, he believed the church should alleviate the plight of the poor. He became a district superintendent in 1938 and, during the Japanese occupation of the Philippines during the Second World War, reported many encounters with the Japanese, who were often searching for guerrillas.

After being elected bishop in 1948, he attended the meeting of the Council of Bishops held in 1950 and was dismayed to learn that the central conference bishops were not allowed to vote. On learning the reason for his unhappiness, Bishop Francis McConnell asked the council to reconsider this practice. The council immediately approved the right of all active bishops to vote, a change formally approved at the 1956 General Conference. Filipino bishops were elected for four-year terms, and Valencia was re-elected for four additional terms and served until 1968. During his tenure, a new arrangement was made with the United Church of Christ in the Philippines regarding comity. A number of educational, health, and social service institutions were established, and the Filipino church grew greatly under his administration. He died in 1994.

Sources: José L. Valencia, *Under God's Umbrella: An Autobiography* (Quezon City, Philippines: New Day Publishers, 1978), pp. 1–118 passim; Nolan B. Harmon, "Valencia, José Labarrette, Sr.," *Encyclopedia of World Methodism*, 2: 2408; Valencia, "Jesus Christ and Ourselves," *Daily Christian Advocate*, 1960 General Conference, pp. 107, 648; email from José L. Valencia, Jr., to editor, Jan. 15, 2004.

work in any locality where there is an established church of a Federation member-church, will confer with the pastor or official representative of the local church in the area as to the advisability of opening up work and organizing a church in the given area."

During the 1950s, Methodists established youth and student centers in several cities that were for social purposes but also educational in deepening an understanding of Christian faith. Mobile clinics were also established in rural areas, which were evangelistic as well as medical in nature. Many secondary schools and colleges were founded from 1948 to 1968 that also had an evangelistic as well as an educational purpose. Rural centers were established in the north in San Mateo, Isabela Province, and in the south in Kidapawan, Mindanao. Laity were trained in the centers, and education was given in agriculture, health, and literacy.

Women were assuming positions of leadership in the Philippines in the 1950s. Doctora S. Florendo, president of the WSCS at Central Church, Manila, became special commissioner for anti-TB work of the Philippines government and also head of the YWCA in the Philippines. Asuncion Peréz, also a member of Central Church, became Commissioner of Public Health and Welfare.[39]

Lands of Witness and Decision

The desire for growth in numbers, the desire to spread into relatively undeveloped territory, and the questions about indigenization led to a special program in 1957 that focused on several places that were identified as lands for witness and decision. Eugene Smith stated its goals: The special program was to maintain the momentum that had been built in the years that followed the war, especially once the rebuilding was well under way. Methodists planned to put more energy into evangelism, using as inspiration the work that J. Wascom Pickett, a Methodist Episcopal Church missionary and bishop in India, had managed to do among the untouchables in India.[40] In addition, the board pledged to recruit more missionaries for increased work in many places in the world, reversing a trend that had seen numbers barely hold steady after finally regaining the prewar numbers. Smith wanted the riches of the U.S. to be shared with the rest of the world.

The board chose four countries as the foci for the new program: Bolivia, Sarawak, the Belgian Congo, and Korea. Each represented particular challenges or emphases. The Board of Missions published a book, *Lands of Witness and Decision*, to help Methodists better understand the diverse history and needs of the lands on which they were to focus. A specialist in each region was asked to write material that would both inform and excite U.S. Methodists about the opportunities.

Although the first Methodist missionary had entered Bolivia from Chile in 1906, the church had stayed confined to a few areas high in the mountains. In addition, it was only 30 percent self-supporting — in contrast to the Filipino church, for example, which by that time was nearly 100 percent self-supporting. The Methodist effort was fueled by concern for scriptural literacy, using as supportive material the Roman Catholic tradition, which focused on hierarchical decision making, as well as by a desire to move into many more towns and cities throughout the country. Bishop Sante Uberto Barbieri, who presided over Argentina, Uruguay, and Bolivia, issued the call to greater mission in his essay, "That Strange Land Called Bolivia."

In Southeast Asia, Sarawak, according to Medical Secretary Harold Brewster, was in a similar position with Methodism in only a small percentage of the country. But the momentum had begun, and the board was optimistic about the gains that could be accomplished. It focused attention on a tribal group known as the Sea Dyaks, or Ibans. Missionaries had started their work in 1938, but in the first eleven years, no one had been baptized. Then, on Christmas Day, 1949, forty-nine people had come forward for baptism. In the eight years since that time, more than three thousand people had joined the Christian movement.

Choosing Sarawak added extra work for the mission interpreters, for few people in the U.S. even knew about this former British colony on the island of Borneo. In addition to interpretation, the proposed ministry included a larger challenge in the areas of education and literature. Fewer than 4 percent of the children were even in school. The results of the work of the previous few years had excited the board, and with this initiative, it looked to Sarawak for continuing results.

Brewster himself believed that the success of the endeavor was very much in the hands of the Methodist Church missionaries, lamenting the lack of a Wesley or an Asbury, men who had roused people to spread the word with fervor. He wrote, "But the Methodist Church of today is a complacent, self-satisfied church, resting comfortably in the assurance that it is the largest Protestant denomination in America." He wondered if the church would be able to catch the vision of the role it could play in places so far away.

Helping to interpret the needs in the Belgian Congo was Bishop Newell Snow Booth. His concerns were echoes of Brewster, for he asked that U.S. Methodists think of the people as living near to them in the neighborhood of the world. He tried to rouse interest and perhaps understanding and sympathy as he described the conditions of confusion in the Belgian Congo as more and more rural people came to urban centers looking for work. He pictured the setting — the once rural chapel and school now completely surrounded by apartments, the quiet of the rural scene now filled with the sounds of constant human activity. He reminded his readers that the money sent by the U.S. church was in addition to the funds that the Congolese raised for themselves. As a church, the Congolese still desired connection with missionaries — at least ones that could serve with the right attitude of mutual confidence and ministry.

Like the Belgian Congo, Korea represented an area of mission and ministry in which the board and the U.S. church had long been active. Choosing it as an area of decision was a way to build on the success of the Christian movement as well as to continue the levels of support needed. Three hundred churches had been destroyed during the war, and the church had succeeded in rebuilding two hundred of them. Brumbaugh drew on his years of experience to highlight the history and needs in this new effort. The number of schools run by missionaries had dropped, leaving fewer opportunities to combine evangelism with education. Korea's inclusion in the list was a signal of concern for continued success and hope that real advances were possible.

When the church published its booklet *Lands of Witness and Decision*, it included a final essay by Pickett, who had achieved such success with the untouchables in India. He addressed growing concerns throughout the church about the fears of Western imperialism in the work of the Methodists. He believed that making the missionary force interracial, as well as including indigeneous leaders at every opportunity, would help to overcome the fears that were growing in many parts of the world. Pickett himself found great joy in evangelism and called others to join in and share those joys.[41]

Changing Roles for Women

When the Woman's Foreign Missionary Society developed in the nineteenth century, it owed its existence to the lack of place for women to be active in the structure of the church's "foreign" work. Not only did women want to be part of this work of the church, but many men also recognized that women could reach other women. The Society was organized in the Methodist Episcopal Church in 1869 and sent its first two missionaries later that year. It served not just as a sending body that expanded the mission of the church in other lands but also as an educational body that provided significant information about Christianity and the world for its members and supporters in the United States. Such organizations for women had been an important part of the work of all the uniting bodies. By the same token, deaconesses and "home" missionaries had required separate organizations to give them visibility, support, and funding. These organizations provided opportunities for women that were otherwise unavailable in the church and in the society. Women responded. Success built success. Women with management skills and interests could follow the promptings of their faith and seek out service in the church that would also provide them with a livelihood. Opportunities to develop policy as well as to engage daily in work that fulfilled their belief in spreading the gospel and furthering the Kingdom of God were available through the missionary societies far more broadly than through conferences and other church organizations.

In 1952, the Commission on Deaconess Work gave new attention to the deaconess office. As they had done with missionaries in the World Division, board and staff examined the numbers of deaconesses working in the field, compared enrollments, and made decisions. In September 1955, the clause requiring compulsory retirement was removed. Less than a year later, ordained women in The Methodist Church were granted full clergy rights, but deaconesses could not have full membership. Numbers continued to decline, not because fewer efforts were made at recruitment, but because women left the office in order to marry or pursue other careers.

Effects of McCarthyism

Senator Joseph R. McCarthy of Wisconsin began making charges of Communism in the U.S. State Department in 1950. As chair of the Senate

Permanent Subcommittee on Investigations, he employed a former Methodist clergyman, J. B. Mathews, as a staff member. Mathews wrote an article for a magazine titled "Reds and Our Churches." In it, he stated that the largest group supporting Communism in the U. S. was composed of Protestant clergy. His was only one of many suggestions that Methodists and others, including other Protestants, Roman Catholics, and Jews, had been sympathetic to Communism and supported it.

In March 1953, the chair of the House Un-American Activities Committee said that his committee might investigate church groups and clergy. In response, Bishop G. Bromley Oxnam of Washington said that the Federal Bureau of Investigation was a better instrument for ferreting out any conspirators than was the House committee. Another member of the committee, Representative Donald L. Jackson of California, inserted a comment in the House record alleging that Oxnam had given "aid and comfort" to Communism. Oxnam replied to the accusations point by point and requested the right to appear before the committee and rebut the charges.

Oxnam appeared before the committee on July 21, 1953. Although the committee counsel made several accusations, Oxnam rebutted them all. At the end of the hearing, the members unanimously adopted a statement that the committee had received "no record of any Communist Party affiliation or membership by Bishop Oxnam." They did not, however, correct their file on accusations against Oxnam. In the wake of Oxnam's appearance, many felt he had vindicated himself and other Protestants who were accused of supporting Communism. McCarthy was finally censured by the U.S. Senate on December 2, 1954, ending his crusade. But throughout the 1950s fervent reactionary groups, some within the churches and some outside, continued to make innuendoes and charges about "Methodism's Pink Fringe."[42]

While McCarthy had raised fears of Communism in the U.S., he had also raised the sensitivity to its spread in many parts of the world. Missionaries saw international Communism in very individual ways that often started with their own theology and politics and then developed through life experiences. Eugene Smith responded to discussions that linked the missionaries with some of the freedom movements. He saw the struggle as not simply about territory but about the struggle for the souls of human beings. Smith laid out a powerful picture of the challenges facing the church, putting them in terms that made the type of response quite clear.

G. Bromley Oxnam testified before the House Un-American Affairs Committee about alleged ties to the Communist Party. Although Oxnam was cleared of any Communist involvement by the committee, any Methodist leader who worked for social justice or was involved in ecumenical affairs was suspect to an ultraconservative Protestantism of the 1950s. *(Photo courtesy of United Methodist Archives and History)*

In the February 1954 *World Outlook* was a picture of a large crowd of Asian people. The caption read, "These are some of the people of Asia. Which path will they choose? This crowd is in China where communism now has the initiative." In boldface, the text read, "The international march of Communism presents the greatest world threat to Christianity since the rise of Islam." The graphic illustrations were matched with an opening story originally told by Pearce Hayes, when he was still a district superintendent in China. Hayes had returned home one day and found twenty Communists camped in his living room. Because they were from the community, he had come to know them during his time in China. They discussed the political developments together; then he asked if they really believed they would conquer the world. They replied that in the end all they had to do was undermine the Christian foundation of the U.S., and everything would crumble.

Smith described the development of Christian missions through the century before returning to the topic of the disciplined Communists, which he claimed could probably be found in every nation in the world. To illustrate his concern, he told a story about a businessman who had visited a Methodist missionary in Sumatra after the war. He toured the facilities and expressed in a letter to the board his concerns about the inadequate equipment, lack of personnel, and crowded conditions and asked that more funding be sent. Five years later he returned to visit the mission again. He found the same conditions with the buildings even more dilapidated. In yet another letter to the board, he described a nearby school with a staff of twenty, "educated with the equivalent of a college degree in the United States, and each of the twenty was a hardened, trained Communist." Smith did not stop with this statement, instead questioning why the U.S. "let the Communists have open highway to the minds of the people in Asia."

Communists were not the only concern. He also raised the specter of Islam, which was converting more persons away from Christianity than Christianity could convert from Islam. He called on Christians to seize again the initiative in the war of ideas. "We have let much of that initiative slip out of the hands of Christians into the hands of the deadliest enemies whom Christ has ever confronted."

At the end of the article, Smith described places where mission work was expanding: Formosa (Taiwan), the Philippines, and Nepal. He then explained that World Service dollars had received a significant cut that had implications for the amount of staffing in some of the locations. In response to the concerns he knew his readers would feel, he called on them to give. The board never just asked for money. Its approach, a sincere one, was that the help of church people was needed not just for money but for prayer and other support as well. His suggestion at this time, however, was also couched in very political terms. Suggesting a revival of the Wesleyan class meetings, he described the ways that it would enhance Methodist church life in the United States. Then he drew the parallel to Communism and the relationship of Communists to their cells. He saw the power that was coming for such a sustaining small group and spelled out the ways it could enhance both individuals and churches.

Smith's article was significant because it was much more overtly political than most of the missionary literature officially published by the board. Individual missionaries sometimes made political comments or interpretations, but rarely in such a protracted manner. It is important also to see it in the context of what had happened within Methodism in the previous four years. As part of the wave of anti-Communist fervor started by McCarthy, the Methodist Federation for Social Action (MFSA) was continually attacked and accused of Communist sympathies. Articles and letters in both the church and the popular press printed false accusations about the head of the organization, Jack McMichael, and the entire MFSA. As a result, the General Conference acquiesced to the political pressures and voted in 1952 to express disapproval of the policies and statements of the MFSA, even asking it to change its name and endorsing a move to evict it from space in the Methodist Building.[43] The implications appeared clear. Not only did the church not stand behind one of its own as he faced the Committee on Un-American Activities, but also it did not seem willing to question the underlying philosophy that was developing.

Later in the decade, however, the focus began to shift. The experiences of the missionaries and their analyses of the struggles for freedom in many places in the world did not always fit the Communist/free world dichotomy of U.S. rhetoric. The introduction to the 1958 report, *The Tasks He Gives*, was written by W. Vernon Middleton and contrasted with the public statements of only a few years earlier. He wrote that Asians and Africans were often confused because the U.S. was not always on the side of freedom but colonialism and exploitation. "Were it not for the courageous efforts and living of our missionaries in those lands, the result would be obviously disastrous for the free world." Further, he reminded the U.S. church that increasing communication meant that more of the world saw not just the positive aspects of their lives, but also a society with increasing problems of alcohol abuse, crime, pornography, and racism.[44]

Increasingly, the reports of missionaries reflected the needs of a U.S. population that was changing. Movement to urban areas increased the challenges for those charged with town and country work. The 1958 report raised the question of how best to provide leadership for the growing number of charge conferences with fewer than five hundred members. Since at least one-third of charges had two hundred or fewer members, the church needed to study how best to provide for them. Photo essays continued to be used in these reports to emphasize the variety and complexity of the mission needs.

A Missionary Newsletter

Knowing how important missionary letters were, the Reverend Kenneth Jones of the board staff made a careful study of many letters, then wrote an evaluation for a June 1958 newsletter that was distributed to all missionaries. He reminded his readers that a letter "has to take the place of your good looks, your pleasant smile, your natural charm. It has to twist people's arms, tug at their hearts, open their purses, and remind them of God's plan of salvation." His article gave many practical suggestions about what to write and how to write it. He summed up the purpose of the letters with a list of reasons, the first of which was to let people at home share in the experiences, then witness the progress, and finally let them feel the challenge. While his list of "do's" makes fairly predictable reading, his list of "don'ts" reveals the variety of letters that were being churned out each year. The "don'ts" included saying too much about the family, elaborating on illnesses, writing travelogues, making emotional pitches for money, and writing more than two pages. These suggestions served to produce a more uniform and probably more widely read type of letter. At the same time, they indicate the professionalism that was expected of the missionaries on many different fronts.

The missionary newsletter reveals some of the details of concerns discussed between New York and missionaries in various places in the world. For example, the same issue of the newsletter carried information about visits from the bishops, noting that these were not planned by the board but set by General Conference.

Another entry in this issue reminds missionaries of the methods for ordering books, again mentioning several in which they might be interested. "It is dangerously easy for us to be busy rather than thoughtful" opens the article. The newsletter sometimes carried reviews or recommendations as a way of keeping missionaries in more remote places apprised of continuing educational opportunities. Just within this issue was a form for ordering volume three of the *History of Methodist Missions* at no charge as well as the news that copies of *The Organization Man* were being mailed to each missionary.

Rounding out the breadth of just this one issue of the field newsletter was discussion of papers being circulated on theology of missions and discussion on economic trends in the U.S., ones that not incidentally meant that giving, especially for Advance Specials, was down. The efforts by the

Betty Thompson, right center, and Arthur J. Moore, Jr., left, are shown in
the press room at the North American Faith and Order Conference, Oberlin,
Ohio, in 1958. Also shown are Elizabeth Gallin, left, and in right background,
Lou Cassells, religion editor, United Press (in white shirt) and George Dugan,
religion editor, the *New York Times*. Moore, the son of Bishop Arthur J. Moore,
became editor of the board mission magazine and Thompson the head executive of mission board communications in The United Methodist Church.
(Photo courtesy of United Methodist Archives and History)

New York staff helped missionaries in a variety of places and situations
throughout the world stay up-to-date on developments, theology, and
general skills, for their work was a model of what they hoped the missionaries would be doing for others.[45]

Preparation for Change

Reports and stories about the mission all over the world were full of activity, with much going on in many places. The Woman's Division filled its
yearly journals with pages of charts and numbers, accompanied by snip-
pets and stories designed to put names and activities onto the numbers.

Yet underneath all this activity was a host of changes that affected the nature and, eventually, the structure of the mission work itself. For those responsible for moving the work of mission forward, the problem was not really that they did not see the changes, but that they were not sure where these changes were taking them. Bishop Dodge, for example, could see how much was happening in Africa that would affect Methodists for years to come, but he could not always know which of the preparations for change he could make that would be the most effective. So much had been built and developed since the end of the war. The leadership in many areas of the world truly was evolving. Still more tumultuous events lay ahead.

CHAPTER 5

New Frontiers

*T*HE ELECTION OF John F. Kennedy as president was heralded as a new era for the United States. The young liberal Democratic Party politician and his glamorous wife symbolized the vigor, beauty, and vision of a U.S. fully recovered from wars and ready to enter the new frontiers of space as well as new frontiers in service to others. Ironically, despite all his seeming differences from his predecessor — the much older, more conservative retired general who had allied with the Republican Party — foreign policy remained the same. Policies that affected "foreign" missionaries and their roles abroad did not change.

The Cold War took new forms. Not only were concerns continually raised about the spread of Communism in Africa and Asia, but also even outer space became a contested arena when the U.S. promised to put a man on the moon. Kennedy campaigned, however, as the man who would conquer new frontiers, calling the country to new arenas of service through the Peace Corps and to new arenas of racial justice in the U.S. The kind of world he heralded was one the missionaries and their supporters — board, staff, and church members — already knew about. But neither government nor church knew how to make smooth transitions to more autonomy for the many colonized places in the world.

The new frontiers, of course, were not limited to scientific accomplishment or the spread of democracy (which really meant capitalism) around the world. Not all persons in the U.S. had shared equally in the economic gains of the postwar period. Conditions in the cities cried out for more attention. In many parts of the country, housing remained substandard and segregated. Schoolrooms in the metropolitan areas bulged, not just from the postwar "baby boom," but also from children whose parents had moved to the city from rural areas or from other countries looking for

In 1962, astronaut John Glenn, right, showed President John F. Kennedy the "Friendship 7" space capsule at Cape Canaveral, Florida. The Methodist Church had provided leadership for the changes symbolized by space flights as part of Kennedy's New Frontier. For these leaders, the new frontiers publicized on the political front had parallels in new mission challenges both in the U.S. and abroad. *(AP/ Wide World Photo used with permission)*

better jobs and a share in the overall prosperity of the nation. The steps toward greater racial equality, slowly taken in the 1950s, publicized the need for more equal access to education and social services. If some viewed them as great achievements or even too much change, others believed they were only the first of the massive changes needed to provide more equal opportunity. The church had provided leadership for the changes; those in leadership positions knew that the task was really only beginning. For them, the new frontiers publicized on the political front were ones they had been able to see all along. Further, these new frontiers had great potential for state and church to work together.

Even as the board, the staff, and the personnel were in the process of working toward greater justice and were spreading scriptural holiness across all the lands, they did not envision all that could happen along the way. Opening new frontiers affected life within the institution as well as the fabric of U.S. society and relationships throughout the world.

Founding of Alaska Methodist University

In October 1960, a year after Alaska became a state, Alaska Methodist University (AMU) opened. This four-year liberal arts school had been conceived in the late 1940s as it became clear that Alaska would eventually become a state. Gordon Gould, who was born in Alaska and had become an ordained Methodist minister, proposed a school while he was a staff member of the Home Missions Division. In 1948, he conducted a needs survey for the division and recommended two major goals. The first was to revive local churches under capable leadership. The second was: "Establish a privately supported church oriented liberal arts college or university to educate and prepare Alaska's youth in Alaska for the future leadership responsibility in Alaska."[1] Although Gould included indigenous peoples in his concept, he apparently did not restrict it to Native Americans; after all, there were many persons in Alaska, like himself, who were "native" but Anglo-European. He did envision a school that "would develop persons who would possess not just the technical skills to harvest the land and the seas, but it would produce those who would develop the vision to plan creatively for a future Alaska society rooted in Christian values."[2]

From there the idea grew, until by the mid-1950s, Methodists in Alaska, chiefly in the Anchorage area, had raised $700,000 for the school. The 1956 General Conference approved a $2 million Advance Special for the school. By the time the school opened, the entire amount had been raised. Although planners had received advice from prestigious Methodist schools, no Native Americans were on the first board of trustees.[3] Nevertheless, land was purchased in Anchorage, buildings were constructed, and the school opened with 141 full-time students.

During the 1960s, Native Americans at the school increased from two in 1963 to twelve by 1968. (They increased to forty-seven in 1971.) Although these numbers were small, they represented as much as 5 percent of the Native Americans who were graduated from high school in Alaska. The retention rate for Native Americans was higher at AMU than at the University of Alaska, and AMU tried hard to make the college conducive to Native American learning.

The number of students enrolled at AMU grew during the 1960s to more than four hundred, but enrollment leveled off after that. A goal was to enroll eight hundred students. Increasing financial difficulties beset the school by the late 1960s. General Conference indicated it would reduce its

The opening of Alaska Methodist University in 1960 expressed a sense of being on the "cutting edge" for Methodists, since Alaska was a new state and the creation of a higher education institution hearkened back to the era of Methodism's greatest accomplishments in global mission. *(Photo courtesy of United Methodist Archives and History)*

support to the school, and it became difficult to find support from other sources. AMU represented, however, a willingness on the part of the whole Methodist Church to have a presence on the frontiers of the nation and to educate Native Americans.[4]

Communication Gaps

As the 1960s began, mission work in Africa was portrayed in increasingly diverse ways. Methods of evangelization vied for space with evaluations of the latest political crisis. Two sets of stories illustrate this contrast.

The Division of World Missions and the Joint Section on Education and Cultivation (formerly Joint Division) met in February 1959 to look at possibilities for an increased audiovisual program in Africa as a way of in-

creasing evangelization efforts. William F. Fore, the director of visual
education, was sent to help clarify basic needs, develop strategy, and even
assist the conferences in developing ministry in this arena. Despite the
difficult travel during his three months (October through December
1959), he visited 80 percent of the missions and interviewed 80 percent of
the staff at those missions. His report to the division and section was both
detailed and forthright, alerting the staff to serious communication needs.

Fore reported a lack of communication among the missionaries, among
the mission stations, and among the mission conferences. Missionaries often struggled to develop programs to meet particular needs, unaware that
others were asking the same questions and finding similar solutions. Hall
Duncan had developed a series of discussion pictures for special use in
African Christian education. These pictures were designed to incorporate images to bridge the historical and cultural gap between African and
European/U.S. understanding. Yet 90 percent of the missionaries had
never even seen the pictures, let alone planned to use them. With this example in mind, Fore concluded that many missionaries were unable to
give priorities or objectives for their work and did not see themselves as
part of an overall plan.[5]

Despite these concerns, Fore saw tremendous opportunities for the use
of mass media. He believed that Christian education curriculum could
easily be developed for use throughout Africa, with modifications for
differing cultures as necessary. Because the U.S. Methodists were the
wealthiest of the mission churches, further development of African curriculum might be shared by several churches, depending on the support
and leadership from the United States. His report underlined several
themes in African mission: communication, isolation, and yet overwhelming potential.

In a parallel concern, missionaries Robert and Thelma Kauffman issued a report on church music in January 1960. They urged missionaries
to search and collect authentic African music and make it available to
others. They also reminded them to be on the alert for composers or persons who could be trained to perform. At the same time, they noted the
problems that existed as those in Africa tried to develop a tradition of
Christian music. Some African converts placed a higher cultural value on
traditional European music and wanted to use it because it made them
feel more equal to the European/U.S. church. Incorporating African traditions meant using rhythms that some indigenous and missionary leaders

considered a concern because they were hypnotic or identified with particular tribes. Even with these concerns, the Kauffmans believed that new
liturgies needed to be developed. These liturgies would be a real contrast
to the European approaches to worship and would also challenge traditional notions. By laying out these visions and concerns, the report gave
critical information to those of the board and missionaries who were interested in developing a truly African church.

Both these reports were helpful to the board, which served as the center of policymaking and communication. But the implementation of the
recommendations remained dependent to a large extent on the individuals in various places who made the time to read, study, and obtain the
resources that were made available. As Fore noted, a large gulf existed between the development of materials and their widespread use. Further,
the recommendations for music carried assumptions about culture and
equality—assumptions not shared by all personnel. For many missionaries, European or Western forms remained the ideal expressions for art.
Discussion of these cultural assumptions was not even attempted in the
reports. Without broader forums for exploring these new frontiers, worship and education developed locally and erratically.

But as the church looked at the small ways it was becoming and could
become even more African in nature, the African people themselves were
in the process of reclaiming their continent after more than a century of
colonization. Unlike events of the previous decades in Asia, where missionaries were able to work without getting very involved, as in India, or
where they had to leave because of military conflicts and then return, as
in Japan and Korea, the missionaries in many African countries found
themselves in the middle of the freedom struggles. Their personal stories
and responses demonstrate the ways the board—and ultimately The
Methodist Church—was challenged to develop policy for new situations.
Events in Africa and in the U.S. became a dialogical challenge that
reached all levels of the church.

Greater Expectations of Missionaries

The Joint Committee on Missionary Personnel made a report at the beginning of the 1961–1964 quadrennium. The sobering description of the
work to be done, expanding and changing in many places in the world, was
matched with the equally sobering numerical reality that the board needed
to continue major recruitment for the years ahead, just to keep up with

the number of scheduled retirements. The committee used the report to describe the kind of person being recruited and to consider general qualities needed in a "foreign" or "home" missionary or deaconess. Summarizing that material reveals the commitment to the goals of indigenization and the sensitivity of the church to the ways that missionary roles had developed whether in the U.S. or in other countries. At the same time, the detail of the demands—none of them easy—contrasts even more with continuing public perceptions that the job of the missionaries was to convert "heathen." Some of the provisions included:

- ability to handle a heavy workload, complicated by the possibility of a trying climate and the need for two or more additional languages;
- working in a part of the world undergoing significant change and development;
- living in the midst of tension, including receiving unwarranted criticism or open antagonism;
- sharing power and authority with local leaders to the point of even working under those leaders;
- working where the job is ever-changing and evolving in ways that no one has predicted;
- working in the U.S., with sensitivity and understanding of one or more minority groups and the particular pressures they face; and
- adaptability for families whose concerns might include child-rearing difficulties, little family time in the busy-ness of missionary demands, isolation when one's spouse travels, and questions of balanced time for women faced with tasks both at home and at work.

This listing was in addition to what had always been expected of Methodist missionaries—religious experience and motivation, adequate professional education and preparation, and good health. The reality of the difficulty behind these "superperson" demands was even more sobering when difficult living conditions and low salary were factored in as part of the conditions. Although the board had set high standards for its recruits for a long time, the changing world demanded even more sensitivity. It was not enough to want to share Jesus with the world—if, indeed, it ever really was—but the board was trying harder than ever to prepare candidates well for what lay ahead.[6]

At the same time, the board was conscious that many questions were being raised about missionaries and their roles. Staff member Melvin O. Williams was sent from the board to visit in both Europe and Asia, asking questions for further discussion. His report to the board noted some of the key areas that he felt demanded more attention and policy concern from New York. At the top of the list was language mastery, which required more time and attention than had been given in the past. Some missionaries preached in the tongue of their listeners or did key translation work, but others learned only enough to get by in the marketplace. Since many African countries were still colonies or were only recently recovering from long colonial periods, European languages were also needed. Other recommendations addressed needed skills and preparation of personnel before being assigned. Giving missionaries more education about the particular countries to which they were assigned was also a concern. Sources of information about Africa were still not easily available; many classrooms did not study African history or geography.

Further, Williams noted that the board needed to make a sharper distinction between the needs in different countries in specific areas. These needs were different not just because the countries themselves, with their differing histories, had different economic needs and development, but because the Methodist mission areas were sometimes urban, and in other places rural. Other variations existed between missions that had more recently been developed and those that had existed since the late-nineteenth century. The African church was also developing with more indigenous leaders in some countries than in others. Reflecting the growing importance of the indigenous churches and pastors, Williams called for more responsibility from those churches in guiding the missionaries in their duties. All of these variations meant that the church needed to be more sensitive to the ways needs varied from one locale to another. Although such an approach would seem to be self-evident, it was not easy, particularly because of pressure to develop overall policies and even overall narratives that could be used in telling the worldwide story to the U.S. church.

Helping the board with these considerations at its January meeting was Dr. José Míguez from the seminary in Buenos Aires. The board was grappling with the role of the missionaries, whose goal had been for many years to work themselves out of jobs. Yet Míguez told the board that the "older" churches still had an important role to play in seminary education, both in providing leadership through the missionaries and in continuing to consult on curriculum, literature, and even methods of contact with other leaders around the world.

At this same staff meeting, Thoburn Brumbaugh reported on his trip to Africa and Asia. Invited to give his observations, he started by emphasizing that greater attention needed to be given in every area of activity to racial inclusiveness and to interracial relationships within the church. His reminder was not new, but it linked together the growing understanding both within the church and without that racial concerns needed forthright action. The Africa recommendations contained his serious concerns about education and literacy as well as the role of the missionaries in working with the local churches. In his travels, he found that there was little correlation among the board, missionaries, and the indigenous churches. To move toward a more indigenous church in particular countries would take more intention than ever. In many places the church had plenty of land, but it was not aiding the growth of the individual communities of faith.[7] He also suggested that individual countries might need to choose missionaries with skills in very specific areas rather than the more general background many brought.

Brumbaugh and Roland Scott, executive secretary for southern Asia, had also visited Asia together. Each presented a report to the board. Brumbaugh had very specific comments for the mission work in each country as he looked to the years ahead. He found a common theme that centered on training and leadership, since concern for the indigenous churches remained paramount for the staff. For example, he called attention to Korea, where church growth was giving excitement to several denominations. Since the church there was autonomous, missionaries and officials continually had to be aware of the lines of authority and the job descriptions. Missionaries served the board, but their day-to-day activities were determined by the Korean church. Brumbaugh was also concerned with keeping the welfare of the Christians and the growth of the church as the major focus of the U.S. church, rather than any political objectives that could easily arise on either side. His position was not a change in policy, but he could now see that it would be increasingly difficult to maintain an apolitical position.

Scott's report likewise focused on increased church development. He wanted annual conferences to be more intentional in moving to support local pastors and in training more leadership. To help meet this goal, the board's responsibility was to provide resources for these more local endeavors. While he was traveling, Scott had paid particular attention to places that received extra funds as Advance Specials. Significantly, he called for changes in the procedures used to determine the way that the money was handled. Advance Specials were a popular way to raise significant amounts of money beyond the appropriations from the general budget because they allowed givers to have a very specific picture of where the money was going and what it could accomplish. At the same time, Advance Specials would sometimes create great inequities in funding. Some missionaries or supporters of particular missions were more eloquent or were related to wealthier churches and districts that could fund substantial amounts. Money flowed to some projects while others, arguably even more needy but lacking such leadership or connections, received little. Scott called on the board to continue the efforts begun earlier; his trip had again demonstrated the need to provide an overall policy that could even out inequities.

Taken together, the reports pointed out the continuing need for missionaries in many of the places, despite the growth of indigenous churches. But many of these individual missionaries needed to address the ways the role of the missionary was continually evolving. The churches needed people with specific skills and leadership in a variety of areas beyond education, medicine, and evangelism. At the same time, while concerns for evangelism remained paramount, the growth of local churches meant that coordination of efforts between staff from the U.S. church and indigenous leaders was even more important. The evaluation brought in from the trips by board secretaries proved invaluable in the months to come as missionaries and staff were challenged in new ways — ways that continued to reflect the evolving role of missionaries and the changing world in which they worked.

In addition, some board structures complicated indigenization and the work of the missionaries. In each global area, a Committee on Coordination, or field committee, had authority over the missionaries and, thereby, superseded the authority of the annual conferences. This structure hindered the growth of the churches. The women under the Woman's Division, however, felt the protection of the committee. They had little representation in many of the annual conferences and were concerned that their work would be lost altogether without the committee.

The conditions in the world were indeed changing. Less than a month after the board met to hear the reports and plan for the year, a group of African-American students sat down at lunch counters in Greensboro, North Carolina, demanding service that had previously been given only to whites. Students at Methodist colleges were a key part of the movement that developed, a movement that challenged the centuries-old racial habits

and patterns of the South and other segregated places in the U.S. It was a
beginning with some violence, with failures and successes, but it accelerated the changes to race relations in the U.S. just at the time when they
were being challenged in new ways in Africa and other places where
Methodists were in mission.

Racial Protests in the U.S.

James M. Lawson, Jr., a young African-American Methodist who had
served in India as a short-term missionary, had gone to Nashville in 1958
for the Fellowship of Reconciliation, a pacifist organization. He entered
Vanderbilt Divinity School, but his focus was to train young African
Americans in Mahatma Gandhi's methods of nonviolent protest for
achieving social change. During 1959 and 1960 he gathered African-
American students from African-American schools in Nashville and
shared with them Gandhi's approach. Lawson joined a talented Nashville
group that included several persons from the Baptist communities of
faith, both African American and white. After the sit-ins at Greensboro,
which began February 1, 1960, the group decided to initiate change by sitting in at lunch counters in downtown Nashville. Even though Nashville
prided itself on being the "Athens of the South," in truth it was as segregated as other Southern cities. On February 13, 1960, the sit-ins in Nashville began with 124 students sitting down at lunch counters.

The students were turned away, and the reaction was at first benign,
but it turned violent. On February 27, the police vacated the downtown
area to allow whites to beat the students and assail them with epithets.
Eighty-one students participating in the sit-ins were arrested. Their treatment aroused only further protests from African-American students, and
many more entered the downtown area to be assaulted and arrested. Under pressure from racist groups in Nashville, Vanderbilt University expelled Lawson, and he too was arrested. His arrest, in turn, triggered
protests by seminarians across the country, and the Nashville sit-ins became part of a wave of protests across the U.S.[8]

When General Conference met in late April, it only slightly acknowledged the civil rights revolution that was beginning. The conference
passed a statement commending college students for "the dignified nonviolent manner in which they conducted themselves," while also commending police for their restraint. Bishop William C. Martin read the

James M. Lawson, Jr.

Lawson was born in Uniontown, Pennsylvania., in 1928, one of nine children of a U.S. Methodist pastor and a Jamaican mother. He took much of his attitude toward others from his mother, who did not believe in violence. Lawson grew up in Massillon, Ohio, where he became a good student in predominantly white schools.

He entered Methodist-related Baldwin-Wallace College in Berea, Ohio, where he joined the Fellowship of Reconciliation (FOR) and became interested in the nonviolent methods of Mahatma Gandhi. He met A. J. Muste, the executive secretary of FOR, and others in the pacifist movement, including James Farmer, Bayard Rustin, and Glenn Smiley.

Although he initially registered for the draft, he became a conscientious objector at the time of the Korean War and was sentenced to three years in federal prison. Baldwin-Wallace refused to grant his degree because of his prison sentence. Entering prison in April 1951, he served until May 1952, when he was paroled. He returned to college to obtain his degree, then became a short-term missionary of The Methodist Church to Nagpur, India, where he was an instructor at a Presbyterian school, Hislop College. Lawson was surprised to find that some Western missionaries did not like Gandhi and considered him a troublemaker. But Lawson considered that Gandhi had exemplified Jesus' teaching of love.

Lawson returned to the U.S. in 1956, did postgraduate work at the Oberlin Graduate School, and also received a degree from Boston University. He met Martin Luther King, Jr., who urged him to find a way to serve in the South. Lawson accepted an invitation from FOR to develop nonviolent methods for African-American students in Nashville, Tennessee. In the fall of 1959, he began voluntary training workshops for college students there, and shortly after the Greensboro sit-ins, Nashville students started sit-ins on February 13, 1960. In the ensuing months, students continued to protest, and the lunch counters were desegregated, but not before Lawson was expelled from Vanderbilt and jailed.

Lawson participated with King and others in the civil rights protests throughout the 1960s. He was a founding member of Black Methodists for Church Renewal in 1968. In 1974, he was appointed pastor of Holman United Methodist Church in Los Angeles, where he served for many years. He served the denomination as a member of its agencies and continued to articulate concerns for justice in the U.S. and peace abroad. In October 1996, he received the distinguished alumnus award from Vanderbilt University, despite never having received a degree there.

Sources: David Halberstam, *The Children* (New York: Random House, 1998); *Who's Who in Methodism* (Chicago: A. N. Marquis Co., 1952); *Central Christian Advocate* 131 (October 15, 1956): 18; *Christian Advocate*, March 7, 1968.

James. M. Lawson, Jr.
*(Photo courtesy of United
Methodist Archives and History)*

Episcopal Address, which recalled earlier positions of discrimination as
"unfair and unchristian." The effectiveness of such denominational pronouncements was shown in 1963 when twenty-eight Methodist clergy in
Mississippi signed a statement affirming it and were put under such pressure that most had to leave the state.[9] The conference approved Amendment IX, which abolished the Central Jurisdiction in principle. But there
were no ringing calls for justice for the oppressed, no dramatic speeches or
protests calling for the end of segregation.[10]

The 1960 General Conference also received the report of the so-called
Commission of Seventy, which "delighted southern whites, satisfied most
white jurisdictional critics, but disappointed black Methodists."[11] The
commission recommended that the Central Jurisdiction be retained but
changes made to promote a unified church. Harold Case, president of
Boston University, asked the conference to set a target date for the abolition of the jurisdiction. The conference rejected this motion but created
another commission to use Amendment IX to speed integration in the
church.

This commission, known as the Commission of Thirty-Six for its six members from each jurisdiction, produced a plan by 1961 but set no target date. Essentially the plan called for the Central Jurisdiction annual conferences to transfer into the other jurisdictions. One problem with the plan was that it would have meant that some Southern black churches would have belonged to jurisdictions outside the South. The Central Jurisdiction held a historic meeting in Cincinnati in March 1962 in which it rejected the commission's plan and called for placing all black and white Methodists in one geographic area into the same jurisdiction.[12]

Africa—Unrest in the Belgian Congo

The Republic of the Congo, created from the former Belgian Congo and part of French Equatorial Africa, gained independence on June 30, 1960. The continuing unstable situation was discussed at length and possibilities from the change anticipated at the General Conference in May in the U.S. A resolution welcomed the new country into the "fellowship of independent nations" and commended the Methodist conference there on its celebration of fifty years of ministry. From the outside these two themes of a half-century of Methodism and independence had resonance within the U.S. But as the time of independence approached, the board released a confidential memo to the Council of Bishops, the editors of the various publications, and the conference missionary secretaries. In this piece, the board acknowledged the reports of instability and even danger. Cautioning that this information might have been exaggerated or in error, it nonetheless wanted to be alert to possible new developments that might quickly change the conditions.

Since the missionaries had also discussed the situation, acknowledged the potential danger, and decided to stay, the board supported their decision and prepared for any emergencies. The board reiterated the policy statement of May 1958, which emphasized safety as the major concern:

> Naturally, missionaries are not expected by the Board to remain in places where the situation becomes such that their lives are in danger. It is important, on the one hand, that undue haste be avoided. This only serves to undermine confidence and an effective Christian witness among the very people we are called to serve. . . . When any situation becomes serious enough for withdrawal to be considered, it is expected that before any action is taken, the missionary (or missionaries) seek

counsel, as far as possible, from State Department representatives and from bishops and district superintendents, and when possible consult the Executive Secretary, who will be keeping in touch with the situation. When evacuation is deemed necessary, it will generally be sufficient that the missionary go to another point in the same country or to some near-by point in another country rather than return at once to his [sic] home in the United States.[13]

While such policy was well known to the missionaries, it needed to be stated for those in the U.S. who were concerned as they read the newspaper reports and wondered how the missionaries were affected. The board closed its official statement with concern not just for the missionaries but for all the African Christians and church leaders. Because of the immediacy of the situation, the board sent a cable to remind the missionaries of the policy, making them aware again that the primary decision about evacuation would be left up to them.

Independence was exciting, but the unrest was real to those who lived and worked in the newly formed Republic of the Congo. After discussion and serious consideration, Methodists decided to go ahead with their planned annual conference for July. In the midst of these preparations, they discovered that the bishop, Newell Booth, was missing. The confusion that resulted was described vividly in the letters that missionary Dorothy Gilbert wrote home, detailing the uncertainty of the days. She explained that the missionaries were aware of the concerns of their families in the U.S. as well as of their coworkers throughout the world because of all the confusing news coming out of the country. They knew it was important to keep sending news, but it was not always possible. The missionaries finally made radio contact with the U.S. on July 9, sending word to Mel Blake, executive secretary for Europe, North Africa, Liberia, and the Congo, that they and their families were safe and saw no trouble nearby. Making the contact was important because unrest had continued, and the news of violent incidents was reaching the world. In addition, New York-based staff members of the Presbyterian Church had been trying to reach the U.S. ambassador for news, only to be told that he had no contact with the province where the missionaries were located.

In contact once again and with plans for the coming conference, as they gathered to worship the next morning after this important communication, the congregation lustily sang, "Anywhere with Jesus I can safely go." When the missionaries finally made radio contact again, they heard that the U.S. consul was advising all nonessential U.S. personnel to leave. This notice caused some apprehension but also some lighthearted joking about who and what was nonessential. Discussion continued. To go ahead and have the conference without Bishop Newell Booth was a sign that ministry continued despite danger. But the danger was too real and too near to move ahead in a foolhardy manner. Finally, the missionaries decided to pack and go to Katako Kombe, Republic of the Congo, from whence they would be sent on to other ministries. Some began the heartrending task of turning over the work to the Africans, all of whom were staying behind. Others packed for the trip, knowing that the limit for suitcases was twenty-two pounds. Because they had heard that they were eventually going to Southern Rhodesia (now Zimbabwe), where it was winter, they tried to find what little warm clothing they had. According to Gilbert, most of the Africans were bewildered by the decision. They had no enmity toward the missionaries themselves and did not understand why they felt threatened. The essence of a Tuesday afternoon conversation when the missionaries announced they were following the advice of the consul demonstrates the painful dilemma:

> *African district superintendent to missionaries:* Where is your courage now?
> *Missionary:* We are willing to die for Christ but not willing to die because our skin is white.
> *African DS:* Were you sent by your government or by God?
> *Missionary:* Our presence could be harmful to Africans as well.

With great difficulty, the missionaries stuck to their decision and, after a sunrise communion service the following morning, prepared to board the planes. As the very final arrangements were being considered, several of the men decided to stay behind to operate the radio. When they announced their decision, their wives announced that they wanted to stay as well. Then Woman's Division missionaries spoke up, also wanting to stay. The decision to leave had been a tenuous one, after all. But all the women of both divisions were told they had no choice and must evacuate. Reluctantly, they boarded the planes. The gender roles, which were often contested or broken down by those in mission abroad, returned with full force in time of danger.

The planes arrived in Salisbury, Southern Rhodesia, in the middle of the night. By Friday, the refugee missionaries had dispersed to new assignments and begun to discuss future plans. Meanwhile, in Leopoldville, unbeknownst to all of them, Bishop Booth had heard all the radio transmissions but had not been able to send word of his whereabouts. He was determined not to give up the ministry in the Republic of the Congo.[14]

In contrast to the ultimately difficult discussion as the missionaries prepared to leave was the editorial that appeared a few days later in the *New York Herald Tribune*. Rarely did the popular press attempt to portray the work of the missionaries, but the small article made a strong, if somewhat Western-biased, statement. Commenting that many thought that missionaries had disappeared from the scene, it praised the recent "dramatic examples of their courage and devotion."

Meanwhile, Dr. Harold N. Brewster, medical secretary of the board, had flown to Malange, Angola, where he was met by some of the missionaries who were arriving from the Republic of the Congo. They had decided to leave their posts after hearing that a garrison had mutinied. Before he reached Malange, nearly two hundred missionaries from different groups and places had already arrived. He heard stories of increasing difficulties and concerns that many African Christians had shown hostile attitudes to the missionaries who were leaving. At one place, the Africans had actually tried to prevent the missionaries from getting in their cars to leave. These differing responses to the crisis between indigenous people and missionaries highlighted again the challenges faced by the leadership of the emerging church.

Brewster's report provided a picture of the confusion that often surrounded rebellion as rumors and counterrumors fueled actions in an ever-accelerating progression. He helped to bring home the reality of the differences. Using this information, however, he also focused on what had become a continuing theme, questioning the directions of the mission work. He had done it several times before, feeling that he represented, not just a few of the missionaries, but those in the church who were not in sympathy with the policies of the board. In this case, he reported that some missionaries had said that if they could get back they would get out of all institutional work, reorganize, and concentrate on evangelism and Christian nurture. These missionaries felt that many Africans were being attracted by the benefits of education in order to get better jobs, rather than by the gospel. They believed the institutional work of the church fostered a materialistic philosophy.

Brewster did not attribute these comments to any particular group of missionaries. Instead, he took advantage of his report back to the

Interdivision Committee on Foreign Work to indicate a perceived need for a policy shift. At the same time, he was primarily telling a story of people under duress and fear, trying to find some explanation for what was happening to them. In a further paragraph, he critiqued the setup at Quessua, Angola: "Quessua impressed me as being a prime example of the 'mission station approach.' Its thousands of acres of land with only a fraction (although an increasing fraction) of it being used; its colony of Christian farmers who are granted the privilege of the use of the land; its large schools providing education for Christian children makes me wonder if we are not in a rather paternalistic position here. I wish I could see more clearly how this extensive program really helps in evangelism and Christian nurture. I say this not in any sense of criticism of the fine, devoted, missionaries and African pastors and teachers. This is one station where I did not hear any criticism of missionaries by fellow missionaries!"

His report also described Umtali, Southern Rhodesia, where the sporting goods stores had sold out of ammunition to the white Rhodesians. He found it ironic to have Republic of the Congo missionaries sent there, because its political situation was already much more bitter than the one in the Congo.

He made his own recommendations about the choices the board and the missionaries faced, telling them that time was running out—and missionaries could feel this. Some were frightened and reacted with hostile attitudes toward Africans. These missionaries, he stated, should be brought home "for their *own* good, as well as for the good of the work."

In his role of reporting for the board, Brewster was much more blunt about the difficulties than the missionaries had been in their letters home. He saw the Methodist Church in Katanga, Republic of the Congo, split over the political situation. Tribalism and regionalism played a role in nearly all aspects of life, making much more difficult the work of the church. He noted that the best-qualified person to head up the school system was considered an outsider just because he had not been born there. As he traveled, he saw many market areas with little business because most Europeans had fled, leaving thousands of gutted homes and no one in the streets. The missionaries continued to adapt as best they could.

In August, Booth met with some of the missionaries. They decided that the women and children should return to the U.S., but that the bishop and sixteen of the men would return to the Central Congo to supervise the Kindu District from Tunda. Finally, in September, Africans and missionaries were able to gather for annual conference, two months late but celebrating 100 percent attendance.

Booth took time to announce once again in the full conference session why the missionaries had left: disturbances and terrible things had happened elsewhere, and the U.S. Government had ordered all U.S. citizens to leave (his report contained a question mark by the word "ordered," which itself is in quotes). He continued to explain that much trouble in the Belgian Congo was due to disobedience to the government, thus missionaries needed to obey their own government to set a good example. Finally, he spoke again for the missionaries who left because they truly believed African Christians might have been exposed to real danger if they tried to protect missionaries. Until the bishop made these public explanations, the conversations about the missionaries' hurried departure had continued to be a sore point among many of the Africans. The bishop's statements helped to clear the air, except among the African Christians from Wembo Nyama. The conference leader from there was strongly anti-missionary. At one point in the proceedings, John Wesley Shungu, superintendent of the Wembo Nyama District, refused to translate this leader's question to the bishop because it was "too insulting."

Another issue the church had to consider was the reopening of schools. The government said there was no money to pay teachers' salaries. Booth suggested that the students pay some tuition and that the teachers take a pay cut—a shocking idea to many. Brewster's fears that Christianity had strong economic meaning were not unfounded. At the conference there was only time for the immediate decisions that needed to be made. The possibility of deeper discussion of theological and economic implications was not addressed.

Meanwhile the hospitals were barely functioning—no operations were performed, even though the doctors wanted to stay rather than go to Rhodesia, as the bishop wished. Brewster gave his report to the committee in New York in September. He concluded by asking, "What has this taught us?" He listed three points: (1) Missionaries should be given some choice in whether to stay or evacuate during crisis. (2) Women and children should have left (in the recent crisis), but men should have the privilege to stay. (3) Missionaries who go back should not climb into the same saddle again. They should share authority with those who had carried on while they were gone.

The board needed to rethink its policies regarding housing and transportation for workers, whether missionary or indigenous. Missionaries remained vastly privileged in comparison with indigenous people, who would now have to perform the bulk of the work; thus the board needed to decide how to help them.

He went on to comment that the Central Congo church was in bad shape as far as paid ministry was concerned. In fact, no students were receiving pastoral training. Further, he believed the country would be in chaos for years to come. Since the worst conditions would be in the cities, the best possibilities for church development lay in the rural areas. He wrote that if the missionaries were willing to accept a simpler lifestyle and be equal partners, then there was opportunity, but they should not stay too long.[15]

Brewster's report provided an important counterview to comments by both the staff and a number of the missionaries and leaders in the field. On the one hand, he identified difficulties that missionaries faced as they tried to work collegially with their African counterparts. While the philosophy of the work was not really in question, the funding and the personnel needed during the transition to a more indigenous leadership were. In addition, there was a difference between policy and implementation. Individuals came into mission at different times. Although they made reports, met with staff, and stayed in contact with the board, they did not all share the same philosophy and theology. As the conditions of their work changed, some made radical shifts in thinking and personal approach; others did not change at all. Some missionaries gave lip service to development but were content to live with a model that allowed them a larger share of the power. Many continued the practices they found when they arrived of living in separate settings, often much nicer than what their African counterparts could afford. Bishop Ralph Dodge's practice of living with the people he visited was not adopted by many of the missionaries. In some areas, even more separation between missionaries and the indigenous people was common. For example, in Southern Rhodesia, where the missionary lot was much better than in Angola or Algeria, Africans had to come to the back door when they visited the missionary residence. That door had a small flap that the missionary would open to talk through to the Africans.[16] Colonialism remained more than just a way of governing.

Brewster's report did not discuss all these difficulties and practices. Although he was more willing than others to acknowledge the gap in faith and practice, he did not deal head-on with the political difficulties and situations faced by missionaries and Africans alike. His bias was clear, but he left behind Methodist missionaries who faced a variety of difficult situations that were not merely related to whether or not they were doing evangelistic work. Broader analysis was needed. In addition, the assumption that women and children should, of course, leave too easily dismissed the deep commitment and courage of the women. Despite the gender bias so common in the U.S., personnel of the Woman's Division were accustomed to being in leadership roles with power and authority. They were not willing to be taken for granted as lightly as Brewster and others might have wished. Missionary wives also carried professional loads in their service. As part of the team, sharing in difficulties and deprivations as well as accomplishments, many were accustomed to equal participation in decision making and danger.

By late October 1960, more of the missionaries had once again returned to the Republic of the Congo. The disruptions continued, however, creating a climate of uncertainty and discomfort. In January, the missionaries were evacuated again. While the staff in New York monitored the situation as much as possible, missionaries were often the ones who ultimately had to make decisions about what they would do and why. Letters from some of the Republic of the Congo personnel reveal the various decisions and reasoning.

Charles and Mildred Reeve represent one such response. They had been part of the group evacuated originally but had returned to Katako Kombe. When the unrest continued, affecting their young son, they chose to return to the U.S. and work on translations of the Bible and other materials, hoping to return as soon as things had quieted down. Alexander and Hazel Reid had also been evacuated. When they met with Booth, he indicated that they were allowed to give personal preferences for their next appointment. Because they had been through several evacuations, they were told that if they wished, they could choose to leave for a furlough. Despite this appealing offer, they decided to stay and do work within five miles of the Republic of the Congo border, finally taking a position in the United Free Church. Not long afterward, they received a sobering message from a pastor friend in the former Belgian Congo: "Your residences are no longer residences. You did well to have left when you did."[17]

Rolla Swanson wrote home about the difficulty of getting medical supplies. The unavailability of gasoline meant that obtaining any kind of supplies was often a problem. But she told her readers, for whom the Republic of the Congo and its unrest must have seemed far away, that she was proud of the Christian leaders who were speaking out without fear of the consequences.[18]

Missionaries in the Republic of the Congo were not the only ones facing crisis decisions during those months. In South Africa, a missionary died as a result of injuries from an attack. Both South Africa and Southern Rhodesia continued to be dangerous places for missionaries, as the African population seethed under the racist restrictions and oppression of more than a century of colonial domination.

Considering Change Together: Africa Consultation

The eruption of violence in several places in Africa helped the board and the missionaries to examine the realities of the policies under which they worked. With each event, they scrambled to respond to the individual situation, treating it as the exception to missionary policy and experience. Overall change was not contemplated. Reflecting on this, Blake wrote that the underlying message to the younger churches was still: "This is our structure—see how you can fit into it." By February 1961, the Interdivision Committee on Foreign Work was ready to concede that while new approaches were needed, finding the best solutions would not happen in New York but in the contested areas of the world where the church was struggling for identity. The committee proposed consultations—one for Africa within the year, one in Latin America in 1962, and another in Asia in 1963. The first one would be held in the Republic of the Congo.

Preparations for an Africa consultation in Elizabethville began immediately. When greater violence erupted in Angola, the committee planning the consultation realized that participants from that country probably would not be able to attend. So they debated how to proceed. In the end, they felt the need for such a meeting was urgent enough to go ahead without Angola. One letter they received told them, "You're nuts for trying to have a Consultation in any form, let alone trying to have it in Elizabethville." But Tracey Jones, executive secretary for policy and planning in Southeast Asia, felt differently. When he arrived in Elizabethville, he met with Tshombe Moise, who had just been released from prison, felt the tension in the air, and said, "This is just the place to have the Consultation."[19]

This 1964 map shows
The Methodist Church
strategically positioned
for the future of Africa
(shaded areas), but the
extent and placement of
the church's missions
also exposed missionaries
and African Christians to
danger in the volatile aftermath of the independ-
ence of African states in
the 1960s. (*Map courtesy
of United Methodist
Archives and History*)

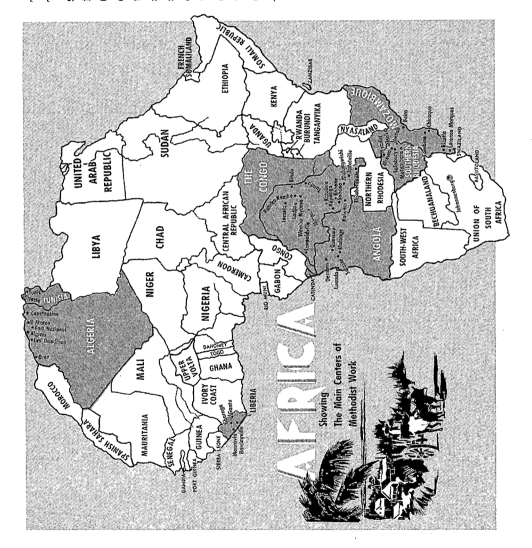

Twenty-one representatives from the African churches attended the consultation. These included seven laymen, seven laywomen, and eight members of the clergy. Nine missionaries attended—four from the Woman's Division and five from the Division of World Missions, all five of whom were clergy. Nine members of the consultation's advisory committee (which included representatives from Asia and Latin America as well as from Europe and the U.S.) made the trip, as well as six members of the staff of the Board of Missions and four members of the board itself.

Because the consultation had been arranged in such a hurry, no agenda awaited the participants when they arrived. Within three days, the participants had managed to identify the major issues confronting them and divided into groups to begin the work of formulating proposals and possible solutions. The U.S. delegation experienced a real difference in its evaluations and perceptions of what it meant to be in mission. Blake described this change using a metaphor: Instead of being a wheel with the hub in New York and spokes reaching out to various areas around the world, the board was part of a universe of constellations, with the U.S. being only one of many and the center of control in God's hands.

The recommendations of the consultation reveal the underside of missionary activities even when official policy was favoring indigenization. Calling for a transfer of responsibility to Africans, the participants made it clear that they still desired missionaries but that Africans themselves wanted to move into leadership roles. Although the goal of giving leadership to the churches in each country had been stated policy by the board for many years, the implementation was slow at best and usually only partial. Participants gave examples of the current practices. A job might be assigned to an African, but the bookkeeping or financial responsibilities would be retained by the missionary. Others told of being given a position once held by a missionary that involved travel. The car the missionary had used, however, was not transferred to the African, and he had to travel everywhere by bicycle. These examples and others revealed a pattern that kept control in the hands of the missionaries, even when many of the duties and responsibilities were being transferred to Africans. Creating a general policy had not been enough.

The consultation participants reviewed the written materials guiding the organization of the annual conferences. They suggested ways that these rules might be seen as guidelines for the annual conferences to use for experimentation, finding what best served their local ways of operating.[20]

Funding issues consumed much of the time and discussion. Several recommendations emerged that indicated the difficulties with the current
pattern. Many of the funds received by both the Woman's Division and
the Division of World Missions were designated for particular agencies
and institutions. Sometimes funds were even designated for a particular
part of a building. But workers in the ministry locations needed more
flexibility in handling finances and asked that more funds be undesig-
nated. They also asked that the treasurers of the annual conferences in
Africa be the ones to disperse the funds rather than having some of the
checks sent directly from New York to the local site. These kinds of recommendations were a challenge for the staff and board, who knew that
successful fund-raising techniques were often particular and designated.
Raising the money in the U.S. had always depended on fostering identification of the givers with particular needs and projects. Pictures and personal stories had kept specific projects and places well defined for the
faraway donors. To loosen these ties was a risk.

Perhaps the biggest development was the location of the meeting itself.
Gathering in the Republic of the Congo made the policies of evacuation
much more real than the participants would have felt in a retreat center in
the U.S. They reflected on the recent experiences and suggested amend-
ments to the evacuation policy. In particular, they cautioned against haste,
also suggesting that evacuation be to points nearby rather than all the way
back to the U.S. Indeed, the statement opened with the words, "Danger in
itself is not necessarily a cause for evacuation. The Kingdom of God may
be advanced by missionaries and the church suffering together." These
words were both descriptive and prophetic.

The Angolan Struggle for Freedom

Another center of Methodist work, Angola, was also becoming increasingly unstable. In April 1961, Methodists suffered their first losses. During
a rash of violent incidents, two African pastors were killed, as well as two
children of one of the district superintendents. When the U.S. voted in
the UN to call for an investigation into events in Angola, angry whites attacked the Methodist building in Luanda. No one was killed, but the lines
were being drawn between the colonial government and the indigenous
people. Methodist missionaries showed their sympathy for and identification with the people.

Despite censorship by the Portuguese, more and more reports of the violence reached the outside world. Angola was very much a colony, with four million Africans and 300,000 whites. Protestant missionaries had been there for nearly eighty years, becoming close to many of the Africans as they worked together to build churches. The Portuguese were primarily Roman Catholic, so colonial officials were not part of Protestant churches and ministries. This religious difference made the Portuguese government wary of the Protestants and their work. But times were changing for all Christians. While the Roman Catholic Church had received many favors from the government in the past and had a virtual monopoly on education, even this church was no longer able to remain silent about human rights abuses and the increasingly difficult conditions of the masses.

The first outbreak of violence, in April 1961, was not an isolated incident. The month went on with continued violence in both the Republic of the Congo and Angola. From New York the staff issued press releases that described the looting of the missionary residences in the Congo and further killings in Angola. The Portuguese military forces, joined by civilians, participated in the bloodshed, staging hurried trials and then quickly executing the accused. The victims of these actions included eight Methodist pastors. Of the thirty-three indigenous Methodist pastors, almost all were exiled, jailed, or killed.[21] The violence was growing closer and closer to the lives of the missionaries. In addition, at the northern end of the African continent, troops took over Algiers, also creating an unstable situation for the missionaries there.

As spring turned to summer, the troubles in Angola increased. On July 14, Raymond E. Noah, missionary from Kansas who had been in Angola since 1950, was arrested by the secret police and held incommunicado for twenty-eight days. He managed to smuggle out a letter that told of his situation. It arrived in New York a week later. The Portuguese did not even announce his arrest until July 27. They charged him with having aided three Angolan students to escape the country. He admitted that he had, indeed, given them money to leave the country and thus be able to accept scholarships they had earned for schools outside Angola; but he denied charges of smuggling guns and ammunition. Those charges, in fact, were dropped for lack of evidence. Even so, Noah was transported to Lisbon and deported.

As such incidents increased, articles about missionaries continued to appear in the popular press. An article from the *Wall Street Journal*, August 14, 1961, laid out both the dilemmas and the often unrecognized assets of the missionary force. When violence had broken out in the Belgian Congo, the U.S. State Department had suddenly realized that it did not know where all U.S. personnel were or how to get them out. Technically, they were the responsibility of the embassy, but officials had never bothered to become aware of the numbers or the locations.[22] Once they did pay official attention, the actual numbers startled them. Of the 1,100 people from the U.S. in Southern Rhodesia, for example, 710 were missionaries. After what had happened in the Belgian Congo, the State Department representatives in Rhodesia sent their consular officer around to visit all of them and learn what he could about their situations.

At the same time, the missionaries often felt the need to keep as much distance as possible from the government officials because they needed to establish autonomy and develop the trust of those with whom they worked. They even asked Peace Corps personnel to stay away from the missions because their success rested on representing the church and not the U.S. Government. Dr. M. E. Culver at the Epworth School in Salisbury told the *Journal* reporter that his concern was for the long process of earning the Africans' trust. He had to prove his competence, showing that he was not just another white man out to take advantage of the African people and their land. The article observed that Culver and others tried to play it down the middle but, "as with many American clergymen, their sympathies are on the side of the African and his demands for equal rights." Board Secretary Mel Williams was also quoted in the article, telling how missionary trainees were encouraged to participate in civil rights protests in the U.S. "A jail sentence here may mean brotherhood when he's in Africa."

Forty years later, Fred Brancel reflected on the developments in Africa at that time and named exactly the same events as the article mentioned to illustrate what was important about the ways missionaries were interacting with the African people during this period. The development of the civil rights movement in the U.S. was a parallel to the deepening independence efforts in Africa. Missionaries home on furlough could see it happening. Others made the connection as they read the news from home and corresponded with friends and relatives. While the representation of the missionaries in the article did not fit all those working in

Africa, it was prophetic of the years ahead, as missionaries were swept up in the struggles of Africans to regain their land and their culture throughout the continent.

The article also did not explore the important aspects of theology that motivated Methodists and others to step out from traditional colonial roles, begin to work with Africans as equals, and identify in their struggle. That theology did not often appear in literature or reports. But when questioned, missionaries were quick to articulate a view of human beings as equal children of God and an understanding that they were called – as all Christians were called – to work for the coming of the Kingdom of God on earth. Making lives better and creating better social situations were as much a part of the ministry as were preaching, flannel board presentations, and ministry to and care of the sick.

Finally, and importantly, the article also made public again what had been long-standing policy for the board: the Africanization of the church. Methodists continued to work at reorganizing the church system so that eventually Africans would run everything.

Resolving the Noah situation did not end the crisis in Angola that year. On September 5, four more missionaries were arrested. Wendel Golden and Marion Way, Jr., were in Luanda; Brancel and Edwin LeMaster were in Quessua. All four were taken to prison. The Portuguese had a long list of charges against them: running a school for terrorists, storing arms in a nearby mountain, teaching courses with hidden meanings, importing refrigerators filled with guns, planning secretly to blow up a mine. No evidence was produced for any of these charges; the real objective of the Portuguese was to get the missionaries out of the country. The missionaries, too, were aware of their real crime – they were teaching Angolans to read, write, and think for themselves. At the same time, the tactics the Portuguese had chosen to get rid of them shocked and sickened the missionaries. For example, one of the specific charges against Brancel and his wife Margaret was that they had taken four students into their home and urged them to join the terrorists. When he heard their names, Brancel knew it was a trumped-up charge because he did not know any of the students. But in backing up their charges against the missionaries, the Portuguese involved innocent Angolan Christians. One day, the secret police brought in before the four men the church leader who had allegedly made the accusation. Bruised and frightened, he trembled as he repeated his charges against the missionaries. To see the way that people were being played off one another was harder for the missionaries to endure than their own arrest had been. Later they saw the man being taken away, trying to gesture to them that he had been beaten and forced to make the false confession. The missionaries were not able to find out what happened to him, but the particular accusation was never repeated.

During their prison term, the prisoners were taken every other day to see the U.S. consul so that he could verify that they had not been beaten. Despite their own protection from abuse, the missionaries found their incarceration difficult in ways that went beyond the physical confinement. From their cell they could hear the cries of Angolans, some whom they knew, being beaten and tortured. One of them was a beloved Methodist leader. Although he was later released, it took many years for his physical and spiritual wounds to heal.

After less than two weeks, the four missionaries were secretly put on a plane, flown to Lisbon, and imprisoned there. Their families, still in Angola, did not know where they were. Conditions in the prison in Lisbon were not difficult physically. Each day the head of the prison came to visit with them. After they had been there a couple of weeks, however, Way became ill. Prison officials treated him for malaria, but he developed pneumonia as well. After another week, the prisoners were able to reach the U.S. consulate, which sent a doctor and the U.S. ambassador. The doctor treated Way, and the ambassador assured the four men that once the authorities had completed their investigation, they would deport the missionaries. He thought it would be soon. Knowing international law, the missionaries guessed that they would be held in prison the full three months legally allowed with official charges being brought against them. They began to anticipate their release.

Instead, six more long weeks went by while the missionaries waited in prison. Officials in New York continued their efforts to free them, using the opportunity of interest from the mass media to publicize their work throughout Africa. The *Christian Century* ran articles two weeks in a row in November that explored in more detail the political situation leading up to the arrests. Changes taking place in the U.S. were part of this context. In May, Alan Shepard completed a brief suborbital flight that was the official U.S. entry into the space race. The Cold War, increasingly more evident around the globe, had entered a new phase.

Critical to the discussions taking place in Africa and elsewhere were the concerns about Communism and the possibility that the missionaries were part of its spread. These articles provided a chance for board staff to provide explanations with accurate information. George Daniels laid out the arguments in a November 15, 1961, *Christian Century* article, reporting that Portugal had quickly blamed the violence on Communist-inspired agitators from the Belgian Congo [*sic*]. He quoted the board's response: "All the leaders of the Nationalist Movement are well known Angolans, some trained by the Protestant Church and some trained by the Roman Catholic Church." Further, the board had made its position clear in September when it stated that the civil war was actually the result of postponing reforms needed for Africans and the Portuguese alike.

Bishop Dodge wrote a guest editorial that appeared in the magazine the following week. Because he had started his mission ministry in Angola, his analysis spoke even more personally of the difficulties placed on missionaries by the Portuguese government. He reflected on the dilemma missionaries had faced for many years: "The outspokenness . . . has surprised both friends and opponents. Heretofore the missionaries have suffered in silence with the people of Angola. All at once they have become vocal in bringing recent events in Angola before the conscience of the civilized world for judgment." Years before, the Templins, serving in India, had taken a stand with a freedom movement. They were whisked away almost as soon as possible. Times had indeed changed.

Some of the factors Dodge pointed out in his article made this difference in attitude easier to understand. In Angola, the government actually encouraged destruction of Protestants' property. When the mob attacked the center in Luanda, for example, they did so under police escort. The violence followed years of religious discrimination against Protestants throughout the country. Yet another factor was the government's denial of entrance to news reporters or other outsiders who might tell the story to the outside world. The missionaries knew they were the ones in the best position—sometimes the only ones—to provide critical information.

Several other factors also affected the way the incident was viewed. Education had become a political act, and the missionaries were ready to accept the consequences for it. Within the U.S., awareness of racial discrimination and injustice was at a much more sensitive level than it had been before the Second World War, when the Templins had taken their stand. Also, more and more people evaluated the church's work as one part of the fabric of the whole society. So both functionally—as missionaries interacted daily with Africans—and philosophically—in board decisions and policy — Christian witness was accepted as a political act with possible consequences. Even so, Christian values served to limit political acts in particular ways. For example, Dodge's article reminded readers that "the truly Christian position must be one of nonviolence," a standard he held for Africans and Portuguese alike.

Brancel, for one, was flattered that the Portuguese blamed the missionaries for the uprisings. He believed, as did many Methodists, that if one were preaching and spreading the gospel, those who heard it would not be subservient to colonial or despotic governments. This was a theological argument about liberation based on Gospel and Old Testament passages that missionaries and indigenous Christians lived out before it became known to the rest of the world as Liberation Theology. In other ways as well, the missionaries made their attitudes clear. For example, many of those in power referred to the indigenous tongue in Angola with a Portuguese word that meant "language of the dogs." The Methodists were not among them. They continued to preach that in Christian teaching all people were worthy. The missionaries were pleased that Angolans were speaking up and taking risks and tried to give their support whenever possible.[23]

Despite the difficulties in Angola, the board continued to look for positive developments in other parts of Africa. In October 1961, it announced the continuing Methodist ministry in the Republic of the Congo, despite the absence of the missionaries and the persecution of some of the remaining clergy. The Reverend Pierre Shaumba, a Crusade Scholar, and the Reverend Victor Wetshi, pastor of the largest Methodist church in Kindu, emphasized their desire for the missionaries to return, even as they reported on ministers who had been beaten and thrown into prison. They believed missionaries were still needed in the growing church.

Meanwhile, the Angolan saga continued. On December 2, the secret police came to the Lisbon prison and released the missionaries, putting them on planes to join their families. At the airport, an embassy official met with them one last time and told them it was their own choice whether or not to talk about their experiences. To the four men, this was easy to answer. As LeMaster expressed it in the article he wrote for the *Saturday Evening Post*, "We arrived . . . and began talking immediately. We are still talking." The May 12 issue featured a full four-page spread with ample opportunity for him to explain to the public the details of the political situation in Angola. During the spring, the missionaries spoke in

churches and public meetings, wrote articles, and even appeared on the
Today show on television.

These efforts were an important response of the board. The missionaries stayed on the payroll, but their families were transferred to the United
States. The men divided into two teams to travel in the U.S., each team
taking half.

Often they were asked about the spread of Communism. Cold War
rhetoric and concerns dominated the dialogue in the United States. Brancel spoke for the missionaries when he said that they considered Portugal
itself to be the best advocate for Communism in Angola. By ignoring the
lack of education, poverty, and filthy conditions that colonialism had
created, they encouraged the Africans to find any system they could to
give them support. The missionaries were always ready to back such statements with details about the conditions they had endured and events they
had witnessed. At the same time, their news did not always fit the popular
images of Communism and development that were popular in the U.S.
mass media. Interpretation was sometimes very difficult, and their message was unpopular.

The schedule that the board arranged for the missionaries took them
to some local churches as well as to many campuses, which were the
main centers for social action during the period. The grueling schedule
was made easier because the men believed that the attention they were
giving to the problems of colonialism would be a positive thing. They
were also able to see and comment on the parallels with the civil rights
movement under way in the United States. But despite their dramatic
story and best efforts, they saw little direct change in U.S. foreign policy.
Even so, Brancel spoke for all of them years later when he called it a privileged experience.

Education and Politics in Africa

After his election to the episcopacy in 1956, Dodge continued the kind of
work common to African bishops: visiting pastors, planning conferences,
and making decisions. But gradually his efforts were more and more visible
in their support for the independence movements. He explained that he
got swept up in politics as a result of the call of the gospel: "I think anyone
does. You're always going to find things you can't agree with it. Which way
do you go? I decided to go the way it should be rather than the way it
was. God would be in support of independence."[24]

Such an attitude did not mean Dodge engaged in explicit political activity, such as organizing or lobbying. Looking back years later, he explained that he never had a particular plan, even though he was aware of the political ramifications of some of the things he did, such as riding the buses with the Africans. Another very visible activity was his effort to get educational training for young Africans. For him there was no question: Africans were capable people, even though the government wanted to look at them as inferior. "I wanted training for Africans just as well as for my own children." It made the only sense to him; it was part of the good news, the gospel. Similar attitudes about the importance of education in the development process were expressed in such publications as the *Africa Christian Advocate*, a periodical with most of the articles still written by missionaries. For example, an editorial in the summer 1961 edition pushed for African self-government. It identified the role of the church as providing better preparation for more Africans to be leaders.

Dodge continued to find every possible way he could to get training for young Africans. His immediate success was noteworthy; its effects were long lasting. At one time, more than two hundred Africans sent through Methodist Church channels were studying in the United States. Many returned to their countries to give leadership and direction to the growing churches. His belief and efforts to widen the educational opportunities were not always shared, even by some of the other missionaries. Some saw them as too political; others thought that the action of sending students overseas was too risky. No one was quite sure where it would lead. Not everyone saw the potential for the church to lead the way to a radical transformation of society, and even fewer thought it desirable. In his book *The Unpopular Missionary*, Dodge asked that if the church were willing to do it in the area of the training ministry, why not give the Africans opportunities to develop skills in various fields? Without advocating independence outright, he helped to build support for providing the tools that would be needed in an independence movement. For him even the parallels with the desegregation movement in the U.S. were secondary to his focus on the development of the African people.

Stephen Supiya, reporter for the *African Daily News*, illustrated the way that education and the political struggles actually divided the missionaries from one another as well as dividing the missionaries from the Africans. He reported that the church had originally built schools and that Africans had "continued to love the missionary until a few years ago, when the Africans and many of the missionaries came to a crossroads owing to the fact that the majority of the missionaries refused to support the Africans' political struggle to gain prestige, equality, and self-determination."[25] Missionaries who put themselves on the line were not criticized publicly by their colleagues. But many questioned their activities privately. Dodge was used to this, but he and others refused to alter their activities.

Besides his public activities, in 1962 Dodge edited a series of booklets aimed at keeping the church at the heart of all the change he was working to achieve. Each small pamphlet was titled, "The Church and . . . ," with an evocative cover and a foreword by an appropriate African. The booklets ranged from the more-usual church literature on "The Church and Tobacco" to "The Church and Multiple Society," with a picture of black and white men; "The Church and Politics," with a picture of a rally; and even "The Church and Non-Violence," with a drawing of black and white men shaking hands and the words, "There is a better way than war." The foreword in this pamphlet was written by Dr. T. S. Pariirenyatwa, deputy president of the Zimbabwe People's Union. Inside were quotes from the Methodist Social Creed and statements about non-violence as a way of life.

The pamphlets were another subtle part of the involvement of Methodists in the independence struggles. Each month during 1962 brought concerns, news, and changes that kept both the staff and the missionaries in Africa in communication and discussion about the appropriate response. This response was not just a way to answer the questions that were raised in Africa, but also a way to portray these developments for the whole Methodist Church, particularly as racial issues were dividing segments of society in the United States. To be on the side of racial integration and inclusivity was to separate oneself from many professing Methodist Christians in the United States. The racial confusion in the U.S. affected the interpretation of mission focus abroad.

But politics did intrude. Bishop Dodge was refused visas to both Angola and Mozambique. Methodist staff members in Angola suddenly faced the hard choices their colleagues in the Belgian Congo had experienced only three years earlier: stay and possibly compromise Angolan Christians, or go and wonder if one was deserting one's calling. By the end of the year, only five of the twenty-five were left.

Methodists in the U.S. did not always appreciate the fact that their church journals and leaders brought news of the conditions in Africa. While much of the discontent took the form of mutterings after services or church meetings or often just plain apathy about the issues, occasionally Methodist mission work was singled out for particular attention in the press. An example of this was the way that columnist Dorothy Barrow responded to the Georgia Methodist Student Movement in her December 1961 column in the *Savannah Morning News*. The students had drafted a resolution censuring Portugal for the repressive measures in Angola. Barrow reacted by making the usual charges of involvement with Communism against the students. But she did not stop there. A few months later she personally attacked Dorothy McConnell of the Woman's Division in her column, raising questions about McConnell's loyalty and Christianity. While some would have wished to ignore these attacks, hoping that most readers were too smart to fall for them, local pastors knew from past experience that unanswered attacks could sometimes gain a life of their own and have long-lasting ramifications. In this case, the Reverend C. E. Steele, pastor of the Park Avenue Methodist Church in Valdosta, Georgia, sent newspaper clippings to the board office, asking them to reply to the editor and not let the matter go unanswered. He wrote his own letter to the paper and soon received a letter from the columnist herself. In it, she continued to make her charges of godless Communism against the student groups and deplored the way the church was repressing any questions that might be raised about their liberal teaching. While some claimed that Barrow's was a minority opinion among Methodists, hers was a voice with a certain amount of power and authority. The charges she raised were more formal and public statements of the feelings that circulated informally in many local churches. Christianity and opposition to Communism were closely intertwined in many books, conversations, and speeches. Staff members and returning missionaries who presented a picture different from the one with two opposing and very different sides — Communism or freedom — risked misunderstanding and even the kind of public condemnation that Barrow had made about McConnell. Answering such attacks took time and effort. In this case, the board referred the matter to Mrs. Porter Brown, general secretary of the Woman's Division, who then took more time and effort to form a reply.[26]

Eugene Smith's views demonstrated the shift in philosophy and action that the board felt it needed to make in the face of developments in Africa. The board staff member wrote that as world events, especially shifts in boundaries and ruling powers, provided new situations, the church in the U.S. responded with interest but opposition, desire for new information but apathy, energy for the new but wanting the old to fit into the same patterns. Those in charge were becoming increasingly aware that the old patterns for mission and evangelization were not sufficient, Smith wrote, and he made several key points, including the conviction, "The status quo promises to be that commodity probably most conspicuously absent in the future which we are entering."[27]

Smith believed that the board needed to find better ways for a shift of initiative to the younger churches. While verbal support was sometimes given to this transfer of power, indicating that it was indeed important, most often the older, established churches retained the patterns of operation that had provided them with power and prestige in the past. Giving away power was hard. But without that, Smith stated, the initiative could not reside where it needed to be. He announced four steps the board was taking to assist in the shift that had been talked of for so long.

The first step was to take an audit. Smith recognized the cultural gulf that accompanied such a request from the board: "The entire concept of an audit of funds violates deeply the traditional pattern of leadership in Asia and Africa." But he was willing to risk that as a way for the younger churches to have control of the funds they desired.

Second, Smith announced the series of consultations that would take place in Asia, Africa, and Latin America, not in the U.S., where they had often been held. The board would send listeners, but participants from those areas would plan the program and its content. Both of the consultations that had been completed resulted in more power shifted to the annual conferences of those areas. Yet another step by the board was precipitated by the growing sensitivity to the complexion of the majority of the missionary force. In a time when race was playing a major role in the U.S. as well as in many of the countries struggling for independence, the whiteness of the majority of the workers needed analysis and discussion. As younger churches developed their own sending capacities, the possibility for mission to be done in a crossnational collaborative way increased. Already Sarawak provided an example. Six different missionary boards from different countries were sending personnel there. But more intentional work was needed.

Finally, Smith emphasized the need for the U.S. church to continue ecumenical efforts as well as to shift its thinking. The board thought of itself as working with Methodists in particular parts of the world, knowing that other denominations were following the same pattern. Smith called for churches in a given area to work on their own models of evangelization and for the board to work cooperatively with them as needed. This self-development shifted the responsibility and focus away from the leadership in the U.S.

The changes that Smith laid out were ones that many of the missionaries and board members could see when they looked for next steps in the development in many of the areas of the world. But these proposed changes were not popular with everyone. Older missionaries sometimes felt that their work was devalued or that those in New York (or the younger churches) did not understand how much guidance was still needed. For some, the changes did not fit their understanding of the kind of ministry to which they were called and committed. When it came to raising funds, these approaches also seemed risky. Many local church people looked forward to visits from the missionary, with illustrated talks on the needs of persons living in remote corners of the world. The model of giving from those "with" to those "without" was accompanied by an unnamed, but very real, understanding of power that resided in the "withs." With images of violent freedom struggles in Africa and India being shown on their televisions, it was easy for U.S. Christians to listen to government officials debate the same topic in the secular arena and agree, "They aren't ready." Further, maintaining control by the U.S. church ensured that U.S. (Western) values and patterns would dominate the emerging African church. Few could picture any other kind of church.

Wider discussion of these ideas as articulated by Smith became even more possible when Dodge's book *The Unpopular Missionary* was published in 1964. The short book was written for a large audience, carefully laid out in organized chapters in easy-to-read prose. But the message, like Smith's, was not as easy to digest.[28]

Dodge again reminded the U.S. church, his primary readership, that in Africa the missionaries were often of the same race as the colonizers, making it easy for Africans to identify them with oppressive governments. In addition, their salaries, while small by U.S. standards, provided a more comfortable living style than most Africans enjoyed, and missionaries often received privileged positions on committees. They were asked to identify with the local people, but they were put in positions that actually increased their aloofness and decreased their effectiveness. In Dodge's mind, too often words of faith substituted for the necessity of living the faith, which he defined as living together with the people. An example, not in his book but illustrative of his point, was that of the Brancels, who had made many efforts in their work in Angola to be a part of the society. Other missionaries criticized them for sending their children to the local schools and allowing them to find friends among their African neighbors. So great was the criticism that the Brancels had even wondered if they would be reassigned when their first term was up. Missionaries, especially those who had entered the field in earlier times with outwardly different standards, felt the criticism of the ideas Dodge was presenting in the book.

Further, he criticized the church everywhere for being too cautious. Out of his own experiences, he wrote, "There is a time for the Christian to stand up and proclaim justice from the housetops, even though he knows his residence permit may be revoked." At the same time, he reiterated the need to live the gospel each day and even to choose times to remain silent. In his own way, Dodge was voicing concerns close to the heart of Methodism. John Wesley never meant his approach to be that of a comfortable, quiet faith, but one that voiced the concerns of the world. Wesley himself had been vocal in opposition to slavery, although this attitude was not adopted by many of the Methodists in the U.S. For readers in the U.S., Dodge's words were about Africa, but they could also be applied to what was happening around them. Christians were being asked to speak and act in ways that put them at variance with some of the powers and norms in the culture. While the opening section was a strong critique, Dodge followed it up with positive comments about the witness of the mission work. Missionaries were proclaiming Jesus Christ, translating and distributing the Bible, sponsoring a variety of medical programs, continuing education efforts, and building cultural bridges. In addition, they were empowering indigenous peoples to participate in the changes that were sweeping across Africa and elsewhere. Dodge wrote that the church should be alarmed when no change was taking place in its areas of work. He believed that radical reformers were part of the needed social change and criticized those who believed reports of "the red herring of communism."

After his assessment of the present situation, he wrote of his vision of the future, a vision shared by Smith and many within the board. He urged continuing training of leadership by sending students abroad for study, relinquishing the reins of power by tapping into local sources, and sharing the burden by continuing to work on joint projects. This refrain of shared power echoed from reports, through books, and ever so slowly into the practice of the church.

With such books and articles, the board was able to inform the general church of its policy and directions and to educate the public about the needs of the world. While these developments really continued a pattern of shifting power that was fairly well established, they began to take on a different look as U.S. society began to reflect more and more of the upheaval going on throughout the world. Change was not just across the ocean.

Poverty and Justice in the U.S.

"Changes have come—but not fast enough nor far enough! ... The Church, including The Methodist Church, has not always been *out front* where the going is hard. Maybe the time has come not only to take stock of the progress over the past decade but to 'determine to move' forward *now* as the New Decade confronts us."[29] With such statements Thelma Stevens, head of the Department of Christian Social Relations, continued to challenge Methodist women to work for change in church and society. Support for the sit-ins and other protest activities of these years was mixed in churches in all parts of the United States. The Woman's Division played an active role in education, but support at the staff level was not always reflective of support in the local units.[30]

The women and men who served as church and community workers for The Methodist Church followed a tradition of individuals in service to the church who often used anecdotes as the most effective way to explain their mission. Such stories captured the connection with individuals that gave life to reports that were otherwise full of numbers and facts. Ministry on the U.S. front did not carry the aura of adventure or difference that could be used in compelling ways in the stories from other countries. Because projects in the National Division were jointly supported by local churches and annual conferences, problems and policies were also more localized. Awareness of the U.S. work remained local; the stories and pictures became necessary to carry the concern more broadly.

Often stories would appear in reports and journals, though the pictures were captured year in and year out in the magazine. Occasionally devotional booklets or other publications would collect the stories. Several such typical stories were collected in booklet form from the residents of

Brooks Howell retirement home in 1986. These vignettes represent the lives of church and community workers during the 1960s.

Far from the clashes over race and even farther from the growing prosperity of much of the nation lay many of the Appalachian communities where church workers spent their days in the early 1960s. Those days were very full because each worker traveled to several different communities over rutted mountain roads, making visits, helping with various services, and being in ministry in the many tiny congregations that hung on precariously to life. One such congregation, not atypical, had half a dozen members, all but one quite elderly. That one exception had not been able to follow the hope of better opportunities in the cities because of poor health. For evident reasons, the church members felt despair over the future of their congregation.

K. M. (no other name given), the community worker in one area, did not agree that no young people remained to carry on the life of the church. With the permission of church members, she scheduled a gathering for young people one Wednesday evening. On the preceding days she and the younger members drove over the mountain roads, inviting everyone they saw, assuring them that the gathering was open to everyone, not just church members.

When Wednesday evening arrived, they were startled to find that the small church was packed. More than seventy young people and children were in attendance. For many it was the first time they had ever been invited to a gathering just for young people, and they were full of excitement and anticipation. K. M. faced a dilemma. She had not prepared for such a large group. She had not anticipated the range in age from four to the early twenties. With aplomb, however, she led the group in more than an hour of singing. The audience loved it. And it was the beginning of weekly meetings that averaged between fifty and seventy-five. K. M. planned more activities and found that other adults volunteered to come and help. A few of the young people found their way back to church on Sunday morning. These were not startling numbers; after all, many of the young people were already active in other churches. The size of the crowds was, however, enough to give life and hope to the half-dozen elderly members who had feared their church would die. New life had, indeed, come.

Working in the Ozarks, K. M. had similar experiences. In her new assignment, she planned to start a Bible school, even though she was told there was not much chance of success. Inviting the young people of the community came easily for her, even though long-time members were convinced that not many children would come. When Monday night came, however, eighty-one children had arrived for the promised program. Once again she was in a one-room church, surrounded by eager youth, with no help but what she could provide for herself. She opened the evening with lots of singing, then directed the young people to areas around the room where she had placed materials for activities. She noted that three adults were sitting in the back of the room, observing everything. The second night, five adults sat together at the back. After the singing, she approached them, asking if they would help at some of the activity stations. By the third night, the adults were pitching in without having to be asked. When the next summer arrived, adults eagerly asked if there was to be another Bible school. That year and every year thereafter, she had plenty of help in teaching.

Methodist women continued to be active in mission in urban areas as well. Josephine Beckwith, an African American who had served in several cities, wrote in 1959 that the changes that were taking place were not just about economic needs. She called for broadening services that would not be paternalistic but would allow for individuals to develop self-respect and independence.[31]

By the early 1960s, Puerto Rican immigration to New York City and New Jersey had created new Spanish-speaking churches. Refugees from Cuba and Latin American countries were also part of this migration. The Methodist Church of Cuba lost about half of its 5,000 members between 1961 and 1965. Most went to the U.S., although some had left the church to become part of the Castro revolution. But sixty-one of seventy pastors emigrated, leaving only a few in the country.

Puerto Rican migration alone accounted for some fifty to sixty thousand persons annually during the 1950s, leading to the claim that one in ten persons in New York City spoke Spanish. Spanish-speaking ministries were established in Manhattan, Queens, Brooklyn, and the Bronx by The Methodist Church. Although there had been Spanish-speaking Methodist churches in New York since the time of the First World War, they remained small. The Reverend Alberto Baez, a Mexican immigrant, served the First Spanish Church in Brooklyn for forty-one years before retiring in 1961. The Reverend Ernest Vasseur from Cuba replaced him. The Woman's Division assigned Beatriz Wright, a Dominican, to work with the South Third Street Church in Brooklyn. Spanish-speaking ministries also received the support of the New York and New Jersey annual conferences.[32]

Methodists in Texas were engaged in a conflict resembling the civil rights conflicts in the South. Following the successful strike led against grape growers in California in 1965–1966, led by César Chávez, organizers led Hispanic citrus workers in the Río Grande Valley of south Texas to strike for higher wages. Most Methodists were Anglo, and both Methodist clergy and laity sympathized with the fruit growers, many of whom were also Methodists. The Reverend Leo Nieto, also a Methodist and director of the Migrant Ministry of the Texas Council of Churches, said, "I am neutral on the side of the farm workers." His position was criticized by both the Reverend Ted Grout of the Río Grande Conference and the Reverend Sam L. Fore of the Southwest Texas Conference, the predominantly Anglo conference.[33]

When the workers organized a march to Austin, they asked for support for food money for their families from the denominations. The Woman's Division contributed $300 to the workers, who also received support from the Río Grande Annual Conference. The council of churches, attempting to mediate, was caught between its support of the migrant workers and a hope that it might be a reconciling agent with the farm owners and the Texas Rangers, who were accused of violence against Hispanics and who took the side of the owners. Although the results of the strike were ambiguous, some political reforms were made in some counties, giving Hispanics a voice in changing an oppressive situation.[34]

Strategies of the denomination for its Hispanic constituency varied. In 1955, the Río Grande Conference decided to remain a separate conference, whereas the Latino American Provisional Conference in California had merged with the predominantly Anglo Southern California–Arizona Conference in 1956. The numbers of Hispanics in the California conference began to decline, even though Hispanics were a growing presence in the state. During the following decade they were joined by immigrants from many Central American and South American countries. The Río Grande Conference continued to grow and in 1960 had 14,447 members.[35]

Cubans who had fled the Castro regime now became a larger part of The Methodist Church in Florida, which had a long-standing relationship with the church in Cuba. Frances Gaby and Lorraine Buck, the former

When Mexican-American workers in the citrus fields of South Texas protested their working conditions in the 1960s, The Methodist Church was deeply divided, since many orchard growers were Methodists and the area was the center of the Río Grande Conference, Methodism's Spanish-speaking conference. *(Photo courtesy of United Methodist Archives and History)*

missionaries to Cuba, worked in Miami in 1963 at the Methodist Committee on Overseas Relief (MCOR) center to relocate Cuban refugees. Besides providing basic supplies for the refugees, who frequently had to flee wearing only shirts and shorts, they handed out Bibles and *The Upper Room*, the Methodist devotional booklet. Some refugees were relocated inland to places like Stillwater, Oklahoma, and Dallas, Oregon, but many preferred to stay in Miami. By June 1963, some 1,500 Cuban Methodists had been relocated through the center. There were an estimated one hundred thousand Cubans in Miami.[36]

The growing crisis in U.S. cities led to the formation of the Metropolitan Urban Service Training (MUST) project. An ecumenical effort in which Methodists were a major partner, it had a board led by the Reverend George W. Webber, who had become known through his work in the East Harlem Protestant Parish. As the associate general secretary in the National Division, J. Edward Carothers would write that MUST taught Methodists the strengths and weaknesses of their system. Methodist clergy were not prepared well for the tasks of leading in a situation of conflict, which characterized the urban situation. Congregations also sometimes were intimidated by the enormity of the task they faced and had to learn to identify a limited agenda. Eventually many urban congregations were led to the realization that they needed to work with others in a cluster of churches. Their encounter with poverty, discrimination, and the other problems of the city also drove them back to their theological and biblical foundations. Some kind of continuous training in the social task seemed to be required. But, concluded Carothers, "the renewal of the clergy and laity in Methodism is possible and the local congregation is still the training ground for the Christian's life."[37]

A Latin America/Caribbean Consultation

The context for the consultation in Latin America was different from those in Africa and Asia because the majority of the populace was already Christian. Protestant churches created institutions and preached their message to persons who had many symbols and reminders of faith all around them. But the actual process of developing the churches was similar to that of the churches in Africa and Asia. All needed to become more independent and move local persons into positions of power. Although societies differed in their levels of development and education throughout the continent, the move of the church to more indigenous leadership was more dependent on the individuals involved—both the missionaries and the local people—than on the particular country or society. For example, although Panamá was a country with greater freedom than Perú, the local leaders of the Peruvian Methodist church more quickly moved into positions of power.

Missionaries in many Latin American countries received assignments to specific schools, institutions, or churches. Like missionaries in other parts of the world, they often lived in enclosed areas on the grounds of the institutions they served. Service staff helped with the shopping, child care, and other necessities of the household. Since most women were also assigned teaching positions or other roles in the work of the mission, this extra help was necessary and did not usually provide them any more leisure time than national women. Peruvian missionary Joanne Russell related how necessary the help was, because in addition to raising her children and teaching in the church-supported high school, she also helped with evening literary work and visits to a mission church at some distance from the school.[38]

Members of the church in Latin America met in 1962 to do their evaluative work in the consultation. Although The Methodist Church continued a significant program throughout the continent, it faced different issues in this region than those in other mission locations. Even though more mission churches were being started in the region, the work continued to center on institutions, particularly schools. Significant social needs lent urgency to the call for more missionaries, but expansion of the worshiping bodies was slow. Even with those differences, the consultation in Latin America had much in common with the one held by Africans a year earlier.

Once again the difference in stated policy—indigenization—and practice was noted in the suggestions that came from the consultation. In Latin America, the Committee on Coordination, or field committee, of the board had the same effect experienced by those in the other global areas.

Financial concerns joined the gender concerns. As with mission locations elsewhere, Latin American churches struggled with the specific designations of most of the funding they received. They wanted autonomy to be speeded up by allowing more discretion for the funds to go to the local receiving bodies. In addition, the churches called on the board to be aware of the difference in salaries between missionaries and Latin American workers. The disparity in salaries created a feeling of hierarchy among the workers that hindered their ability to accomplish the tasks of ministry.

Personnel issues were a parallel concern. Latin American Methodists wanted to hold more of the key positions, ones that had been held by missionaries for many years. The consultation also wrestled with concerns about pastoral care of both missionaries and Latin American workers. Superintendents, whether missionary or local, often had large numbers of persons and sometimes large areas under their care.

Other concerns raised at the consultation involved the goals for growth and development proposed by some of the conferences. The gathering allowed Methodists to raise common concerns and gave the board another venue for receiving information to inform its own development and policy.

Talking about the common concerns helped. But individual personalities remained a strong determinant of experience and policy. On the one
hand, missionaries were often strong people. They had to be to buck the
desires of their families and friends and go off to a strange place. Missionaries who were interviewed years later stressed over and over the importance of the calling by God that motivated them. To answer that call, they
had learned to be strong, to forge ahead for what they thought was right.

But the same quality that got them to Latin America, or wherever they
were sent, could easily work against them as the church tried to evolve
into a more indigenous organization. Missionaries clashed over policies.
Some depreciated the abilities of the local people, arousing the ire of coworkers. Some could not envision having a Latin American "over me!"[39]
Policies that looked good in New York were less appealing to some
charged with implementing them.

This era was both the time of the greatest number of missionaries sent
by Methodists and the time of most effort to encourage indigenous leadership. These two realities led to discomfort and controversy in nearly all
the areas.

By 1960 the U.S. Government was urging the churches to move missionaries out of Cuba. There the small seminary was left to run on its
own, as the missionaries gradually and reluctantly followed the orders to
leave. The church in Cuba became autonomous in 1964, and the departure of the missionaries had one healthy effect: Indigenous leadership assumed control of the church. In 1968, Cuban Methodists elected the
Reverend Armando Rodríguez as presiding bishop. Perhaps equally as
significant was that Bishop Alejandro Ruíz of México was present to
officiate and consecrate Rodríguez.[40]

Growth in México

The Woman's Society of Christian Service, called *Sociedad Feminal* in
México, raised funds for many projects. The society supported four deaconesses in rural churches, provided scholarships for girls to attend a deaconess school, contributed to the deaconess retirement fund, supported a
missionary to Latin America, helped to pay for a translation of the Bible
into indigenous languages, and gave money for new churches and an or-
phan's home, which opened in 1960. The Wesleyan Service Guild, called
the *Legión Blanca de Servicio*, sponsored other projects, such as holding

monthly worship services in rural Protreros, which had no church. Although these kinds of developments might have seemed mundane in the context of the U.S. church, for a one-time mission church they were signs of maturity. The church still received U.S. missionaries, but as Sra. Celia Hernández, president of the Frontier Federation society, remarked, "It is better to stand on one's own feet." In 1963, the women were host to the Latin American Congress of Methodist Women, held in México City.[41]

New church buildings were also being constructed. Methodism was growing in Monterrey, a city with an increasing population. The Reverend Edgardo García came to Monterrey in 1958 and served a mission on the eastern edge of town in a poor area known as "La Ville de Guadalupe." Soon he had a congregation of sixty, and the one-room chapel that was being used for youth work and Sunday school had expanded. García obtained a piano, and since no one else could play it, he took lessons and began playing for worship. The enthusiastic hymn-singing of the congregation attracted passers-by—a completely different reaction from what was experienced in previous years, when suspicious Roman Catholics were known to cross the street before walking in front of a Protestant church. The El Divino Redentor congregation built a new church building with the help of funds from the Division of World Missions in New York. La Trinidad, a large downtown church in Monterrey, added a three-story educational building. In the western suburbs, a new congregation was started with the assistance of U.S. missionaries Beth and Robert Conerly. In a slum called San Nicolás, a Woman's Division missionary, Pauline Willingham, developed an educational ministry with more than a hundred children. Monterrey Methodist laity also went out into the surrounding towns and villages to preach in rural churches. Thus the church continued to extend itself in both urban and rural areas during the early 1960s.[42]

Increasing Indigenization in Asia

Committees for each of the area consultations planned the proceedings in accordance with their particular concerns. Asian Methodists had more time to think about their consultation than had those in Africa or Latin America, and thus planned accordingly. The disparate nature of Methodism in Asia dictated the necessity of clarity about the various concerns, something that the planners decided could happen only in small groupings. Having determined that, the planners asked each region to hold its own consultation prior to the larger meeting. This preliminary conference gave regional churches much more time to air their concerns and their victories. The reports contained many items with suggestions for direction and guidance for the specific annual conferences. But some of the material related directly to the workings of the board and its personnel.

In India, church leaders met in April 1963 at Pachmarchi for ten days — a time to worship together and consider the issues they were facing. They published their report in a small booklet and sent their delegates on to the Asia consultation with many insights and ideas. First, they again asked that the role of the Western missionary change, making the adjustment to a subordinate position in the church. Although this had been a policy for many years, leaders in the Indian church still struggled to find a balance. One particular area was fund raising. Missionaries were still charged with fund-raising responsibilities, particularly for institutions. Some Indians felt that this worked against the local church and evangelistic efforts in those areas. Missionaries seemed to have more sources from which to raise money than did the Indian Christians.

Another area of concern was the relationship of missionaries and institutions from the two divisions. The problem was not cooperation, which was generally good. Rather, because the board had moved to a more equitable salary structure, some resented the better position of the single women of the Woman's Division of Christian Service (WDCS), compared to that of the married men of the Division of World Mission (DWM), who had to support families with their salaries. Yet this difference in the standard of living did not show up on paper.

Because the Woman's Division was not dependent on funds that could be raised locally, its projects had a great financial edge over conference-related projects. Administratively, these projects still functioned as mission work compared to other work Indian Christians were doing. Church members also complained that the Woman's Division work was aimed at women and children and was not well integrated with other projects. These comments point to a split created by the relative wealth of the Woman's Division, a problem that continued to haunt the efforts of indigenization. But the report at the consultation cautioned against making money the only divider: "It was noted that often in contrast to the institutions under the supervision and direction of the DWM, those of the

WDCS outclass the former in standards of administration, education, staffing, and facilities. Only a small part of the reason is related to money."[43] But it was related to money. The ability of the Woman's Division to raise funds over the years meant that their buildings and institutions had been maintained at a much higher level. Their role for many years as one of the major providers of education for the women of India meant that they had an educated pool of persons from whom to choose leaders for the next generation. Money had been important; money continued to be important.

The church in Sarawak also met to prepare for the larger consultation. In September, participants drew up a list of concerns that called for the annual conference to have more control over the property, including the missionary housing, and the job assignments. They wanted the bishop, the district superintendent, and local leaders to be able to plan the assignments of missionaries.

Members of the Filipino Methodist Church also met for a few days in September to plan their recommendations. They wanted money issues and mission board structures to be addressed at the consultation.

The experiences of the Asian churches were summed up in the reports presented at the consultation. Although their histories and current political situations differed, the younger churches of Asia and Africa both looked at the "problem" of the missionary. The frank assessment spoken at the consultations was not denied in board and general church materials, but it was rarely mentioned with the same bluntness. The reports from these consultations thus remain important sources to use in reviewing the official reports and pronouncements.

Board staff member Robert Turnipseed's assessment was a major presentation at the Asian consultation in Malaysia in late November. He included the concerns of the receiving churches in what to do with the missionary and the concerns of the missionaries in understanding their role. He painted a picture of isolation from both church at home and church of the mission assignment, loss of morale or conviction about the direction of the work, and even a dulling of the impulse to Christian witness. Although his assessment was not without positive statements, he raised these serious concerns and questions in order to help the entire board focus on moving toward a new way of thinking. He challenged the old philosophy that missionaries were to work themselves out of a job, noting that more properly people should view it as one Christian turning

Richard Deats

Deats grew up in a Methodist family in Texas and attended McMurry College in Abilene, Texas, in the early 1950s. There he became active in the Methodist Student Movement, which was beginning to voice concerns about civil rights and racial justice, holding its first interracial meeting at McMurry. A visit from Muriel Lester, who was active with the International Fellowship of Reconciliation, changed his life. She talked about the inner life of prayer and the Sermon on the Mount, bringing to Deats and others her passion for world peace. He was inspired by the vision of "the brotherhood of man under the fatherhood of God" and bought and read all of her books. While attending Perkins School of Theology to study social ethics, he met Walter Wink. They began to talk about going to Brazil as missionaries. When Deats made contact with the Methodist Board of Missions and began to explore the idea further, the Philippines was mentioned. The idea of ministering there appealed to him because the culture shared Roman Catholic and Hispanic elements with Texas.

Following seminary graduation and marriage, he moved to Boston University, where he completed requirements for his Ph.D. in 1959 before leaving for an assignment as a student worker in the Philippines. When he arrived there, however, he received a telegram from Bishop José Valencia that read: "Assignment as pastor at Knox begins this Sunday." Knox was in downtown Manila, the largest English-speaking church in Asia; it had four congregations, each with its own pastor who preached in his own language. In his congregation was the president of the seminary, who invited Deats to teach a course. By his

(Continued on next page.)

over certain responsibilities to another (newer) Christian. This more collegial model was not new, but its mention as something for the future rather than a present reality indicated how difficult the transition continued to be.

At the close of the consultation, the participants issued a statement that summed up the important points. First was the recommendation that any annual conference not already autonomous should begin to study the possibility as soon as possible. They asked that the Board of Missions make a statement to support this recommendation. In addition, the consultation recommended that each annual conference establish its own board of missions and that exchanges of speakers, personnel, preachers, participants in work camps, and even newsletters begin as soon as possible between the conferences.

(Richard Deats, continued from preceding page)
second year in the Philippines, he was the full-time social ethics professor at the seminary.

The philosophy with which he entered missionary service was shared by many in the church. As the war in Vietnam began to heat up, he got together with a small group to form a committee of Americans for Peace in Indochina. They sent a letter to other missionaries, asking them to take seriously the political situation and the stance of their faith. A group of seventeen met together to stand in vigil outside the U.S. embassy. Their actions galvanized William Pickard, who had followed Deats at Knox. He sent out a counterstatement, seeking support for the war. Deats and his friends were in turn shocked at this uncritical response to the actions of the United States. They viewed imperialism wherever it occurred as a sin. With such thinking by others in the church, he appreciated the support he received from Tracey Jones, Charles Germany, and others on the Board of Missions.

Not all his efforts went into teaching or even actions for peace. He and his family learned as much as they could about Filipino culture. His wife, Jan, a professional musician, taught music at the seminary. She also wrote books about Filipino music. Like others of his generation, Deats believed that part of his job description was to work himself out of a job. So when Larry Gomez, a Filipino, finished his Ph.D. studies, Deats and his family prepared to leave the Philippines. Richard eventually went to work for the Fellowship of Reconciliation, from which he retired in 2005.

Source: Author interview with Deats, November 2000.

The relationship with the board was addressed in detail. Participants raised an issue that was shared by receiving churches in other places in the world — one that had been raised earlier by the churches in Africa. Advance Specials had proved a very effective way to raise funds. But as recipients found out, they were especially effective when someone related to a particular Advance Special fund went on a speaking tour or connected with a list of individuals and churches, giving them specific details of what was needed. Thus the funding for the specials remained quite uneven.

Other recommendations focused on proposals for partnership with the board, including the appointment of an Asian area secretary.

For many years the board had used educational and medical institutions as concrete evidence of the success of missions in some countries. Such institutions were often doubly satisfying because not only did they contribute to societies in very tangible ways, but also their structures, buildings, and very physical presence made a continuing witness to the presence of Christianity and its work. Pictures of the work and personnel of these places were featured prominently in the various publications of the board. Institutions also added problems for the local churches, however, that were only sometimes noted by the board and rarely by anyone else. Often the institutions overshadowed the local congregations and became the focus of the community. The institution was how the ministry or mission was defined. By trying to address this problem, the consultation was calling yet again for more examination of these relationships.

Japan's experience was the most visible example of the way Christians worked ecumenically in some of the younger churches. The United Church had been functioning since before the war, working out many of the difficulties that resulted from multiple boards and sending agencies, but its efficacy was not universally acknowledged. Although 80 percent of Japanese respondents thought the most significant role of the missionaries was to represent the ecumenical church, only 38 percent of the missionaries agreed. Denominationalism continued to have less meaning in cultures where Christianity remained a small minority.

The Japanese report also expressed sympathy for the missionaries. Many times the church failed to give the missionaries a clear assignment. Wanting to be in control, the local churches pushed them to the periphery, not fully taking them into their lives. Sometimes the missionaries also had trouble identifying with the life of these local churches, exacerbating the level of marginalization that had already been created.

The real evolution of the Japanese church and the role of the missionaries were summed up in the report in a way that was beginning to be true in many places in the world: "In the church in Japan today, missionaries from other countries are needed, not because there are no Japanese ministers, but because we need the Christians with different gifts, including traditions and nationality and mentality, in order that the church in Japan may partake in the immeasurable riches of Christ hidden in the Church in the world."

Comparing the conclusions of the consultations with the policy directions laid out by Smith, Dodge, and others now reveals a fairly consistent pattern of concern and evaluation. The goals of indigenization remained before many of the leaders. But the practical application was harder. The old systems had allowed power to congregate in various institutions and

with various people, both indigenous leaders and missionaries. Giving up
the power was far more difficult to manage than the consultations that
were called to discuss it. Policy was easier to change than were attitudes.

Letters from Southern Rhodesia

Because missionaries had their own lists of supporters in addition to those
WSCS units and church committees that supported the work of the
board, letters continued to play an important role in telling the story.
These became more sophisticated over the years, thanks both to better access to technology and to the awareness of the church of what was effective and useful. At the same time, missionaries retained a personal
approach in their letters that illustrated the variety of concerns and approaches that were all part of the mission work. Several letters, all from
Southern Rhodesia and written in the period of a few months from 1963
to 1964, give a glimpse into the way missionaries were telling their stories.

In her letter of November 1964, Margaret Jones Brancel reflected on
doubt and change. The family was at its third assignment in as many years,
affecting the children's schooling, and husband Fred's work, as well as her
own. Fred was managing twenty-seven schools. Her own work was in
Umtali, where she gave leadership to a girls' hostel that served African
girls who were working in town and needed a homelike place to live.
Ironically, not much later the Brancels were moved again (their twenty-
first move in fourteen years) to Mtoko, where both of them had teaching
responsibilities. Three of their four children moved from a European
school for missionary children to a church-run school, where they were
the only non-African children.

Because Fred had been imprisoned in Angola only two years before,
many of their friends and relatives raised questions and concerns about
their safety and the political situation. In this letter, the Brancels reminded
them that the long-range view about the future of the region was optimistic. At the same time, they used the letter to detail gifts and to thank
their many supporters. Such gifts included money for roofing materials, a
well and pump, a sewing machine, a typewriter, and even a car that was
left behind for the new manager at the previous location. These concrete
items gave their supporters a real picture of the basic needs and a possibility to feel like part of the work. Missionaries had to think carefully about
the items they took with them and the distribution of items that were

seemingly plentiful in the U.S. and other places but often lacking in many of the assigned settings.

While their letters featured pictures of work in Umtali, another letter written from Umtali at this same time was sent on the usual African stationery, which featured a drawing of huts and people in an African landscape. This letter, from Helen and Larry Eisenberg, contained a range of personal information for those who knew the family well, as well as many facts that inform the work being done. For example, the letter opened with news about Helen's teaching work, noting that a Southern Rhodesia Christian Council survey had determined that 75 percent of the Africans there were illiterate. This condition had implications for the work of the missionaries who had put much effort into publications of tracts and translations. It also helped the U.S. readers to maintain perspective on the challenges of the setting.

Details of other work also helped readers in the U.S. to expand their ideas about mission. When Larry's preaching work was highlighted, its ecumenical nature became quite evident without naming it as such. In the time covered, he preached at services for the Baptists, the Assembly of God members, and the British Methodists. Such examples of the lived-out oneness of the Christian family helped readers at home to grow in their own understanding. It also meant that missionaries in Africa, like many of their counterparts in Asia, lived and worked where denominations did not necessarily keep Christians divided in worship or work.

Political events were not ignored. In a section of the letter labeled "Agony of the Soul," they wrote, "Here in Southern Rhodesia the struggle for soul expression continues. The 'haves' want to hold onto what they have; the 'have-nots' are restive. Africans, held down for generations, long desperately to express themselves freely in uniquely African ways."

Even more specific were their comments about Bishop Dodge's recently published book, *The Unpopular Missionary*. Particularly revealing of their own experiences and observations were the lines they wrote to compare the appointment of the missionary to that of the parish pastor. The Eisenbergs noted that the minister is merely moved if he or she is not liked, but that the missionaries could be eliminated altogether if enough people voted against them on the Committee of Coordination. They asked the church to consider this development carefully, concluding, "this new element often leaves the individual missionary feeling alone and unsupported by the very agency that recruited him for life."

A letter from Clagett and Patricia Taylor gave their readers much more detail about the political situation and the hardening of positions as Africans sought to have more participation in the government of their own countries. They detailed the Africanization that was taking place within the structures of the church, part of the policy of the Methodist board and its partners. Their frustration with the time of transition was clearly stated in the last paragraphs of the three-page letter, where they laid out the realities of their position – a position shared by Christians in many places. Christianity was seen as "white man's religion," and all whites were assumed to be Christians. The kind of government and business dealings that were often practiced seem to be in direct contradiction to Christianity and dumbfounded the Africans. Missionaries became implicated in the unjust practices. The Taylors included a familiar statement, "When the white man came to southern Rhodesia, he had the Bible and the African had the land. Now he has the land, and the African has the Bible." It summed up for them the dissonance that was also part of their African experience.

A follow-up to the concerns raised by such letters was sent out by the board in early 1965, noting that after reading missionary letters, many people desired to be helpful beyond their usual gifts through World Service and the Woman's Society pledge to missions. The letter was from Abel Muzorewa, a young man who had been sent to study in the U.S., returning to Southern Rhodesia to a list of duties that included pastor, a secretary of the conference, a committee member, and a speaker. The Advance Special authorized reception of funds to purchase a car, noting the differences in the way African pastors were paid compared to their U.S. counterparts. Such a letter gave those interested in mission very specific ways to participate and a feeling of even greater connection with the African Christians themselves.

European Churches, East and West

Although seemingly forgotten by Methodists in the free world, many Methodists continued to struggle for existence under totalitarian regimes in Europe. Poland seemed to have the most tolerant government, and at an annual conference in 1960, some sixty ordained and lay preachers attended. The church maintained a girls' home at Konstancin, a suburb of Warsaw, supported partially by the WSCS. Its most visible success, however, was the English Language College in Warsaw. With an annual registration of six thousand students, it claimed to be "the largest school of its type in the world given over *exclusively* to the teaching of the English language."[44]

Methodism in other countries barely managed to keep the flame of faith alive. The church in Finland built a home for the aged in 1963. Others in Bulgaria, Hungary, Macedonia, and Yugoslavia were reduced to mere remnants, but remnants who endured. The Czechoslovakian church continued to meet annually, at least through 1962, when the church had 2,500 members. The church elected a new superintendent, the Reverend V. Hunaty, one of the founders of the church. Contact had been lost with the churches in the Baltic states in 1940, but in 1962 the church in Estonia managed to hold its first annual conference since the Second World War. The Soviet Union, de facto ruler of the Baltic states, legalized the church. Odd Hagen, the Scandinavian bishop, was allowed to visit Estonia and reported that the membership was growing.

In the 1960s, the Swedish church was declining, the Norwegian church was stable, and the church in Finland was growing. The Scandinavian churches were sending missionaries and funds to other countries, however, and some new local churches were being built. Danish Methodists were running a high school in their country with its own dormitories, mostly with their own funds but also with some help from the Advance. Evangelistic teams were being employed in both East and West Germany, and German Methodists were looking forward to union with the Evangelical United Brethren church, which had long had work in Germany. The West German churches had contributed to a publishing program in Argentina. The Swiss church sent twenty-seven missionaries to North Africa, Republic of the Congo, Rhodesia, and Argentina. Austrian Methodists were developing lay training. A small group of Methodists continued to meet in Hungary. Kharyew, a seminary outside Warsaw, was opened in Poland. Joseph Szczepkowski was re-elected as superintendent in Poland. "The churches in most of the Eastern European countries are permitted to carry out their worship and other activities relatively freely, as long as they do not attempt to make public propaganda," a 1965 report stated.[45]

All these new frontiers of growth and development were exciting for those associated with the board. They had weathered crises, supported much church growth in many places, and worked hard to find ways to put the ideals for shared leadership into practice, whether at home or abroad. Work at many institutions in the U.S. had continued to grow, paralleling educational and social service growth throughout society. But just as the exploration of new frontiers in U.S. foreign policy had unexpected consequences and events, so also the reevaluations of work abroad began to have echoes in New York.

CHAPTER 6

Unease – Growing Pressures
in the U.S. and the World Beyond

NE OF THE EASIEST questions for people who were adults in the United States in 1963 remains, "Where were you when JFK was shot?" Yet while President John F. Kennedy's assassination was a defining moment for the nation as a people, it was not a defining moment for the new frontiers he had promised to explore. Civil rights legislation passed more easily in the wake of the country's loss of its charismatic leader, and campaigns for voting rights grew more vigorous. The space program continued. But the new frontiers brought their own problems and challenges. President Lyndon B. Johnson's War on Poverty gave hope not only to many groups that had long been suffering but also to organizations such as the Woman's Society of Christian Service (WSCS) and workers in the National Division who were no longer so unnoticed and alone in their efforts in city, town and country, and rural life. Yet with the hope came raised expectations. Those who were suffering economic distress, often with a racial component, looked for the day when they would share in the riches they saw around them. Groups like the WSCS felt that they were on a tide that would bring real change to society.

Other events during that year and early 1964 went almost unnoticed or, at the least, undervalued. Betty Friedan wrote *The Feminine Mystique*, which called into question many of the assumptions about gender relationships and the role of women. Rachel Carson's book *Silent Spring* was receiving attention, the opening shot in what became a growing concern for the environment. Military advisers were asked to put Vietnam on their itinerary. The seeds of future upheavals were being sown.

The Sameness of Mission

Despite all these political and cultural changes, most missionaries were able to go about their work in the same way that they and their predecessors had done for many years. On any given day, men and women would awaken in homes that increasingly resembled those of the middle-class citizens of the countries in which they lived. Eating a mix of familiar foods from "back home" and the foods favored locally, missionaries prepared for their days. If some had only to walk across the compound to school or an office, others traveled the crowded streets of large cities or embarked on another trip through rural areas of forest, desert, jungle, or plains to more remote Christians who were awaiting the medicine, the gospel, and the warmth they would bring. As communication systems became more accessible, missionary families were able to stay in even closer touch with those they had left behind. For most, the days were joyful, full of the tasks and challenges of their profession.

Just as life changed for missionary families living in countries outside the U.S., so also it changed for the nationals, indigenous Christians who were assuming more and more control of the work of the church, control that finally included finances. Bishops and district superintendents were chosen from the trained clergy of Asia, Africa, and Latin America, gradually replacing U.S.-born leadership. In the colleges, schools, and hospitals, support dollars continued to come from the U.S., but more and more often those in charge of distributing these funds were nationals. In the U.S. itself, ethnic minorities and women also found increasing opportunities for leadership on boards and staff positions in the agencies.

Such changes meant that the need to communicate all of this work was ever present. In 1965, the Methodist Board of Missions published a book called *The Methodist Story* to explain more graphically how mission dollars had been used in the previous quadrennium. Twenty-two stories collected from missionaries and nationals from around the world filled the pages. Hoping for even wider distribution through church newsletters, the editors gave permission for reprinting any of the stories. The range was intentionally wide and inclusive:

An Eskimo woman became a nurse in Alaska.
From Japan, a story of "Walking in the Footsteps of Jesus Chicken
    Farm" told of a man who had polio and turned to Christianity.

An African ministry was told from the point of view of the truck "Blue Angel," which took medicines to persons in outlying areas. "Blue Angel" emphasized that medical help was accompanied by help in finding a more abundant way of living.

Prayer life at Cedar Creek Church in Oklahoma showed that parishioners had many needs. One woman prayed that her husband would join the church. Soon after he did, he also found a job.

After a fire destroyed a girls' school in Chile, the women who ran the school received help in recovery, and they also built a dental clinic.

Such examples reassured Methodists that their money was bringing both spiritual and physical relief in settings around the world.

Redefining Mission: Africa

Africa provided the dramatic stories and the worries during the early part of the decade, but the full meaning of some of the changes became part of the reevaluation and rededication of the final quadrennium of The Methodist Church.

One of the best examples of how revolution and change allowed for a new angle of vision for the mission work came from Algeria. After independence was declared in 1962, the missionaries had to reassess their work and its location again, deciding to reopen some of the sites that had been closed during the conflict. With the French leaving, the nature of the work was also altered. As Gerhard G. Hennes reported in June 1964, some of the changes were material — such as new coats of paint — and some were theological. Despite much effort, the work had not produced converts. This failure was more noticeable when there were no French-speaking people coming to services or participating in any of the Christian work. Algeria now had only one religion: Islam. The challenge for the church came in finding a balance between the *church* — small and unsure, an almost invisible minority in a Muslim land — and the *service arm* of the church — large and vigorous, with 274 people on the payroll to help with its clinics, schools, reforestation projects, and milk programs.

But even doing social work was different in this culture. As missionary Marston Speight explained, the Muslim culture has an unself-conscious integration of religion into life.[1] Christians felt it as well, acknowledging that one did not divide the work into social at some times, Christian gospel other times. In the Muslim environment, no one thought it odd or intrusive to talk about the things of God, the things of faith. Muslims actually expected Christians and others to be outspoken and positive about their faith. Speaking in Arabic made it even easier, because the language was full of vocabulary about God. While many missionaries felt this integrated approach to their work wherever in the world they were, few lived in a culture that was mirroring their attitude. Usually the biggest gap came in trying to explain the integrated nature of life, work, and faith to the local church in the U.S.

Speight and his wife, Elizabeth, found that the cultural difference went even deeper than just making it easy for them to talk about faith matters. This integrated approach helped them to learn more about their own faith, bringing back together what had been split in the secularization of Western culture. A gap sometimes developed as missionaries moved back and forth between the U.S. and other cultures. Much emphasis was usually placed on what the missionaries had given up or missed most when they left their own culture. Few people asked about or realized what they had come to value in other cultures that might make it hard for them to move back to the U.S.[2]

In reality, some aspects of life in Algeria were not so difficult. Fresh vegetables and meat were always available. Missionaries lived in nice houses with central heating. Not only had the French built good roads, but they also had a good bus system. City living did not differ in material comforts from middle-class city living in the United States. Missionaries in the mountains (the Woman's Division had a hospital in the mountains) faced more primitive conditions, just as did those in the rural U.S. at the time. Algeria was an example of the way that much of the missionary mindset within the U.S. church had stayed fixed on images of physical difficulty. For a number of missionaries, the hardest challenges were cultural and demographic, which meant that they were part of minority groups in countries still loosening the bonds of their colonial pasts.

The goal of The Methodist Church for Algeria was similar to that in every part of the world: to build a church. But the realities of the culture caused those in mission to change their interpretation of this understood goal. Instead, they defined their work as becoming true witnesses to Jesus Christ and having faith in him. They began to talk about what it meant to proclaim that message by their life and words in the framework of the Islamic world. Defining mission in this way helped them to continue to find meaning in work that did not yield the same signs of success that they had been taught to look for, such as growth in worshiping congregations and increase in numbers of converts.

Defining the goal this way had real ramifications in the way missionaries approached their work. In great contrast to early missionaries, who would go out to street corners and preach in the hope of making converts, these missionaries were willing to go a long way in discussions with Muslims and others to find a common ground. At the same time, however, they were aware that because they were strong Christians, they would reach a point where they could no longer find common ground. In trying to bridge the gap, the missionaries sought to understand why others did not accept Christ rather than just imposing their way of thinking. Their goal was to make the best witness possible of their own faith and leave the outcome to God. Sometimes there were little hints that progress was being made, barriers being broken down. These were exciting moments for the missionaries who had redefined their understanding of mission.

Not everyone agreed with this approach; some of the missionaries left because they felt that no progress was being made. Others remained evangelistic, publishing their ideas in *World Outlook* and the *International Review of Mission*.

As the North African missionaries conferred with the board, they presented their change in thinking and their approach. They found that the staff of the board was very understanding and supportive of what they were trying to do. But others were not so open. One deputation reacted with belligerence, "No converts! What are you doing?!" Some colleagues would point to the handful of converts almost as "trophies." They believed that as long as they were nurturing even a small group of people, they would be able to get generous material support. Missionaries such as the Speights asked serious theological questions about their work and their purpose. To stay was to understand that God's action in the world and their work were not restricted by the pattern of response (or nonresponse) from those whom they were seeking to convert. Service to God was learning how to be with people, to see oneself as a guest. They learned to define "missionary" as "one who crossed boundaries for Christ's sake."

The Algerian experience allowed missionaries and others in the church the chance to think about faith and action in a different way. Leaving the outcome to God, a common expression of Christians, was not an act of

faith in the way that the Speights and others chose to make it for their
work. In a denomination and culture that carefully evaluated numbers and
results, they were living out a belief that there were other ways to measure
success — namely, through faithfulness. This view remained a minority
opinion, however, with discussion seldom reaching the local church level.

Concerns about the mission work in Algeria continued among many in
the church, however. With political tensions no longer drawing attention,
the continuing evaluation was still important enough to involve discussion
in *Together,* a denominational magazine. Several Methodist Church staff
toured the area in 1967 to inspect the evangelism efforts and the social
work. They saw the changes that had occurred since the French had left;
for example, the Roman Catholic cathedral in Algiers had become a
mosque. They considered the same questions that had been asked since
the Second World War, but now they asked about even more probing concerns. Dr. J. Harry Haines, head of the Methodist Committee on Overseas Relief, suggested that Muslims had never really felt that Christians
were interested in them for their own sake. Indeed, that was the issue
some Methodists began to raise about the mission work itself. The evangelistic fervor that Lester Griffith, missionary in North Africa, had been
able to maintain over his years of ministry was at odds with this increasing
sensitivity. The Reverend David Butler, a missionary in Algeria, talked
about the work as service given in love and not as a gimmick to gain converts. He wondered if Christ really wanted conversion at all costs.

But the dilemma remained. Social work seemed like a weak crutch on
which to justify mission. And the theological questions that were being
asked in the U.S. culture, where religious columns in newspapers and
journals were featuring news about Eastern religions and the "God is
dead" movement, were important to consider in making the practical decisions about the nature of mission and its place in the life of the church.
What made Christianity unique? What did it mean to claim the lordship
of Jesus Christ? Missions board staff member Melvin Blake spoke for
many when he commented that when Christian missionaries abandoned
the concept of the uniqueness of Christianity, they had no business in
North Africa.

Missionaries like Sue Robinson were part of the discussion. She had
been in North Africa for many years, serving both in institutions and
through her example. One story told about her was about the time she
sent a note to an elderly woman. Unable to read the note herself, the

woman took it to the mayor. After reading the note to her, the mayor asked, "Who is this person?" She replied, "The only person who has been kind to me for the last five years of my old age." The mayor responded, "When you see Miss Robinson, thank her for me."

Robinson knew that what was happening in Algeria had not produced many visible results. While she could point to various social service achievements and the continued need that inspired the missionaries to further service, she was aware that there were few conversions. "We leave the results to the Lord," she stated in her reports.

The dialogue about mission in Algeria made its way into the popular press as well. The missionary couple Dr. Ronald and Jewell Dierwechter relocated to Algeria in 1963 to help establish a hospital. With the help of their funding base in the U.S., they were able to install an operating room, buy instruments, and set up six beds for patient recovery. In their first nine months, they performed more than a hundred operations. At the same time, they were mindful that they were to work themselves out of a job, so they began a training program for several young people. Their success led them to dream of building a regular hospital, even though socialized medicine was part of the life in the new Algeria. When the hospital was finished, their efforts were recorded in the *New York Times* in 1966. The *Times* quoted Dierwechter as saying "proselytizing is a dead dodo today."[3] Instead, they considered themselves to be part of a new wave dedicated to helping Africans build better countries.

They were not alone in their assessment of what was important. Looking back years later, the Speights reflected on their time in North Africa and what it had come to mean. "At present one can say that the skills that people were able to bring to the development of the Tunisian nation were the best outcome of the Christian mission."[4]

In many ways the Algerian missionaries had the clearest challenge. They were a tiny minority in a large population with a strong religious commitment and increasingly available social services. The questions about their role and purpose seemed huge. The dilemma they faced was not so different from that in many other areas where The Methodist Church had long been active. In India and Japan, for example, Christians remained a small percentage of the population. More and more often, the church, whether locally or through its agencies, raised questions about the purpose of mission, about the definition of success, and even about theology.

Tracey K. Jones, by then associate general secretary, heard the concerns and saw the dilemmas. In 1963, he published *Our Mission Today: The Beginning of a New Age*, in which he addressed a number of these issues. The book was controversial, provoking even more discussion about the meaning of mission. In many ways, the book illustrated the gap between the growing convictions about the direction of many missionaries, staff, and board members and leadership in the church that was not as involved with mission. He opened with the thesis that the old era had ended; no longer were white males with a special calling being sent to save souls in uncivilized lands. The obsolescence of this view of mission had been long held among those most concerned with mission. But he was correct in noting that somehow if the old era had ended (decades before), the understanding of many in the church had not yet changed.

Jones further indicted the church for its lack of inclusivity and its loss of sense of mission. He questioned, "Is there anything more tragic in any part of the world than 'to belong' to a local congregation that does not know why it exists, is exclusive in membership, and has no distinctive quality of life in its members?"[5] He redefined the mission field as any place where people talk to one another about human existence. Citing the changes in demographics, he called on all Christians to begin to think of themselves as missionaries. By the year 2000, he predicted, Christians would be able to talk with persons of other religions quite easily because they would be part of their neighborhoods and communities.[6] With these changes in mind, he called on the church to continue in its tasks of liberation—a liberation that was not about Westernization, as many had thought it was in the past.

This call to servanthood was built on the theology and concerns that had been building within the board and its staff for a number of years. Missionary reports provided backing and context for the proposals and analyses that Jones was making. The succinct statements in the book represented a growing theological understanding and tradition that was being applied to a very particular moment in history. The controversial response illustrated yet again that the public view of missions had not kept pace with the realities that informed the work of the board.

The All Africa Conference of Churches began to fulfill its promise as a vehicle for development of the churches. It distributed nearly $1 million in 1967 through one of its committees. The funds were dedicated to refugee aid, development, and scholarships in fifteen countries.[7]

The religious effects of mission education became evident in 1964 when Escrivâo Anglaze Zunguze of Mozambique became the first African elected a bishop. He presided over an area in the South East Africa Methodist Conference that included parts of Mozambique and South Africa. He was a strong preacher and singer and impressed the Council of Bishops and also General Conference.[8]

African Methodists found other new leaders. In 1965, Stephen Trowen Nagbe, Sr., became the first Liberian to be elected bishop. He had been educated in African schools and was ordained by Bishop Prince A. Taylor, Jr., in 1958. After studying at Gammon Theological School and receiving a master's degree from Boston University School of Theology, he returned to Liberia and served as a pastor. William S. Tubman, a Methodist layman, continued to serve as president of Liberia.[9]

Mission education proved to have both secular and sacred influences in Mozambique. Dr. Eduardo Mondlane had gone to the Cambine Methodist Boys' School and was also a Crusade Scholar. In 1962 he founded the Front for the Liberation of Mozambique (FRELIMO), which began an armed struggle against the Portuguese. During the war, Mondlane was assassinated. Mozambique did not win its independence until 1975.[10]

John Wesley Shungu also went to Old Umtali for his theological education. He served as a pastor and superintendent of churches and also biblical professor at Wembo Nyama Bible School in the Belgian Congo. He went to the 1952 and 1956 General Conferences and was a participant in the Board of Missions consultations in Africa, Latin America, and Asia from 1961 to 1963. He was elected bishop in 1964.[11]

Southern Rhodesia did not enter into independence easily. A British colony, its leaders approved a constitution in 1961 that guaranteed continued control by whites. When Great Britain applied pressure, the colony declared independence in 1965; missionaries were deported, and a civil war began. After Ralph Dodge was prevented from giving episcopal supervision, Abel Muzorewa was elected bishop in 1968 and became involved in the political process, which led to the independence of Zimbabwe in 1980. When he returned to Southern Rhodesia from the U.S. in 1963, Muzorewa joined the struggle for human rights in addition to assuming many duties for the church. He was a pastor and also served as youth secretary of the Christian Council of Rhodesia.[12] While working as minister of youth education, he chaired the Language Committee, responsible for training missionaries, and was a member of the trustees and

Escrivâo Anglaze Zunguze

Born in Mozambique in 1914, Zunguze became a Christian through his wife, Thelma, who was a graduate of the Hartzell's Girl School in Chicuque. He was educated at a Methodist Episcopal Church school in Inhambane province, at the Cambine mission, and Old Umtali in then-Southern Rhodesia (now Zimbabwe), where he studied theology. During the early part of the twentieth century, African Methodists in Mozambique agitated for control. In the 1920s and 1930s, the Portuguese colonial government placed restrictions on Methodists because of their sympathy with forced laborers. These dynamics undoubtedly influenced Zunguze's thinking as a young man and prepared him well for the struggles ahead. He entered the ministry in 1946 and was ordained elder in 1950. He served as pastor of the Cambine Methodist Church, one of the largest churches in Mozambique. He was a delegate to the Africa Central Conference three times from 1948 to 1956 and was elected a delegate to the Methodist General Conference in 1960 and 1964. He was elected bishop in 1964, the first African to become a bishop in The Methodist Church. Although the Portuguese government had prohibited him from leaving Mozambique in 1964, he was named to the Commission on Ecumenical Affairs at the 1968 General Conference. He died October 26, 1980.

Sources: Nolan B. Harmon, "Zunguze, Escrivâo Anglaze," *Encyclopedia of World Methodism*, 2: 2632; *Daily Christian Advocate*, 1968 General Conference, p. 807.

the Auditing Committee. Because he needed a car for his many speaking engagements, the Board of Missions authorized an Advance Special in April of 1965 to raise the money.

Southern Africa: More Challenges

Work continued, but in many places on the continent so did the political difficulties. Yet another first in the life of the church missions was recorded in July 1964, when Bishop Ralph Dodge arrived one day at his office in Salisbury, Southern Rhodesia. Officials from the government met him and presented him with an order to leave the country in fourteen days. Dodge requested an extension of the time so that he could stay for his daughter's wedding the following month. The government refused to allow this request but told him he could come back for the wedding. He

Escrivâo Anglaze
Zunguze. *(Photo cour-
tesy of United Methodist
Archives and History)*

signed the documents and was surprised when thirty minutes later, the
man returned. He had brought the wrong document with him before;
Dodge had to sign yet another one promising he would leave. When news
of his expulsion was made public, fifty-eight members of the clergy, of
both races, practically all the clergy in the city, marched through Salisbury to deliver a manifesto to the prime minister's office. Joshua Nkomo,
top nationalist leader, wrote a glowing tribute to Dodge from his detention cell and managed to smuggle it out. After long prayer meetings, many
missionaries and African church leaders donned black sashes and stood in
protest. Hundreds came to send him off at the airport.[13]

Dodge moved to Zambia, where he continued his episcopal duties. On
site in Salisbury, African nationals carried on much of the administrative
work. The Reverend Jonah Kawadza, Dodge's administrative assistant, directed day-to-day operations, meeting with government officials, attending ecumenical meetings, and representing the church wherever needed.
Isaac Musamba directed the financial affairs.[14]

Political developments were only the most dramatic and visible parts of continuing missionary activities. Consultations, visits, and other forms of reports and analyses appeared in literature and on mission personnel desktops in a seemingly unending stream.

In 1966, the Woman's Division sponsored a conference in Mindelo, Cape Verde Islands, attended by equal numbers of African and U.S. women. Looking ahead to the expected merger with the Evangelical United Brethren Church (EUB), persons in ministry in Sierra Leone were also included. The African women expressed their concern for continued relationships and for scholarships and training for the women. They asked for sincere communication and the exchange of ideas, as well as noting the need for continued material aid.

The following year, another delegation of women went to Africa, conferring with twenty-five Methodist, four EUB, and fourteen other church and civic groups. Staff member Rose Catchings summarized the findings, which included the desire for self-rule, the concern about economic injustice, and the dependence on and yet separateness from the missionaries. She concluded that several critical problems needed to be addressed, particularly the confusion as the societies changed from traditional ways, urbanization, and the inadequacy of the educational preparation of many who were in leadership. The report suggested that funding be increased so that 60 percent would go to leadership training (rather than 50 percent) and that the 20 percent spent on literacy and literature be reduced to 5 percent so that the remaining amount would go for workshops and other unmet needs.

Another study and report published in the *Africa Christian Advocate* reflected a similar shift in the needs. Medical missionaries reported the need for continued help with medical training, but the training of new personnel was also sorely needed, since more and more services could be provided by Africans.

At the board level, many of the concerns were with the broader scope of mission, the balance of power, and the balance of materials and personnel. But missionaries and church members were continually challenged as they tried to live out the gospel. At Epworth Theological College in Salisbury, children of the African seminary students and the faculty (usually white) were enrolled in what was believed to be the only interracial kindergarten in Southern Rhodesia. Earlier a similar program in an elementary school in Nyadiri had to be phased out because the government disapproved. The Salisbury kindergarten opened so that seminary students' wives could work on their own educations, often being taught by faculty wives.[15]

Although Dodge was gone from Salisbury, the church continued to challenge the status quo. In his role at the board, Tracey Jones called for more voting rights and adjustments to the Land Distribution Act. Roy Harrell, an employee of the U.S. Department of State, explained in an article in *World Outlook* that the situation of rule by minority whites had been supported by many of the churches in Southern Africa, a situation that caused many Africans to have little respect for the church because it did not appear to live up to its convictions. Africans believed that the true church would have supported the cause of the blacks. Harrell wrote that whites claimed that religion should have nothing to do with politics; religion is a private matter between God and each person. "This is absurd. . . . Whites also state the purpose of the discriminatory legislation is to preserve Western civilization and the Christian heritage. No Christian worthy of the name should want his religion preserved in this way."[16]

The Church of India as a Sending Church

In India, The Methodist Church, numbering about 600,000 members, was divided into eleven conferences, which met together as a central conference. Board of Missions personnel continued to provide leadership in many of the institutions as well as for some of the churches. Even with efforts to make the churches and their institutions self-supporting, money from the U.S. still played a significant role. At the quadrennial conference of the Southern Asia Central Conference in January 1965, Bishop Gabriel Sundaram delivered the episcopal address the four bishops had composed together. In it he praised the continuation of work from the Board of Missions, including a small increase in personnel. Institutions of The Methodist Church, many with leadership from the missionaries, continued to provide important educational and medical opportunities. Within these opportunities was further Christian witness — daily service of worship in the schools, for example. Scholarship help for medical students was another way the board stayed involved.

But the India church was more than a receiving church for the U.S. missionaries. It also sent its own missionaries to other areas. These included a couple named Joseph, who went to Sarawak, and another named Jordan, who went to Fiji, as well as efforts in Nepal and Goa. India,

Leila and Tom Brown

Leila (Lee) came out of Middleville Methodist Church in Michigan, a small-town rural congregation that was on the cutting edge of theology and was proud of its contributions to Methodist ministry and mission. She first heard about the short-term program from the Reverend Charles Swann, her college sociology professor, whose parents had been missionaries in India, because he featured stories about India in many of his lectures. Yet when she announced her intention to enter missionary work, not only were her parents surprised, but also her other sociology professor told her it was not a very usual thing to do and asked what she was running away from. The "3's" (three-year missionaries) were part of the same training program as long-term missionaries, spending six weeks in Hartford in training sessions of the Methodist Board of Missions led by the Germanys. There Lee met Tom Brown, who was in training for work in Malaysia.

She first went to a school at Lal Bagh in Lucknow, India. There she was assigned to teach art. Lal Bagh, a secondary school, was located in the heart of Lucknow, so she and her students were able to walk to all the art exhibits that came to town. Such public visibility was frowned on by the families of some of the students. Lee told of one Muslim student who refused to wear her burqa, considered necessary covering when in public. The other girls in the class carefully surrounded her whenever they had to walk to an exhibit so that no relative would ever know that she had been out in public. But such acts of subterfuge were rare. Indian independence was still new, and most missionaries were aware of the need to affirm the "Indianness" of their endeavors.

Lee left India to marry Tom, who had finally reached Malaysia after two years of delays because of difficulties with his draft board. Her marriage meant transferring from the Woman's Division to the World Division.

Malaysia had not yet achieved independence from the British. The Browns lived in a compound with other Methodists, including the Tamil-speaking and English-speaking ministers. After a furlough in 1959, the Browns lived in a suburb of Kuala Lumpur. They saw the church and its members becoming more and more independent of foreign workers and recognized that the time had come for change. Returning to the U.S. in 1965 did not end their ministry or the effects of their time with the Board of Missions. Because of their experiences in Southeast Asia, the Browns were asked questions about Vietnam and became involved in antiwar meetings.

Source: Author interview with Browns, January, 2001.

though still not producing all the Christian leaders it needed within, was nonetheless taking the next step and reaching out to others in the region. The quadrennial gathering gave the church another opportunity to review its mission and set priorities. With membership numbers at a plateau, the bishops pledged again to focus on evangelism.

Korean Missionaries

India was not the only country that was both sending and receiving missionaries. Chae-Ok Jun was sent by Ewha Women's University to Karachi, Pakistan, in 1961. Although only 1.5 percent of the population of Pakistan was Christian (97 percent was Muslim), some five hundred persons a year were converted to Christianity. Jun found practices in Muslim Pakistan similar to old Korean customs, in that women were not treated as humans. She was "confused" by female circumcision, polygamy, and arranged marriages. Nevertheless, she taught English in a girl's school, and, "During her teaching work, she began the Bible class and introduced Jesus to her women students." Later she established a Bible school for both men and women. Sung-Wook Kim, a pastor and medical doctor who spoke both English and Chinese, went to Sarawak in 1963 through the Chung-Dong Korean Methodist Church. The Chinese-speaking population comprised some 40 percent of Malaysia. In 1965, Bon-keun Chang was sent to Bolivia. Three Ewha graduates, all laity—Ok-Eui Kim, Nam-Soon Kim, and Mi-Yoon Chang—were appointed to Pakistan at the same time.[17] The Korean church continued to ask the board for missionaries to serve on its campuses and to help with the underserved rural areas.

Pamphlets and small booklets helped to pass this information along to the U.S. church, maintaining a level of interest and commitment. The materials were increasingly sophisticated in their use of photographs and color, but they often retained the same storytelling devices the board had used for many years.

The Philippines: Connected but Indigenous

Methodists had not joined the United Church of Christ in the Philippines when it was formed in 1948, but they cooperated with the National Council of the Churches in the Philippines, which was formed in 1963.

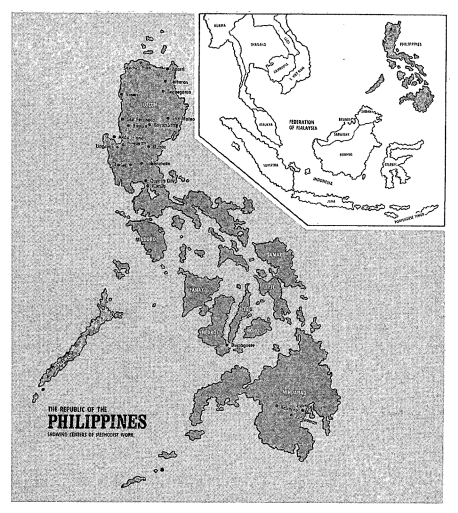

Methodism in the Philippines in 1965 was organized as a central conference, that is, a conference subordinate to the U.S. church, and yet it grew in numbers, engendered significant leaders, and expressed a typically Wesleyan approach that included both evangelism and social concerns. *(Map courtesy of United Methodist Archives and History)*

Relations between Roman Catholics and Protestants had improved by the 1960s. Methodist teacher Emerito Nacpil went to the Second Vatican Council, and spiritual retreats and other meetings were held between Roman Catholics and Protestants. The emphasis of Filipino Christians on ecumenicity was mitigated, however, by the arrival and activity of new missionary groups that proselytized both other Protestants and Roman Catholics.

Methodists, like other Christian groups, continued to work through hospitals like Mary Johnston in Manila and through schools established by the churches. Especially supportive of indigenous leadership develop- ment were theological schools like Union Theological Seminary. Biblical translation was also a continuing activity and was important because of the many dialects and languages in the Philippines. Filipino Christians be- gan to send missionaries to other countries in the 1950s, and by 1967 the Methodist Church had sent seventeen missionaries to other places.

Although Filipinos had their own bishop, José Valencia, who was suc- ceeded by Benjamin Guansing in 1967, the Filipino Methodist church was still dependent on U.S. support and remained a central conference. This situation led other Asian churches to complain that Filipino churches were merely extensions of the U.S. churches. Leaders in the Methodist Church in the Philippines seemed undaunted by this criticism and contin- ued to maintain relations through the Methodist General Conference and the Board of Missions.[18]

Growing Methodism in Polynesia

Methodists had been in Hawaii even before the Spanish-American War, and Hawaii was made a mission in 1939. After its central role in the Sec- ond World War, it remained a base for U.S. forces. Methodists in Hawaii had a dual mission, serving both the indigenous population and the U.S. population, many of whom were transient because of the high number of military bases. Even though Hawaii became a state in 1959, Methodist missionaries were still being sent there into the 1960s. The membership of The Methodist Church was growing, and it was facing some of the same problems that congregations on the mainland experienced. For example, in its twenty-six congregations in 1963, twelve had church schools larger than the membership of the churches. In some communities, Methodists worked out comity agreements with other Protestant denominations. Hawaii became an entry point into the U.S. for other Polynesians and Asians, and some of the ministries of the church were conducted in lan- guages other than English — in Samoan, for example, for immigrants.[19]

The International Missionary Council organized an All-Pacific Chris- tian Conference in Western Samoa in 1961. The Reverend Setarcki

Tuiloveni, a Methodist, was elected chair. Work was also done at the conference in planning a Pacific Theological College, to be located in Fiji.
The Fiji Islands had become almost entirely Christian by the 1940s. The
Methodist Church in Fiji became a conference of the Methodist Church
of Australasia in 1964.[20]

Japan: The Kyodan in Mission

Isamu Omura, a Methodist who had been dean of the Aoyama Gakuin
School of Theology, served as moderator of the Kyodan from 1962 to
1966. Another Methodist, Masahisa Suzuki, was elected moderator following Omura. The Kyodan continued to work on self-development (65
percent of the Kyodan support in 1966 came from within Japan, a great
increase from previous years) and also continued to participate in ecumenical venues. A Kyodan observer went to Vatican II. Exchanges took
place between Methodists and Presbyterians in Korea and Japan, and between Japan and Okinawa. (A union between the two united churches in
Japan and Okinawa occurred in 1968.) Even though Japanese Christians
were well established in leadership positions in the Kyodan and its membership was well educated, compared to other mission churches, as late as
1968 some four hundred missionaries were serving in Japan from many
different Christian groups. Most of them were from North America.

The Kyodan also began sending missionaries to other countries. By
1966 it had "nine missionaries in South America, ten in North America,
two in Thailand, two in Okinawa, one in India, two in Egypt." Sixteen
other Japanese missionaries were serving at the Relief of Leprosy in Asia
in India, and others were part of medical teams in other Asian countries
through the Japan Christian Medical Association. Aoyama Gakuin students also showed a sense of responsibility for the rest of the world by
sending books for a new Methodist college in the Philippines and by raising funds for a famine in India. Yet in 1964 only 5 percent of its entering
students were Christian. By their graduation, 10 percent were Christian.
In the mid-1960s, 45 percent of the faculty were Christian.[21]

Solidarity in Latin America and the Caribbean

The emergence of several strong Latin American and Caribbean leaders
demonstrated that former mission churches were assuming global leader-

Emilio Castro, a
Methodist from
Uruguay, had served as
a pastor, bishop, and
ecumenical leader in
South America when
he became a leader of
the World Council of
Churches. *(Photo cour-
tesy of United Methodist
Archives and History)*

ship. Emilio Castro, for example, a Uruguyan Methodist, served as a pastor in Bolivia and then returned to Montevideo, where he spoke on
the radio about his concerns for peace and justice. He helped to create
Church and Society in Latin America and was elected the first bishop of
the Methodist Church in Uruguay when it became autonomous in 1969.
His growing ecumenical interests led him to participate in the formation
of the Consejo Lainoamericano de Iglesias (CLAI) and to involvement in
the World Council of Churches (WCC).[22]

Mortimer Arias was part of this same effort to shape both church and
society. Although he noted that Protestant numbers had grown in Latin
America from little more than one-half million members in 1937 to nine
million in 1961, he asked: "Are Latin American Protestants involved in
society or alienated from it? Are they bolstering the status quo or fostering revolution?" His portrayal of Latin American Christians seemed similar to that of Christians in North America: absorbed in church life but not

participants in shaping society. In the 1960s, "the door is opening for Evangelical [Protestant] women to work in secular structures on the same level as men." Arias, a Methodist pastor in Uruguay, interpreted an ecumenical gathering in Uruguay in late 1967 by writing, "There was a repeated warning: service projects must not become instruments to preserve the status quo. At the same time, there was definite pronouncement in favor of *Christian* action at all levels." This warning was immediately relevant to the tendency of Christian missionaries to serve the poor but remain silent about the structures that oppressed them. It would become relevant later in the century as North Americans developed the short-term volunteer service project as a model to replace support of long-term mission.[23]

An expression of this sense of solidarity was the formation of the Consejo de Iglesias Evangelicas Metodistas de America Latina (CIEMAL). Some of the organizing for the council took place in 1968, and it was formally established in 1969. All of the Latin American countries in which Methodism had missions—Argentina, Bolivia, Brazil, Chile, Costa Rica, Panamá, Perú, and Uruguay—became autonomous during this period. Newly elected bishop by the preceding Latin American Central Conference were Frederico Pagura of Buenos Aires (assigned to Panamà and Costa Rica) and Raimond A. Valenzuela of Cuba (assigned to Chile). The purposes of CIEMAL called for the member churches to plan, set strategy, develop programs, and support one another. An assembly would meet every five years, and between assemblies a Directive Committee would serve. Elected as first chair of this committee was Eduardo Gattinoni of Argentina. The intent was to seek inclusion of the churches in the Caribbean later.[24]

Methodist churches in the Caribbean, many of which had ties with the British Methodist Church, formally became autonomous in 1967 as the Methodist Church in the Caribbean and the Americas. The Methodist Church and later The United Methodist Church continued to have warm relations with these churches, especially in places like Jamaica, from whence many immigrants to the U.S. had come. In the Dominican Republic, Methodists participated in the Dominican Evangelical Church along with EUBs, United Presbyterians, and Moravians.[25]

René Bideaux was one of the first persons commissioned by his annual conference for missionary work. By the time he entered service in 1959, the plan of working toward indigenous leadership was much more

Lloyd Knox

Lloyd Knox used his skills and leadership in two different societies. He and his family had gone to Cuba, where he taught in the Evangelical Theological Seminary in Matanzas. In September 1960, the U.S. embassy sent word that all U.S. citizens needed to leave Cuba. But the embassy did not provide assistance for that to happen. Buying a ticket home meant paying in U.S. dollars. But missionaries had no dollars, because their pay went straight to the banks of the countries where they served. Finally the Board of Missions sent U.S. currency to Knox, but by the time the money arrived, the earliest ticket reservation he could make was for more than a year later. Although he thought Castro's regime might fall during that time, he used connections through an uncle to get a ticket. When it was time for his plane to leave, 250 students and faculty from the school came to see him off. Leaving was emotionally difficult. He had been part of the school and called to the work; he felt like a shepherd leaving his sheep.

His next assignment was at the Instituto Superior Evangélico de Estudios Teológicos (ISEDET) in Buenos Aires. Despite the similarity of language, he found many cultural differences. Argentina was a more closed society, a man's society. He later described his tenure as paternalistic, "The way missionaries were always looking out for people." The seminary itself was more European in its approach (academic and philosophical) than evangelistic. This perspective mirrored the culture, which also embodied the values of nineteenth-century rationalism. These traits as well as the presence of the established Roman Catholic Church made development of the Protestant churches difficult. But Vatican II and Liberation Theology actually served to bring the two groups closer together.

Argentina was also a society with many immigrants, especially German, Eastern European, and Russian. Services of worship were in English as well as Spanish, though Knox felt that the board was foolish to continue to support bilingual worship. He did preach in Spanish and noted that when he got stuck for a Spanish word, someone in the congregation would call it out.

Despite the paternalistic nature of the culture and the country, Knox worked with many women who became licensed preachers. Unmarried women in particular were sent to rural areas because church leaders with children tried to stay near the better schools. Like most missionaries, Knox found many ways to be in ministry. In addition to his teaching, he wrote and distributed a magazine to support the mission efforts.

Sources: Interview with Edith L. Knox by Ben Houston, January 13, 2001; interview with James Lloyd Knox by Ben Houston, January 14, 2001.

focused. He went to Costa Rica and spent five years at a school that was designed to train and develop leaders for the country. When he left, he was replaced by a Costa Rican.

Bideaux's experiences mark the ambivalence and even conflict as the shift toward more and more autonomy became pronounced. He found that some persons in the church in Latin America still wanted a strong missionary force to help raise money and provide leadership. Others advocated a paternalistic set of responsibilities.

Latin American Methodists continued their mission to one another during the 1960s. Pablo Monti, a physician from Argentina, went to Bolivia to serve as an adviser to Methodist work there. María Barbosa, a Puerto Rican, became a teacher at El Vergel agricultural center in Chile. Dr. Humberto Cicchetti and his wife, from Argentina, served in their own country with the Tobas people. This ministry received a gift from the East Asian Christian Council in another sign of churches in mission to one another. Although Latin Americans largely supported this work on their own, Ruth Clark from the U.S. and Elizabeth Stauffer from the Methodist Church of Switzerland also worked with the Cicchettis in the Tobas ministry.[26]

The quadrennial report of the board in 1968 noted the growth in school enrollment in Latin America, all the way from the primary grades up to the university level. Ironically, at the same time, the report called attention to the growth in illiteracy. The ecumenical movement of which Arias and Castro were so much a part also had an effect in Chile, where a theological community included Methodists, along with members of eight other Protestant churches. The Bolivian church was reported to be growing, as was the church in Perú, although the latter was very small, consisting of some 3,000 members.

The Methodist Church in Brazil was developing new ministries and also exploring ecumenical cooperation. Two clergy educational institutions were to be merged and a lay training program established. Methodists hoped to carry out these ventures with other denominations. A new graduate school of social work was being planned for Porto Alegre by the Methodists and other churches. A rural community development project was taking place in Matto Grosso. Literacy work and curriculum development were increasing. All these developments were marked in the context of the celebration in 1967 of the centennial of the Methodist Church in Brazil.[27]

Convergence of Issues in México

The conference of the Mexican church was organized as efficiently as was its colleague in the U.S., with boards of evangelism, Christian education, missions, literature, and institutional work. Several of the institutions had been founded early in the nineteenth century with support from the U.S. churches, and they became centers around which the church in México built significant ministries for the urban poor. Centro Cristiano in Chihuahua had a day nursery and gymnasium. Centro Social in Monterrey became known for its English program. Centro MacDonell in Durango had adult education courses, including English instruction, and also a large clinic. Centro Social Roberts in Saltillo provided dormitories for college women, since Saltillo was a higher-education center. On the border near McAllen, Texas, the Centro Social in Reynosa also emphasized education, especially for women. Sanatorio Palmore, which was the only Methodist-related hospital in México, not only provided much-needed health care for some 175 communities in the Sierra Madre Occidental region, but also trained young Tarahumaras in medicine, who then returned to serve in isolated villages. In 1967, Marjorie Ruegger was overseeing public health at the hospital, along with two doctors and two nurses.

The colleges that had been founded through Methodists in the years before 1939 also continued to serve, and the church had student hostels and rural work as well. The need to provide support to the directors of these institutions led to a 1966 conference in Monterrey. That year the General Conference of the Methodist Church of México established a Board of Institutions in order to coordinate and promote the work of the institutions. The directors who served were mostly laity.

Deaconesses of the Mexican church also served through the institutions. Guadalupe Carrasco was appointed by Bishop Alejandro Ruíz to Casa Hogar, Puebla, where she did personal counseling and organized services of worship. Others served as rural pastors on the weekends. Piedad Pérez, for example, was serving a small church at Tequesquiten near Cuernavaca, where she met with the Woman's Society and served "as the minister (except for burial, marriages and baptisms)." Deaconesses were trained at the Methodist Deaconess School in México City.

Among the leaders of the Methodist Church in México during the 1960s were the Reverend Manuel Flores, president of the Union Seminary in México City. The school incorporated the seminary work of

Alejandro Ruíz,
bishop of the Methodist
Church of México in the
1960s, led the church in
extending its rural min-
istries, establishing a
Board of Social Concerns,
and dividing the church
into two annual confer-
ences, Frontier and Méx-
ico. *(Photo courtesy of
United Methodist Archives
and History)*

Episcopalians, Lutherans, Baptists, Presbyterians, Congregationalists,
and Disciples of Christ, as well as Methodists. Flores had gone to Brazil as
part of his interest in art and in the 1940s had served as executive secretary
of the Board of Christian Education. Another significant leader was the
Reverend Gustavo A. Velásco, who served as church historian and public
relations director of the church. Since tourism was a large industry in
México, the church sought to serve tourists and interest them in church
life. Velásco noted the value of an information center run by the Roman
Catholic Church and sought to establish a similar one for Methodists.
Velásco also developed a way for Methodist clergy and their families to be
included in Mexican social security.[28]

In México, often regarded as part of Latin America, the themes of
indigenization, the role of missionaries, and institutional development
characterized church life. Animosity between Roman Catholics and
Protestants was also changing. Both groups participated in the 1968 Week
of Prayer for Christian Unity. Protestants were also engaged in an International Border Consultation, formed in 1967. Some nineteen denominations participated in joint attention to problems such as the lack of clean

water, opportunities for work, and prostitution. Dr. Ernesto Contreas, a Methodist layman and cancer specialist, worked on these issues as well as on alcohol and drug abuse.[29] Another sign of the health of the Methodist Church in México was its sending of Ulises Hernández to Ecuador. After studying medicine, Hernández went to seminary and served as a pastor. He and his wife went to Quito, the capital, in 1965 and worked with the United Evangelical Church of Ecuador with the support of Methodist and Waldensian churches in Latin America.[30]

The U.S. Church: A Split Personality

In contrast to their growing marginalization in many countries where they were active in the world, Methodists were finding their long-time concerns at the center of changing domestic policy in the U.S. This situation created its own set of challenges. The 1965 annual report reminded readers of the twofold nature of the task of the National Division—working through local churches to meet human needs and working with human needs in "order to arouse the concern of the local churches for their new tasks." Such a phrase summarized the changing realities for U.S. Methodism. On the one hand, many who staffed church positions, whether as WSCS officers, national staff, or board members, had been actively expanding the church's outreach ministry in directions established nearly one hundred years before by the deaconesses and the "home" missions societies. On the other hand, many persons in churches kept their distance from the ministries that were always "somewhere else to those less fortunate." What changed in the 1960s was that the ministries of many churches came closer and closer to home. Using a systemic analysis of society, looking at institutions as well as individuals, implicated the Christian community for its complicity in racism, classism, and eventually sexism. Hearing of the changes that needed to be made so close to home was different from hearing about the suffering of people in faraway lands. But this news and its accompanying descriptions were not always welcomed.

In their reports, staff members recognized the links between the church's efforts and those in the public arena. In a rare moment of combined effort, the elected officials of the nation had taken on the responsibility of caring for the welfare of all citizens. Thus churches and other nonprofit organizations were no longer the only ones in the social welfare sector. The 1965 report made a connection with the government's War on

Poverty; the specifics in the City Work unit of the Section of Home Fields reveal the various efforts in which the church was involved. These included a ministry to skid row dwellers in Denver; a legal aid clinic at a church in Detroit; school readiness in South Bend, Indiana; a group ministry for struggling churches in St. Louis; and an interracial community center in Phoenix. The kinds of ministries were the same that the National Division had always supported; the division was not changing, but its context was. No longer was the church (not just The Methodist Church but many churches) the only highly visible player in the societal game. Society, through governmental agencies, was taking the responsibility in greatly expanded forms. At the same time, the need for increased focused work of the church arose because of the increasingly tenuous nature of social structures in many places. Many church people plunged in with energy and enthusiasm as they recognized more and more areas of human need that were being exposed by the U.S. national — and thus more public and visible — awareness of racism. The rhetoric of the day, the New Frontier's having given way to the Great Society, made it hard to ignore the poverty and economic inequality of the country.

Even as these shifts were taking place, not all agreed that these areas of need were the places the church should be in active ministry. The institutional nature of the National Division allowed the church to maintain a split personality. Local work continued because its supporting theology could range from evangelical to what was labeled "liberal." Taking a harder look at society might have produced a more radical reordering of priorities but remained removed from general discussion in the churches, even when staff or board members could see the need.

Supporting mission schools and colleges continued to be under the National Division, even with the new structure. This part of the board's work remained more easily understood and supported. Meanwhile, Goodwill Industries — at least those local units of it that were still related to the division — analyzed its operations for ways to meet the ever-emerging social needs in many parts of the country. One concern was that the changes in minimum-wage laws would affect the operations. Funding was not yet available for other envisioned partnership projects, but board staff members held out possibilities. The climate seemed right for more extensive work.

The same style was followed in the 1965 Church Extension Report. Likening the staff to modern-day circuit riders, the report described a va-

Leo Nieto was a Methodist clergy leader in *"la lucha,"* the struggle for social justice. He offended Anglos and conservative Hispanics in his outspoken partisanship on behalf of the citrus workers in Texas, but he was admired by those fighting for the rights of the workers. *(Photo courtesy of United Methodist Archives and History)*

riety of projects in various stages of vision and completion. This bigger picture gave inspiration and pride to Methodist readers.

Building on the growing awareness of the problems of urban areas in the U.S., the National Division reported the ways in which the church was working in partnership with both congregations and programs in various cities. The overall message it wanted to send was that The Methodist Church was playing an important role in the urban life of the country. From the point of view of the staff, this was very true. Travel and correspondence were demanding; projects and personalities differed greatly. But in contrast to the world mission work, which was looking for new models, many of the National Division projects had always been driven by long-established institutions or communities. The actual problems of the cities and rural areas might be somewhat different, but the *method* of responding was not. At the same time, the shortcomings of the decentralized nature of the work gave real truth to the report statement, "There isn't a Methodist in the nation who knows all that is going on in this unit alone."[31]

As societal conditions and values received increasing pressures and challenges in the press, in speeches, or even on the political front, no one in the division — staff, field workers, or board members — was charged with developing an overall response. In the short run, this omission presented no problems. But the long-term results would bring a more mixed review. If part of the identity of Methodism was its connectedness, its decentralized national ministries gave an anecdotal identity. Reading the report from the National Division reveals that the church was very aware of questions being raised about inclusion of various ethnic groups, the role of women, sensitivity to persons who were disabled, and other oppressed groups that were finally finding a voice. But the nature of the ministry, especially after the change in the organization of the Woman's Division, made it easy for local churches to stay disconnected. This, in turn, defused any pressure to have more overarching discussions about the systemic changes. When these discussions did happen, there was no immediate way to translate them into the church's mission.

Other attempts to respond to the changes and pressures brought short-term results but had a more mixed long-term legacy. Jack Rogers, who spent most of his life working for National Division ministries, was critical of some of the attempts made by the division in those years. Because the church wanted to empower the very people whom many of these agencies served, he saw that they sometimes gave jobs to people who were not yet ready to manage or to carry such a broad responsibility. In some cases, property deteriorated. Support for these newly empowered persons was often lacking within the established structures. Other shifts during the era also affected the way that many of the institutions operated. The board wanted to move away from funding institutions to funding programs. This meant that staff persons at the various agencies often had to do more fund raising, taking time away from other supervisory activities.

Since the deaconesses were part of the National Division, they also were affected by the staff realignment. In 1965, the Commission on Deaconess Work, a denominational body that was advisory to the division, initiated a self-study to look at the question of what was an appropriate appointment and how it related to congregations. Other questions were also studied — administrative ones that looked at the needs of retirement funds for a group that had received abysmally low salaries, for the most part, during its members' service; and pragmatic ones that questioned the future of the role in the church as fewer women chose that path of service.

No easy answers were found. Even so, deaconesses continued to fill important positions in many agencies of the church.

The National Division related to the mission conferences within the U.S., which comprised Alaska Mission and Oklahoma Indian Mission conferences. As noted, a major development in Alaska was the university, although missionaries continued their work among Native Americans there. The Oklahoma Indian Mission Conference (OIMC) had continued to grow through the 1950s and 1960s and in 1968 reached its apogee at 12,000 members. The first Native American to receive a degree from a Methodist school of theology was Robert Pinezaddelby, who was graduated by Perkins School of Theology in 1953. He served as pastor and district superintendent in the OIMC.[32]

In other places, the ministry with the Lumbees continued. Some Lumbees became part of the Methodist Episcopal Church in 1900. Ten churches with several hundred members were located in Robeson County, North Carolina, and one of them, Prospect, at one time was reported to have more Native American members than any church in North America. The Lumbee community, though small, showed its sense of dignity and power in 1958 when it broke up a Ku Klux Klan rally in Robeson County. Two Klan leaders were convicted of inciting a riot and sent to prison.[33]

Hispanic Women

Hispanic Methodist women began to become more visible by 1960 at the beginning of what was called "years of the Liberation Movement." To be sure, women had been active in several conferences since the 1939 union. Elida García de Falcón had translated the Woman's Division program book into Spanish, beginning in 1943 and continuing through 1964, assisted by her daughter, Clotilde Falcón Náñez, who was a member of the Woman's Division from 1964 to 1968. In 1952, Mary Lou Santillán (later Baert) became the first woman missionary sent from the Río Grande Conference. She went to Cortazar in rural Guanajuato state, México, where she taught Bible studies and led worship. She then served in México City on the church's Board of Christian Education under Manuel Flores. She wrote curriculum materials for youth and children. After that she was transferred to Saltillo and worked at Centro Social Roberts. Finally, she returned to México City and helped to establish a Board of Literature and Publications for the Mexican church. She trained editors and writers and

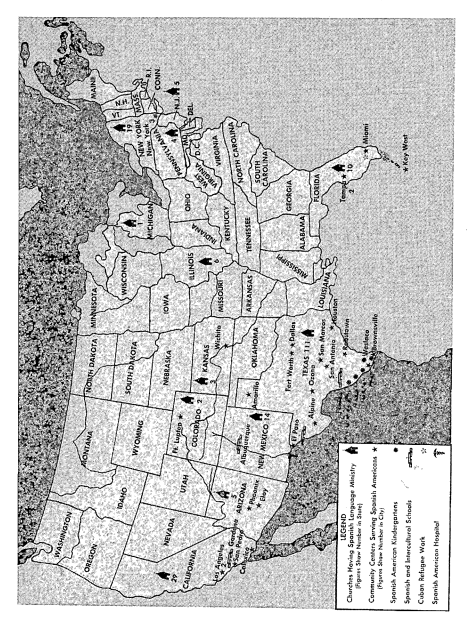

This 1964 map shows that Methodists had ministries with Hispanics in the Southwest and West who had a long presence in the U.S. but also with the new immigrant Puerto Ricans in the East, other Hispanics in the Midwest, and Cuban refugees in Florida. (*Map courtesy of United Methodist Archives and History*)

LEGEND

Churches Having Spanish Language Ministry ★
(Figures Show Number in State)

Community Centers Serving Spanish Americans ★
(Figures Show Number in City)

Spanish American Kindergartens

Spanish and Intercultural Schools

Cuban Refugee Work

Spanish American Hospital

Elida García de Falcón, Clotilde Falcón Náñez, and Minerva Garza

A remarkable line of Hispanic women gave leadership to developments in the Río Grande Conference. Elida García was born in Guerrero, México, in 1879. She was orphaned at the age of ten and emigrated to the U.S., where she went to school at Holding Institute and Southwest Texas State College. She married Antonio Falcón. A teacher, writer, and poet, she was the first to translate the Woman's Division program book into Spanish, accomplishing this task in 1943. She continued this work with her daughter, Clotilde Falcón Náñez, until 1970.

Clotilde Falcón was born in Río Grande City, Texas, in 1908. She received her undergraduate degree in Spanish from the University of Texas and a master's degree in Ibero-American civilization from Southern Methodist University. She taught in public schools in Texas and also at Trinity University and Pan American University. She married Alfredo Náñez and taught in conference and jurisdictional schools of Christian mission. From 1960 to 1962 she served as jurisdictional secretary of publications and was a member of the Woman's Division from 1964 to 1968. She became president of the Río Grande Conference Women's Society of Christian Service (WSCS) in The United Methodist Church, serving in 1976 and 1977.

Minerva Náñez, the sister of Alfredo Náñez, was born in 1920. She married Oscar F. Garza. In 1944 she became the first person from the Southwest Mexican Conference, which later became the Río Grande Conference, to attend the South Central Jurisdiction school of mission. She led her district's first school of mission in 1945 and the first conference school of mission in 1958. She was an officer of the conference WSCS from 1944 to 1970. She held offices in other Hispanic organizations, including service as president of Union Femenil Cristiana de Texas, and was a member of the Church Women United executive council. In addition, she wrote historical articles on the history of Hispanic women for the Woman's Division.

Sources: *They Went Out Not Knowing: 100 Women in Mission* (New York: General Board of Global Ministries, 1986), pp. 15, 40, 46; Minerva N. Garza, "The Influence of Methodism on Hispanic Women Through Women's Societies," *Methodist History* 34 (January 1996): 78–89.

developed bibliographies of available material in Spanish. She returned to the U.S. in 1965. Hispanic women were generating young leaders during the 1960s who were to serve the mission of the church in many different capacities in future years.[34]

A Turning Point: The 1964 Restructure

While each decade in the life of The Methodist Church brought with it changes in structure, the most profound changes for the mission work were those adopted in the 1960s. Previous changes had been important— sometimes at the national level, as in 1952, and sometimes at the local level, as legislation in 1956 continued to help local women's units shape their work to match the priorities of the national office more easily and to move gradually away from groups like the Ladies Aid that no longer fit the definitions of service groups.

In 1960, the Woman's Division recommended to the board that the division be authorized to restructure, with the aim of creating an office of general secretary, making it similar to other divisions of the board. Previously only the other divisions of the board had general secretaries to head them, and in the Woman's Division the heads of each section had been designated as executive secretaries, functioning collegially in making decisions. The system worked well, but it was different from that used in the other divisions. In addition, it gave the women more voices on the floor of General Conference, since all executives had speaking privileges. Since fewer than 10 percent of the voting conference delegates were female, the women felt that having five possible speakers instead of one helped give a little gender balance. Writing about it later, Thelma Stevens noted, "The new policy . . . gave the division one voice at General Conference. Men thought that was appropriate and so it came to be."[35]

As a follow-up to the discussion begun there, in 1963 the Board of Missions named a special committee to study and recommend further structuring changes. The committee was chaired by the president of the board, Bishop Richard Raines, and was composed of staff and elected members of the board.[36] In its discussions, the committee evaluated the functioning of the board, noting several problems: dual administration for programs outside the U.S., multiple approaches to local churches in the U.S., lack of opportunity for board members to be involved in policy, and relation of churches outside the U.S. to other boards and agencies of the church. At the same time, the group agreed that the Woman's Division needed to be preserved and listed several ways of strengthening it: increasing women members of the board and requiring that two of the four principal administrative positions be occupied by women; requiring that one-third of the supervisory staff be women; and requiring that at least 40 percent of the board elected staff be women.[37] The final proposal included these requirements along with the recommendation for a general secretary for the whole board, a unified mission administration, and a Joint Commission for Education and Cultivation. The deaconesses were put under the jurisdiction of the National Division. Finally, to protect control of their financial responsibilities, the Woman's Division was allowed to choose what projects in the work of the World Division and National Division it wished to support and to allocate those funds for a prescribed period. The sending function of the division was discontinued, however. Instead, all program administration of the projects was lodged in either World or National divisions, with these new entities designated as the sending agencies.

The recommendations represented some compromises and movement toward streamlining administrative work at a time when such aspects of the church's work were increasingly scrutinized. At the same time, the finished product was difficult for many to accept. Tracey Jones remembered it as "tricky to bring in the work of the women."[38] Thelma Stevens wrote, "Pros and cons were heard, at least they were expressed."[39] Further, she explained that the safeguarding attempts were only partial. Even with them, the reduced size of the board and staff meant that men still had a numerical majority on the board and in all units except for the Woman's Division. The previous pattern had been that units functioning on behalf of the whole church, other than those in the Woman's Division, had tended to exclude women. It was hard for the women to trust that this would change overnight, even with the partial guarantees. Board member (and Woman's Division member) Virginia Laskey later told staff members that notes from the meetings had mysteriously been lost.[40] Even with these grave concerns, Stevens and others saw as positive the discussions that led to the provisions for greater gender equity in the top administrative positions.

Despite the misgivings of some of the women, the proposed changes were approved by the Board of Missions by a vote of 84–7, with 53 either absent or abstaining. (The changes still had to be approved by General Conference.)

Other minutes and reports carry evidence of the sense of loss for many of the women because of the administrative changes. One report noted that in the past staff members who had leadership in division-related projects were often invited to the annual meetings of the board, especially when one of the plenaries featured that part of the mission. This practice worked because, "They were 'our workers' and that was 'our work.' But suddenly in 1964, they were all shifted." In some cases, men took over the supervisory positions, giving a different feel to the work. Even retirees quickly noticed the changes, because small things such as monthly letters from the Committee on Spiritual Life no longer arrived. Lifelong workers for the Woman's Division felt cut off. Even when board staff (nearly all of whom were men) visited the retirement homes (and they rarely did), the women there did not feel that the men were a connection to the Woman's Division. As the new divisions developed their own pattern of meetings, reports, and even celebrations, the Woman's Division members felt even more disconnected from the work they were funding.

While the losses were great and felt by women for a long time, the administrative changes did give more focus to the work. All work outside the U.S. was under the World Division, with the work grouped in smaller units under a single area secretary. The Woman's Division had three sections: Program and Education for Christian Mission, Christian Social Relations, and Finance. This structure helped Christian Social Relations become more prominent and to continue to give leadership at a time when society was examining many of the areas in which it specialized. The new structure was designed to reduce the competition between U.S. social relations and projects outside the U.S.

At the time of the restructure, there were 1,468 missionaries, of whom 381 were single women. When the churches united in 1939, the Woman's Division related to 1,839 missionaries and deaconesses. This number went down to 578 women missionaries outside the U.S. in 1950 and continued to decrease noticeably. Although many factors changed the number of single women entering missionary service — once one of the few fields offering many ministry options — some pointed to the recruitment changes that were accelerated by the restructure as the major factor in this decline. Previously, the Woman's Division had followed up interest at the local and conference levels, inviting women to special events and giving them a chance to learn more about the work. When the division was no longer directly involved, this level of personal solicitation was also lost.[41] In addition, women who had been raised with an awareness of the Woman's Division and its work no longer felt a direct link between their choices of service and the organization.

The changes had influence beyond even the work of the board. In Korea, the missionaries continued to relate to the Korean Methodist Church, with its structures and committees. But Margaret Billingsley reported in 1967 the difference in the women's ability to participate that followed the reorganization three years before. Conference members no longer considered women who served under the former Woman's Division as possibilities to serve on committees. One member announced on the floor of the conference that it was no longer necessary to have anything that was considered to be woman's work. His comments and the work in question were referred to a committee that was composed entirely of men.

Billingsley was quick to note that the issue actually went even deeper. As the board policy had pushed for allowing the indigenous churches to give leadership, missionaries had held back in ways that were almost uncomfortable. Many had entered the field because they wanted to be part of shaping ministry and service within the church. They found it unnatural not to take a role in shaping the church and community. It was a kind of self-denial that no one had anticipated in being part of missionary service.

This effect of a structural change in the U.S. church on mission in other parts of the world was another of the difficulties that continued to be part of the crosscultural dialogue. As questions arose in U.S. society about race and gender, they were mirrored in the structures and concerns of the church. When these structural changes did not match the values and mores of churches in other cultures, no one quite knew what to do. Trying to avoid the cultural imperialism of the past, the women sometimes hesitated to apply the same pressures they were willing to use in their own setting. But the result, as Billingsley's comments indicate, was unsatisfactory and even questionable.

General Conference accepted the changes the board had proposed. It approved the plan that organized the Board of Missions Board of Managers with five bishops; members elected by jurisdictional conferences; twenty-one laymen, at least three from each jurisdiction; twenty-one women, at least three from each jurisdiction, elected by the Woman's Division; and six young people, evenly split between men and women. General Conference also voted to add a list of fifteen functions to help explain the work of the board, in addition to "the aim of missions," a summary that was already in the *Discipline:* "The supreme aim of missions is to make the Lord Jesus Christ known to all peoples in all lands as their divine Savior."[42]

The functions were to help persons come to a knowledge of Jesus Christ as Lord and Savior; to respond to God's action in Christ through engaging in religious, educational, social, medical, and agricultural work in every part of the world; to promote and support all phases of missionary and church extension activity in the U.S. and other countries; and to allow the board to have oversight of all this work and to coordinate it; to make policy; to recruit and train workers for it; to maintain institutions; to raise funds; and to engage in ecumenical activities. (Curiously, the functions used some suspiciously archaic language, like "determine the fields to be occupied.")

As if that were not enough, the *Discipline* also specified functions for the Woman's Division, which seemed to make women's work indirect and tangential. Women were to interpret mission, to provide resources and opportunities for mission, "promote plans for securing funds" (rather than raising funds per se), "to project plans toward leadership development of women" (instead of simply developing leadership), and so on.[43]

The Second Charter on Racial Justice

In 1962, the Woman's Division adopted a second Charter on Racial Justice and sent it on for adoption by General Conference in 1964. With the passage, the division requested to work jointly with the Department and the Division of Human Relations and Economic Affairs of the Board of Christian Social Concerns. In 1964 the Woman's Division proposed programs to merge all conferences of the Central Jurisdiction into regional jurisdictions. Another major area of concern was the racial integration of all institutions of The Methodist Church. Local churches were also tasked to develop inclusive membership and fellowship.

The inclusive nature of these goals, continuing the long tradition of the Woman's Division, did not receive the full support of the church. For example, in 1965 the Section of Christian Social Relations of the Woman's Division had to carry on alone in consultations to support merger of the Central Jurisdiction conferences because some area bishops and district superintendents refused to support the Board of Christian Social

Betsy Ewing

Ewing came out of the Methodist Episcopal Church, South, although it became part of The Methodist Church when she was a teenager. As she was growing up, she planned to go to Scarritt College. She not only completed her education there but stayed on for fifteen years to work with alumni as well.

Even though she went to a high school where students were segregated by gender and worked most of her life with women's organizations, Ewing and her work are part of the church's struggles with gender and gender roles.

When the Board of Missions went through its major restructure in 1964, it "radically changed the internal workings of the board and relationships." Before men had "done their thing" at their headquarters in Philadelphia, women had "done theirs" in New York. She accepted the invitation to head up the deaconess program. The deaconesses had always been women, but as the board integrated various programs, it also opened this field of service for men, calling them "home missionaries."

She also saw the differences as two systems of missions were brought together. The men had always been part of helping to raise the money through developing lists of friends and donors. Women had raised money through the local church groups and the structures that were in place at every level of the church. She saw the positive way the restructuring helped to unify missions. One of her concerns was communication. When she was growing up, she always heard people complain, "Oh, those people in Nashville!" She wanted to be a liaison, to continue to communicate with people, even those who seemed to feel that the board was always dictating all the decisions.

Always a leader, she attended her first international meeting in West Berlin in 1963. She wanted to host a meeting in the U.S. and invited the organization to come. That meant, however, that she had to bring together a national organization to prepare for the 1966 meeting. Later she went on to be president of Diakonia, an ecumenical experience that she felt really helped and enriched her work on the board, where eventually she became an administrative executive in New York.

Ewing appreciated the variety of organizations she worked with during her ministry—Scarritt-Bennett, the Board of Missions, Diakonia—all doing the same thing in different ways. As she looked back over her work, she noted how rewarding it had been. She was committed to what she was doing, got a lot of support, and found people to be very gracious. The challenge of working with people was one that she took on and mastered.

Source: Interview with Ewing by Melynn Glusman, January 18, 2001.

Theressa Hoover began as a field worker for the Woman's Division and eventually ascended to its top leadership position. She consistently asserted the rights of African Americans and other minorities and pressed for the church's attention to women, children, and youth. *(Photo courtesy of United Methodist Archives and History)*

Concerns in its sponsorship. A Racial Witness Relief Fund was established to aid pastors and others who suffered economic retaliation for their work on behalf of racial justice. But no funding mechanism was provided. Lack of wholehearted monetary support was also given to the National Council of the Churches of Christ in the U.S.A., whose Commission on Religion and Race depended on denominations for its funding. In The Methodist Church, such funding was left to general agencies to give whatever they could from their budgets. The $10,000 contributed by the Methodists, in contrast to $60,000 from the United Presbyterians or even the $5,000 from the much smaller Evangelical United Brethren Church, was an embarrassment to the board, which worked so hard on these concerns. Such funding actions sent a mixed message. With no clear authority other than General Conference, staff members and boards were viewed as being in the position to speak for the whole church, even if technically they did not. Local church members who did not support such actions made their displeasure known.

Undeterred by the foot-dragging of the denomination, the Woman's Division continued to look for ways to witness to its ideals of racial understanding and integration. For a long time, the women had used stockholdings as a way to witness to their social beliefs; policies prohibited the ownership of alcohol, tobacco, or munitions stock. As it sought ways to make meaningful statements about values in a society increasingly aware of racial tension, the division used Kodak and General Motors stock to call attention to the needs for greater racial domestic justice.

Abolition of the Central Jurisdiction

In 1964, some Central Jurisdiction conferences began transferring into other jurisdictions. James S. Thomas, an African American, was elected bishop and assigned to the Iowa Area in the North Central Jurisdiction. Changes began taking place in other jurisdictions as well, but no changes were taking place in the South. Meanwhile, nonviolent protestors were attacked in Selma, Alabama, and other places; Congress passed the 1964 Civil Rights Act and the 1965 Voting Rights Act; and two bishops,

At Selma, Alabama, March 9, 1965, John Lewis (light coat, center), leader of the Student Nonviolent Coordinating Committee, cringes as a state trooper swings his club during a protest march for civil rights. *(Photo © Topham/ The Image Works, used with permission of the Image Works, Inc.)*

James S. Thomas

Thomas was born in Orangeburg, South Carolina, and was ordained and became an elder in the South Carolina Conference of the Central Jurisdiction in 1944. After serving as a pastor, he taught at Gammon Theological Seminary. He became associate director of the Department of Educational Institutions of the Board of Education of The Methodist Church in 1953. During these years, he wrote thoughtful articles about the Central Jurisdiction, suggesting that its existence contradicted American principles of equality.

Thomas was chair of the Committee of Five, which was created by the 1960 General Conference to develop a plan of desegregation for the denomination. The committee was the group that initiated the call to the Central Jurisdiction's leaders to discuss desegregation. The meeting that took place in Cincinnati in March 1962 was decisive in the approach the church finally took toward desegregation. By rejecting the previous plan that divided the Central Jurisdiction among the other jurisdictions, the conference effectively called for the abolition of the Central Jurisdiction.

Thomas was elected bishop in 1964 and was assigned to the Des Moines Area of the Iowa Conference in the North Central Jurisdiction. He subsequently served as bishop of the East Ohio Conference, from which he retired in 1988. He published *Methodism's Racial Dilemma* in 1992.

Sources: Nolan B. Harmon, "Thomas, James Samuel," *Encyclopedia of World Methodism*, 1: 2336; Peter C. Murray, "The Racial Crisis in The Methodist Church," *Methodist History* 26 (October 1987): 3–14; James S. Thomas, "The Christian Bases of Race Relations," *Central Christian Advocate* 130 (February 1, 1955): 4–5, 22.

African-American Charles F. Golden and white James K. Mathews, were denied entrance to Galloway Methodist Church in Jackson, Mississippi.[44] These events placed tremendous pressure on U.S. Methodists, who seemed to be intentionally delaying ending segregation in the body of Christ.

The 1964 General Conference approved a procedure that would lead to union with the Evangelical United Brethren Church (EUB). Implicit in the plan was the abolition of the Central Jurisdiction. EUBs were vehemently opposed to the separation allowed in the Central Jurisdiction. But because differences within The Methodist Church were still strong, the Council of Bishops attempted to mediate between Southerners and the rest of the church. Their effort failed. A new Commission of Twenty-Four

James S. Thomas. *(Photo courtesy of United Methodist Archives and History)*

created at the 1964 General Conference drew up an "omnibus" resolution that would transfer the black annual conferences into predominantly white annual conferences. The major objection on the part of African Americans like John T. King and Dennis R. Fletcher, both members of the commission, and of Bishop Charles Golden was that the resolution set only a "target date" of 1972 for the final merger of Southern conferences and did not mandate it. Nevertheless, the resolution was approved at a special 1966 General Conference held to work toward the Methodist-EUB merger.

The resolution still had to be approved by a two-thirds majority by the annual conferences. It barely received approval in the white Southeastern Jurisdiction, but three black annual conferences presided over by Golden failed to approve it. Other black annual conferences approved the resolution, however, and since the merger of the two denominations was also approved, the Central Jurisdiction ended in 1968 as part of the merger.[45]

In 1967, while the debate over racism in The Methodist Church was still going on, James M. Lawson helped to organize a conference of black Methodists in Cincinnati. Addressed by James Farmer, the founder of the

Congress on Racial Equality, and Stokely Carmichael, the conference wrestled with questions about the role of blacks in the church. Although the group was critical of the failure of the church to support urban blacks in their mission, it also struck a repentant note: "We said at Cincinnati that for too long we have played the game of being churchmen in The Methodist Church; participated in the politics of seeking prestige and position without sacrifice and obedience." Creating a new organization, Black Methodists for Church Renewal (BMCR), the conference raised questions that would continue to preoccupy the church in implementing desegregation, particularly the hiring of minorities at The Methodist Publishing House. The disappearance of the Central Jurisdiction did not mean the end of the struggle for true racial justice within the church.[46]

Using the Connection for Interpretation

By the 1960s, the church had developed a complex system for interpreting mission to local churches. The Interboard Committee on Missionary Education worked to see that mission was included in the curriculum resources created by the Methodist Board of Education. In 1964, the Board of Missions actually created its own office for curriculum resources, which produced not only print materials but also slides, photographs, and other audiovisuals. The National Division Office of Campus Ministry cooperated with the Division of Higher Education of the Methodist Board of Education to educate those in the Methodist Student Movement about mission and to recruit missionaries from colleges. Linking to past ties with the ecumenical movement, the office supported international students and had summer projects.

The Joint Commission on Education and Cultivation published books in astonishingly high runs: *The United States and the New Nations*, for example, sold 46,000 copies. Similarly, the number of filmstrips had increased so that 13,000 were distributed in 1965. Films were being produced in cooperation with TRAFCO. Some were done ecumenically. The photo laboratory made almost 15,000 prints in 1965, used not only in board magazines but also in curriculum materials and secular publications. (The number of annual conference papers was then very small.) The commission also had its own news service, department of field interpretation (which oversaw the missionaries' itinerating to local churches in the U.S. while on leave), and the Advance. In 1965, a quarter of the income for the

World and National divisions, nearly $9 million, was received from the Advance. The commission also did educational work: It cooperated in ecumenical conferences on the Christian world mission, in which more than 2,000 Methodists participated in 1965.

The World Division also worked in mass communication and global literacy. Much of the literacy work was done through the World Council of Churches. Publications in Portuguese were being produced for use in Mozambique and Angola, and the board was exploring the possibility of printing materials in the Kru language of Liberia. Besides the board work in literacy, some of the churches in developing countries were doing their own literacy work. In particular, Alfalit was working in the rural areas of Bolivia by 1968. The EUB work in Sierra Leone and Methodist work in Liberia was being consolidated. British and U.S. missions were cooperating on literacy in the Sudan United Mission in Nigeria. Staff member Doris Hess reported that radio studios had been established in twelve countries, from Korea to Brazil. She worked with the World Association for Christian Communication to train Christians globally to work on mass communications and to produce programs. Shortwave radio stations had been established in the Philippines and in Addis Ababa, Ethiopia, by 1968. The latter had the capacity to broadcast as far as India.

By 1968, the board was beginning to move from film to a new medium. "The Action of the General Conference on Civil Disobedience" was produced on videotape and distributed to conference and district meetings.[47]

Conflict over Vietnam

The 1964 presidential election was termed a landslide as the incumbent, Lyndon Johnson, was aided by depictions of his opponent as a trigger-happy, nuclear war proponent. No mention was made during the campaign of the advisers who were making their way to Southeast Asia to become involved in various national struggles. But in the months following the election, the involvement of U.S. troops in Vietnam became more widely known.

Much of the response in the U.S. came under the leadership of the Board of Christian Social Concerns, but the Board of Missions responded as well. In particular, the Woman's Division began to organize educational materials and discussions about the facts of the war. And in their locations throughout the U.S. and the rest of the world, missionaries felt the impact in greater and lesser degrees. Missionaries in Asian countries very early became aware of what was happening in Vietnam. In Japan, fifth-grade missionary children were debating the intervention of the U.S. as early as 1964. Missionary John W. Krummel wrote in 1968: "Vietnam! The most ubiquitous topic of conversation in Tokyo today."[48] Many missionaries quickly became involved in protests and marches against the war. From their vantage point, so much nearer the conflict than people in the U.S., the involvement looked to be a big mistake and a tragic misreading of the political situation. Some missionaries did favor U.S. policy, however.

For protesting missionaries, participating in marches and protests did not mean they were breaking the pledge they had taken. Certainly the actions were very political, but they were aimed at the U.S. Government, not the government of the host countries. In the Philippines, missionaries also staged protests at the U.S. embassy, being clear that their message was to their own government, not the Filipinos. When Frank Kuhlman was asked whether the board had ordered him to stop, he replied that if they had, he would have felt he had to leave church service because he and his family felt so strongly about their opposition to the war.

The war was experienced most strongly by those serving in Asia. Kuhlman noted that being in Asia increased the sense of outrage that Americans were killing untold numbers of Asians and continually trying to justify it. Missionaries who became involved in protests were a small portion of the total number around the world, but their actions and witness became an alternative source of information to those in the U.S. church.

By 1968, the war in Southeast Asia had affected U.S. life in untold ways. The U.S. church had no consensus to offer about race, urban problems, war, or the role of women. All were being contested in the society at large and in the church. Even with conflict on the streets and in its committees, efforts to make life better for people continued under the leadership of the Board of Missions. The board would be taking new form as the life of The Methodist Church ended and a new church was born from the merger with the Evangelical United Brethren — The United Methodist Church.

CHAPTER 7

The Church — Mirror or Beacon?

*I*N 1905, John R. Mott published *The Evangelization of the World in This Generation.* Such an ambitious statement needed explanation, even in a time and place that were quite optimistic about the future of Christianity. In defining what he meant, he noted that he was not expecting the conversion of the world, but "to bring the Gospel to bear on unsaved men."[1] The distinction that he makes is important in evaluating the mission of the church. While he expected that conversions would follow the preaching of the gospel, he cautioned against determining the success of the mission by numbers of conversions. "We are not responsible for the results of our work, however, but for our fidelity and thoroughness."

"This generation" of Mott had passed even by the birth of The Methodist Church — and yet another had come and gone by its end. But an institution can and does evaluate itself. Mott's words remained imbedded in the thinking, if not the writing, of many associated with mission. They believed that the outward results were not always the full indicator of the goals or even the accomplishments of those bringing the gospel to the world. To be true to their vision, an evaluation must first be made on their own terms.

On this level it is not difficult to give strong positive marks to the Board of Missions of The Methodist Church for its accomplishments. Both in the United States and abroad, personnel ran schools and hospitals, preached the gospel, and helped in the development of societal institutions. While the numbers of persons paid through the Board of Missions declined over that period, the change was part of a plan to allow local churches and institutions to assume more and more of the responsibility and day-to-day operations. In short, the church announced a plan for its mission, gave particular attention and emphasis to allowing the work to evolve into local care, and proceeded to go out and to the best of its ability implement that plan. Adopting the language that casts history as story gives a particular view to what happened. Although the narrative is full of details of interest, the plotline appears rather thin and unpromising of the tension and conflict necessary to maintain interest in the sense of a traditional novel. Theologically, The Methodist Church remained quite consistent for its entire existence. Further, the goals of the board, stated so succinctly in 1939, remained at the heart of all the work and discussion:

- making the Lord Jesus Christ known to all peoples,
- persuading them to become his disciples,
- gathering these disciples into Christian churches,
- enlisting them in the building of the kingdom of God,
- cooperating with these churches,
- promoting world Christian fellowship, and
- bringing to bear on all human life the spirit and principles of Christ.

Given the outside forces and the possibilities for rethinking the task in the face of many difficulties and changes, the church held fast to its purpose.

A main feature of classic story lines, however, is the way the main character overcomes the challenges and disruptions of life. Viewed on that level, the story offers far more scope for evaluation. Several themes that have continually recurred in each era of this twenty-nine-year span can be examined and evaluated. These themes or questions include: How did the *structures* created for The Methodist Church help or hinder the work of mission? How much of the *policy* of indigenization was actual reality? Was it truly accepted by the missionaries and by the church as a whole? What were its ramifications? How did the *role* of missionaries change, and where did those changes come from? The 1964 board integration significantly shifted *power*. What impact did this have as the church prepared for yet another merger?

Strengths and Weaknesses of Methodist Structure

The 1939 reuniting of three bodies that had been apart for one hundred years did not erase one of the major differences that had driven them apart. Attitudes about race had caused the split one hundred years before. Attitudes and actions about race still differed widely when these bodies came back together. Rather than be deterred in their unification efforts, leaders made a compromise, one that had long-lasting ramifications for The Methodist Church. For one thing, the issue of race was not confronted directly. Creating the Central Jurisdiction and continuing it throughout the life of The Methodist Church allowed many members to ignore or feel comfortable in their attitudes about the underlying racism of church and society. In many cases, they could ignore that racism when they participated in church matters. Equally important, the regional structures — jurisdictions — that were created in part to deal with this racism had a mixed impact on the growth and development of the church as a whole. On the positive side, they allowed for more participation of persons beyond their efforts and work in the local churches. Both clergy and laypersons had an increased number of opportunities to exercise leadership talents. More programs, gatherings, and services of worship all became possible. The connectional nature of the church was strengthened on a regional basis. In the Central Jurisdiction, many members who might otherwise have been denied leadership opportunities because of their race also had the chance to bring their gifts and talents to the church on a larger scale. But the separation delayed the kind of ordinary encounter for many lay and clergy across racial lines that might have provided a model for the larger U.S. society, which was struggling with the same issue.

Even more important, the separation into jurisdictions and the accompanying legislation divided the church in new ways. Bishops served regionally rather than nationally within the United States. Board members were elected throughout jurisdictions rather than nationally. Top agency staff was no longer elected but was chosen by each agency. Reunification arguably brought with it greater fragmentation than any of the uniting bodies had experienced previously.[2] The price for the continuing racism of the church was initially paid by African-American Methodists, who once again had evidence that they were not equal in the community of faith. For them and for all other Methodists, the costs of racism were a long-term fragmentation that had far-reaching consequences.

On an administrative level, the reuniting brought together staff from the three bodies. Driven by the immediacy of the Second World War and the strong leadership of Ralph Diffendorfer, the Board of Missions incorporated changes and growth with seemingly little difficulty. Reports and analyses were initially dominated by decisions about the war, then by action for the recovery efforts. The structure was the tool for addressing the

Annual conference and jurisdictional boundaries of The Methodist Church, 1956. The heavy lines show the borders of the jurisdictions, from left to right: Western, South Central, North Central, Southeastern, and Northeastern. As the inset shows, the Central Jurisdiction, which covered the entire continental U.S., had slightly different boundaries for its annual conferences. *(Map courtesy of United Methodist Archives and History)*

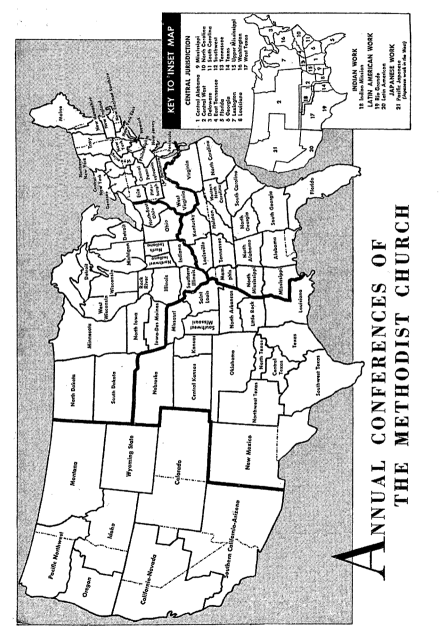

ANNUAL CONFERENCES OF THE METHODIST CHURCH

KEY TO INSET MAP

CENTRAL JURISDICTION

1 Central Alabama
2 Central West
3 Delaware
4 East Tennessee
5 Florida
6 Georgia
7 Lexington
8 Louisiana

9 Mississippi
10 North Carolina
11 South Carolina
12 Southwest
13 Tennessee
14 Texas
15 Upper Mississippi
16 Washington
17 West Texas

INDIAN WORK
18 Indian Mission

LATIN AMERICAN WORK
19 Rio Grande
20 Latin American

JAPANESE WORK
21 Pacific Japanese
(Japanese work in the West)

more immediate concerns of personnel and property. Fine tuning of the tool itself was delayed for several years.

But by 1968, the impact of the changes initiated in 1939 was much more visible. The division by race and region that had begun with the new structure had spread to gender and other forms of identity and community. The resulting power of the board from the 1939 regionalization of bishops was perceived to be a concern by a significant number in the church. Conversations about the ways to curb that power became more frequent, often detracting from some of the real accomplishments of the boards and agencies. Seen in the larger context of a society that was also much more visibly aware of its fragmentation and diversity, the church on this issue was yet again a mirror of the tensions and issues of the late 1960s, despite significant efforts of some groups, including the Board of Missions, to provide leadership. The church's form of regional organization intensified rather than minimized the fracturing of the social structure. To a large extent, however, the church generally identified the issues that were creating the tensions as those specific social issues, whether racism or sexism, rather than as coming from the very core of its being, its own organization, its own form of blaming the victim. This avoidance of its internal nature sometimes served to marginalize and politicize those who took on the social battles. The power struggles over race or gender, for example, were seen as having been caused by oversensitivity to race or gender rather than inhering in the structure of the institution as well as the society in which it existed.

At the same time, from its beginning, the Woman's Division, in particular, had been looking ahead, recognizing that institutional change needed to accompany ordinary changes in attitudes. The concerns that led to the Racial Charter and beyond came from an awareness that society was already fractured and split in ways that had long gone unacknowledged. Leadership from the Woman's Division, supported and informed by work of the other divisions, gave the church a voice and a visible presence during the time of change and upheaval. Theologically, the women were prepared. In working ecumenically in areas of race and justice, the empowerment from the board and the connectional nature of the church further enhanced the leadership of Methodists.

Thus the new structure, implemented in a complexity of national and international events, worked in ways its proponents could not have seen. Designed to empower regional groups and even to help maintain power where it had always been lodged, the structure eventually allowed more national backing for efforts that undermined the power of the status quo. Further, its regional, interest-group nature became the example for those desiring change (women and various ethnic groups, for instance) to find ways to organize and work in caucuses and task groups that clearly defined their own interests.

The Powerful Minority of Women

Related to the effects of the reunification structure on the national/regional character of the church were the specific provisions for the Woman's Division. The first assault on its separate funding powers had come as early as 1884 in the Methodist Episcopal Church, but the women had managed to maintain their financial autonomy.[3] At the time of reunification, when other denominations were combining the general and women's missionary boards and budgets, the women remained firm about the need for separate organizations and managed again to keep their financial autonomy. Tight structure and specific programs gave the programs of the Woman's Division a recognized place in local churches and conferences. With such an identity, financial giving stayed sufficient to allow the women to maintain a significant level of programming in mission, both within the U.S. and globally. The women used clearly defined lines of communication between local and national offices so that information and education materials flowed to local groups. National assemblies and leadership training opportunities assured commitment to the programs planned nationally and enhanced personal relationships across conference and jurisdictional lines. Careful planning and moving ahead with mission only when the money was in hand led to the perception that the women were the ones with money. This perception had consequences.

Mission work through the Woman's Division tended to be tied to institutions and agencies with a history, whether in the U.S. or abroad. The price of stability was a reluctance to venture out too far into new programming. Money was there, but when new projects were being planned, it was often the World Division that responded more readily with money rather than the Woman's Division. While the women gained a reputation in some areas for being "liberal," in terms of finance they operated with "conservative" principles. This variance sometimes created friction in local areas, but it had very specific benefits for women, who still did not oc-

Thelma Stevens, a Southerner, was the head of the section on Christian Social Relations of the Woman's Division. She developed policies that ensured racial integration in Woman's Division events, though the denomination resisted her efforts to make all the church's national meetings integrated. She also led Methodist women in gaining equity within the Board of Missions and in working on larger issues of justice and poverty. *(Photo courtesy of United Methodist Archives and History)*

cupy many positions of importance. Having the money put the women in a position of relative power within the church structure. Throughout the life of The Methodist Church, women were a minority on boards and agencies, but they maintained both a higher profile and much more actual power on the Board of Missions. On the one hand, this reality continued some gender identification of mission as women's work and became a convenient place to funnel talented women. The desire of women to be active in the church did not have to "threaten" other boards when there was a specific place for them. On the other hand, the nature of keeping all mission work under one board prevented total "ghetto-ization." Men and women worked together. At its best, the board became a model of the way that power could be shared.

The reorganization of 1964 was a response to these realities and perceptions. Ironically, the loss of autonomy came only a year after *The Feminine Mystique* began to raise the consciousness of many North American women about power and control in society. The sensitivity of the larger society, as well as the dedication, memories, and work of the women themselves, kept the change from significantly affecting the numbers and even influence of the women who were active in the church; but it was experienced as real loss by many who lived through it. One might argue that the societal advances in understanding the potential of women and their contributions helped to minimize potential harmful results of the restructure. Women now had other opportunities to participate fully in the life of the church. But changing rules—such as allowing ordained women to be full members of the annual conference (1956)—did not mean that women enjoyed equal access to all parts of church structure. The reorganization, although in keeping with the church's philosophy, did not reflect the realities of power and access. In 1964, women still did not have equal status in either local churches or on national boards.

The Complex Situation of Methodist Women

Assessing the function of the Board of Missions to the developing role of women, beginning with the Second World War, remains a matter of theological perspective. Using midcentury Methodist theology, informed by such persons as Georgia Harkness, gives one such perspective. In these terms, Christianity functions to allow all human beings to develop their full potential as children of God even if it moves them beyond traditional roles and stereotypes.

The assumption of the Woman's Society of Christian Service (WSCS) and the Woman's Division itself was that women were eager for spiritual development, community service, and greater knowledge of the world. Magazines, study books, reading lists, speakers, and events educated women on complex issues of foreign policy, biblical interpretation, and problems within the U.S. While a segment of U.S. culture was being reminded weekly through television that *Father Knows Best*, Methodist women in leadership assumed that they were among an audience that was open and continually interested in education, service, and mission. Monthly meetings at the local level allowed women the possibility of staying in touch with issues. The women's groups of the uniting churches all brought similar histories of both education and action. Review of their history at assemblies and gatherings and naming names of leaders of the past kept before them a legacy of power and influence. This historical memory helped to keep the church in the forefront of possibilities of leadership and training for women.

Rose Thomas, center, was one of several African Americans who were sent by The Methodist Church to areas outside the U.S. in the 1950s and 1960s. Here she is shown with students in a primary school in Angola in 1961. African Americans became valuable representatives of the church in Africa during the turbulent period when countries were gaining their independence from colonial rulers. *(Photo courtesy of United Methodist Archives and History)*

Actual service in either "foreign" or "domestic" mission only intensified these possibilities. Particularly in missions outside the U.S., where they single-handedly ran schools and hospitals, women could exercise far more authority and power than was available in much of secular U.S. culture.[4] In domestic work as well, women not only ran institutions but also had many opportunities to participate in team ministries that carried responsibility. With this structure for its mission work, the church was modeling a more inclusive division of labor than was accepted in most of society.

To view this one branch of the church as merely a more comfortable place for women desiring positions of power would be to ignore the deeper dimension of the work. The life of The Methodist Church as a denomination divides almost exactly in half between a time when women were denied full membership and benefits as members of the ordained

Tracey K. Jones, Jr.

By the time Jones started his time with the board as a commissioned missionary, he already had overseas experience, having lived in Canton, China, for
eleven years while his father worked there with the YMCA.

Jones was among the first group of new missionaries for the new Methodist
Church; eight were commissioned by Bishop Arthur J. Moore in 1940. When he
finally left China, as did all the missionaries because of the Second World War,
he took with him perspectives on how more independent churches and institutions could evolve from the missionary structure.

Because he had the opportunity to develop greater language skills during
the war, when he was finally able to enter China again he went to west China,
spending a year as liaison with the bureau of foreign affairs of the Chinese
government. He was one of several missionaries who served in such secular
posts during the time of war recovery. Once he was released from his duties by
the government, he went to Nanking to resume work for the church. Recovery
work surrounded him. Always he worked with and under Chinese leaders who
had survived the war. Indigenization was not just a goal or a concept but a
pragmatic necessity.

Jones joined other missionaries in trying to make sure that their work and
any solutions they suggested fit into Chinese values. For example, personal
relationships were extremely important. Jones learned always to look for what
he thought of as "the Chinese solution." He tested himself not by how fast
things were going but by whether new leadership was evolving.

Leadership in postwar China was developing in ways that no one had really
envisioned. Jones remembered that he had watched Chiang Kai-shek and Mao
Zedong with U.S. General Albert C. Wedemeyer, drinking a toast to the new
China. At the time neither Jones nor anyone else really dreamed that it would
be Mao and his ideas that would emerge triumphant.

In the years that followed, Jones continued to work in Asia, serving six
years as Asia secretary of the Board of Missions. In his book *Our Mission Today* (1964), which sold a quarter of a million copies, he used China as an example of the way Christianity did not have to be defined with culture. He wrote
that Western Christians could learn from the Chinese, who had faced many
hardships as their churches were weakened, silenced, or manipulated. The
same year the book was published, Jones became associate general secretary
of the agency, the same time that the Board of Missions significantly restruc-
tured itself, changing the power dynamics between men and women.

As a leader of the Board of Missions, he believed that decentralization was
characteristic of creative missionary periods and worked hard to let each divi-

sion have as much autonomy as possible. Just as his book was not universally greeted with enthusiasm, so also Jones found that his ideas were controversial. The main obstacle was the differing worldviews within the church itself. Theological pluralism was matched by a political and social pluralism that was increasingly visible on international issues as well as issues within the United States. Others did not want to change the way things had been done. Jones's vision and life experiences gave him the stature needed to keep the church moving forward.

Sources: Interview with Jones by Ben Houston, January 18, 2001; articles, letters, and papers of Jones in United Methodist Archives and History.

clergy ranks and a time when they finally achieved it, though the number of those who chose ordination and full membership remained small. Although women could be ordained and preach, the very structure meant that such models were seen and experienced by only a few.[5] For women called to be in Christ's service, the most visible structure in which to interpret their call remained that of the Board of Missions. Validation and acceptance there freed their energies for the real work of evangelization and service.

On a counternote, one can look at the way the church as a whole adapted to the growing concerns over women, jobs, and greater equality. The beginnings of this awareness came during The Methodist Church era. Surprisingly, the Wesleyan Service Guild, established specifically for working women, did not become revitalized and grow as a result of the interests and pressures of society. The elements were in place to make an impact on society, but in this case, it did not happen in a dramatic way.[6]

Charges that the boards and agencies of the church were out of step with local churches — in this as in some of the international concerns — ignore other realities within Christianity, and Methodism in particular. At this time, relatively few pastors or even theologians were providing the necessary scholarly and pastoral support for a less misogynist view of women within the faith. While the Woman's Division provided the framework compatible to a growing understanding of the expanded possibilities for women, biblical studies and theological conversation that would have supported the framework were rarely found in local churches. Methodist students attending church-related liberal arts colleges had the opportunity to learn about biblical criticism and modern theology, but few local churches presented opportunities to study these disciplines on a regular basis for the laity.

This schizophrenic attitude about women and their role in the church in many ways left the Woman's Division isolated and feeling unheard and unheeded when the reorganization occurred in 1964.

Experience and Authority of Board and Staff

Empowered on behalf of the church, the board and its staff provided stability both of personnel and of policy throughout the period. Relating to the field personnel may have become easier with greater and greater communication capabilities and shrinking travel times, but it was still fraught with the difficulties that always exist when lines of authority are drawn among persons separated by distance. In general, those with authority for board or staff managed to walk a line that allowed greater power to missionaries at key times, while standing ready to make tough decisions at others. Examples that have been mentioned include decisions left to missionaries about evacuation and also decisions about buildings and institutions that were made by staff in consultation with on-site personnel. Both written and oral research reveal a pattern of generally good relations between the missionaries and the board and staff. This amity appears in part to have resulted from the open lines of communication and respect.

A major reason for the level of understanding and trust, however, was that staff area secretaries tended in this period to be chosen from among persons who had been missionaries in those areas of the world. The personal knowledge — of missionaries for the secretary and of secretaries for the nature of the work — lessened the possibility of tensions developing and helped to solve problems when they did. This attention to the relational aspects of the work paid benefits in smoother functioning for the work and ultimately in greater energy given for the work itself. The staff also benefitted from relative longevity of those filling most of the positions. The high level of competence of the personnel made long tenure positive rather than negative.

In addition, board members often brought knowledge and experience to their positions. In the Woman's Division, for example, women were often active on local and conference levels for many years, giving them a

Tracey K. Jones, Jr.
(Photo courtesy of United Methodist Archives and History)

wide knowledge of the workings of the church and even long background in the area of mission studies.

Missionary Status and Indigenization

Evangelizing the world, as Mott described, was still at the heart of the work missionaries were called to do. Such a simple statement does not lend itself well to carefully written job descriptions. In reality, the nature of many of the placements was such that the job description changed in detail quite frequently. Persons recruited into "home" missions often started with a willingness to work wherever they were sent. Further education followed. Such was the case with those called to "foreign" mission as well. With such conditions, what is remarkable is the way that missionaries reported fairly unanimously that not only were they well prepared for the jobs they had to do, but also that there were not many surprises about what they did. Training that focused on exposing the new missionaries to a variety of peoples and cultures helped to bridge the gap between the backgrounds of the missionaries and the people with whom they would work. Most missionaries outside the U.S. attended language schools, sometimes for as long as a year, so that they were able to start the job with the skills to converse with local populations. Missionaries in the U.S. were able to attend training schools that gave them needed information for the areas where they worked. In addition, the staff occasionally sent books, articles, and other study materials to the missionaries. Those home on furlough could also attend workshops and retreats. As for support, most missionaries felt that they received it in a variety of ways. As a system, the Board of Missions took very seriously its supportive role. Furloughs served not only to inform churches about mission work but also to give a change to persons who might otherwise become worn from the variety of stresses that accompanied the job.

While many individual missionaries did not personally experience great changes in their roles throughout this period, the role of missionaries in general was changing, though still with its center as the evangelization of the world. More and more persons were recruited for specific skills, though medicine and education remained primary. The National Division continued to focus on many social work areas but also recruited persons with technical and agricultural backgrounds, as did the World Division.

A key factor was the oft-repeated phrase that missionaries were to "work themselves out of a job." Although not everyone liked the concept, agreed with it, or even interpreted it in similar ways, it expressed the heart of the theological basis for the work. Missionaries, whether in the U.S. or outside, were to be working hand in hand with the people. As more training or knowledge was available to the local people, as more people in the area committed themselves to Christianity and the work of The Methodist Church, the missionaries, as outsiders, were to withdraw.

Assessing the success of this part of the ministry is central to an overview of the legacy of the board for The Methodist Church. Both the philosophy and its implementation provided part of the groundwork on which the mission work of the new church — The United Methodist Church — was built.

Preparation and expectations for the work stayed "in sync" with the experiences of those who answered the call, but the spectrum of theology and approach to the work remained wide and varied. Some workers saw themselves in a strictly evangelical role, emphasizing Bible translations, preaching, and conversion. Others, especially those called to medical or teaching ministries, participated in the evangelical activities but with a different perspective. They believed in demonstrating Christ's love through action, participated in local church activities, but left much of the direct evangelization to indigenous Christians. Missionaries with these varied perspectives often worked near one another or on shared projects. Few changed their perspectives about the nature of mission work, even after many years. Diversity of beliefs among those who answered the call remained a characteristic of the missionary force.

The roles of the missionaries were further complicated by the triumph of the U.S. in the Second World War. This victory intensified for some the claims of superiority of "Western civilization" and all that accompanied it. The juxtaposition of the freedom of the West with the political constraints of Communist regimes further complicated discussions about values and cultures.

These attitudes were reflected in the work of some within the church around the world. The tension between what it meant to be Western and what it meant to be Christian remained. Pressure to adopt Western dress, Western art, and Western cultural values came not just from the missionaries but also from sources within the cultures. Consciously or not, however, many missionaries did participate in emphasizing these attitudes. Sensitive language about difference was as slow in reaching mission discussion as it was in reaching secular foreign policy circles.

A number of the missionaries recruited just after the war brought with them, however, a deepened sensitivity to culture and the ways that Christianity could root itself and flower in unexpected color and design. They were in conflict with older missionaries because they chose to live another way and to encourage national Christians to develop further their own traditions. These conflicting views were less visible for a long time because many missionaries worked fairly independently or primarily with indigenous people. Newer missionaries were also reticent about their views because of the greater longevity of their superiors in the places of work.

At the same time, the importance of the translation work in contributing to the overall goals of the church should not be underestimated. Through the diligence of these workers, more and more people around the world were able to read the gospel and worship in their own language. Lamin Sanneh has explored the theological and cultural importance of this aspect of missionary endeavor. While immediate social changes were not always evident, he emphasizes another level of contribution: "In Bible

Indigenous leaders in countries outside the U.S.
represented the success of one of the mission
goals of The Methodist Church. As these leaders
gained responsibility in their churches, they
proved the wisdom of policies that subordinated
the role of white, Western missionaries to that of
indigenous Christians. Shown here, top left to
right, are Liberian Bishop Stephen T. Nagbe,
Japanese educator Yoshi Tokunaga, Mexican missionary Ulises Hernández, and Czech leader
Joseph P. Barták, with daughters Marian and Helen, son Paul, and Mrs. Barták. *(Photos courtesy of
United Methodist Archives and History)*

translation, hitherto taboo ethnic groups and their languages and cultures were effectively destigmatized while at the same time superior cultures were stripped of their right to constitute themselves into exclusive standards of access to God."[7]

The tensions and differences in these attitudes were mirrored in indigenous Christians as well. In some of the locations, Christians were second-, third-, or fourth-generation. Some of these had adapted many of the Western values and attitudes as their own. With these beliefs, some of these Christians had acquired enough power or position that they felt threatened by discussion of indigenization. In their minds, the old ways of their own culture had been repudiated. Christianity had provided the explanation for the problems of the past. The easiest way to create new possibilities was to let go of the past completely. These long-time Christians had become comfortable with Western dress and ideals, even seeing their use as a way of showing modernity and sophistication. Others were participating in liberation or modernization movements in their culture that viewed Christianity as part of the imperial or colonial structures. They sought a way to define Christianity in compatible terms with these movements. Many other Christians sought a comfortable middle ground for both inherited beliefs and new ideas. The variety of responses from indigenous Christians gave missionaries a confusing message about how to be most effective.

Thus the discussion of further indigenization of the church did not have the same meaning to all persons. Some could picture themselves with the power and prestige formerly owned by the missionaries; others wanted a church more truly reflective of their own culture. The consultations of the early 1960s — one each in Africa, Asia, and Latin America — represented an important shift for the church. Each of the three events allowed much more time for indigenous Christians to organize, speak, and give direction to the future. Power and control questions emerged before and during these consultations. But in general, the church — and its many members and parts — was slow to appreciate that the next steps involved a paradigm shift rather than indigenous Christians doing what missionaries had formerly done.

One example of a possible paradigm shift was the way the Kyodan, the Japanese church, grew and developed during the entire life of The Methodist Church. Methodists were nearly always active in ecumenical endeavors both nationally and internationally, but the Japanese experience allowed a living out of ecumenism that had not yet been tried in most locations. The Kyodan had its own unique limitations and problems. Yet while mission personnel and Japanese Christians contributed significant writing and speaking on the benefits of ecumenism and their experiences, most in the church did not look to the Japanese model for future directions for the church. Ignoring the Kyodan, however benignly, deprived Protestant Christians of a successful model or new paradigm that focused on similarities rather than differences.

Methodists in North India, for example, chose not to join a united church effort, a decision that most missionaries watched with concern. Staying in The Methodist Church ensured that the bishops and other conference personnel were paid salaries equivalent to their counterparts in other places in the world, most significantly in the United States. The Methodist Church, while aware of the difficulties this differential caused, had not successfully addressed the money and power issues that were involved for conferences making decisions about independence from the U.S. church.

Thus indigenization as a process had a cost to the mission churches that some in power were unwilling to pay. Administrators and leadership personnel received both social and material benefits from the links to the U.S. church. With their concern for continuing mission efforts, board officials were often reluctant to ask embarrassing or difficult questions. Methodists were committed to all their churches. For all the best reasons, some churches had enjoyed significant material benefits without an accompanying accountability. One had only to look at the facilities and the surrounding non-Christian population to believe that more money could only benefit the work and help the churches to grow in number and influence.

In retrospect, the reasons for this lay far more in the lack of theological and ethical discussion around culture and definitions of progress and development both in the U.S. and abroad than in serious lack of attention to financial details. The pattern of Western missionaries going to *other places*, despite all the growing racial and cultural awareness, was still firmly entrenched in most discussions and from most persons participating in those discussions. And while theologians in India and other areas of world mission were beginning to find a voice, their distinctiveness was slow to be seen, valued, or realized.

Informal review of most of the literature backs up this analysis. *World Outlook* contained numerous stories of the ways that indigenous Christians (and locals in the case of the National Division) were giving leadership to the work. But the descriptions were always written in Western cultural terms. Rarely did the articles give any time or space to the ways the Western church (or in the case of U.S. mission, the dominant middle-class culture) might be changed by these persons and events. Only occasionally did readers see representations of Christianity that were unfamiliar. Instead, photographs of frame churches in Africa looked almost as though they could have been taken in areas of the Midwestern United States. Under mission sponsorship and direction, young girls sewed Western-style clothing. Sunday school children usually looked at the same blond, blue-eyed Jesus whether they were in rural Africa, urban India, inner-city Detroit, or Southern California. The voices of change of those who had learned from the missionary experience and wanted something different were lost in the continuing patterns that favored a primarily Western cultural church with a gradually indigenous leadership and direction.

In all this, The Methodist Church was no worse than other denominations or than other institutions from U.S. culture. But although the church favored turning over power to local churches — a significant step — it was also unable to break free of many of the patterns from the past. If missionaries were encouraged to think of working themselves out of a job, as indeed they were, the full impact of this goal was not explored from either end.

In a more tangible way, the role of missionaries shifted as technological advancements allowed easier communication and travel. Where once missionaries left the U.S. and returned once or twice at most, now missionaries had more frequent furloughs. Lifetime service was still the norm, but as mission churches made decisions and shifted responsibilities, personnel were assigned to a wide range of sites and positions. In addition, the early incorporation of a program for short-term missionaries had positive consequences. A number of these persons signed on as full-term missionaries when their terms were up. Others were able to use their experience as involved laity and clergy. They provided yet another link between home churches and the worldwide variety of work of the church.

Paradigm Shifts

That said, the role of the missionaries shifted during this period in some ways that continued to be significant. The involvement of the missionaries in the life of the country as well as the church, the continuing movement out of compounds and into the communities, and the awareness that one answered to the indigenous church as well as to the board began a process of evolution in mission that took the church in unexpected directions. Some of these changes have remained controversial into the life of The United Methodist Church.

Perhaps the most controversial development was one that came not from a changing policy at the board level, but from developments within various sites where mission personnel worked. Before entering their fields of work, missionaries agreed not to get involved in local politics. When the Templins did so in India, the bishop arranged for their return to the United States. By the 1960s, missionaries involved in societal developments were in a different position, however. In many places, speaking out against racism or working for greater economic opportunities was seen as an extension of the gospel, just as feeding the hungry had been in the past. While study of Liberation Theology was occasionally part of this, missionaries and indigenous people came to this position from their own experiences and analysis. Workers for the National Division also experienced theological growth and development that led to greater social action.

The most dramatic result was the imprisonment of the four missionaries in Angola. While the process was tainted by the actions of the Portuguese and the actual charges false, the colonial government accurately saw that the work of the Methodists was indeed a threat to colonial society as the Portuguese had constructed it. The line between active political work, seemingly so clear in 1940 when considering the ministry of the Templins, and gospel-based action in life that undermined authorities was disappearing, not by deliberate intent of the missionaries to mix in local politics, but by their attempt to be faithful to the gospel as they understood it. The faithfulness that informed actions in their relationship with the indigenous people, but that still did not cross the line into active political work, put them at odds with the principalities and powers of the areas where they worked. Earlier missionaries had been sure that Christianity would have a significant impact on previously non-Christian nations. The moment for that impact had arrived. Because it looked different from the vision of those early missionaries and many of those still in the churches, it was not always recognized.

In the end, the real shift was not just what happened in Angola or other places where the work of the missionaries brought attention from those in power. It was what happened when the missionaries returned to the U.S. By sending three of the men who had been imprisoned on speaking tours, the board was accepting a role of making change in the U.S. a response to a particular situation in the world. In the words of Fred Brancel, the board and the missionaries thought that their speaking about the Angolan colonial experience would make a difference. By calling attention to the abusive powers of the Portuguese government to Christians, the board believed it could change the public perspective on developments in Africa and ultimately influence U.S. policy. In the short term, the speaking tours did not have this effect. Foreign policy proved harder to affect and change. The power of mainstream religious bodies as a force had begun to wane.

But the tours brought something more effective and dangerous to powers of injustice. Although missionaries had long seen themselves in the role as interpreters of the Christian experience and even of the cultures where they worked, now they played a role in providing politically sensitive information with potential to make a change in U.S. culture.[8] Such information and the accompanying social analysis meant that a significant group of missionaries found themselves in exactly the opposite position as those seen in the novel *Hawaii* and some of the other stereotypes common in the culture. Neither hand in hand with corporate interests nor simply defining mission and spiritual life in a narrow and limiting way, this group of missionaries provided information counter to much that was available to Christians in the United States. Further, they saw the links between the racial unrest in the U.S. and the freedom struggles in other parts of the world. Articles, speeches, and interaction with and by these missionaries had the potential to put the church in a more specific political situation, one in fact that was closer to points of view earlier espoused by the Methodist Federation for Social Action.[9]

Drawing on this kind of information had implications for the church not just in the arena of racial justice at home and abroad but also in the foreign policy arena, as had been attempted with the speakers on Angola. As the conflict in Southeast Asia developed, many in the U.S. began to ask for more information than was readily available through the usual print and broadcast media, which came to be seen as primarily sources of information approved by the government. A small number of missionaries in Asia, raising questions about the war, were also able to provide alternatives to the analysis of the social and political situation in that part of the world. Again, the potential for a significant source of information outside the sources commonly available lay within the Board of Missions. Access to such information created a worldview, especially for board and staff members, that was less consonant with the primarily middle-class members of what had been a middle-of-the-road church. The amount of information and lack of consensus on its meaning and use also made the interpretive task more difficult. The gap between denominational staff and church members was not always recognized as one of the results of the knowledge and perspective difference created by these different information sources. The worldview, usually ecumenical as well, was not valued in society in general. Although Methodists had the potential for great leadership, they had only a small number of ready followers, whether in the denomination or in society.

Describing the legacy from all this depends on one's theological approach. For those who see within the gospel the call for liberation of all persons — liberation that moves from personal to social and political — The Methodist Church discovered and developed resources that had the power to further the growth of the Kingdom of God on earth. This introduction of resources was particularly meaningful because The Methodist Church had instituted a new liturgical season in the 1939 *Discipline*. Kingdomtide was designed as a time to focus on Scripture that took the words of Jesus seriously in the reshaping of society and the determining of Christian behavior. For a church without strong liturgical or even theological identity, Kingdomtide was a significant offering to the wider church. Mission work at home and abroad was clearly part of the building of the Kingdom.

Yet by naming this development as important, one creates a basis for seeing how the church fell far short of its own potential. A growing number of personnel did ask questions about culture and politics that moved them out of the "middleness" that characterized most of U.S. Methodism. Leaving behind this middle had the potential of significant loss of identity for Methodists.

This middle nature of Methodism has been noted by many sociologists and church historians. Until this time, Methodism had remained the largest Protestant denomination because its very nature was middle class, middle of the road, found in every part of the United States. Movement on social issues by the General Conference was slow and careful. Wesley's dictum to "think and let think," though unknown as such to many Methodists, prevailed, creating a wide spectrum of theological, political, and intellectual beliefs. Methodists remained identified by their polity and, to some extent, their worship style. But unlike the Methodists of Wesley's time, U.S. Methodists reflected the values of the culture. Any serious move away from those values had the potential to put those parts of the church at odds with the total membership.

Thus the potential for radical leadership for justice and social change was tempered by the realities of the church's identity and polity. At the same time, the Board of Missions, by its openness to experiences of its personnel, provided one source of growing understanding of theologies of liberation as well as a significant source of information about the operation of powers and principalities in many parts of the world.

This opening to the broader world was matched on the U.S. mission side in part by growing racial understanding and developing concerns about women and their role in society. Again the Woman's Division, based on its experiences, began to provide more literature and leadership for questions being raised in U.S. culture. Both the prophetic voice that the women had been using on racial issues and women's role and the history of training women for important leadership positioned Methodist women to be major contributors to the changes in society. At the same time, the pull of the vast middle of the church acted to moderate ideas that veered too far in one direction. Change was slow to come. Women who wanted to become part of the secular women's movement often felt they had to hide their Christianity or find sources of support for their spiritual life.

Despite the efforts of the Woman's Division, many women were unable to uncover the support they needed and began to leave the church. Openness at the board and staff level did not always translate into a welcome note for women at the local church level or even information to support them. Challenges to the middle came from the other side of the political spectrum as well. With changes in society coming rapidly in the 1960s, many other women felt threatened and confused, unable to sort out the varied messages. They asked churches to be a safe refuge from the change of secular society. Being confronted with questions about liberation did not feel like "good news."

The potential for what was being called a more radical discipleship in the church was also tempered by a lack of significant theological developments translated into discussions for local churches. Even biblical criticism, nearly one hundred years old in seminary classes, was not well known among the laity. Harkness was one significant theologian of the midcentury who took seriously the need for the laity to understand their heritage. She wrote and published many books that gave a sound theological grounding accessible to laity. Although she was popular, she was only one voice. Without adequate theological and biblical foundations being developed in local churches, the experiences and ideas of the missionaries made less impact on the laity and on The Methodist Church as a whole.

Thus by the end of the life of The Methodist Church, there were often fairly wide differences between some of the denominational leadership, who often had more access to training and resources, and local leadership, who either had fewer resources or were not encouraged to find them. Because the church had always operated with a wide latitude in the theological spectrum, this difference was not immediately seen to be a problem. But it did mean that as the church entered into a new alliance, becoming a new church, it brought in a less well-defined theology and approach than was immediately apparent. Even the tools for analysis of theological and biblical understanding had been politicized, so that their use was seen as a choice or a political statement rather than a necessity.

The tensions in the U.S. can be seen in part both to herald and to reflect the pluralism of the culture, though not defined as such at the time. This pluralism, long a reality, became harder to ignore after the Second World War. Some staff and personnel of the board had held serious discussions about what it meant to be Christian as a minority group as well as what it meant to begin to work with other major religions. As noted, the Japanese experience for Christians, as well as insights from those working in Algeria, were part of this discussion. But the time was not yet right for the discussion to make its way into the church. This offering from mission experience, which could have put the church at the forefront in embracing new realities, would have to wait. The church had opportunities to be a beacon, and its hesitation mirrored a society that was overwhelmed by all the change that was taking place. Instead of truly making a paradigm shift, the church retained its old patterns.

Transformation of the Other

In addition to shifts in the way mission work was conceived and executed, the church was also part of a broader cultural shift as communications increased, making the world seemingly smaller. Perception of the division between peoples continued to fluctuate along political, cultural, and philosophical lines, most commonly noted in the form of race; but also following the Second World War, it was discussed in broad ideological terms. Through the opening provided by the statement of purpose of the board, staff and personnel worked to create an "us" of worldwide Christians that became real for a growing number of U.S. Christians. This identification process meant that written materials and proposed legislation increasingly focused on the partnership of Methodists in endeavors, whatever the location of the work or the background of the workers. This goal was seldom the reality in practice that its proponents might have wished, but it served the purpose of pushing the church closer to understanding mission as global partnership.

As the church prepared to enter a new liaison in 1968, this partially finished process of the "other" becoming "us" was thrown into another mix. Some mission churches were forming their own bodies; others were staying tied to what would become The "United" Methodist Church. "United" was a key word that continued a verbal heritage from the Evangelical United Brethren Church as well as one that made a statement about the intent to honor the importance of each tradition. "United" also reflected achievement for the Board of Missions. Although some of the churches differed much more than they had in 1939 over dress and worship practices, the worldwide church as a denomination was in a closer place in shared experiences and inclusive leadership. The unexpected turns in the story of the Board of Missions add much interest but no change in the outcome.

At the same time, the need for an "us" was growing stronger in an increasingly secular world. The possibilities for fracture, sown in the structure, were not diminished by this changing identity. The lack of agreement on how even to evaluate theological and biblical traditions was not addressed during this period, leaving an ever-greater task to the new church. The risks that the board had been willing to take with its programs and with its vision were more vulnerable to attack from within the church as the church felt itself to be under attack and declining in influence and numbers. The pain in the Woman's Division over the changes in 1964 had not waned by 1968, sapping energy at a time when it was most needed to address changes in the culture. The diversity within Methodism meant that the board was increasingly the recipient of criticism from within its own body, but with no consensus on the criticism itself.

Even acknowledging these realities, it is impossible to conclude any narrative about the work of Methodist mission on a low note. Through war and violence, through famine, through urban decay and rural poverty as well as through joy in worship in many styles and tongues, through healing, through education of thousands of talented young people, the work of Christ in the world was accomplished. Methodists around the world were empowered in new ways to work together administratively, to seek solutions theologically, and to cooperate in reforming the nation and spreading scriptural holiness across all the lands of the earth. Often a mirror of society, they also succeeded as a beacon of the love of God.

[Appendixes]

The appendixes have many gaps because of the lack of records in given years, most notably in Appendix 2 for 1960. Appendix 2 is an attempt to make public the names of those who served in the mission of The Methodist Church outside the United States. Names were taken from yearly reports, directories, and gazetteers published by the Methodist Board of Missions and now at United Methodist Archives and History, Madison, N.J. Many of the names are spelled inconsistently in the sources. The editors and author have made every attempt to find the correct spelling. It is regrettable that the first names of wives were not included in the sources. The hope and intention is that, flawed as they are, the records will still be helpful to those seeking information on the history of mission of The Methodist Church.

APPENDIX I

Numbers and Placement of Missionaries, 1941–1967

	1941		1942		1943		1944	
	Foreign Missions	Woman's Division	Foreign Missions	Woman's Division	Foreign Missions	Woman's Division	Foreign Missions	Woman's Division
AFRICA								
Algeria			NA	NA	NA	NA	8	8
Angola	9	6					13	5
Belgian Congo	48	14					44	15
Liberia	13						17	
Portuguese East Africa							13	6
Southern Rhodesia							26	14
Tunisia							2	
ASIA								
Borneo							2	
Burma	14	9					12	9
China	31	40					140	156
India							126	163
Japan							27	40
Korea							8	41
North China	37	33						
Malaya							23	17
Philippines							12	11
Sumatra							6	2
EUROPE								
Belgium							4	
Bulgaria							2	3
Czecho-Slovakia							4	
Poland							4	2
LATIN AMERICA								
Argentina							13	5
Bolivia							13	
Brazil							39	27
Chile							20	
Costa Rica							4	
Cuba							21	17
México							8	27
Panamá							4	
Perú							9	9
Uruguay							4	5

*NA = Not Available

	1945		1946		1947		1948	
	Foreign Missions	Woman's Division	Foreign Missions	Woman's Division	Foreign Missions	Woman's Division	Foreign Missions	Woman's Division
AFRICA								
Angola	NA	NA	15	5	16	5	17	5
Belgian Congo			52		61		72	
Central Congo				15		16	37	14
Liberia			15		15		15	
North Africa			10	8	11	6	11	4
Portuguese East Africa			14		13		13	
Southern Congo							29	
Southern Rhodesia			32	14	33	16	32	16
Southeast Africa				6		8		8
ASIA								
Burma			12	7	8	5	8	5
China			131	136	141	139	142	133
India			138	156	154	150	150	152
Japan			27	40	22	37	20	39
Korea			1	45	32	43	28	36
Malaya			39	13	35	13	46	13
Philippines			12	12	10	13	16	13
Sumatra			6	2	7	1	8	1
EUROPE								
Belgium			4		4		4	
Bulgaria			4	2	1	3		2
Czécho-Slovakia			4		4		4	
Poland			4	2		2	4	2
LATIN AMERICA								
Argentina			12	4	13	4	13	4
Bolivia			11		9		12	
Brazil			38	23	44	26	38	29
Chile			23	15	23		24	
Costa Rica			4		7		5	
Cuba			16		18	15	16	16
México			8	26	6	25	6	22
Panamá			6		8		7	
Perú			10	8	12	12	13	12
Uruguay			2	5	4	5	6	7

	1949		1950		1951		1952	
	Foreign Missions	Woman's Division	Foreign Missions	Woman's Division	Foreign Missions	Woman's Division	Foreign Missions	Woman's Division
AFRICA								
Angola	17	7	19	7	21	11	21	10
Belgian Congo								29
Central Congo	37	17	43	16	48	22	52	
Liberia	16		23	1	27	5	26	5
Mozambique						11		10
North Africa	9	8	14	9	21	14	25	13
Portuguese East Africa	13		10		16			
Rhodesia	38	17	44	20	58		58	
Southern Congo	29	4	27	3	43	5	41	
Southern Rhodesia						24		26
Southeast Africa		8		8			20	
EASTERN ASIA								
Borneo						2	10	3
China General		4						31
East China	26	29	20	25	10	16	8	
Foochow	25	21	27	15	11	9	4	
Hinghwa	9	7	10	6	6	5	4	
Japan	2	55		57	65	70	63	75
Kalgan	11							
Kiangsi	19	14	7	12	2	7	2	
Korea	28	35		30	28	12	31	18
Mid China	12	12	10	11	6	4	4	
North China	6	27	16	21	5	11	5	
Okinawa					4		7	
West China	38	15	12	16	7	10	2	
Yenping	31	3	6	3		2		
SOUTHEAST ASIA								
Burma	8	5	10	5	11	8	11	9
Formosa							2	
Malaya	39	12	46	16	59	20	54	27
Philippines	20	13	22	17	23	24	24	28
Sumatra	8	1	7	1	10		12	2

	1949		1950		1951		1952	
	Foreign Missions	Woman's Division	Foreign Missions	Woman's Division	Foreign Missions	Woman's Division	Foreign Missions	Woman's Division
SOUTHERN ASIA								
Bengal	8	9	12	10	14	8	15	8
Bombay	10	16	13	19	12	15	11	15
Central Provinces	16	14	19	17	29	18	24	17
Delhi	16	22	20	22	32	31	33	31
Gujarat	15	13	14	12	15	12	11	11
Hyderabad	10	7	12	7	9	8	10	8
Indus River	21	8	22	10	21	15		18
Lucknow	11	17	15	16	17		18	
North India	26	38	27	38	31	37	28	37
Pakistan						6	22	9
South India	10	13	15	17	20	20	19	18
India - General	4		4		16		14	
EUROPE								
Austria						4	4	
Belgium	4		4		4		4	
Bulgaria		2						
Czecho-Slovakia	4		4		2		2	
Poland	6	3	2		2			
LATIN AMERICA								
Argentina	14	3	12	3	16	7	17	7
Bolivia	21		27		32		38	
Brazil	47	31	46	32	63		69	36
North Brazil						20		
Central Brazil						11		
South Brazil						11		
Chile	31		31		35	1	33	1
Costa Rica	6		4		6		8	
Cuba	14	19	17	20	20	24	25	22
México	8	24	10	27	10		8	31
Central México						13		
Frontier México						20		
Panamá	5		7		9		7	
Perú	11	12	12	11	13	10	16	10
Uruguay	6	7	6	8	11	11	12	10

	1953		1954		1955		1956	
	Foreign Missions	Woman's Division	Foreign Missions	Woman's Division	Foreign Missions	Woman's Division	Foreign Missions	Woman's Division
AFRICA								
Angola	NA	NA	24	10	25	8	23	9
Belgian Congo			59	39		28		
Belgian Central Congo				21	57		57	20
Belgian Southern Congo			43		46		44	12
Liberia			26	5	22	6	25	7
Mozambique				10		9		7
North Africa			20	11	23	9	22	12
Southern Rhodesia			62	25	60	27	59	27
Southeast Africa			24		27		25	
EUROPE								
Austria			3		3		4	
Belgium			4		4		4	
Czecho-Slovakia			2					
EASTERN ASIA								
Japan			78	70	75	67	75	65
Korea			36	25	40	32	48	36
Okinawa			7		7		8	
CHINA AND SOUTHEAST ASIA								
Burma			13	8	13	6	13	9
Borneo (Sarawak)			11	5	12	6	15	5
China			22	18	10	16		15
Formosa			4		4		4	
Hong Kong			2		2		4	
Malaya			52	32	57	31	51	29
Philippines			28	23	28	22	28	21
Sumatra (Indonesia)			13	2	13	2	15	2

	1953		1954		1955		1956	
	Foreign Missions	Woman's Division	Foreign Missions	Woman's Division	Foreign Missions	Woman's Division	Foreign Missions	Woman's Division
SOUTHERN ASIA								
Bengal	NA	NA	14	8	15	9	12	8
Bombay			11	15	13	12	15	11
Central Provinces (Madhya Pradesh)			22	12	22	13	20	9
Delhi			35	30	35	29	40	22
Gujarat			11	9	7	9	8	9
Hyderabad			11	16	11	6	10	5
Lucknow			18	20	17	21	15	26
Nepal								1
North India			25	34	21	27	23	24
Pakistan			28	9	30	9	33	11
South India			18	17	19	18	17	17
India - General			19		19		20	
LATIN AMERICA								
Argentina			16	7	16	7	16	7
Bolivia			34		33		42	1
Brazil			74	33	71	33	70	31
Chile			30	1	33	1	33	2
Costa Rica			11		11		13	
Cuba			28	20	28	23	26	21
México			8	27	8	25	10	26
Panamá			8		11		11	
Perú			18	10	15	11	16	12
Uruguay			9	7	9	7	9	9

	1957		1958		1959		1960	
	Foreign Missions	Woman's Division	Foreign Missions	Woman's Division	Foreign Missions	Woman's Division	Foreign Missions	Woman's Division
AFRICA								
Angola	24	7	33	8	30	5	30	5
Belgian Central Congo	58	22	59	21	60	22	66	22
Belgian Southern Congo	46	12	48	13	46	10	52	11
Liberia	27	7	26	8	23	5	23	7
Mozambique		8		8		7	35	7
North Africa	22	11	18	12	19	13	19	13
Southern Rhodesia	59	27	56	27	55	27	57	28
Southeast Africa	27		35		35	.		7
EUROPE								
Austria	4		3		3		6	
Belgium	4		7		6		6	
EASTERN ASIA								
Japan	81	62	71	51	84	58	84	50
Korea	49	37	42	33	48	33	52	32
Okinawa	8		7		8		8	
CHINA AND SOUTHEAST ASIA								
Burma	11	7	11	7	10	6	8	6
Borneo (Sarawak)	19	5	20	7	21	11	28	11
Formosa (Taiwan)	6		8	1	10	1		
Hong Kong	2	3	4	2	4	3	16	4
Malaya	47	21	41	21	45	19	49	19
Philippines	27	15	31	16	33	15	38	13
Sumatra (Indonesia)	15	2	9	3	11	3	11	3

	1957		1958		1959		1960	
	Foreign Missions	Woman's Division	Foreign Missions	Woman's Division	Foreign Missions	Woman's Division	Foreign Missions	Woman's Division
SOUTHERN ASIA								
Agra	NA	NA	14	12	12	12	10	12
Bengal	11	7	9	7	9	6	11	7
Bombay	14	9	8	6	8	6	8	6
Madhya Pradesh	20	6	17	6	13	6	6	
Delhi	44	23	22	8	22	6	20	9
Gujarat	8	8	8	5	8	5	8	5
Hyderabad	10	2	8	3	4	3	4	3
Lucknow	14	13	8	10	8	9	4	9
Nepal			4		4		4	
North India	22	20	18	17	16	19	16	17
Pakistan	31	11	23	14	35	13	37	13
South India	19	17	16	15	12	13	12	14
India - General	22	8	11		11	6	25	
LATIN AMERICA								
Argentina	16	4	15	3	14	4	14	4
Bolivia	43	1	42	4	44	5	48	5
Brazil	67	25	63	22	65	20	55	22
Chile	33	2	29	26	27	2	32	2
Costa Rica	11		13		15		15	
Cuba	26	22	26	26	27	25	37	24
México	6	29	6	33	8	36	6	35
Panamá	14		15		9		13	
Perú	15	11	16	11	15	9	15	8
Uruguay	11	6	9	6	9	4	9	4

	1961		1962		1963		1964	
	Foreign Missions	Woman's Division	Foreign Missions	Woman's Division	Foreign Missions	Woman's Division	Foreign Missions	Woman's Division
AFRICA								
Angola	28	4	NA	NA	24	3	8	2
Central Congo	74	22			18	16	43	10
Southern Congo	67	10			109	9	66	5
Liberia	26	9			25	14	26	9
North Africa	21	12			26	13	28	10
Rhodesia	71	29			103	35	94	22
Southeast Africa (Mozambique)	35	8			39	8	32	7
EUROPE								
Austria	5				4		6	
Belgium	6				2		3	
EASTERN ASIA								
Japan	102	59			86	50	91	50
Korea	59	27			56	34	55	31
Okinawa	10				15		13	
CHINA AND SOUTHEAST ASIA								
Burma	11	6			11	2	7	2
Sarawak (Borneo)	29	10			30	13	29	11
China	4							
Hong Kong - Taiwan	17	3			26	13	45	15
Malaya	65	21			52	17	44	12
Philippines	37	11			39	11	34	10
Sumatra (Indonesia)	12	2			10	3	23	1

	1961		1962		1963		1964	
	Foreign Missions	Woman's Division	Foreign Missions	Woman's Division	Foreign Missions	Woman's Division	Foreign Missions	Woman's Division
SOUTHERN ASIA								
Agra	14	11	NA	NA	10	9	10	8
Bengal	9	5			9	5	11	4
Bombay	6	6			4	3	2	2
Madhya Pradesh	4	5			4	4	4	4
Delhi	18	6			16	6	18	4
Gujarat	6	6			10	4	12	5
Hyderabad	4	5			6	4	6	3
Lucknow	7	7			8	6	8	5
Nepal							6	
North India	8	10			12	6	12	5
Pakistan	40	13			44	12	49	12
South India	14	13			18	15	16	15
India - General	26				22	1	19	
LATIN AMERICA								
Argentina	19	6			21	7	32	6
Bolivia	54	7			58	7	58	10
Brazil	60	20			74	21	73	17
Chile	35	4			35	3	37	6
Costa Rica	19	1			22	3	17	3
Cuba	32	24						3
México	8	36			6	32	8	26
Panamá	9				12		12	
Perú	18	9			25	11	23	10
Uruguay	10	4			16	6	13	8

	1965 Foreign Missions	1965 Woman's Division	1966 Foreign Missions	1966 Woman's Division	1967 Foreign Missions	1967 Woman's Division
AFRICA						
Angola	10	1	2		1	NA
Central Congo	55	8	63		59	
Southern Congo	85	10	13		59	
Liberia	24	7	40		2	
North Africa	27	10	36		32	
Rhodesia	94	19	51		83	
Mozambique	34		48		24	
South Africa					13	
Zambia			6		4	
EUROPE						
Austria	6		6		6	
Belgium	2		2		2	
EASTERN ASIA						
Japan	83	46	123		113	
Korea	53	25	89		90	
Okinawa	14		8		8	
CHINA AND SOUTHEAST ASIA						
Burma	6	2	3			
Sarawak (Borneo)	31	12	50		47	
Hong Kong	13	8	20		20	
Taiwan	23	7	35		24	
Malaysia	48	9	56		52	
Philippines	33	12	58		57	
Sumatra (Indonesia)	18	1	16		16	
Vietnam			1			

	1965		1966		1967	
	Foreign Missions	Woman's Division	Foreign Missions	Woman's Division	Foreign Missions	Woman's Division
SOUTHERN ASIA						
Agra	8	7	NA	NA	NA	NA
Bengal	11	4				
Bombay	2	1				
Madhya Pradesh	4	5				
Delhi	18	5				
Gujarat	12	8				
Hyderabad	6	5				
Lucknow	8					
Nepal	6		3		8	
North India	16	3				
Pakistan	31	13	51		39	
South India	16	14				
India - General			170		170	
LATIN AMERICA						
Argentina	26	6	27		31	
Bolivia	54	11	69		76	
Brazil	70	14	81		78	
Chile	36	6	42		39	
Costa Rica	12	4	21		20	
México	10		40		38	
Panamá	12		12		13	
Perú	21	10	34		35	
Uruguay	15	7	21		18	

APPENDIX 2
Missionaries outside the U.S., 1944–1964

Foreign Missions Division 1944

AFRICA

Algeria
Douglas, Rev and Mrs Elmer H
Hansen, Rev and Mrs Hans L
Heggory, Rev and Mrs Willy N
Kellar, Rev and Mrs F J
Angola
Blackburn, Rev and Mrs L E
Dodge, Rev and Mrs Ralph E
Elding, Rev E E and Mrs (R.N.)
Fields, Rev and Mrs C W W
Kemp, Alexander (M.D.) and Mrs
Klebsattel, Rev and Mrs August
Shields, Miss Irene W
Belgian Congo
Anker, Rev and Mrs H P
Ayres, Rev H C and Mrs (R.N.)
Bartlett, Rev and Mrs Elwood R
Brastrup, Rev J E
Chappell, Rev and Mrs C W
Davis, Rev and Mrs J J
DeRuiter, Rev and Mrs William
Everett, Rev and Mrs E I
Everett, Miss Helen N (R.N.)
Hamelryck, Mrs Paul A
Hartzler, Rev and Mrs C C
Hartzler, Rev and Mrs Omar L
Hughlett, W S (M.D.) and Mrs
Jensen, Miss C Marie
Lerbak, Miss Anna E (R.N.)
Lewis, W B (M.D.) and Mrs (R.N.)
Lovell, Rev and Mrs Eugene H
Lovell, Rev and Mrs Marshall W
Piper, Dr and Mrs Arthur
Piper, Miss Ruth B (R.N.)
Reid, Rev and Mrs A J
Sheffey, Chas P M (Dr) and Mrs
   (R.N.)
Stilz, Rev and Mrs E B

Townsley, Rev and Mrs Inman U
Wheeler, Rev and Mrs Henry T
Liberia
Black, Miss Mildred A
Cofield, Mr and Mrs B B
Embree, Rev and Mrs R L
Harley, Dr and Mrs G W
Longstaff, Miss Ruth E
Mitchell, Miss S Susan
Persons, Rev and Mrs Maurice E
Price, Rev and Mrs F A
Smith, Rev and Mrs S R
Wengatz, Rev J C and Mrs (R.N.)
Portuguese East Africa
Fuller, Rev and Mrs Charles (R.N.)
Gillet, Rev and Mrs Ira E
Keys, Mrs Pliny W
Knutsson, Rev Per A
Persson, Rev and Mrs J A
Pointer, Rev James D
Rea, Rev and Mrs J S
Stauffacher, Dr C J and Mrs (R.N.)
Southern Rhodesia
Anderson, Dr and Mrs A Garfield
Bourgaize, Rev Wilfred
Culver, Rev and Mrs Maurice
Gates, Rev and Mrs R C
Hamrick, Mr and Mrs W D
Hanson, Miss Ruth E (R.N.)
Hassing, Rev Per and Mrs (R.N.)
James, Rev and Mrs Henry
Murphree, Rev and Mrs M J
O'Farrell, Rev and Mrs T A
Roberts, Rev and Mrs G A
Roberts, Mr Tudor R
Rydell, Miss Rosa C
Sells, Rev and Mrs E L
Taylor, Rev and Mrs H E
Tunisia
Kelly, Mr and Mrs C Guyer

ASIA

Borneo
Summer, Rev and Mrs G V
Burma
Boyles, Rev and Mrs J R
Clare, Rev and Mrs M A
Harwood, Rev and Mrs M A
Manton, Rev and Mrs Frank E
Olmstead, Rev and Mrs C E
Spear, Rev and Mrs Ray F
China
Aeschliman, Rev and Mrs E J
Anderson, Rev and Mrs S R
Backus, Dr and Mrs R W
Bankhardt, Rev Frederick
Berckman, Rev and Mrs J H H
Berkey, Mrs Marguerite L
Billing, Mr and Mrs A W
Bishop, Mr and Mrs Merlin A
Breece, Mr and Mrs T E
Brewster, Dr and Mrs Harold N
Burkholder, Rev and Mrs M O
Caldwell, Rev and Mrs H R
Calhoun, Rev and Mrs E C
Clay, Dr and Mrs Ernest H
Cole, Rev and Mrs Winfred B
Coole, Rev and Mrs Arthur B
Coole, Rev and Mrs Douglas P
Davis, Rev and Mrs W W
Day, Rev and Mrs J Wesley
Dennis, Rev L R and Mrs (R.N.)
Dewey, Rev and Mrs Horace E
Dixon, Rev and Mrs J W
Downie, Dr and Mrs Gerald L
Dyson, Rev and Mrs J W
Ferguson, Rev and Mrs F C
Fuller, Mr and Mrs Glenn V
Gale, Rev F C and Dr
Gaw, Miss Evaline
Hale, Rev and Mrs L L
Hanson, Rev and Mrs P O
Hanson, Rev and Mrs R E
Hawk, Rev and Mrs J C
Hayes, Rev and Mrs E Pearce

Henry, Rev and Mrs R T
Hibbard, Rev and Mrs E R
Holland, Rev and Mrs L W
Houston, Miss O Coral
Humphrey, Rev and Mrs L W
Jarvis, Dr Bruce W
Johnson, Rev and Mrs W R
Jones, Rev and Mrs F P
Jones, Rev and Mrs Tracey K
Lacy, Rev and Mrs Henry V
Leitzel, Mrs Ruth L
Lijestrand, Dr and Mrs S H
Magnet, Dr and Mrs F P
Paty, Dr and Mrs Robert M
Perkins, Dr and Mrs E C
Pilley, Mr and Mrs John A
Ploeg, Miss Deanetta (R.N.)
Ploeg, Miss Elizabeth (R.N.)
Pyke, Rev and Mrs F M
Pyke, Rev James H
Rappe, Rev and Mrs C B
Rice, Dr E L and Mrs
Sawyer, Miss Myra L (R.N.)
Schubert, Rev W E
Sheretz, Rev and Mrs D L
Simester, Miss Edith W
Simpson, Mr and Mrs Willard J
Smith, Rev and Mrs W M
Sone, Rev and Mrs H L
Steward, Mr and Mrs A N
Stockwell, Rev and Mrs F Olin
Stokes, Rev and Mrs C D
Stowe, Rev and Mrs E M
Thouroughman, Dr and Mrs J C
Trimmer, Dr and Mrs C S
Watters, Miss Hyla S (M.D.)
Weed, Miss Alice L
Weiss, Dr Ernest and Mrs (R.N.)
Wiant, Rev and Mrs Bliss M
Wiant, Mr and Mrs Paul
Williams, Rev and Mrs E J
Winans, Rev and Mrs E J
Winter, Rev and Mrs C E
Worley, Rev and Mrs Harry W

India
Aldis, Rev and Mrs Steadman
Aldrich, Dr and Mrs H C
Amrein, Rev and Mrs A S
Atkins, Rev and Mrs A G
Auner, Rev and Mrs O M
Badley, Rev and Mrs T C
Badley, Mr Theodore T
Becker, Mr and Mrs Arthur L
Bell, Rev and Mrs W W
Bisbee, Rev and Mrs R D
Clemes, Rev and Mrs S W
Conley, Rev and Mrs Carl H
Cracknell, Miss Wilhelmina (R.N.)
Davis, Rev and Mrs Orville L
Dewey, Rev and Mrs Halsey E
Dye, Rev and Mrs William
Ebright, Rev and Mrs D F
Emerson, Rev and Mrs H M
Fleming, Dr and Mrs R L
Forsgren, Rev and Mrs C O
Garden, Rev and Mrs George B
Griffiths, Rev and Mrs W G
Hall, Sherwood (M.D.) and Mrs (M.D.)
Hanson, Rev and Mrs Harry A
Harper, Rev and Mrs Marvin H
Heins, Rev and Mrs C P Jr
Herrmann, Rev C C
Hollister, Rev and Mrs John N
Jones, Rev and Mrs E Stanley
Keislar, Rev and Mrs Marvin A
Kinder, Rev and Mrs J L
King, Rev and Mrs E L
Kumler, Rev Marion L
Lacy, Mr and Mrs Henry A
Linn, H H (M.D.) and Mrs
Lipp, Rev and Mrs Charles F
Mathews, Rev James K
McEldowney, Rev and Mrs J E
McLaughlin, Rev and Mrs W J
Minnis, Rev and Mrs J F
Moffatt, Rev and Mrs E M
Nave, Rev and Mrs J W
Patterson, Rev and Mrs John

Perrill, C V (M.D.) and Mrs (M.D.)
Perrill, Rev and Mrs Fred M
Pledger, Rev and Mrs W F
Ross, Rev M D and Mrs (R.N.)
Rugg, Rev and Mrs E M
Scholberg, Rev and Mrs H C
Scott, Rev and Mrs Roland W
Seamands, Rev and Mrs E A
Sheets, Rev Sankey L
Smith, Rev and Mrs Edgar H
Stubbs, Rev and Mrs David C
Stuntz, Rev and Mrs C B
Swan, Rev C L and Mrs (R.N.)
Templin, Rev and Mrs L G
Thoburn, Rev and Mrs C S
Thoburn, Mr and Mrs Wilbur C
Thompson, Rev George B
Townsley, Rev Hendrix A
Tweedie, Rev and Mrs E R
Wagner, Rev and Mrs Paul E
Whetstone, Rev and Mrs Wood K
Wilkie, Rev and Mrs J H
Williams, Rev and Mrs F E C
Williams, Rev and Mrs F G

Japan
Best, Rev and Mrs Earl V
Cobb, Rev and Mrs John B
Harbin, Rev and Mrs Andrew Van
Harker, Rev Rowland R
Iglehart, Rev and Mrs Edwin T
Martin, Mr and Mrs J Victor
Melson, Rev and Mrs Davis P
Ogburn, Rev and Mrs Nicholas
Shaver, Rev and Mrs Issac L
Smith, Mr and Mrs Roy
Spencer, Rev and Mrs Robert S
Stewart, Rev and Mrs Stephan A
Thompson, Rev and Mrs
    Everett W

Korea
Amendt, Rev and Mrs Charles C
Demaree, E W (M.D.) and Mrs
Jensen, Rev and Mrs A K
Peters, Rev and Mrs Victor W

Malaya
Amstutz, Rev and Mrs H B
Baughman, Rev Burr H
Blasdell, Rev and Mrs R A
Hoover, Mrs Ethel M
Ingerson, Mr and Mrs C Dudley
McGraw, Rev and Mrs Eugene O
Mosebrook, Rev and Mrs Charles
Patterson, Rev and Mrs C D
Peach, Rev and Mrs P L
Reinoehl, Rev and Mrs W S
Schmucker, Rev and Mrs P H
Thompson, Rev and Mrs Tyler
Youngdahl, Miss Elsa
Philippines
Billings, Rev and Mrs Bliss W
Brush, Rev and Mrs Francis W
Holter, Rev and Mrs Don W
Moore, Rev and Mrs Joseph W
Riley, Rev and Mrs Herbert J
Tuck, Rev and Mrs Ernest E
Sumatra
Alm, Rev and Mrs K Ragnar
McFerren, Rev and Mrs D D
Ostrum, Rev and Mrs Egon

EUROPE

Belgium
Thomas, Rev and Mrs W E
Thonger, Rev and Mrs W G
Bulgaria
Pratsch, Rev and Mrs A W M
Czecho-Slovakia
Barták, Rev and Mrs J P
Vancura, Rev and Mrs Vaclav
Poland
Chambers, Rev and Mrs Edmund
Warfield, Rev and Mrs G P

LATIN AMERICA

Argentina
Aden, Mr and Mrs Fred
Howard, Rev and Mrs G P
Norris, Rev and Mrs J M

Peterson, Mr and Mrs H H
Stockwell, Rev and Mrs B F
Truscott, Rev and Mrs B R
Welsey, Rev A F
Bolivia
Anderson, E W (M.D.) and Mrs
Beck, F S (M.D.) and Mrs
Beck, Miss Miriam A (R.N.)
Dickson, Rev and Mrs Murray S
Herrick, Rev and Mrs J S
MacDonald, Miss Jean C
Smith, Rev and Mrs L B
Smith, Rev Stephan P
Brazil
Betts, Rev and Mrs D L
Borchers, Rev and Mrs W G
Bowden, Rev and Mrs Jalmar
Buyers, Rev Paul E
Clay, Rev and Mrs C W
Cooper, Rev and Mrs C L
Dawsey, Rev and Mrs C B
Ellis, Rev and Mrs J E
Hubbard, Rev and Mrs C E
Lehman, Rev and Mrs H I
Long, Rev and Mrs C A
Moore, Rev and Mrs W H
Morton, Rev and Mrs D W
O'Neal, Rev and Mrs Ernest E
Ream, Mr and Mrs A W
Rogers, Rev and Mrs W F
Saunders, Rev and Mrs J R
Schisler, Mr and Mrs W R
Smith, Rev and Mrs C l
Smith, Rev and Mrs W K
Chile
Bauman, Rev and Mrs Ezra
Bullock, Rev and Mrs D S
Carhart, Rev and Mrs W D
Crawford, Rev and Mrs R L
Depler, Miss Hazel M
Hauser, Rev and Mrs S P
Irle, Mr and Mrs C A
Miller, Rev and Mrs Leon
Prouty, Miss Florence J (R.N.)

Reed, Mr and Mrs E E
Skinner, Miss Achsah M
Smith, Miss Jennie M
Costa Rica
Eaker, Rev R C and Mrs (R.N.)
Kesselring, Rev and Mrs R A
Cuba
Anderson, Rev and Mrs L P
Bardwell, Rev and Mrs H B
Board, Rev and Mrs J G
Daily, Rev and Mrs M C
Evans, Rev and Mrs Garfield
Mitchell, Rev Paul D
Neblett, Rev and Mrs S A
Snyder, Mr and Mrs L H
Stewart, Rev and Mrs C D
Stokes, Rev and Mrs M B
Stroud, Rev and Mrs J E

México
Davis, Rev and Mrs M C
Hauser, Mr and Mrs J P
Kellogg, Mr and Mrs C R
Newberry, Mr and Mrs L B
Panamá
Herschell, Miss Gladys I
Keyser, Miss Elsie J
Smith, Mr and Mrs Matthew D
Perú
Carey, Mr and Mrs J C
Goddard, Miss Nelle B (R.N.)
Plyer, Rev and Mrs H E
Shappell, Rev and Mrs J E
Yoder, Rev and Mrs H W
Uruguay
Legg, Rev and Mrs J T
Smith, Rev and Mrs E M

Woman's Division 1944

AFRICA

Algeria
Anderson, Mary
Narbeth, E. Gwendoline
Robinson, Martha
Van Dyne, Frances
Webb, Nora
Whiteley, Martha (R.N.)
Wolfe, Ruth S
Wysner, Glora M
Angola
Crandall, Violet
Cross, Cilicia
Glidden, Zella
Miller, Alpha
Nelson, Marie
Belgian Congo
Cary, Doris E (R.N.)
Dalbey, Elizabeth
Eye, Kathryn (R.N.)
Foreman, Flora (R.N.)
Kelly, Lorena

Martin, Edith
Moore, Mary E (R.N.)
O'Toole, Ruth (R.N.)
Parham, Catherine
Rees, Dorothy
Robken, Norene
Smith, Arza Maude
White, Annimae
Winfrey, Annie Laura
Zicafoose, Myrtle
Portuguese East Africa
Bartling, Clara J (R.N.)
Lang, Victoria (R.N.)
Michel, Mabel
Miller, Lucile
Northcott, Ruth
Thomas, Ruth
Southern Rhodesia
Clark, Grace
DeVries, Evelyn
Deyo, Marguerite
Fuller, Marjorie
King, Sarah
Parks, Edith

Parmenter, Ona (R.N.)
Pfaff, Jessie A
Quinton, Frances
Reitz, Beulah
Scovill, Ila M
Tubbs, Alice E (R.N.)
Whitney, Alice E (R.N.)
Wildermuth, Helen

ASIA

Burma
Cavett, Maurine
Ebersole, Stella
Kintner, Lela L
Mitzner, Armanda
Oldfather, Jeanette
Power, Elsie M
Reid, Mabel J
Stockwell, Grace L
Winslow, Hazel B
China
Abel, Edith
Adams, Marie
Adams, Uniola (R.N.)
Aldrich, Sylvia
Alsrup, Alice
Apple, Blanche
Ashby, Elma (R.N.)
Avett, Louise
Battin, Lora I (R.N.)
Bedell, Mary
Blackford, Mary
Boeye, Katherine
Bost, Ethel
Bradshaw, Eloise
Brethorst, Marie
Burdeshaw, Rhoda
Butler, Rosa May
Carlyle, Elizabeth (R.N.)
Cole, Marion
Cone, Gertrude
Cowan, Celia
Craig, Jean
Crane, Emeline

Culley, Frances (R.N.)
Daniels, Ruth N
Danner, Ruth M (R.N.)
Danskin, Elsie
Desjardins, Helen
Dickson, Mary Lois
Dyer, Clara Pearl
Echols, Virginia
Eide, Mary E
Eno, Eula (M.D.)
Eriksen, Alma (R.N.)
Evans, Florence (R.N.)
Ferris, Helen
Fosnot, Pearl
Foster, Lorena (R.N.)
Frantz, Ida
Fredericks, Edith
French, Clara
Gish, Ruth
Glenn, Sarah (R.N.)
Graf, Martha
Green, Alice
Gress, Ruth
Griffin, Pansy
Hansing, Ovidia
Hawk, Mary Ellen
Hemenway, Ruth (M.D.)
Herbert, Anne (R.N.)
Highbaugh, Irma
Hobart, Elizabeth
Hollows, Bessie
Holmes, Marion
Hood, Mary (R.N.)
Jaquet, Myra
Jones, Dorothy
Jones, Edna
Jones, Jane D
Jones, Mrs Pearl W (R.N.)
Kesler, Mary G
Killingsworth, Louise
Killingsworth, Mathilde
Knobles, Lillian
Knox, Emma
Koether, Luella

Lane, Ortha M
Lawrence, Birdice
Lefforge, Roxy
Lind, Jenny
Mace, Rose
Manly, Marian E (M.D.)
Mann, Mary
Mason, Pearl
Mayes, Susie
McCain, Pearle
McCutchen, Martha
McIntosh, Elizabeth (R.N.)
Merritt, Edna
Miller, Geneva E (R.N.)
Mitchell, Laura
Morgan, Julia (M.D.)
Nagler, Etha M
Nelson, Lena
Nevitt, Jane Ellen
Nowlin, Mabel
Nutting, Clara A (M.D.)
Palm, Emma (R.N.)
Parsons, Maud
Peacock, Nettie
Pittman, Annie M
Plum, Florence
Powell, Alice M (R.N.)
Prentice, Margaret M (R.N.)
Proctor, Orvia
Reik, Elsie
Richey, Elizabeth
Robinette, Gusta
Robinson, Louise
Rossiter, Henrietta
Rowland, Jean
Rue, Margaret
Russell, Mary K
Savage, Eugenia
Schleman, Laura
Search, Blanche
Seeck, Margaret
Shearer, Mary
Shelton, Mittie
Sia, Ruby
Simpson, Cora (R.N.)

Smith, Clara Bell
Smith, Ellen
Smith, Florence
Smith, Joy L
Smith, Muriel
Smith, Myrtle
Snow, Myra
Stahl, Minta
Stahl, Ruth
Stallings, Nina
Stanford, Sue
Staubli, Frieda (R.N.)
Stephans, Lillie L
Studley, Ellen M
Suffern, Ellen H
Surdham, T. Janet
Swift, Margaret
Thomasson, Leona
Thompson, May Bel
Townsend, Mollie (R.N.)
Trotter, Charlotte
Troutman, Evelyn I
Troy, Nina
Tucker, Maragaret E (M.D.)
Tuttle, Lelia J
Twinem, Marguerite E (M.D.)
Van, Amber
Waldron, Rose
Wallace, Ethel
Watrous, Mary
Webb, Lucy Jim
West, Hester (R.N.)
Westcott, Pauline
Wheeler, Maude
White, Mary Culler
Whitmer, Harriet
Wilcox, Alice A (R.N.)
Wilson, Emma
Wilson, Frances (R.N.)
Winn, Mary B
Witham, Lois E
Wolcott, Jessie
Woodruff, Mabel
Youtsey, Edith

India

Abbott, Anna Agnes
Abbott, Edna May
Albertson, Mildred L
Albertson, Miriam A (M.D.)
Austin, Laura F
Bacon, Edna G
Bacon, Nettie A
Ball, Jennie L
Barber, Emma J
Barry, Elda Mae (R.N.)
Bass, Allie May
Bates, Grace M
Beach, Lucy W
Beale, Elizabeth M
Becker, Gertrude A
Beecher, Barbara H
Bishop, Beulah V (R.N.)
Blackstock, Anna G
Blackstock, Constance E
Boles, Lula A
Boyde, Mary L
Bradley, Edna I
Bragg, Jessie A
Bugby, Margureite M
Burchard, Mary A (M.D.)
Buss, Helen S
Buyers, Anna P (R.N.)
Calkins, Ethel M
Campbell, Louise
Carr, Rachel
Chilson, Elma M
Christensen, Lydia D
Clancey, Kathleen
Clark, Faith A
Clinton, Emma Lahuna
Coleman, L Maxine
Collins, Irma D
Colony, Lucile
Comstock, Joy E
Corner, S Marie
Corpron, Ruth A
Cox, Ruth M
Coy, Martha M
Crawford, Janette H

Crouse, Margaret D
Davis, Grace C
Dimmitt, Marjorie A
Dodd, Stella L (M.D.)
Dome, Alice Mae
Doyle, Gladys
Doyle, Letah M
Drescher, Mildred G
Dunn, Olive
Elliott, Bernice E
Emery, Phoebe E
Ericson, Judith
Eveland, Ruth
Everley, Garnet M
Fales, Cora M
Farmer, Ida A
Fehr, Helen E
Field, Ruth
Forsyth, Estella M
Gabrielson, Winnie
Gallagher, Hannah C
Gordon, Mary V (R.N.)
Green, Lola M
Greene, Leola Mae
Griffin, Alta I
Hadden, G Evelyn
Harrod, Anna M
Heist, Laura
Hermiston, Margaret I W
Hoath, Ruth A
Hobson, Ruby L (R.N.)
Holder, M. Edna
Holland, Mrs Alma H
Holland, Opal
Honnell, Grace L
Huffman, Loal E (M.D.)
Huibregtse, Minnie
Hunt, Ava F
Hutchens, Edna M
Johnson, Frances E
Justin, Catherine L
Kennard, Ada Marie
Keyhoe, Katherine
Kinzley, Katherine M
Kipp, Cora I (M.D.)

Kleiner, Clara
Klingeberger, Ida M
Kriz, Josephine R
Lacy, Edith (M.D.)
Landrum, Margaret
Lantis, Aldine L
Lawrence, Mabel C
Leavitt, Ollie R
Logue, Eva K (R.N.)
Lorenz, Theresa (R.N.)
Low, Nellie M
Manchester, Ruth Coe
Masters, Florence F
McCall, Meriel
McCartney, Blanche L
Miskimen, Mildred
Moore, Mary Ellen
Morrow, Julia E
Moses, Mathilde R
Munson, Kezia E
Nelson, Ada M
Nelson, Caroline C
Nelson, Dora L
Nelson, Maude V (R.N.)
Oldroyd, Roxanna H
Palmer, Pearl E
Parks, Vera E
Perrill, M. Louise
Perry, Ella L
Pierce, Mildred L
Pool, Lydia S
Porter, Eunice (R.N.)
Precise, Myrtle L (R.N.)
Precise, Pearl E
Rexroth, Emma K
Richards, Gertrude E
Richardson, Faithe
Richmond, Mary A
Robbins, Anna A
Robinson, Ruth E
Ross, Elsie M
Ruggles, Ethel E
Salzer, Florence
Saunby, Dora C (R.N.)
Schaefer, Carolyn E

Schlater, Irma (R.N.)
Sheldon, Mabel M
Shepherd, Mildred
Shoemaker, Esther (M.D.)
Simonds, Mildred
Smith, Grace Pepper
Smith, Jennie M
Stallard, Eleanor
Stewart, Emma
Sutherland, May E
Swan, Hilda M
Swords, Lilly G
Thoburn, Isabella
Tirsgaard, Maren M
Tower, Rita B (M.D.)
Wallace, Margaret
Warner, Marian
Warrington, Ruth A
Waugh, Nora B
Webb, Gladys M
Welles, Doris I
West, Nellie M
Westrup, Charlotte (R.N.)
Whiting, Ethel L
Williams, Laura V
Wilson, Retta I
Winslow, Annie S
Wright, Mildred V
Japan
Anderson, Myra
Byler, Gertrude
Carroll, Sallie
Cheney, Alice
Cooper, Lois
Couch, Helen
Curry, Olive
Curtice, Lois
Draper, Winifred
Feely, Gertrude
Fehr, Vera
Field, Ruth
Finch, Mary
Finlay, Alice
Hempstead, Ethel
Hodges, Olive

Holland, Charlie
Hudgins, Mildred
Johnson, Katherine
Kemp, Eva Deane
Kilburn, Elizabeth
McMillan, Mary
Moore, Helen
Paine, Mildred A
Peavey, Anne
Peckham, Caroline
Peet, Azalia
Pider, Myrtle
Searcy, Mary
Simons, Marian
Starkey, Bertha
Stevens, Catherine
Tarr, Alberta
Teague, Carolyn
Tumlin, Mozelle
Wagner, Dora
Whitehead, Mabel
Wolfe, Evelyn
Korea
Alt, Grace E (R.N.)
Appenzeller, Alice
Beaird, Marjorie
Billingsley, Margaret
Black, Nannie
Butts, Ethel (R.N.)
Chaffin, Mrs Anna
Cherry, Mabel
Church, Marie
Conrow, Marion
Cooper, Kate
Dyer, Nellie
Foster, Susie Peach
Hall, Ada B
Hankins, Ida
Hauser, Blanche (R.N.)
Howard, Clara
Hulbert, Jeannette
Kostrup, Alfrida (R.N.)
Laird, Esther
Lee, Rubie
Loucks, Blanche

Lund, Pearl
McHugh, Patricia
McMakin, Alice
McQuie, Ada
Moore, Sadie M
Morris, Harriett P
Oliver, Bessie O
Roberts, Elizabeth (R.N.)
Rosenberger, Elma (R.N.)
Rosser, Helen (R.N.)
Rowland, Elston (R.N.)
Smith, Bertha
Smith, Euline
Wood, Grace
Young, Mary
Malaya
Bloxsom, Bonita C
Bunce, Thirza E
Corbett, Lila M
Craven, Norma B
Dirksen, Mechteld
Harvey, Ruth M
Kerr, Mildred
Marsh, Mabel
Nelson, Eva I
Olson, Della
Olson, Emma
Rank, Minnie
Sadler, Eva M (R.N.)
Urech, Lydia
Philippines
Atkins, Ruth
Blakely, Mildred
Carson, Anna (R.N.)
Cornelison, Bernice
Davis, Hazel
Deam, Mary L
Dingle, Leila
Erbst, Wilhelmina
Evans, Mary A
Thompson, Armenia
Walker, Marion
Sumatra
Chadwick, Freda
Redinger, June

EUROPE

Bulgaria
Carhart, Esther
Reeves, Mrs Florence
Turner, Mellony F
Poland
Browne, Sallie Lewis
Lawrence, Ruth

LATIN AMERICA

Argentina
Boyles, Helen
David, Muriel G
Donahue, Katherine M
Edmeston, Rhoda C
Givin, Olive
Knapp, Lena C
Brazil
Anderson, Ruth
Baxter, Mary Jane
Bennett, Sarah
Best, Louise
Brown, Mary Sue
Brown, Rosalie
Clark, Mary Helen
Cobb, Allie
Dawsey, Sarah
Denison, Alice
Epps, Leila
Farrar, Verda
Ferguson, Lydia
Harris, Anita
Holt, Nancy
Hyde, Eva
Jarrett, Rachel
Kennedy, Gertrude
Mathis, Maude
McFadin, Monta
McKinney, Ruth
McSwain, Mary
Oberlin, Gladys
Peterson, Elizabeth
Simmons, Alberta

Terry, Zula
Varn, Clyde
Cuba
Bailey, Barbara
Buck, Lorraine
Chalmers, Clara
Clay, Ione
Cook, Eulalia
Diggs, Ruth
Earnest, Elizabeth
Fernández, Sara
Gaby, Frances
Hulbert, Esther
Kelly, Juanita
Kenyon, Carrie C
Lewis, Lucille
Malloy, Anges
Neal, Mattie
Nelson, Augusta
Shanks, Leora
Sharpe, Dreta
White, Mary Lou
Williamson, Ethel
Woodward, Mary
México
Arbogast, Gertrude (R.N.)
Baird, Mamie
Booth, Virginia
Byerly, Ruth E
Callahan, Ola E
Cupp, Reba
Deavours, Anne
Dyck, Anna Bell
Dyer, Addie C
Eldrige, Emma
Fox, Lillie F
Hall, Pearl L (R.N.)
Hodgson, Helen M
Hoffman, Jeannette
Ingrum, Dora L
McAllister, Hazel
McKimmey, Tommie Orlene
Nixon, Irene
Pearson, Mary

Potthoff, Edna (R.N.)
Rawls, Lula D (R.N.)
Schmidt, Dora
Seal, May Bel
Shepherd, Elsie M
Thomas, Ethel
Vail, Lucile
Warner, Ruth V
Panamá
Rea, Caroline L
Perú
Fulton, Frances
Hahne, Jane
Hanks, Gertrude

Johnson, Geraldine
Korns, Bonnie
Kutz, Semeramis C
Overholt, Treva
Vanderberg, Martha
Vandergrift, Frances
Widger, Emma A
Uruguay
Brand, Bernice
Craft, Angeline
Derby, Marian L
Hoerner, Lena M
Reid, Jennie

Foreign Missions Division 1948

AFRICA

Angola
Blackburn, Rev and Mrs L E
Blake, Rev and Mrs Charles M
Dodge, Rev and Mrs Ralph E
Elding, Rev E E and Mrs (R.N.)
Hartzler, Rev and Mrs Omar L
Kemp, Alexander H (M.D.) and Mrs
Klebsattel, Rev and Mrs August
Shaad, Rev and Mrs Loyd O
Shields, Miss Irene W
Belgian Congo
Akerberg, Dr and Mrs Ake
Anker, Rev and Mrs H P
Ayres, Rev H C and Mrs (R.N.)
Bartlett, Rev and Mrs Elwood R
Brastrup, Rev John E
Brinton, Rev and Mrs Howard T
Chappell, Rev and Mrs C W
Davis, Rev and Mrs J J
Deale, Dr and Mrs Hugh
DeRuiter, Rev and Mrs William
Everett, Rev and Mrs E I
Everett, Miss Helen N (R.N.)
Hamrick, Rev and Mrs William D
Hughlett, W S (M.D.) and Mrs

Jensen, Miss C Marie (R.N.)
Johnson, Rev and Mrs Louis
Jones, Mr Everett R
Lerbak, Miss Anna E (R.N.)
Lewis, W B (M.D.) and Mrs (R.N.)
Lovell, Rev and Mrs Eugene H
Lovell, Rev and Mrs Marshall W
Maw, Rev and Mrs Joseph H
Persons, Rev and Mrs Maurice E
Piper, Dr and Mrs Arthur
Piper, Miss Ruth B (R.N.)
Pottenger, Mr and Mrs James L
Randall, Mr and Mrs Darrell D
Reid, Rev and Mrs Alexander J
Ridgway, Alton (M.D.) and Mrs (R.N.)
Roberts, Rev and Mrs Emery M
Robinson, Mr and Mrs Lawrence
Smalley, Mr and Mrs Ray L
Stadius, Dr and Mrs Karl G
Stilz, Rev and Mrs Earl B
Townsley, Rev and Mrs Inman U
Wegnatz, Rev J C and Mrs (R.N.)
Wheeler, Rev and Mrs Henry T
Woodcock, Rev and Mrs Everett L
Liberia
Argelander, Rev and Mrs Frank A
Beck, Miss Blanche
Black, Miss Mildred A

Britt, Rev Charles
Cofield, Mr and Mrs Bonnie B
Gray, Mr and Mrs Ulysses S
Harley, Dr and Mrs G W
Kelley, Rev Robert W and Mrs (R.N.)
Mitchell, Miss S Susan
Smith, Rev and Mrs Samuel R

Portuguese East Africa
Gillet, Rev and Mrs Ira E
Keys, Mrs Clara M
Knutsson, Rev Per A
Mitchem, Mr and Mrs Arthur L
Persson, Rev and Mrs J A
Pointer, Rev James D
Randall, Mr and Mrs Darrell D
Rea, Rev and Mrs J S
Stauffacher, Dr C J and Mrs (R.N.)

Southern Rhodesia
Blomquist, Rev and Mrs Lennart
Bourgaize, Rev Wilfred
Culver, Rev and Mrs Maurice E
Eriksson, Rev and Mrs Kaave E
Fuller, Rev Charles E and Mrs (R.N.)
Gates, Rev and Mrs Robert C
Hanson, Miss Ruth E (R.N.)
Hassing, Rev Per and Mrs (R.N.)
Huie, Rev and Mrs Carl W
Jackson, Mr and Mrs Frank S
James, Rev and Mrs Henry I
Murphree, Rev and Mrs Marshall J
O'Farrell, Rev and Mrs T A
Roberts, Rev and Mrs G A
Roberts, Rev and Mrs Q C Jr
Roberts, Mr and Mrs Tudor R
Sells, Rev and Mrs E L
Sheldon, Dr and Mrs John
Thacker, Mr and Mrs Jewel E

ASIA

Burma
Clare, Rev and Mrs M A
Harwood, Rev and Mrs M A
Manton, Rev and Mrs Frank E
Spear, Rev and Mrs Ray F

China
Aeschliman, Rev and Mrs E J
Anderson, Rev and Mrs S R
Backus, Dr and Mrs R W
Bankhardt, Rev Frederick
Berckman, Rev and Mrs J H H
Berkey, Mrs Marguerite L
Breece, Mr and Mrs T E
Brewster, Dr and Mrs Harold N
Clay, Dr and Mrs Ernest H
Cole, Rev and Mrs Winfred B
Coole, Rev and Mrs Arthur B
Coole, Rev and Mrs Douglas P
Davis, Rev and Mrs W W
Day, Rev and Mrs J Wesley
Dennis, Rev L R and Mrs (R.N.)
Dewey, Rev and Mrs Horace E
Dixon, Rev and Mrs J W
Downie, Dr and Mrs Gerald L
Dyson, Rev and Mrs J W
Ferguson, Rev and Mrs F C
Flaherty, Mr Donald
Foster, Rev and Mrs William
Gale, Rev F C and Dr
Gilkey, Mr William
Haines, Rev and Mrs Joseph Harry
Hale, Rev and Mrs L L
Hanson, Rev and Mrs Richard E
Harris, Mr and Mrs Thomas A
Harvey, Rev Earl E Jr
Havighurst, Mr Robert
Hayes, Rev and Mrs E Pearce
Henry, Rev and Mrs R T
Hibbard, Rev and Mrs E R
Holland, Rev and Mrs L W
Hollister, Rev and Mrs George W .
Houston, Miss O Coral
Humphrey, Rev and Mrs L W
Jarvis, Dr Bruce W
Johannaber, Rev and Mrs Charles F
Jones, Rev and Mrs F P
Jones, Rev and Mrs Tracey K
Kennedy, Rev Arthur C Jr
Knettler, Rev and Mrs Edward K
Lacy, Rev and Mrs Henry V

Leitzel, Mrs Ruth L
Lijestrand, Dr and Mrs S H
Manget, Fred P (M.D.) and Mrs
McCoy, Rev Lewistine Mr and Mrs
    (R.N.)
MacInnes, Mr and Mrs Donald E
Overholt, Rev and Mrs William W
Perkins, Rev Edward C (M.D.)
    and Mrs
Phillips, Rev J Carlisle
Pilley, Mr and Mrs John A
Ploeg, Miss Deanetta (R.N.)
Ploeg, Miss Elizabeth (R.N.)
Pyke, Rev and Mrs Frederick M
Pyke, Rev James H
Rappe, Rev and Mrs C Bertram
Schubert, Rev and Mrs William E
Sheretz, Rev and Mrs Dwight L
Simester, Miss Edith W
Simpson, Mr and Mrs Willard J
Smith, Rev and Mrs Wesley M
Sone, Rev and Mrs Hubert L
Steward, Mr and Mrs Albert N
Stockwell, Rev and Mrs F Olin
Teele, Dr and Mrs Roy
Thoroughman, J C (M.D.) and Mrs
Trimmer, Clifford S (M.D.) and Mrs
Watters, Miss Hyla S (M.D.)
Weed, Miss Alice L
Weiss, Ernest W (M.D.) and Mrs
    (R.N.)
Wiant, Rev and Mrs Bliss M
Wiant, Mr and Mrs Paul
Winans, Rev and Mrs Edward J
Winters, Rev and Mrs Charles E
Workman, Rev and Mrs George B
Worley, Rev and Mrs Harry W
India
Acton, Rev and Mrs J P
Aldis, Rev and Mrs Steadman
Aldrich, Herschel C (M.D.) and Mrs
Atkins, Rev and Mrs Arthur G
Auner, Rev and Mrs Orval M
Badley, Rev and Mrs Theodore C
Bell, Rev and Mrs William W

Bisbee, Rev and Mrs Royal D
Boyles, Rev and Mrs J R
Branch, Rev and Mrs M Wells
Bunce, Rev and Mrs H Ross Jr
Conley, Rev and Mrs Carl H
Cracknell, Miss Wilhelmina (R.N.)
Dewey, Rev and Mrs Halsey E
Dye, Rev and Mrs William
Ebright, Rev and Mrs Donald F
Emerson, Rev and Mrs Henry M
Finley, Rev and Mrs Lester
Fleming, Mr Robert L and Mrs (M.D.)
Forsgren, Rev and Mrs Carl O
Garden, Rev and Mrs George B
Ginn, Mr Wesley D and Mrs (M.D.)
Griffiths, Rev and Mrs W G
Hall, Sherwood (M.D.) and Mrs
    (M.D.)
Hanson, Rev and Mrs Harry A
Harper, Rev and Mrs Marvin H
Harwood, Rev Sprigg
Heins, Rev and Mrs Conrad P Jr
Herrmann, Rev and Mrs C C
Hoffman, Mr and Mrs Nelson M
Hollister, Rev and Mrs John N
Howard, Rev Arthur W and Mrs
    (R.N.)
Jones, Rev and Mrs E Stanley
Keislar, Rev and Mrs Marvin
Kinder, Rev and Mrs James L
King, Rev and Mrs Earl L
Lacy, Mr and Mrs Henry A
Lightfoot, Rev and Mrs LeRoy
Linn, Hugh H (M.D.) and Mrs
Linn, Mr and Mrs Kennie M
Lipp, Rev and Mrs Charles F
Lott, Miss Elizabeth Warren
Marble, Rev and Mrs Robert V
McEldowney, Rev and Mrs James E
McLaughlin, Rev and Mrs W J
Minnis, Rev and Mrs Jesse F
Moore, Rev Richard W
Nave, Rev and Mrs J W
Neufeld, Rev Harold M
Nilsson, Rev and Mrs Sten G

Patterson, Rev and Mrs John
Perrill, Charles V (M.D.) and Mrs
    (M.D.)
Perrill, Rev and Mrs Fred M
Pledger, Rev and Mrs W F
Presler, Rev and Mrs Henry H
Reed, Mr and Mrs Ned R
Ross, Rev Marcellus D and Mrs (R.N.)
Rugg, Rev and Mrs Earle M
Rugh, Rev and Mrs Donald E
Scheuerman, Mr and Mrs Lee N
Scott, Rev and Mrs Roland W
Seamands, Rev and Mrs David A
Seamands, Rev and Mrs E A
Seamands, Rev and Mrs John T
Sheets, Rev Sankey L
Smyres, Rev and Mrs Robert W
Staley, J S (M.D.) and Mrs
Stuntz, Rev and Mrs Clyde B
Swan, Rev Charles L and Mrs (R.N.)
Templin, Rev and Mrs Leslie G
Thoburn, Rev and Mrs C Stanley
Thoburn, Mr and Mrs Wilbur C
Thompson, Rev and Mrs G Barney
Titus, Rev and Mrs Murray T
Townsley, Rev and Mrs Hendrix A
Tweedie, Rev and Mrs Earl R
Unruh, Rev and Mrs Irvin A
Wagner, Rev and Mrs Paul F
Westmo, Rev and Mrs Gustaf C
Whetstone, Rev and Mrs Wood K
Wilkie, Rev and Mrs J H N
Wolcott, Rev Leonard T

Japan
Cobb, Rev and Mrs John B
Germany, Rev and Mrs Charles H
Harbin, Rev and Mrs Andrew V
Harker, Rev Rowland R
Hughes, Mr Lee B
Iglehart, Rev and Mrs Edwin T
Judy, Rev and Mrs Carl W
Shaver, Rev and Mrs Isaac L
Smith, Mr and Mrs Roy
Spencer, Rev and Mrs Robert S
Thompson, Rev and Mrs Everett W

Korea
Amendt, Rev and Mrs Charles
Anderson, Rev Earl W (M.D.)
    and Mrs
Anderson, Rev and Mrs L P
Brannon, Rev and Mrs Lyman C
Burkholder, Rev and Mrs M Olin
Jensen, Rev and Mrs A Kristian
Moore, Rev and Mrs James H
Peters, Rev and Mrs Victor W
Sauer, Rev and Mrs Charles A
Shaw, Rev and Mrs William E
Snyder, Rev and Mrs Lloyd H
Stokes, Rev and Mrs C D
Turner, Rev and Mrs Archer R
Williams, Rev and Mrs F E C

Malaya
Amstutz, Rev and Mrs Hobart B
Baughman, Rev Burr H
Blasdell, Rev and Mrs Robert A
Depler, Miss Hazel M
Dodsworth, Rev and Mrs Marmaduke
Eklund, Rev and Mrs Abel
Foss, Rev and Mrs Carlton H
Foster, Rev and Mrs William H
Ingerson, Rev and Mrs C Dudley
Kesselring, Rev and Mrs Ralph A
Kuehn, Rev and Mrs Herbert F
McGraw, Rev and Mrs Eugene O
Peach, Rev and Mrs Preston L
Peterson, Mr and Mrs Herbert H
Reinoehl, Rev and Mrs Waldo S
Runyan, Rev and Mrs Theodore
Schmucker, Rev and Mrs Paul H
Snead, Rev and Mrs Paul
Thompson, Rev and Mrs Tyler

Philippines
Billings, Rev and Mrs Bliss W
Houser, Rev and Mrs Otto N
King, Mr and Mrs Russell

EUROPE AND NORTH AFRICA

Belgium
Thomas, Rev and Mrs W E
Thonger, Rev and Mrs W G

Czechoslovakia
Barták, Rev and Mrs J P
Vancura, Rev and Mrs Vaclav
North Africa
Aurbakken, Rev Hans L
Douglas, Rev and Mrs Elmer H
Heggory, Rev and Mrs Willy N
Kellar, Rev and Mrs F J
Kelly, Mr and Mrs C Guyer
Smith, Rev Edgar H and Mrs (R.N.)
Poland
Chambers, Rev and Mrs Edmund
Warfield, Rev and Mrs Gaither P

LATIN AMERICA

Argentina
Aden, Mr and Mrs Fred
Howard, Rev and Mrs George P
Norris, Rev and Mrs John M
Ramey, Rev and Mrs Arthur G
Stockwell, Rev and Mrs B Foster
Truscott, Rev and Mrs Basil R
Williams, Rev Paul Stark
Bolivia
Beck, Frank S (M.D.) and Mrs
Dickson, Rev and Mrs Murray S
Herrick, Rev and Mrs John S
Holt, Rev and Mrs William
MacDonald, Miss Jean C
Robison, Rev W T
Smith, Rev and Mrs LeGrand B
Brazil
Andrews, Rev and Mrs William E
Betts, Rev and Mrs Daniel L
Bowden, Rev and Mrs Jalmar
Buyers, Rev and Mrs Paul E
Carr, Rev and Mrs Wesley M
Clay, Rev and Mrs Charles W
Cooper, Rev and Mrs Clyde L
Dawsey, Rev and Mrs Cyrus B
Ellis, Rev and Mrs James E
Hubbard, Rev and Mrs C E
Legg, Rev and Mrs J Thoburn
Lehman, Rev and Mrs H I
Long, Rev and Mrs Charles A

Middleton, Rev and Mrs Loyde M
Moore, Rev and Mrs W H
O'Neal, Rev and Mrs Ernest E
Peterson, Rev and Mrs Arthur T Jr
Ream, Mr and Mrs Albert W
Rogers, Rev and Mrs William F Jr
Saunders, Rev and Mrs John R
Schisler, Mr and Mrs W R
Schisler, Mr William R Jr
Smith, Rev and Mrs Wilbur K
Wisdom, Rev and Mrs Robert W
Chile
Bauman, Rev and Mrs Ezra
Carhart, Rev and Mrs Walter D
Crawford, Mr and Mrs Randall L
Hauser, Rev and Mrs Scott P
Irle, Mr and Mrs Charles A
Major, Rev and Mrs James E
Mason, Rev and Mrs Walter F
Miller, Rev and Mrs Leon
Peet, Miss Alice Lida
Prouty, Miss Florence J (R.N.)
Reed, Mr and Mrs Elbert E
Wade, Mr and Mrs Martin G
White, Rev and Mrs David C
Costa Rica
Eaker, Rev Robert C and Mrs (R.N.)
Smith, Miss Jennie M
Ward, Rev and Mrs Joseph C Jr
Cuba
Bardwell, Rev and Mrs H B
Daily, Rev and Mrs Maurice C
Evans, Rev and Mrs Garfield
Milk, Mr and Mrs Richard G
Smith, Rev and Mrs Irving L
Stewart, Rev and Mrs Carl D
Stokes, Rev and Mrs M B
Stroud, Rev and Mrs John E
México
Davis, Rev and Mrs Milton C
Kellogg, Mr and Mrs Claude R
Matzigkeit, Rev and Mrs Wesley M
Panamá
Arms, Mr and Mrs Wallace R
Fiske, Rev and Mrs Louis M

Herschell, Miss Gladys I
Smith, Mr and Mrs Matthew D
Perú
Bower, Mr and Mrs Edwin T
Landis, Mrs Frances C
Miller, Miss Elizabeth W
Nothdurft, Rev and Mrs Ivan H
Patton, Rev Carl Jr

Plyler, Rev and Mrs Henry E
Shappell, Rev and Mrs John E
Yoder, Rev and Mrs Howard W
Uruguay
Lee, Rev and Mrs Lawson
Nyberg, Rev and Mrs Warren A
Smith, Rev and Mrs Earl M

Woman's Division 1948

AFRICA

Angola
Crandall, Violet
Cross, Cilicia
Glidden, Zella
Miller, Alpha
Nelson, Marie
Central Congo
Cary, Doris E (R.N.)
Dalbey, H Elizabeth
Eye, Kathryn (R.N.)
Foreman, Flora (R.N.)
Homfeldt, Ethel
Kelly, Lorena
Martin, Edith
Moore, Mary E (R.N.)
Parker, Anne
Rees, Dorothy
Smith, Arza Maude
White, Annimae
Winfrey, Annie Laura
Zicafoose, Myrtle
North Africa
Anderson, Mary
King, Mrs Anna
Webb, Nora
Whiteley, Martha (R.N.)
Southeast Africa
Bartling, Clara J (R.N.)
Lang, Victoria (R.N.)
Michel, Mabel
Miller, Lucile

Northcott, Ruth
Thomas, Ruth
Southern Congo
Montgomery, Thelma
Parham, Catherine
Southern Rhodesia
Ashby, Elma (R.N.)
Clark, Grace
DeVries, Evelyn
Deyo, Marguerite
Hackler, Frances
King, Sarah
Parks, Edith
Parmenter, Ona (R.N.)
Pfaff, Emma
Pfaff, Jessie A
Reitz, Beulah
Scovill, Ila May
Taylor, Lois Mildred
Tubbs, Lulu
Whitney, Alice E (R.N.)
Wildermuth, Helen

ASIA

Burma
Cavett, Maurine
Ebersole, Stella
Kintner, Lela L
Reid, Mabel J
Winslow, Hazel B
China
Abel, Edith
Adams, Marie
Adams, Uniola (R.N.)

Aldrich, Sylvia
Alsrup, Alice
Apple, Blanche
Avett, Louise
Battin, Lora I (R.N.)
Bedell, Mary
Blackford, Mary
Bost, Ethel
Bradshaw, Eloise
Brethorst, Marie
Butler, Rosa May
Carlyle, Elizabeth (R.N.)
Cole, Marion
Cone, Gertrude
Cowan, Celia
Craig, Jean
Culley, Frances (R.N.)
Daniels, Ruth N
Danner, Ruth M (R.N.)
Danskin, Elsie
Desjardins, Helen
Dickhaut, Olivia
Dyer, Clara Pearl
Eide, Mary E
Eriksen, Alma (R.N.)
Evans, Florence (R.N.)
Ferris, Helen
Fosnot, Pearl
Foster, Lorena (R.N.)
Frantz, Ida
Fredericks, Edith
French, Clara
Fulton, Frances
Gautier, Linnie Lou
Gish, Ruth
Glenn, Sarah (R.N.)
Graf, Martha
Gress, Ruth
Griffin, Pansy
Gruber, Miriam Jean
Hansing, Ovidia
Harris, Ruth
Heinsohn, Judith
Herbert, Anne (R.N.)

Highbaugh, Irma
Hobart, Elizabeth
Hollows, Bessie
Holmes, Marion
Jaquet, Myra
Johannaber, Elizabeth
Jones, Jane D
Jones, Mrs Pearl W (R.N.)
Kesler, Mary G
Killingsworth, Louise
Killingsworth, Mathilde
Knobles, Lillian
Koether, Luella
Lane, Ortha M
LaRue, Eunice
Lind, Jenny
Main, Mrs Idabelle Lewis
Manly, Marian E (M.D.)
Mann, Mary
Mason, Pearl
Mayes, Susie
McCain, Pearle
McCutchen, Martha
Mercer, Evelyn
Merritt, Edna
Miller, Geneva E (R.N.)
Mitchell, Laura
Mitchell, Mary
Mortimer, Mrs Elizabeth
Nagler, Etha M
Nowlin, Mabel
Nutting, Clara A (M.D.)
Palm, Emma (R.N.)
Parsons, Maud
Pittman, Annie M
Prentice, Margaret M (R.N.)
Proctor, Orvia
Reed, Mary Frances
Reik, Elsie
Richey, Elizabeth
Rippey, Hazel
Robinette, Gusta
Rossiter, Henrietta
Rowland, Jean

Rue, Margaret
Russell, Mary K
Savage, Eugenia
Schleman, Laura
Seeck, Margaret
Shearer, Mary
Sia, Ruby
Smith, Clara Bell
Smith, Florence
Smith, Joy L
Smith, Muriel
Smith, Myrtle
Stahl, Ruth
Stallings, Nina
Stanford, Sue
Staubli, Frieda (R.N.)
Steinheimer, Mary (M.D.)
Stephens, Lillie L
Studley, Ellen M
Suffern, Ellen H
Surdam, T Janet
Swift, Margaret
Thompson, May Bel
Townsend, Mollie (R.N.)
Trotter, Charlotte
Troutman, Evelyn I
Tucker, Maragaret E (M.D.)
Twinem, Marguerite E (M.D.)
Van, Amber
Waldron, Rose
Wallace, Ethel
Watrous, Mary
Webb, Lucy Jim
Wheeler, Maude
Whitmer, Harriet
Wilcox, Alice A (R.N.)
Wilson, Emma
Winn, Mary B
Witham, Lois E
Wolcott, Jessie
Woodruff, Mabel
Youtsey, Edith
India
Abbott, Anna Agnes

Abbott, Edna May
Albertson, Mildred L
Althouse, Mildred L
Austin, Laura F
Bacon, Edna G
Ball, Jennie L
Barry, Elda Mae (R.N.)
Bates, Grace M
Beach, Lucy W
Beale, Elizabeth M
Bearden, Dorothy
Becker, Gertrude A
Beecher, Barbara H
Blackstock, Anna G
Blackstock, Constance E
Blasdell, Jennie
Boles, Lula A
Bomar, Minnie Mae
Boyde, Mary L
Bradley, Edna I
Bragg, Jessie A
Bugby, Margureite M
Burchard, Mary A (M.D.)
Buss, Helen S
Buyers, Anna P
Calkins, Ethel M
Calkins, Helen
Campbell, Louise
Chilson, Elma M
Christensen, Lydia D
Clancey, Kathleen
Clark, Faith A
Coleman, L Maxine
Collins, Irma D
Comstock, Joy E
Corner, S Marie
Corpron, Ruth A
Cox, Ruth M
Coy, Martha M
Crawford, Janette H
Davis, Grace C
Dimmitt, Marjorie A
Dodd, Stella L (M.D.)
Doyle, Gladys

Doyle, Letah M
Drescher, Mildred G
Dunn, Olive
Elliott, Bernice E
Emery, Phoebe E
Eveland, Ruth
Everley, Garnet M
Fairbanks, Elizabeth
Fales, Cora M
Farmer, Ida A
Fehr, Helen E
Field, Ruth
Gallagher, Hannah C
Gordon, Mary V (R.N.)
Greene, Lola M
Greene, Leola Mae
Griffin, Alta I
Hadden, G. Evelyn
Harrod, Anna M
Heist, Laura
Hoath, Ruth A
Hobson, Ruby L (R.N.)
Holder, M Edna
Holland, Alma H (Mrs)
Honnell, Grace L
Huffman, Loal E (M.D.)
Huibregtse, Minnie
Hunt, Ava F
Hutchens, Edna M
Johnson, Frances E
Johnson, Mrs Harriet F
Justin, Catherine L
Kennard, Ada Marie
Keyhoe, Katherine
Kinzley, Katherine M
Kleiner, Clara
Klingeberger, Ida M
Kriz, Josephine R
Lacy, Edith (M.D.)
Landon, Louise
Landrum, Margaret
Lawrence, Mabel C
Leavitt, Ollie R
Lewis, Nellie E (R.N.)

Logue, Eva K (R.N.)
Lorenz, Theresa (R.N.)
Manchester, Ruth Coe
Mansfield, Marietta
Martyn, Florence (R.N.)
Masters, Florence F
McCall, Meriel
McCartney, Blanche L
Morrow, Julia E
Moses, Mathilde R
Munson, Kezia E
Nelson, Ada M
Nelson, Dora L
Norris, Kathleen A (R.N.)
Oldroyd, Roxanna H
Overby, Elizabeth (R.N.)
Palmer, Florence K
Palmer, Pearl E
Parks, Vera E
Perrill, M. Louise
Perry, Ella L
Pierce, Mildred L
Pool, Lydia S
Porter, Eunice (R.N.)
Precise, Myrtle L (R.N.)
Precise, Pearl
Rexroth, Emma K
Richardson, Faithe
Robbins, Anna A
Robinson, Ruth E
Ross, Elsie M
Ruggles, Ethel E
Saladin, Louise
Salzer, Florence
Saunby, Dora C (R.N.)
Schaefer, Carolyn E
Sheldon, Mabel M
Shepherd, Mildred
Shoemaker, Esther (M.D.)
Sluyter, Eunice
Smith, Grace Pepper
Smith, Jennie M
Stallard, Eleanor
Stewart, Emma

Sutherland, May E
Swords, Lilly G
Thoburn, Isabella
Tirsgaard, Maren M
Wallace, Margaret
Ward, Mrs Olive Gould
Warner, Emma E
Warner, Marian
Warrington, Ruth A
Webb, Gladys M
Webster, Lucille
Welles, Doris I
Wells, Evelyn
West, Nellie M
Westrup, Charlotte (R.N.)
Whiting, Ethel L
Williams, Laura V
Wilson, Retta I
Wright, Mildred V

Japan

Anderson, Myra
Bailey, Barbara
Brittain, Blanche
Byler, Gertrude
Carroll, Sallie
Cheney, Alice
Cooper, Lois
Curry, Olive
Draper, Winifred
Feely, Gertrude
Fehr, Vera
Field, Ruth
Finch, Mary
Finlay, Mary
Hempstead, Ethel
Holland, Charlie
Holland, Opal
Hudgins, Mildred
Johnson, Katherine
Kemp, Eva Deane
McMillan, Mary
Moore, Helen
Paine, Mildred A
Peavey, Anne
Peckham, Caroline

Peet, Azalia
Pider, Myrtle
Schwab, Elsa
Searcy, Mary
Simons, Marian
Starkey, Bertha
Stevens, Catherine
Tarr, Alberta
Teague, Carolyn
Tumlin, Mozelle
Wagner, Dora
Warne, Eleanor
Whitehead, Mabel
Wolfe, Evelyn

Korea

Alt, Grace E (R.N.)
Appenzeller, Alice
Beaird, Marjorie
Black, Nannie
Boyles, Helen
Butts, Ethel (R.N.)
Chaffin, Mrs Anna
Church, Marie
Conrow, Marion
Cooper, Kate
Diggs, Ruth
Dyer, Nellie
Foster, Susie Peach
Hall, Ada B
Hauser, Blanche (R.N.)
Howard, Clara
Hulbert, Jeannette
Jackson, Carrie
Laird, Esther
Lee, Rubie
Lund, Pearl
Mauk, Mary Vic
Maynor, Mrs Velma
McHugh, Patricia
McMakin, Alice
McQuie, Ada
Miller, Ethel
Moore, Sadie M
Nelson, Maude V (R.N.)
Oldfather, Jeanette

Oliver, Bessie
Roberts, Elizabeth (R.N.)
Rosser, Helen (R.N.)
Smith, Bertha
Wood, Grace
Malaya
Corbett, Lila M
Craven, Norma B
Dirksen, Mechteld
Harder, Ann
Harvey, Ruth
Kenyon, Carrie C
Marsh, Mabel
Mitchell, Mabel
Nelson, Eva
Olson, Della
Rea, Caroline L
Sadler, Eva
Urech, Lydia
Philippines
Blakely, Mildred
Carson, Anna (R.N.)
Cornelison, Bernice
Davis, Hazel
Deam, Mary L
Dingle, Leila
Evans, Mary A
Klepper, Madaleine
Lefforge, Roxy
Moe, Carol E
Odec, Bertha (R.N.)
Rowland, Elston (R.N.)
Walker, Marion
Sumatra
Chadwick, Freda

EUROPE

Bulgaria
Turner, Mellony F
Wolfe, Ruth S
Poland
Browne, Sallie Lewis
Lawrence, Ruth

LATIN AMERICA

Argentina
Abrams, Josephine
Donahue, Katherine M
Givin, Olive
Knapp, Lena C
Brazil
Anderson, Ruth
Asher, Helen
Baxter, Mary Jane
Bennett, Sarah
Best, Louise
Bowden, Mary Elizabeth
Bowden, Sarah Frances
Brown, Mary Sue
Brown, Rosalie
Clark, Mary Helen
Dawsey, Sarah
Denison, Alice
Epps, Leila
Farrar, Verda
Ford, Florence
Harris, Anita
Hesselgesser, Irene
Hyde, Eva
Jarrett, Rachel
Kennedy, Gertrude
Locke, Sarah Louise
Mathis, Maude
McFadin, Monta
McKinney, Ruth
McSwain, Mary
Oberlin, Gladys
Simmons, Alberta
Terry, Zula
Traeger, Gazelle
Cuba
Buck, Lorraine
Chalmers, Clara
Clay, Ione
Cook, Eulalia
Earnest, Elizabeth
Fernández, Sara
Gaby, Frances

Hein, Marjorie
Hulbert, Esther L
Kelly, Juanita
Malloy, Agnes
Moe, Gertrude
Neal, Mattie
Nelson, Augusta
Shanks, Leora
Sharpe, Dreta
Woodward, Mary
México
Arbogast, Gertrude (R.N.)
Baird, Mamie
Booth, Virginia
Byerly, Ruth E
Callahan, Ola E
Deavours, Anne
Dyck, Anna Bell
Eldrige, Emma
Gibson, Clara
Hall, Pearl L (R.N.)
Hodgson, Helen M
Ingrum, Dora L
McKimmey, Tommie Orlene
Nixon, Irene
Pearson, Mary
Rawls, Lula D (R.N.)

Schmidt, Dora
Seal, May Bel
Shepherd, Elsie E
Thomas, Ethel E
Vail, Lucile
Warner, Ruth V
Perú
Farr, Geraldine
Fenner, Esther Gene
Games, Mary Helen
Greve, Ella
Hanks, E Gertrude
Koch, Alverna
Kutz, Semeramis C
Meier, Opal
Overholt, Treva
Sandfort, Dorothy A
Vanderberg, Martha
Vandergrift, Frances
Uruguay
Brunken, Viola
Derby, Marian
Hoerner, Lena M
Kress, Maylah
Lynch, Gladys G
Nelson, Dorothy
Person, Ulla

Foreign Missions Division 1952

AFRICA

Angola
Andreassen, Rev and Mrs Harry P
Blackburn, Rev and Mrs L E
Blake, Rev and Mrs Charles M
Brancel, Mr and Mrs Frederick C
Cooper, Rev and Mrs Edgar R J
Hole, Mr Charles W
LeMaster, Rev and Mrs E Edwin
Noah, Rev and Mrs Raymond E
Nordby, Rev and Mrs J M A
Schaad, Mr and Mrs Loyd O
Shields, Miss Irene W
Way, Mr Marion Jr

Belgian Congo
Central
Akerberg, Ake (M.D.) and Mrs
Anker, Rev and Mrs H P
Ayres, Mr and Mrs Henry C
Bitsch-Larsen, Immanuel (M.D.) and Mrs
Bright, Mr Robert E
Chappell, Rev and Mrs C W
Davis, Rev and Mrs J J
Davis, Rev and Mrs Joseph
Deale, Hugh S (D.D.S.) and Mrs
DeRuiter, Rev and Mrs William
Hamrick, Mr and Mrs W D
Hughlett, W S (M.D.) and Mrs
Johnson, Rev and Mrs Louis C
Law, Mr and Mrs Burleigh A

Lewis, W B (M.D.) and Mrs (R.N.)
Lovell, Rev and Mrs Eugene H
Lovell, Rev and Mrs Marshall W
Maw, Rev and Mrs Joseph H
Mothersbaugh, Mr Jesse M
Reeve, Rev and Mrs Charles W
Reid, Rev and Mrs A J
Ritter, Mr and Mrs Darrell Max
Shaffer, Mr and Mrs Harrison L
Stilz, Rev and Mrs Earl B
Townsley, Rev and Mrs Inman U
Weaver, Mr Charles F
Wheeler, Rev and Mrs Henry T
Young, Mr and Mrs Jesse M
Southern
Bartlett, Rev and Mrs Elwood R
Bastrup, Rev John E
Brinton, Rev and Mrs Howard T
Burlbaugh, Mr and Mrs Alfred G
Davis, Rev and Mrs William D
Deschacht, Mr and Mrs Louis
Enright, Rev and Mrs Kenneth D
Everett, Rev and Mrs Kenneth D
Hardee, Howard D (M.D.)
Hartzler, Rev and Mrs Omar L
Henk, Rev and Mrs Wallace E
Lerbak, Miss Anna E
Little, Mr and Mrs Harry
Nelis, Mr and Mrs Marc
Persons, Rev and Mrs Maurice E
Piper, Miss Ruth B
Pottenger, Mrs James L
Ridgway, Alton H (M.D.) and Mrs
Roberts, Rev and Mrs Emery M
Robinson, Rev and Mrs Lawrence
Shryock, Mr John E
Smalley, Mr and Mrs Ray L
Whelchel, Rev Albert F
Woodcock, Rev and Mrs Everett L
Liberia
Black, Miss Mildred A
Booher, Mr Harold H
Britt, Rev and Mrs Charles R
Carey, Mr and Mrs Robert Dale
Carson, Rev and Mrs John Walter

Cofield, Mr and Mrs B B
Gray, Rev and Mrs Ulysses S
Harley, Rev George W (M.D.)
    and Mrs
Kelley, Rev and Mrs Robert W
Mitchell, Miss S Susan
Smith, Rev and Mrs Samuel R
Strom, Mr and Mrs John W
Sundar, Rev and Mrs Paul N
Tross, Friedrich C (M.D.) and Mrs
Watters, Hyla S (M.D.)
Southeast Africa
Adolfson, Rev and Mrs T E V
Gillet, Rev and Mrs Ira E
Greenberg, Mr and Mrs Harry
Helgesson, Mr and Mrs Alf Gustav
Kaemmer, Mr John E
Kemling, Rev and Mrs Max Vernon
Kemp, Rev Alexander H (M.D.) and
    Mrs
Knutsson, Rev and Mrs Per A
Persson, Rev and Mrs Josef A
Rea, Rev and Mrs Julian S
Whitney, Mr Gilbert L
Rhodesia
Aeschliman, Rev and Mrs Edward J
Anfinsen, Rev and Mrs Hans F
Blomquist, Rev and Mrs Lennart G
Boucher, Rev and Mrs Arnold R
Bourgaize, Rev Wilfred
Carr, Mr and Mrs Galen M
Culver, Rev and Mrs Maurice E
Eriksson, Rev and Mrs Kaare E
Fuller, Rev Charles E and Mrs (R.N.)
Gates, Rev and Mrs Robert C
Griffin, Rev and Mrs Hunter D
Hanson, Miss Ruth E (R.N.)
Harper, Rev and Mrs Kenneth E
Hassing, Rev Per and Mrs (R.N.)
Higgs, Mr and Mrs Barnie A
Huie, Mrs Carl W
Jackson, Rev and Mrs Frank A
Janssen, Mr and Mrs Ivar W
Johnson, Mr J Morgan
Kinyon, Mr and Mrs Wallace V

Leiknes, Rev and Mrs Asbjorn
Mansure, Rev and Mrs Arthur L
Murphree, Rev and Mrs Marshall J
Roberts, Rev and Mrs Q C Jr
Roberts, Mr and Mrs Tudor R
Sells, Rev and Mrs Ernest Lawrence
Sheldon, John Fisk (M.D.) and Mrs
Sheretz, Rev and Mrs Dwight L
Smalley, Rev and Mrs Bruce Alan
Stine, Rev and Mrs Ovid A
Thacker, Mr and Mrs Jewel E
North Africa
Aurbakken, Rev and Mrs Hans Lorents
Bres, Rev Paul H
Butler, Mr David Wendell
Carlo, Mr Joseph M
Chambers, Rev and Mrs Edmund
Douglas, Rev and Mrs Elmer H
Griffith, Rev and Mrs Lester E
Heggory, Rev and Mrs Willy N
Holmes, Mr James B
Kelly, Mr and Mrs C Guyer
Reinertsen, Rev and Mrs F Arne
Smith, Rev and Mrs Edgar H
Sullivan, Mr Gordon E
Teigland, Rev and Mrs Thorlief
Williams, Rev and Mrs R Ward

EUROPE

Austria
Argelander, Rev and Mrs Frank A
Barták, Rev and Mrs Joseph P
Belgium
Thomas, Rev and Mrs William E
Thonger, Rev and Mrs Wiliam G
Czechoslovakia
Vancura, Rev and Mrs Vaclav

CHINA

East China
Anderson, Rev and Mrs Sidney R
Henry, Rev and Mrs Robert T
Smith, Rev and Mrs Wesley M
Thoroughman, J C (M.D.) and Mrs

Foochow
Lacy, Rev and Mrs Creighton B
MacInnis, Mr and Mrs Donald E
Hinghwa
Phillips, Rev and Mrs James Carlisle Jr
Winters, Rev and Mrs Charles E
Kiangsi
Weiss, Ernst W (M.D.) and Mrs (R.N.)
Mid-China
Johannaber, Rev and Mrs Charles F
Jones, Rev and Mrs Francis P
North China
Gilkey, Mr William E
Kennedy, Rev and Mrs Arthur C Jr
Wiant, Rev and Mrs Bliss M
West China
Stockwell, Rev and Mrs F Olin

BORNEO

Coole, Rev and Mrs Douglas P
Dennis, Rev and Mrs Louis R
Harris, Mr and Mrs Thomas A
Overholt, Rev and Mrs William W
Pilley, Mr and Mrs John A

BURMA

Clare, Rev and Mrs Maurice A
Hollister, Rev and Mrs George W
Howard, Rev Robert C
Jones, Rev and Mrs Haniel
Manton, Rev and Mrs Frank E
Spear, Rev and Mrs Ray F

FORMOSA

Knettler, Rev and Mrs Edward K

MALAYA

Amstutz, Rev and Mrs Hobart B
Baughman, Rev Burr H
Berckman, Rev and Mrs J H H
Blasdell, Rev and Mrs Robert A
Day, Rev and Mrs J Wesley
Dodsworth, Rev and Mrs Marmaduke
Eklund, Rev and Mrs Abel

Foss, Rev and Mrs Carlton H
Foster, Rev and Mrs William H
Goltz, Mr Charles Robert
Haines, Rev and Mrs J Harry
Jones, Rev and Mrs Tracey K Jr
Kesselring, Rev and Mrs Ralph A
Knutsen, Rev and Mrs Kjell C
Kuehn, Rev and Mrs Herbert F
Lundy, Rev and Mrs Robert F
Mark, Mr and Mrs Herman J
McGraw, Rev and Mrs Eugene O
Miles, Mr Teddy Cole
Peterson, Mr and Mrs Herbert H
Reinoehl, Rev and Mrs Waldo S
Runyan, Rev and Mrs Theodore
Shumaker, Mr and Mrs Charles E
Snead, Mr and Mrs Paul K
Sone, Rev and Mrs Hubert L
Teilmann, Rev and Mrs Gunnar J
Thomas, Miss Margaret E
Wahl, Mr and Mrs Bernard C
Wiant, Mr Paul P
Williamson, Mr Andrew J

SUMATRA

Alm, Rev and Mrs K Ragnar
Dixon, Rev and Mrs Edward E
Hamel, Mr and Mrs Albert W
Klaus, Rev and Mrs Armin V
Lager, Rev and Mrs Per-Eric A
Pyke, Mr and Mrs James H

JAPAN

Adams, Rev and Mrs Evyn M
Bascom, Mr and Mrs Gilbert E
Basinger, Mr Robert R
Berkey, Mrs Marguerite L
Best, Rev and Mrs Ernest Edwin
Bray, Rev and Mrs William
    Davenport
Browning, Rev and Mrs Willis P
Cobb, Rev and Mrs John B
Des Autels, Rev William W
Dornon, Mr Ivan Forest

Dunton, Mr and Mrs Rupert C
Elder, Mr and Mrs William Milton
Germany, Rev and Mrs Charles H
Harbin, Rev and Mrs A Van Jr
Hayes, Rev and Mrs E Pearce
Housman, Mr H Burton
Hughes, Mr Lee B
Johnson, Mr and Mrs Keith W
Kreps, Mr and Mrs Leslie R
Linde, Mr Richard
McMullen, Mr John Lester
McWilliams, Rev and Mrs Robert W
Palmore, Rev and Mrs P Lee
Parrott, Mr and Mrs George W
Parsons, Mr and Mrs Norman W
Pray, Mr Martin B
Reid, Mr J David
Saito, Mr and Mrs Morse T
Sawada, Mr Ben
Shaver, Rev and Mrs Issac L
Skillman, Mr and Mrs John H
Squire, Rev John Robert
Stubbs, Rev and Mrs David C
Swift, Mr E Lawrence
Teele, Mr and Mrs Roy E
Thompson, Rev and Mrs Everett W
Weiss, Mr Gerald W
Williams, Mr and Mrs F E C
Winans, Rev Edwin J

KOREA

Amendt, Rev and Mrs Charles
Anderson, Rev and Mrs Leonard P
Appenzeller, Rev and Mrs Henry D
Burkholder, Rev and Mrs M Olin
Cooper, Mr Lee Ronald
Jensen, Rev and Mrs A Kristian
Judy, Rev and Mrs Carl W
Payne, Mr and Mrs Donald T
Sauer, Rev and Mrs Charles A
Schowengerdt, Mr and Mrs Dean
    Louis
Shaw, Rev and Mrs William E
Spitzkeit, Rev and Mrs James W

Stokes, Rev and Mrs Charles D
Taylor, Rev and Mrs Lyman P
Turner, Rev and Mrs Archer R
Zellers, Mr and Mrs Lawrence A

OKINAWA

Barberi, Mr and Mrs Mario Charles
Bell, Mr and Mrs Otis W Jr
Hambrick, Mr Charles
Rickard, Rev and Mrs C Harold

PHILIPPINES

Bush, Rev and Mrs Richard C Jr
Case, Mr Norman D
Clark, Rev and Mrs Byron W
Dewey, Rev and Mrs Horace E
Foster, Mr and Mrs William A Jr
Hartman, Gerald V (M.D.) and Mrs
Holt, Rev and Mrs John B
Lundy, Mr and Mrs John Thomas
Lung, Rev Thomas W
Moore, Rev and Mrs James H
Mosebrook, Rev and Mrs Charles
Reeves, Mr Don Theodore
Spottswood, Rev and Mrs Curran
Wiant, Mr B Leighton

INDIA AND PAKISTAN

Bengal
Dewey, Rev and Mrs Halsey E
Griffiths, Rev and Mrs Walter G
Hastings, Mr Joseph E
Jones, Mr William Wayne
Larsson, Rev and Mrs John A
Morgan, Rev Homer LeRoy
Nilsson, Rev and Mrs Sten G
Rees, Rev and Mrs Oscar W
Workman, Rev and Mrs George B
Bombay
Fuller, Rev Glenn S
Garrison, Rev and Mrs Maran S
Minnis, Rev and Mrs Jesse F
Reynolds, Mr and Mrs Charles
Unruh, Rev and Mrs Irvin A

Wagner, Rev and Mrs Paul F
Central Provinces
Carney, Rev and Mrs Harry Arnold
Ehrensperger, Mr Harold A
Emerson, Rev and Mrs Henry M
Harper, Rev and Mrs Marvin H
Hogg, Rev and Mrs (M.D.) William
    Richey
Lanham, Rev and Mrs Raymond E
Marble, Rev and Mrs Robert V
Martin, Rev and Mrs Tunnie Jr
McEldowney, Rev and Mrs James E
Presler, Rev and Mrs Henry H
Scott, Rev Julius S
Smith, Mr and Mrs Arthur R
Thoburn, Rev and Mrs C Stanley
Delhi
Allen, Rev and Mrs Daniel D
Allison, Mr John Richard
Dye, Rev and Mrs William
Finney, Rev and Mrs John Wilton
Hall, Sherwood (M.D.) and Mrs (M.D.)
Johns, Mr and Mrs H Drewer
Kawata, Mr and Mrs Kazuyoshi
King, Mr and Mrs Russell H
Meacham, Mr and Mrs Stewart
Pickett, Mr Douglas R
Powell, Mr and Mrs Lyle H
Rugh, Rev and Mrs Donald E
Sill, Mr and Mrs Maurice L
Smyres, Rev and Mrs Robert W
Staley, Joseph S (M.D.) and Mrs
Stoddard, Mr Robert H
Thompson, Rev and Mrs G Barney
Whetstone, Rev and Mrs Wood K
Gujarat
Aldrich, Herschel C (M.D.) and Mrs
Bauman, Rev David B
Finley, Mr and Mrs Lester
Jarvis, Bruce W (M.D.) and Mrs
Johnson, Mr and Mrs Gerhard T
Manning, Rev and Mrs William C
Hyderabad
Garden, Rev and Mrs George B

Hoffman, Mr and Mrs Nelson M
Moon, Rev and Mrs William Rex
Patterson, Rev and Mrs John
Seamands, Rev and Mrs David A
Lucknow
Howard, Mr Arthur W and Mrs (R.N.)
Hulse, Mr and Mrs Bruce T
Hunt, Rev and Mrs John M
Kennedy, Rev and Mrs George T
Kinder, Rev and Mrs James L
Leach, Rev and Mrs Keith Alan
Moffatt, Rev Elbert M
Robinson, Mr and Mrs Ruel A
Tweedie, Mr and Mrs Earl R
Wolcott, Rev Leonard T
North India
Atkins, Rev and Mrs Arthur G
Bunce, Rev and Mrs H Ross Jr
Ebright, Rev and Mrs Donald F
Ginn, Mr and Mrs (M.D.) Wesley D
Hanson, Rev and Mrs Harry Albert
Hills, Rev and Mrs David W
Hollister, Rev and Mrs John N
Jones, Rev and Mrs E Stanley
Lacy, Mr and Mrs Henry A
Nave, Rev and Mrs Julian W
Nave, Mr and Mrs Robert W
Perrill, Charles V (M.D.) and Mrs
    (M.D.)
Petersen, Robert F (D.M.D.) and Mrs
Pomeroy, James M (M.D.) and Mrs
South India
Betts, Reeve H (M.D.) and Mrs
Heins, Rev and Mrs Conrad P
Linn, Mr and Mrs Kennie M
Pickard, Raleigh H (M.D.) and Mrs
Ruggiero, Mr John P
Schneck, Rev and Mrs Alfred F
Seamands, Rev and Mrs E A
Seamands, Rev and Mrs John T
Sturges, Mr and Mrs Richard E
Townesley, Rev and Mrs Hendrix A
India General
Baumgardner, Mr Marion F

Bell, Rev and Mrs William W
Clark, Dr John
Downie, Gerald L (M.D.) and Mrs
Fleming, Mr and Mrs (M.D.) Robert L
Lott, Mr Guy Jr
Norell, Miss Dagmar (M.D.)
Scott, Rev and Mrs Roland W
Terry, Mr and Mrs George L
Pakistan
Ballard, J D (M.D.) and Mrs
Boss, Rev and Mrs Charles Luther
Brush, Mr and Mrs Stanley Elwood
Hammerlee, Rev James Dean
Keislar, Rev and Mrs Marvin
Lockman, Mr John R
Martin, Rev and Mrs John H
Rugg, Mrs Earle M
Scheuerman, Mr and Mrs Lee N
Sheets, Rev Sankey L
Stuntz, Rev and Mrs Clyde B
Thoburn, Mr and Mrs Wilbur C
Trimmer, Clifford S (M.D.) and Mrs

LATIN AMERICA

Argentina
Aden, Mr and Mrs Fred
Asay, Mr and Mrs Archie Delbert
Hoff, Mr Leonard E
Holt, Rev and Mrs William M
Kernahan, Rev Galal J
Norris, Rev and Mrs John M
Robinson, Rev and Mrs Milton H
Stockwell, Rev and Mrs B Foster
Truscott, Rev and Mrs Basil R
Williams, Mr Paul Stark
Bolivia
Beck, Frank S (M.D.) and Mrs
Brown, Paul Franklin (M.D.) and Mrs
Carey, Rev James Eugene
Conger, Mr and Mrs Robert Dale
Dickson, Rev and Mrs Murray S
Haggard, Mr and Mrs Theodore
Hallett, Mr and Mrs John A
Hamilton, Mr and Mrs Keith E

Herrick, Rev and Mrs John S
Kent, Mr and Mrs William M
Maitland, Mr D Ronald
McFarren, Mr and Mrs Charles F
McKelvy, Rev and Mrs George F
Middleton, Rev and Mrs Loyde M
Robison, Rev and Mrs William T
Rusby, Miss Helen
Smith, Rev and Mrs LeGrand B
Smith, Mr and Mrs LeGrand B II
Wheatley, Mr Reginald H
Yoder, Rev and Mrs Howard W
Zimmerman, Mr and Mrs William J

Brazil

Andrews, Rev and Mrs Wiliam E
Betts, Rev and Mrs Daniel Lander
Betts, Rev and Mrs John Nelson
Bowden, Rev and Mrs Jalmar
Clay, Rev and Mrs Charles W
Conrad, Mr Melvin L
Cooper, Rev and Mrs Clyde L
Dawsey, Rev and Mrs Cyrus B
Dawsey, Mr and Mrs Cyrus B Jr
Fry, Mr and Mrs Stanley A
Harrell, Rev and Mrs William A
Hubbard, Rev and Mrs Clement
    Evans
Legg, Rev and Mrs J Thoburn
Lehman, Rev and Mrs Howard I
Lewis, Rev and Mrs Arnold R
Maitland, Rev and Mrs Fred B
McCoy, Rev Lewistine M and Mrs
    (R.N.)
Moody, Rev Howard Jr
Moore, Rev and Mrs Walter H
Paltridge, Mr Arthur E
Peterson, Rev and Mrs Arthur T
Purviance, Rev and Mrs Jay Oliver
Ream, Mr and Mrs Albert W
Reily, Rev and Mrs Duncan A
Renshaw, Rev and Mrs J Parke
Rogers, Rev and Mrs William F
Sauder, Mr Raymond A
Saunders, Rev and Mrs John R

Schisler, Mr and Mrs William R
Schisler, Mr and Mrs William R Jr
Smith, Rev and Mrs Wilbur K
Steele, Mr and Mrs Emmett D
Strunk, Mr Leon E
Sturm, Rev and Mrs Fred G
Tims, Mr James E
Wisdom, Rev and Mrs Robert W
Wofford, Rev and Mrs Warren
Yates, Mr Herbert S

Chile

Acker, Mr J Miles
Arms, Rev and Mrs Paul Ray
Barber, Mr and Mrs Edward Earl
Crawford, Mr and Mrs Randall L
Hauser, Rev and Mrs Scott P
Johnson, Mr Robert James
Major, Rev and Mrs James E
Mason, Rev and Mrs Walter F
Miller, Rev and Mrs Leon
Miller, Mr and Mrs Ralph M
Murphy, C Dennis (D.V.M.) and Mrs
Prouty, Miss Florence J (R.N.)
Reed, Mr and Mrs Elbert E
Sargent, Rev and Mrs Russell E
Tavenner, Mr Herbert G
Valenzuela, Rev and Mrs Raymond A
Waddell, Rev and Mrs Donald W
Wesley, Rev and Mrs Arthur F
Yoder, Mr Ingram C

Costa Rica

Eaker, Rev Robert C and Mrs (R.N.)
Royster, Rev and Mrs Denton P
Snedeker, Rev James H
Weed, Miss Alice L
Woods, Rev and Mrs Marion F

Cuba

Bauman, Rev and Mrs B Franklin
Daily, Rev and Mrs Maurice C
Dyson, Mr and Mrs Joseph W
Evans, Rev and Mrs Garfield
Milk, Mr and Mrs Richard G
Nesman, Mr Edgar G
O'Neal, Rev and Mrs Ernest E

Rankin, Rev and Mrs Victor L
Sherman, Rev and Mrs Ira E
Shulhafer, Rev and Mrs Charles P
Stewart, Rev and Mrs Carl D
Stroud, Rev and Mrs John E
White, Rev and Mrs David C
México
Davis, Rev and Mrs Milton C
Groves, Rev and Mrs John L
Kellogg, Mr and Mrs Claude R
Matzigkeit, Rev and Mrs W M
Panamá
Butler, Rev Charles Owen
Darg, Mr Kenneth F
Fiske, Rev and Mrs Louis M
Frank, Rev William F
Herschell, Miss Gladys I
Ross, Mr Curtis E

Perú
Adair, Mr and Mrs Loyd E
Battles, Rev and Mrs Lonzo Francis
Bower, Mr and Mrs Edwin Thomas
Howell, Mr Oliver B
James, Mr John Cary
Landis, Mrs Frances C
Miller, Miss Elizabeth W
Nothdurft, Rev and Mrs Ivan H
Shappell, Rev and Mrs John E
Williams, Rev and Mrs J G
Uruguay
Carter, Rev William Earl
Crumbley, Rev and Mrs T Askew
Howard, Rev and Mrs T Andrew
Lee, Rev and Mrs Lawson G
Pate, Mr Bart Carter
Smith, Rev and Mrs Earl M
Stockwell, Rev and Mrs Eugene L

Woman's Division 1952

AFRICA

Angola
Bailey, Henrietta
Baker, Marjorie (R.N.)
Bennett, Helen
Bonorden, Ruth
Crandall, Violet
Cross, Cilicia
Glidden, Zella
Miller, Alpha
Nelson, Marie
Smith, Alice
Belgian Congo
Benneis, Jean
Cary, Doris (R.N.)
Cowan, Celia
Dalbey, Elizabeth
Dean, Chlora (R.N.)
Dorrell, Mabel (R.N.)
Eastman, Anne
Eye, Kathryn (R.N.)

Foreman, M Flora (R.N.)
Gilbert, Dorothy (R.N.)
Hartman, Barbara
Homfeldt, Ethel
Jensen, Tove (R.N.)
Kelly, Lorena
Martin, Edith
Miller, Patricia
Moore, Mary (R.N.)
Nordin, Brigit (R.N.)
O'Toole, Ruth (R.N.)
Parham, Catherine
Parker, Annie
Rees, Dorothy
Swords, Maria (R.N.)
Taylor, Charlotte
Van Ooteghem, Simone
Wareka, Joan
White, Annimae
Winfrey, Annie
Zicafoose, Myrtle
Liberia
Adams, Uniola (R.N.)

Browne, Sallie Lewis
Peat, Carrie
Prentice, Margaret (R.N.)
Russell, Mary K
Mozambique
Bartling, Clara (R.N.)
Foster, Ruth (R.N.)
Jonsson, Karin (R.N.)
Lang, Victoria (R.N.)
Michel, Mabel
Miranda, Kathryn
Northcott, Ruth
Sessions, Margaret
Tennant, Mary Jean
Thomas, Ruth
North Africa
Burris, Willodean
Gisler, Emmy (R.N.)
Hasler, Helen
Hull, Donna
King, Mrs Anna
Larsen, Liv
Lawrence, Ruth
Manz, Helene (R.N.)
Narbeth, Gwendoline
Robinson, Mary Sue
Scott, Onie
Short, Margery
Whiteley, Martha (R.N.)
Southern Rhodesia
Aldrich, Sylvia
Ashby, Elma (R.N.)
Ball, Marcia Mary
DeVries, Evelyn
Deyo, Marguerite
Emmert, Helen
Hackler, Frances
Hervold, Signhild
Johannson, Margit (R.N.)
Jones, Pearl Willis (R.N.)
King, Sarah
Nutting, Clara (M.D.)
Otto, Grace
Otto, Vivian

Parks, Edith
Pfaff, Jessie
Pfaff, Lois
Priest, Virginia
Reitz, Beulah
Russell, Esther
Scovill, Ila
Sweeney, Ellen
Taylor, Mildred
Tubbs, LuLu
Whitney, Alice (R.N.)
Wildermuth, Helen

ASIA

China
Bradshaw, Eloise
Butler, Rosa May
Craig, Jean
Danner, Ruth (R.N.)
Eriksen, Alma (R.N.)
Evans, Florence (R.N.)
Fosnot, Pearl
French, Clara
Gress, Ruth
Griffin, Pansy P
Harris, Ruth
Hollows, Bessie
Jones, Jane
Killingsworth, Louise
Killingsworth, Mathilde
Koether, Luella
Manly, Marian (M.D.)
Mann, Mary
Mason, Pearl
Mayes, Susie
Pittman, Annie
Rossiter, Henrietta
Smith, Myrtle
Stanford, Sue
Steinheimer, Mary (M.D.)
Studley, Ellen
Surdam, Janet
Swift, Margaret
Van, Amber

Webb, Lucy Jim
Woodruff, Mabel
Borneo
Apple, Blanche
Graf, Martha
Palm, Emma (R.N.)
Sumatra
Robinett, Gusta
Wolcott, Jessie
Burma
Cavett, Maurine
Ebersole, Stella
Highbaugh, Irma
Nagler, Etha
Oldfather, Jeanette
Proctor, Orvia
Reid, Mabel
Richey, Elizabeth
Winslow, Hazel
Malaya
Addington, Patsy
Blackford, Mary
Clancy, Kathleen
Cole, Marion
Corbett, Lila
Craven, Norma
Desjardins, Helen
Dirksen, Mechteld
Fanjoy, Ruth
Gruber, Miriam
Harder, Ann
Hay, Kitty
Holmes, Marion
Lawrence, Birdice
Loomis, Helen
McCutchen, Martha
Mercer, Evelyn
Mitchell, Mabel
Nowlin, Mabel
Olson, Della
Rea, Lois
Sadler, Eva (R.N.)
Schleman, Laura
Seeck, Margaret

Smith, Florence
Suffern, Ellen
White, Martha
Japan
Adams, Marie
Allum, Iris
Alsup, Alice
Anderson, Margaret B
Anderson, Myra
Archer, Marlene
Bailey, Barbara
Barns, Helen
Bedell, Mary
Billings, Peggy
Bost, Ethel
Bourlay, Constance
Boyles, Helen
Brittain, Blanche
Byler, Gertrude
Carroll, Sallie
Cheney, Alice
Church, Marie
Cooper, Lois
Croskrey, Dorothy
Curry, Olive
Driver, Georgieanna
Eads, Mary Elizabeth
Elston, Gretchen
Endow, Masako
Finch, Mary
Freely, Gertrude
Giles, Rebecca
Givens, Anna
Hampton, Charlie
Hartman, Doris
Hempstead, Ethel
Hendrixson, Gay
Hitchcock, Alice (R.N.)
Holland, Charlie
Jefferson, Alice
Lind, Jenny
Marymee, Delores
McCain, Pearle
McMillan, Mary

McQuie, Ada
Miller, Margaret
Mitchell, Mary
Moore, Helen
Oldridge, Mary Belle
Oliver, Bessie
Paine, Mildred
Parsons, Maud
Peavey, Anne
Peckham, Caroline
Peet, Azalia
Pider, Myrtle
Reed, Gloria
Rieke, Alyson
Rippey, Hazel
Rowland, Jean
Searcy, Mary
Seest, Dorothy
Selvey, Esther
Sowa, Lily
Starkey, Bertha
Sterrett, Mary
Stevens, Catherine
Stevens, Doris
Tarr, Alberta
Teague, Caroline
Towson, Manie
Wagner, Dora
Waldron, Rose
Warne, Eleanor
Westfall, Elizabeth
Whitehead, Mabel
Wilson, Emma
Wilson, Grace
Wolfe, Evelyn

Philippines

Atkins, Ruth
Buckwater, Joan
Culley, Frances (R.N.)
Deam, Mary
Dewar, Fannie (R.N.)
Dingle, Leila
Edwards, Dorothy (R.N.)
Evans, Mary

Hamel, Earlene
Hammond, Thelma
Hanna, Eleanor
Hansing, Ovidia
Hess, Doris
Johannaber, Elizabeth
Klepper, Madaleine
Knehans, Elnora
Lane, Ortha
Lefforge, Roxy
Moe, Carol
Redenbaugh, Eula
Rogers, Betty
Rowland, Elston (R.N.)
Rycroft, Phyllis (R.N.)
Scott, Edith
Seifert, Frances
Stallings, Nina
Walker, Marion
Williams, Jane

Korea

Black, Nannie
Conrow, Marion
Cooper, Kate
Crane, Kathleen
Dyer, Nell
Fulton, Frances
Hall, Ada
Howard, Clara
Hulbert, Jeanette
Laird, Esther (R.N.)
Moore, Sadie Maude
Piper, Florence (R.N.)
Ratliff, Olive (R.N.)
Rosser, Helen (R.N.)
Smith, Bertha
Townsend, Mollie (R.N.)
Weems, Euline S
Wood, Grace

INDIA AND PAKISTAN

Bengal Conference

Boles, Lula
Collins, Irma

Eveland, Ruth
Ferguson, Mary
Holland, Mary
Hunt, Ava
Pierce, Mildred
Welles, Doris
Bombay Conference
Blasdell, Jennie
Campbell, Jean
Corner, Marie
Eide, Mary
Elliott, Bernice
Gish, Ruth
Greene, Leola
Holder, Edna
Kleiner, Clara (R.N.)
Lacy, Edith (M.D.)
Masters, Florence
Nelson, Ada
Stewart, Emma
Sutherland, May
Wright, Mildred
Central Provinces
Becker, Gertrude
Bryce, Theodora
Campbell, Louise
Fehr, Helen
Forssell, Monica
Gleason, Naomi
Green, Lola
Keyhoe, Katherine
Klingeberger, Ida
Landon, Louise (R.N.)
Richardson, Faithe
Ruggles, Ethel
Strong, Dorothy
Wallace, Margaret
Ward, Mrs Olive
Warner, Marian
Williams, Mary
Delhi Conference
Armstrong, Esther
Ball, Jennie
Barry, Elda (R.N.)

Battin, Lora (R.N.)
Biddle, Lois
Bowden, Marjorie
Burchard, Mary (M.D.)
Buss, Helen
Carlyle, Elizabeth
Christensen, Lydia
Clark, Faith
Coy, Martha
Doyle, Letah
Everley, Garney
Gilmore, Colleen
Justin, Catherine
Mansfield, Marietta
Munkerjord, Randi (R.N.)
Palmer, Pearl
Perry, Ella
Porter, Eunice (R.N.)
Robinson, ArDelia
Schaefer, Carolyn
Shepherd, Mildred
Smith, Grace Pepper
Sorenson, Borghild (R.N.)
Swords, Lilly
Time, Helen
Tucker, Margaret (M.D.)
Warner, Emma
Williams, Laura
Gujarat Conference
Barnette, Ellen
Gallagher, Hannah
Heist, Laura
Lorenz, Theresa (R.N.)
Nelson, Dora
Palmer, Florence
Precise, Myrtle (R.N.)
Precise, Pearl
Smith, Marceline (R.N.)
Stahley, Wanda
Van Landingham, Glendene
Hyderabad Conference
Bellinger, Pearl
Harrod, Anna
Huibregtse, Minnie

Kriz, Josephine
LaRue, Eunice (R.N.)
Morgan, LaDoris
Shearer, Mary
Wright, Florence (R.N.)
Lucknow Conference
Backstrom, Rose Marie
Harper, Dorothy
Hobart, Elizabeth
Hutchens, Edna
Jackson, Leila
Lawrence, Mabel
Lewis, Nellie (R.N.)
McCain, Alexa
McCall, Meriel (R.N.)
Parks, Vera
Reid, Mary L
Robbins, Adis
Sheldon, Mabel
Sluyter, Eunice
Strader, Evelyn
Tirsgaard, Maren
Wells, Irene
Whiting, Ethel
North India Conference
Albertson, Mildred
Althouse, Mildred
Bates, Grace
Beach, Lucy
Beecher, Barbara
Boyde, Mary
Bradley, Edna
Cale, Jean (R.N.)
Calkins, Ethel
Cox, Ruth
Crawford, Janette
Dimmitt, Marjorie
Doyle, Gladys
Dudley, Jean
Dunn, Olive
Fairbanks, Elizabeth
Gordon, Mary (R.N.)
Hadden, Evelyn
Hagerstrom, Frieda (R.N.)

Hoath, Ruth
Honnell, Grace
Landrum, Margaret
Larsen, Jenny
Moffatt, Margaret (R.N.)
Naess, Bjorg (R.N.)
Nelson, Maude (R.N.)
Overby, Elizabeth (R.N.)
Penn, Betty
Salzer, Florence
Shelby, Martha
Stallard, Eleanor
Stephens, Eunice
Tillou, Anna
Warrington, Ruth
Webb, Gladys
West, Nellie
Westrup, Charlotte (R.N.)
South India Conference
Anderson, Joy (R.N.)
Bugby, Marguerite
Coleman, Maxine
Comstock, Joy
Corfield, Bertha
Cowan, Nona
Daniels, Ruth
Griffin, Alta (R.N.)
Hobson, Ruby (R.N.)
Johnson, Frances
Leavitt, Ollie
Lipscomb, Laura (M.D.)
Logue, Eva (R.N.)
Munson, Kezia (R.N.)
Norris, Kathleen (R.N.)
Rexroth, Emma
Saladin, Louise
Shoemaker, Esther (M.D.)
Pakistan
Blackstock, Constance
Boss, Margaret
Buyers, Anna (R.N.)
Ferris, Helen
Kellogg, Nancy
Reik, Elsie

Robe, Margaret
Winn, Mary
Wolfe, Ruth

LATIN AMERICA

Argentina
Abrams, Josephine
Eckroth, Laura Lou
Knapp, Lena
Rothrock, Lois
Safstrom, Helen
Woodruff, Patricia
Yeater, Alice
Brazil
Baxter, Mary Jane
Bennett, Sarah
Best, Louise
Betts, Joy (R.N.)
Bowden, Mary Elizabeth
Bowden, Sarah Frances
Brown, Rosalie
Burns, Frances
Carr, Hester
Casner, Anna
Clark, Mary Helen
Coffman, Mary Ruth
Conner, Ruth
Dawsey, Sarah
Denison, Alice
Farrar, Verda
Ford, Florence
Graves, Elizabeth
Harris, Anita
Heath, Betty
Hesselgesser, Irene
Horton, Genevieve
Hyde, Eva
Johnson, Martha
Johnson, Mary Ann
Justice, Margaret
Main, Idabelle Lewis
McFadin, Monta
McKinney, Ruth
McSwain, Mary

Oberlin, Gladys
Schisler, Nancy
Simester, Edith
Simmons, Alberta
Stanley, Estelle
Terry, Zula
Chile
Kutz, Semeramis
Cuba
Beale, Elizabeth (R.N.)
Black, Nancy
Buck, Lorraine
Chapman, Virginia
Clay, Ione
Cook, Eulalia
Davidson, Lois
Donahue, Katherine
Earnest, Elizabeth
Fernández, Sara
Fromm, Marilyn
Gaby, Frances
Hill, Joyce
Hulbert, Esther
Kelly, Juanita
Malloy, Agnes
McDowell, Carolyn
Neal, Mattie Lou
Shanks, Leora
Sharpe. Dreta
Williamson, Ethel
Woodward, Mary
México
Arbogast, Gertrude (R.N.)
Baird, Mamie
Baker, Bertha
Baumbach, Gertrude
Byerly, Ruth
Callahan, Ola
Chalmers, Clara
Curtiss, Joyce
Deavours, Anne
Dickhaut, Olivia (R.N.)
Dyck, Anna Bell
Eldridge, Emma

Fitzpatrick, Mary
Foster, Lorena (R.N.)
Gibson, Clara
Givin, Olive
Hall, Judith
Hall, Pearl (R.N.)
Hodgson, Helen
Ingrum, Dora
McKimmey, Orlene
Nixon, Irene
Pearson, Mary
Rawls, Lula (R.N.)
Redmon, Ramona
Santillán, Mary Lou
Schmidt, Dora
Seal, May Bell
Thomas, Ethel
Warner, Ruth
Willingham, Pauline (R.N.)
Perú
Games, Mary Helen

Greve, Ella
Hahne, Jane
Hare, Naomi
Koch, Alverna
Lorah, Mabel
Meier, Opal
Overholt, Treva
Sandfort, Dorothy
Vanderberg, Martha
Uruguay
Baker, Helen
Bigelow, Frances
Brost, Faye
Burton, Marion
Culver, Elsie
Derby, Marian
Frost, Sylvia
Jordan, Mary
Lynch, Gladys
Nelson, Dorothy

Foreign Missions Division 1956

AFRICA

Angola
Andreassen, Rev and Mrs Harry Peter
Blackburn, Rev and Mrs Linwood Earl
Blake, Rev and Mrs Charles Melvin
Brancel, Mr and Mrs Frederick
    Charles
Cooper, Rev and Mrs Edgar Richard
    James
Kemp, Mrs Alexander Hershman
Kollert, Dr and Mrs Wolfgang
    Friedrich
Kreps, Mr Burl
LeMaster, Rev and Mrs Ernest Edwin
Noah, Rev and Mrs Raymond Eaton
Nordby, Rev and Mrs Jeul Magnar
    Arnt
Schaad, Mr and Mrs Loyd Otto
Schields, Miss Irene Withey

Belgian Congo
Central
Bodley, Mr Donald Albert
Burlbaugh, Mr and Mrs Alfred Gregg
Chappel, Rev and Mrs Charles
    William
Collinson, Mr and Mrs Donald Eugene
Davis, Rev and Mrs Joseph
Davis, Rev and Mrs Julius Johnson
Deale, Dr and Mrs Hugh S
Dechene, Mr Fernand-Rene
DeRuiter, Rev and Mrs William
Duncan, Mr and Mrs Hall F
Hughlett, Mr John
Hughlett, Mr and Mrs William Smith
Johnson, Rev and Mrs Louis Charles
Law, Mr and Mrs Burleigh
Lewis, Dr William Bryant
Lovell, Rev and Mrs Eugene Hendrix
Lundeen, Mr and Mrs Lawrence
    Ernest

Maclin, Mr and Mrs Harry Tracy Jr
Maw, Rev and Mrs Joseph Henry
Noris, Miss Barbara
Reeve, Rev and Mrs Charles W
Reid, Rev and Mrs Alexander James
Sapy, Dr and Mrs Samuel L
Shaffer, Mr and Mrs Harrison Lansing
Smith, Rev and Mrs Edward Franklin
Stevenson, Mr and Mrs James Roland
Townsley, Rev and Mrs Inman Ueber
Walker, Mr and Mrs David Eugene
Weaver, Mr and Mrs Charles Tanner
Wheeler, Rev and Mrs Henry Thomas
Southern Congo
Bitsch-Larsen, Dr and Mrs Immanuel
Bartlett, Rev and Mrs Elwood Robert
Brinton, Rev and Mrs Howard
   Thomas
Broadhead, Mr and Mrs Alfred
   Howard
Davis, Rev and William Darlington
Decker, Mr and Mrs Robert James
Enright, Rev and Mrs Kenneth
   Donald
Freeborn, Dr and Mrs Warren
   Sheldon
Hartzler, Rev and Mrs. Omar Lee
Harvey, Mr William R
Henk, Rev and Mrs Wallace
Hoepner, Mr Pete Edward
Jespers, Dr and Mrs Mark
Lerbak, Miss Anna Elizabeth (R.N.)
Little, Mr and Mrs Harry
Metcalf, Mr and Mrs Robert Bailey
Persons, Rev and Mrs Maurice Eugene
Ridgway, Dr and Mrs Alton H
Roberts, Rev and Mrs Emery
   Morrison
Robinson, Rev and Mrs Lawrence
Smalley, Mr and Mrs Ray Lucius
Starnes, Rev and Mrs Billy McDonald
Wolford, Mr Marvin Stanley
Woodcock, Rev and Mrs Everett
   LeRoy

Liberia
Black, Miss Mildred A
Carey, Mr and Mrs Robert Dale
Cason, Rev and Mrs John Walter
Cofield, Mr and Mrs Bonnie Bryant
Gray, Rev and Mrs Ulysses Samuel
Griffin, Mr Robert A
Harley, Dr and Mrs George Way
Jager, Mr Edward
Mader, Mr and Mrs John Frank
Mitchell, Miss S Susan
Prudhomme, Mr and Mrs Robert
   White
Sundar, Rev and Mrs Paul Nikolai
Watters, Dr Hyla Stowell
White, Dr and Mrs Charles Gordon
Wickstrom, Rev and Mrs Werner
   Theodor
Southeast Africa
Adolfsson, Rev and Mrs Tage
   Erik Valter
Anderson, Mr and Mrs William
   Franklin
Gillet, Rev and Mrs Ira Edmond
Greenberg, Mr and Mrs Harry
Helgesson, Mr and Mrs Alf Gustav
Kemling, Rev and Mrs Max Vernon
Knutsson, Rev and Mrs Per Algot
Mendes, Mr and Mrs Francisco
Mikulaschek, Dr and Mrs Walter M
Perrson, Rev and Mrs Borje Alfred
Perrson, Rev and Mrs Josef Alfred
Rea, Rev and Mrs Julian Stuart
Ream, Mr Carl Milton
Southern Rhodesia
Aeschliman, Rev and Mrs Edward J
Anfinsen, Rev and Mrs Hans F
Blomquist, Rev and Mrs Lennart G
Boucher, Rev and Mrs Arnold Ralph
Bourgaize, Rev Wilfred
Carr, Mr and Mrs Galen McDuff
Culver, Rev and Mrs Maurice Edwin
Eriksson, Rev and Mrs Kaare Emil
Fuller, Rev Charles E and Mrs (R.N.)

Gates, Rev and Mrs Robert Calder
Griffin, Rev and Mrs Hunter Dale
Hanson, Miss Ruth Edith (R.N.)
Harper, Rev and Mrs Kenneth Edward
Hassing, Rev Per and Mrs (R.N.)
Higgs, Mr and Mrs Barnie Allen Jr
Jackson, Rev and Mrs Frank Andrew
Janssen, Mr and Mrs Ivar Wang
Kinyon, Mr and Mrs Wallace Virgil
Leiknes, Rev and Mrs Asbjorn
Manbeck, Mr Deane
Mansure, Rev and Mrs Arthur Lee
Miller, Rev and Mrs Charles Miner
Murphree, Rev and Mrs Marshall
    Jasper
Murphree, Rev and Mrs Marshall W
Piburn, Dr and Mrs Marvin Frank
Roberts, Mr and Mrs Tudor Rhodes
Sells, Rev and Mrs Ernest Lawrence
Sheldon, Dr and Mrs John Fisk
Sheretz, Rev and Mrs Dwight Lamar
Smalley, Rev and Mrs Bruce Alan
Stine, Rev and Mrs Ovid Arthur
North Africa
Albricas, Rev and Mrs Franklin T
Albricas, Rev and Mrs Lincoln Goetz
Aurbakken, Rev and Mrs Hans
    Lornets
Bres, Rev and Mrs Paul Henri Phillips
Douglas, Rev and Mrs Elmer Hewitt
Griffith, Rev and Mrs Lester Edgar
Heggory, Rev and Mrs Willy Norman
Hughes, Mr Billy Ray
Reinertsen, Rev and Mrs Fritz Arne
Smith, Mr Clyde
Teigland, Rev and Mrs Thorleif
Williams, Rev and Mrs Rolla Ward

EUROPE

Austria
Argelander, Rev and Mrs Frank August
Barták, Rev Joseph Paul
John, Mr Emil Paul
Belgium
Thomas, Rev and Mrs William Ernest

Thonger, Rev and Mrs William
    Gilbert

SOUTHEAST ASIA

Borneo
Bain, Mr Milton Stanley
Baughman, Rev and Mrs Burr
    Hastings
Coole, Rev and Mrs Douglas Paul
Dennis, Rev and Mrs Louis Reece
Harris, Mr and Mrs Thomas A
Mark, Mr and Mrs Herman John
Overholt, Mr and Mrs William Walter
Pilley, Mr and Mrs John Allen
Burma
Clare, Rev and Mrs Maurice Amar
Hollister, Rev and Mrs George Wal-
    lace
Howard, Rev Robert Crawford
Jones, Rev and Mrs Haniel
Manton, Rev and Mrs Frank Ernest
Shields, Mr and Mrs Edwin William
Spear, Rev and Mrs Ray Forrest
Formosa
Knettler, Rev and Mrs Edward Karl
MacInnis, Mr and Mrs Donald Earl
Hong Kong
Anderson, Rev and Mrs Sidney
    Raymond
Phillips, Rev and Mrs James Carlisle Jr
Malaya
Amstutz, Rev and Mrs Hobart Bauman
Babcock, Mr Richard Harold
Berckman, Rev and Mrs James Hart
    Hoadley
Blasdell, Rev and Mrs Robert Allen
Brown, Mr Thomas Markwell
Castor, Mr Howard Paul
Foss, Rev and Mrs Carlton Hill
Foster, Mr and Mrs Robert A
Foster, Rev and Mrs William H
Goltz, Mr Charles Robert
Haines, Rev and Mrs Joseph Harry
Jernigan, Rev and Mrs Allen Jr
Kesslering, Mr and Mrs Ralph Adolph

Knutsen, Rev and Mrs Kjell C
Lundy, Rev and Mrs Robert Fielden
McGraw, Rev and Mrs Eugene Oliver
Miles, Mr Teddy Cole
Peterson, Mr and Mrs Herbert Henry
Reinoehl, Rev and Mrs Waldo S
Runyan, Rev and Mrs Theodore
Small, Mr Donald Kenneth
Snead, Mrs Elizabeth Betts
Sone, Rev and Mrs Hubert Lafayette
Stockwell, Rev and Mrs F Olin
Teilmann, Rev and Mrs Gunnar
    Johan Jr
Thomas, Miss Margaret
Wiant, Mr and Mrs Paul Prince
Wilder, Rev and Mrs Craig Sparling
Williamson, Mr Andrew Jackson
Zimmerman, Mr and Mrs Norman
    William

Philippines

Bush, Rev and Mrs Richard
    Clarence Jr
Clark, Rev and Mrs Byron Wallace
DaBritz, Rev and Mrs Robert Edward
Dewey, Rev and Mrs Horace Elliott
Hartman, Dr and Mrs Gerald Vincent
Holt, Rev John B
Lundy, Mr and Mrs John Thomas
Lung, Rev Thomas William
Mosebrook, Rev and Mrs Charles
Pickard, Rev and Mrs William
    Marshall
Spottswood, Rev and Mrs Curran
    Lamar Jr
Webster, Mr Max Ray
Wehrman, Mr and Mrs Richard Leon
Wethington, Rev and Mrs L Elbert
Wiant, Mr Bliss Leighton
Williams, Mr Bertram David Jr

Sumatra

Alm, Rev and Mrs Karl Ragnar
Day, Rev and Mrs Jackson Wesley
Dixon, Rev and Mrs Edward Everett
Flight, Mr Thomas
Hamel, Mr and Mrs Albert W

Klaus, Rev and Mrs Armin Vincent
Pyke, Rev and Mrs James Howell
Shumaker, Mr and Mrs Charles Eli

EAST ASIA

Japan

Adams, Rev and Mrs Evyn Merrill
Bascom, Mr and Mrs Gilbert E
Berkey, Mrs Marguerite Lough
Best, Rev and Mrs Ernest Edwin
Bray, Rev and Mrs William Davenport
Browning, Rev and Mrs Willis
Bruner, Mr and Mrs Glen Willard
Cobb, Rev and Mrs John Boswell
Elder, Mr and Mrs William Milton
Floyd, Mr Roger Wentworth
Gamblin, Mr and Mrs Arthur Ernest
Germany, Rev and Mrs Charles Hugh
Gilkey, Mr William Edward
Harbin, Rev and Mrs Andrew Van Jr
Hayes, Rev and Mrs E Pearce
Hilburn, Rev and Mrs Samuel Milton
Hughes, Mr Lee Burt
Johnson, Mr Keith Willis
Jones, Rev and Mrs Randolph
Joyce, Mr and Mrs James Albert
Kitchen, Rev and Mrs Theodore
    Jackson
Kreps, Mr and Mrs Leslie Ray
McWilliams, Rev and Mrs Robert
    Winter
Moss, Rev and Mrs John Adams
Norris, Mr Douglas Irwin
Palmore, Rev and Mrs P Lee
Palmore, Mr and Mrs Payton L III
Parrott, Mr and Mrs George Wood
Parsons, Mr and Mrs Norman Walter
Rahn, Rev and Mrs Robert William
Reedy, Mr Boyd
Saito, Mr and Mrs Morse T
Sawada, Mr and Mrs Ben
Shimer, Mr and Mrs Eliot Richmond
Skillman, Mr and Mrs John Harold
Stubbs, Rev and Mrs David C
Swain, Rev and Mrs David Lowry

Teele, Mr and Mrs Roy Earl
Thompson, Rev and Mrs Everett
    William
Thompson, Mr Lawrence Herbert
Winans, Rev Edward Jones
Korea
Aebersold, Rev and Mrs John Phillip
Burkholder, Rev and Mrs M Olin
Elrod, Mr and Mrs Jefferson McRee
Harper, Rev and Mrs Charles Henry
Jeffrey, Rev and Mrs Finis
    Breckenridge
Jensen, Rev and Mrs A Kristian
Judy, Rev and Mrs Carl W
Larwood, Dr and Mrs Thomas
    Richard
Moore, Rev and Mrs James H
Ogle, Mr George Ewing
Payne, Mr and Mrs Donald T
Poitras, Mr Edward Whitney
Quinlan, Mr Robert Pendleton
Ratliff, Mr and Mrs Mark Twain
Sauer, Rev and Mrs Charles A
Schowengerdt, Mr and Mrs Dean
    Louis
Shaw, Rev and Mrs William E
Sidwell, Rev and Mrs George
    Lincoln Jr
Spitzkeit, Rev and Mrs James W
Stokes, Rev and Mrs Charles D
Taylor, Rev and Mrs Lyman P
Weiss, Dr and Mrs Lawrence Alfred
Zellers, Mr and Mrs Lawrence A
Okinawa
Barberi, Mr and Mrs Mario Charles
Bell, Mr and Mrs Otis W Jr
Krider, Rev Walter Wesley
Rickard, Rev and Mrs C Harold
Tallman, Mr Lester Earl

INDIA AND PAKISTAN

Bengal
Atkins, Rev and Mrs Arthur George
Dewey, Rev and Mrs Halsey

Griffiths, Rev and Mrs Walter G
Larsson, Rev and Mrs John A
Morgan, Rev Homer LeRoy
Nilsson, Rev and Mrs Sten G
Bombay
Garrison, Rev and Mrs Maran S
Lawson, Mr James Morris Jr
Minnis, Rev and Mrs Jesse F
Reynolds, Mr and Mrs Charles
Taylor, Rev and Mrs Richard Warren
Unruh, Rev and Mrs Irvin A
Wagner, Rev and Mrs Paul
Workman, Rev and Mrs George B
Delhi
Aldrich, Dr and Mrs Herschel Carl
Allen, Rev and Mrs Daniel D
Allison, Mr John Richard
Dye, Rev and Mrs William
Finney, Rev and Mrs John Wilton
Hall, Sherwood (M.D.) and Mrs
    (M.D.)
Johns, Mr and Mrs H Drewer
Kawata, Mr and Mrs Kazuyoshi
King, Mr and Mrs Russell H
Lacy, Mr and Mrs Henry Ankeny
Meacham, Mr and Mrs Stewart
Pickett, Mr Douglas R
Powell, Mr and Mrs Lyle H Jr
Rugh, Rev and Mrs Donald E
Sill, Mr and Mrs Maurice L
Smyres, Rev and Mrs Robert W
Stoddard, Mr Robert H
Thompson, Rev and Mrs G Barney
Welch, Rev and Mrs Carlos Alvin
Whetstone, Rev and Mrs Wood K
Gujarat
Bauman, Rev David B
Finley, Mr and Mrs Lester
Johnson, Mr and Mrs Gerhard T
Manning, Rev and Mrs William C
Hyderabad
Garden, Rev and Mrs George B
Hoffman, Mr and Mrs Nelson M
Moon, Rev and Mrs William Rex

Patterson, Rev and Mrs John
Seamands, Rev and Mrs David A
India General
Bell, Rev and Mrs William W
Downie, Gerald L (M.D.) and Mrs
Fleming, Mr and Mrs (M.D.) Robert L
Fraizer, Mr and Mrs Morris Dean
Garst, Dr and Mrs Ronald Joseph
Gilchrist, Mrs Robert Stanley
Hulse, Mr and Mrs Bruce Thomas
Moffatt, Rev and Mrs Elbert Marston
Norell, Miss Dagmar (M.D.)
Scott, Rev and Mrs Roland W
Terry, Mr and Mrs George L
Lucknow
Howard, Mr Arthur W and Mrs (R.N.)
Hunt, Rev and Mrs John M
Kinder, Rev and Mrs James L
Langner, Dr and Mrs Karl Wilhelm
Leach, Rev and Mrs Keith Alan
Morrison, Mr John Irwin
Robinson, Mr and Mrs Ruel A
Tweedie, Mr and Mrs Earl R
Wray, Rev and Mrs Fred C
Madhya Pradesh
Carney, Rev and Mrs Harry Arnold
Emerson, Rev and Mrs Henry Morse
Harper, Rev and Mrs Marvin Henry
Lanham, Rev and Mrs Raymond Earl
Marble, Rev and Mrs Robert Vernon
Martin, Rev and Mrs Tunnie Jr
McEldowney, Rev and Mrs James E
Presler, Rev and Mrs Henry Hughes
Smith, Mr and Mrs Arthur Riddick
Thoburn, Rev and Mrs C Stanley
North India
Bunce, Rev and Mrs H Ross, Jr
Ebright, Rev and Mrs Donald F
Galloway, Mr Gilbert Mandiville
Ginn, Mr and Mrs (M.D.) Wesley D
Hills, Rev and Mrs David W
Hollister, Rev and Mrs John N
Kintner, Rev and Mrs Dwight Lamar
Nave, Rev and Mrs Julian W

Nave, Mr and Mrs Robert W
Perrill, Charles V (M.D.) and Mrs
    (M.D.)
Pomeroy, James M (M.D.) and Mrs
Rees, Rev and Mrs Oscar William
South India
Betts, Reeve H (M.D.) and Mrs
Heins, Rev and Mrs Conrad P
Linn, Mr and Mrs Kennie M
Mark, Mr Edward Leigh
Pickard, Raleigh H (M.D.) and Mrs
Schneck, Rev and Mrs Alfred F
Seamands, Rev and Mrs E A
Seamands, Rev and Mrs John T
Townsley, Rev and Mrs Hendrix A
Pakistan
Acton, Rev and Mrs Philip John
Ballard, J D (M.D.) and Mrs
Boss, Rev and Mrs Charles Luther
Brush, Mr and Mrs Stanley Elwood
Keislar, Rev and Mrs Marvin
Lockman, Mr John R
Maring, Rev and Mrs Robert Milton
Martin, Rev and Mrs John H
Price, Rev and Mrs Floyd William
Rice, Dr and Mrs Edmond Lee
Rutherford, Rev and Mrs Vincent
    Arnell
Scheuerman, Mr and Mrs Lee N
Sheets, Rev Sankey L
Smith, Rev and Mrs Edgar Hoyt
Stuntz, Rev and Mrs Clyde B
Thoburn, Mr and Mrs Wilbur C
Trimmer, Clifford S (M.D.) and Mrs

LATIN AMERICA

Argentina
Anderson, Rev Gordon Fletcher II
Asay, Mr and Mrs Archie Delbert
Norris, Rev and Mrs John M
Robinson, Rev and Mrs Milton H
Schlager, Rev and Mrs Robert Lee
Stockwell, Rev and Mrs B Foster
Trommer, Rev and Mrs Siegfried Karl

Truscott, Rev and Mrs Basil R
Williams, Mr Paul Stark
Bolivia
Beck, Frank S (M.D.) and Mrs
Boots, Mr Wilson Texter
Caufield, Rev and Mrs Robert Leslie
Conger, Mr and Mrs Robert Dale
Cook, Mr and Mrs Kenneth Severin
Dickson, Rev and Mrs Murray S
Fritz, Rev and Mrs Gary Gruber
Haggard, Mr and Mrs Theodore
Hallett, Mr and Mrs John A
Hamilton, Mr and Mrs Keith E
Kent, Mr and Mrs William M
Marshall, Dr and Mrs Bill Jack
McFarren, Mr and Mrs Charles F
Middleton, Rev and Mrs Loyde M
Pate, Mr John Ervin
Robinson, Rev and Mrs William T
Rusby, Miss Helen
Smith, Rev and Mrs LeGrand B
Smith, Mr and Mrs LeGrand B II
Tinder, Mr and Mrs Cecil Kyle Jr
Wilson, Miss Helen Baird
Yoder, Rev and Mrs Howard W
Zimmerman, Mr and Mrs William J
Brazil
Andrews, Rev and Mrs William E
Betts, Rev and Mrs Daniel Lander
Betts, Rev and Mrs John Nelson
Bowden, Rev and Mrs Jalmar
Clay, Rev and Mrs Charles W
Cooper, Rev and Mrs Clyde L
Davis, Mr and Mrs Robert Spencer
Dawsey, Rev and Mrs Cyrus B
Dawsey, Mr and Mrs Cyrus B Jr
Dennis, Rev and Mrs Everett James
Garrison, Rev and Mrs John William
Harrell, Rev and Mrs William A
Hubbard, Rev and Mrs Clement Evans
Kelly, Mr and Mrs Harold Ray
Legg, Rev and Mrs J Thoburn
Lehman, Rev and Mrs Howard I
Lewis, Rev and Mrs Arnold R
Maitland, Rev and Mrs Fred B

McCoy, Rev and Mrs Lewistine M
Moore, Rev and Mrs Walter H
Peterson, Rev and Mrs Arthur T
Proett, Mr William Wesley
Purviance, Rev and Mrs Joy Oliver
Ream, Mr and Mrs Albert W
Reily, Rev and Mrs Duncan A
Renshaw, Rev and Mrs J Parke
Rogers, Rev and Mrs William F
Saunders, Rev and Mrs John R
Schisler, Mr and Mrs William R
Schisler, Mr and Mrs William R Jr
Smith, Rev and Mrs Wilbur K
Steele, Mr and Mrs Emmett D
Traxler, Rev and Mrs Kenneth Earl
Wisdom, Rev and Mrs Robert W
Wofford, Rev and Mrs Warren
Chile
Arms, Rev and Mrs Paul Ray
Arms, Mr and Mrs Wallace Russell
Barber, Mr and Mrs Edward Earl
Crawford, Mr and Mrs Randall L
Johansson, Mr and Mrs Robert Victor
Jones, Rev and Mrs William Burwell
Lowry, Rev and Mrs David Todd
Mason, Rev and Mrs Walter F
Miller, Mr and Mrs Ralph M
Morse, Miss Cornelia Ada
Murphy, C Dennis (D.V.M.) and Mrs
Owens, Rev Charles E
Prouty, Miss Florence J (R.N.)
Reed, Mr and Mrs Elbert E
Valenzuela, Rev and Mrs Raymond A
Waddell, Rev and Mrs Donald W
Wells, Mr Lewis Thomas
Wesley, Rev and Mrs Arthur F
Yonker, Mr Myron William
Costa Rica
Eaker, Rev Robert C and Mrs (R.N.)
Miller, Rev and Mrs Leon
Royster, Rev and Mrs Denton P
Sargent, Rev and Mrs Russell Edwin
Snedeker, Rev James H
Weed, Miss Alice L
Woods, Rev and Mrs Marion F

Cuba
Bauman, Rev and Mrs B Franklin
Evans, Rev and Mrs Garfield
Floyd, Rev and Mrs Hubert Earl
Milk, Mr and Mrs Richard G
Nesman, Mr Edgar G
O'Neal, Rev and Mrs Ernest E
Rankin, Rev and Mrs Victor L
Sandbach, Mr and Mrs John Richard
Shafer, Rev and Mrs Carl Daniel
Sherman, Rev and Mrs Ira E
Shulhafer, Rev and Mrs Charles P
Stewart, Rev and Mrs Carl D
Stroud, Rev and Mrs John E
White, Rev and Mrs David C
México
Chaffee, Mr and Mrs Arthur William
Davis, Rev and Mrs Milton C
Groves, Rev and Mrs John L
Kellogg, Mr and Mrs Claude R
Matzigkeit, Rev and Mrs W M
Panamá
Butler, Rev Charles Owen
Darg, Mr Kenneth F

Fiske, Rev and Mrs Louis M
Herrick, Rev and Mrs John Sidney
Herschell, Miss Gladys I
Reitz, Rev and Mrs Walter Keller
Reynolds, Mr Albert Leroy
Perú
Adair, Mr and Mrs Loyd E
Battles, Rev and Mrs Lonzo Francis
Bower, Mr and Mrs Edwin Thomas
Brown, Rev and Mrs Edward
    Covington
Miller, Miss Elizabeth W
Nothdurft, Rev and Mrs Ivan H
Pool, Mr Fletcher Michael
Shappell, Rev and Mrs John E
Williams, Rev and Mrs J G
Uruguay
Crumbley, Rev and Mrs T Askew
Lee, Rev and Mrs Lawson Gerald
Smith, Rev and Mrs Earl M
Stockwell, Rev and Mrs Eugene L
Thomas, Mr Fred Arthur

Woman's Division 1956

AFRICA

Angola
Bennett, Doris M
Bonorden, Ruth
Bookman, Ada Mae (R.N.)
Crandall, Violet
Foster, Ruth (R.N.)
Hinds, Marcia J
Miller, Alpha
Sprague, Mary Lou
Ware, Alberteen
Belgian Congo
Central Conference
Bozeman, Mary E
Curry, Mary Jane
Dean, Chlora (R.N.)
Eye, Kathryn (R.N.)

Gilbert, Dorothy (R.N.)
Guess, Lorine
Hartman, Barbara
Homfeldt, Ethel
Jones, A Ruth
Kelly, Lorena
Martin, Edith
Moore, Mary (R.N.)
O'Toole, Ruth (R.N.)
Rees, Dorothy
Reinecke, Sarah
Ulsh, Rosa M
Van Ooteghem, Simone
White, Annimae
Winfrey, Annie
Zicafoose, Myrtle
Southern Conference
Buser, Dorothy
Cowan, Celia

Crooks, F Jane
Geiger, Janette
Harmon, F Marlene
Jensen, Tove (R.N.)
McKay, Florence Ross
Montgomery, Thelma
O'Neal, Dorothy (R.N.)
Parham, Catherine
Taylor, Charlotte G
Whyte, Elizabeth Ann
Liberia
Adams, Uniola (R.N.)
Browne, Sallie Lewis
Hill, E Marie (R.N.)
Peat, Carrie
Prentice, Margaret (R.N.)
Raak, Muriel
Russell, Mary K
Mozambique
Bartling, Clara (R.N.)
Jonsson, Karin (R.N.)
Lang, Victoria (R.N.)
Lewis, Charlotte
Michel, Mabel
Northcott, Ruth
Tennant, Mary Jean
North Africa
Blake, Nancy Lee
Chevrin, Laura
De Yampert, Jean
Furbush, Mary Ellen
Gisler, Emmy (R.N.)
Larsen, Liv
Likes, Lois
Lochhead, Marjorie
Manz, Helene (R.N.)
Narbeth, Gwendoline
Robinson, Mary Sue
Wolff, Marguerite A
Southern Rhodesia
Aldrich, Sylvia
Ashby, Elma (R.N.)
Ball, Marcia Mary
DeVries, Evelyn
Deyo, Marguerite

Hackler, Frances
Hervold, Signhild
Hickock, Dorothy
Johannson, Margit (R.N.)
Jones, Pearl Willis (R.N.)
King, Sarah
Larsen, Jenny H
Lind, Ruth H (R.N.)
Nutting, Clara (M.D.)
Otto, Grace
Otto, Vivian
Parks, Edith
Pfaff, Jessie
Pfaff, Lois
Reitz, Beulah
Russell, Esther
Sawyer, Mildred
Scovill, Ila
Taylor, Mildred
Tubbs, LuLu
Whitney, Alice (R.N.)
Wildermuth, Helen

CHINA AND SOUTHEAST ASIA

China, Hong Kong, Taiwan
Craig, Jean F
Evans, Florence (R.N.)
Gress, Ruth
Harris, Ruth
Highbaugh, Irma
Koether, Luella
Manly, Marian (M.D.)
Mason, Pearl
Mayes, Susie
Smith, Myrtle
Steinheimer, Mary (M.D.)
Studley, Ellen
Surdam, Janet
Swift, Margaret
Van, Amber
Burma
Callis, Elizabeth C
Cavett, Maurine
Clark, Patricia M

Ebersole, Stella
Nagler, Etha
Proctor, Orvia
Richey, Elizabeth
Winslow, Hazel
Wintringha, Jeanne
Indonesia
Robinett, Gusta A
Wolcott, Jessie
Malaya
Barkes, Mary Carolyn
Blackford, Mary
Clancy, Kathleen
Cole, Marion
Desjardins, Helen
Dirksen, Mechteld (R.N.)
Eriksen, Alma (R.N.)
Fritz, Rosalie J
Gruber, Miriam
Harder, Ann
Hessell, Martha
Holmes, Marion
Killingsworth, Louise
Killingsworth, Mathilde
Lawrence, Birdice
Little, Carolee
Loomis, Helen
Mercer, Evelyn
Mitchell, Mabel
Nowlin, Mabel
Parks, Dorothy Ruth
Plant, Carolyn
Sadler, Eva (R.N.)
Schleman, Laura
Seeck, Margaret
Smith, Florence
Suffern, Ellen
Thompson, Ruth
Way, Frances
Philippines
Atkins, Ruth
Casbeer, Sybil
Culley, Frances (R.N.)
Dewar, Fannie (R.N.)
Dingle, Leila

Hammond, Thelma
Hansing, Ovidia
Hess, Doris
Jackson, Beverly
Johannaber, Elizabeth
Klepper, Madaleine
Lane, Ortha
Lefforge, Roxy
Masten, Sallie B
Moe, Carol
Rogers, Betty
Rowland, Elston (R.N.)
Stallings, Nina
Tyson, Dana
Walker, Marion
Ward, Ruth
Sarawak
Atkins, Ellen
Graf, Martha
McCutchen, Martha
Palm, Emma M (R.N.)
Pittman, Annie
Japan
Adams, Marie
Allum, Iris
Alston, Charlotte
Alsup, Alice
Anderson, Myra
Bailey, Barbara
Bandel, Myrtle Elizabeth
Barns, Helen
Bedell, Mary
Bost, Ethel
Boyer, Alice
Boyles, Helen
Brittain, Blanche
Byler, Gertrude
Carroll, Sallie
Chamberlain, Addie K
Cheney, Alice
Clarke, Elizabeth J
Cooper, Lois
Croskrey, Dorothy
Curry, Olive
Dail, Lucy

Eads, Mary Elizabeth
Finch, Mary
Fosnot, Pearl
Foster, Mary C
Freely, Gertrude
Giles, Rebecca
Givens, Anna
Hartman, Doris
Hitchcock, Alice (R.N.)
Howell, Elizabeth
Jefferson, Alice
Jones, Mary Frances
Koch, Joyce (R.N.)
Lind, Jenny
Maiden, Margaret L
Mayer, Margery
McCain, Pearle
McLain, Lula Marie
McMillan, Mary
McQuie, Ada
Meek, Martha
Moore, Helen
Morris, M Geneva
Oldridge, Mary Belle
Paine, Milred
Parrott, Rae Beth
Parsons, Maud
Peavy, Anne
Peckham, Caroline
Reed, Gloria
Register, E Kathleen
Rippey, Hazel
Searcy, Mary
Selvey, Esther
Stevens, Catherine
Tarr, Alberta
Tennant, Elizabeth
Towson, Manie
Waldron, Rose
Warne, Eleanor
Westfall, Elizabeth
Whitehead, Mabel
Wolfe, Evelyn

EAST ASIA

Korea
Billings, Peggy
Black, Nannie
Blom, Betty
Conrow, Marion
Cooper, Kate
Crane, Kathleen
Dyer, Nell
Fulton, Frances
Gledhill, Vivian E
Goff, Maude
Howard, Clara
Hubbard, Dorothy R
Kingsley, Marian E (R.N.)
Laird, Esther (R.N.)
Maw, Thelma
Moore, Sadie Maude
Moss, Barbara (M.D.)
Oliver, Bessie O
Piper, Florence (R.N.)
Ratliff, Olive (R.N.)
Rosser, Helen (R.N.)
Shaw, Marion (R.N.)
Shine, Chasteen
Simester, Edith
Smith, Bertha
Stewart, Ruth (R.N.)
Stockton, Elsie L
Stoffer, Esther
Stuntz, Jane
Swinney, Irene T
Terry, Marilyn
Townsend, Mollie (R.N.)
Wayland, Emma Nell
Weems, Euline S
Whitaker, Faith
Wilson, Emma

SOUTH ASIA

INDIA
Bengal Conference
Collins, Irma
Eveland, Ruth

Felchlia, Irma
Ferguson, Mary
Major, Frances
Naess, Bjorg (R.N.)
Parks, Vera
Welles, Doris
Bombay Conference
Blasdell, Jennie
Corner, Marie
Eide, Mary
Gish, Ruth
Holder, Edna
Kleiner, Clara (R.N.)
Lacy, Edith (M.D.)
Masters, Florence
Nelson, Ada
Stewart, Emma
Wright, Mildred
Delhi Conference
Barry, Elda (R.N.)
Battin, Lora (R.N.)
Biddle, Lois
Bowden, Marjorie
Burchard, Mary (M.D.)
Buss, Helen
Carlyle, Elizabeth
Coy, Martha
Doyle, Letah
Gilmore, Colleen
Johnston, Margaret V
Justin, Catherine
Munkerjord, Randi (R.N.)
Palmer, Pearl
Perry, Ella
Porter, Eunice (R.N.)
Robinson, ArDelia
Schaefer, Carolyn
Shepherd, Mildred
Sorensen, Borghild (R.N.)
Swords, Lilly
Tucker, Margaret (M.D.)
Gujarat Conference
Fairbanks, Elizabeth
Gallagher, Hannah

Heist, Laura
Lorenz, Theresa (R.N.)
Overby, Elizabeth (R.N.)
Palmer, Florence
Precise, Myrtle (R.N.)
Precise, Pearl
Stahley, Wanda
Hyderabad Conference
Bellinger, Pearl
Huibregtse, Minnie
Kriz, Josephine
LaRue, Eunice (R.N.)
Wright, Florence (R.N.)
Lucknow Conference
Bale, Marie Finger
Barber, Kathryn
Beecher, Barbara
Boles, Lulu A
Crawford, Janette
Himmitt, Marjorie
Hindley, Frances (R.N.)
Hobart, Elizabeth
Hollows, Bessie
Hunt, Ava
Hutchens, Edna
Jackson, Leila
McCall, Meriel (R.N.)
Reid, Mary L
Robbins, Adis
Salisbury, Sara
Salzer, Florence
Sheldon, Mabel
Sluyter, Eunice
Strader, Evelyn
Tirsgaard, Maren
Wallace, Margaret
Wells, Irene
Whiting, Ethel
Wiggins, Mae
Williams, Laura
Madhya Pradesh
Becker, Gertrude
Campbell, Louise
Fehr, Helen

Gleason, Naomi
Klingeberger, Ida
Landon, Louise (R.N.)
Strong, Dorothy
Warner, Marian
Williams, Mary
North India Conference
Albertson, Mildred
Althouse, Mildred
Bates, Grace
Boyde, Mary
Bradley, Edna
Cale, Jean (R.N.)
Calkins, Ethel
Cox, Ruth
Doyle, Gladys
Gordon, Mary (R.N.)
Grams, Hildegard
Hoath, Ruth
Honnell, Grace
Mann, Una J
Mansfield, Marietta
Nelson, Maude (R.N.)
Penn, Betty
Shelby, Martha
Stallard, Eleanor
Tillou, Anna
Warrington, Ruth
Webb, Gladys
West, Nellie
Westrup, Charlotte (R.N.)
South India Conference
Anderson, Joy (R.N.)
Baldwin, Virginia
Bugby, Marguerite
Coleman, Maxine
Comstock, Joy
Corfield, Bertha
Daniels, Ruth
Griffin, Alta (R.N.)
Hobson, Ruby (R.N.)
Huitema, Wemelina (M.D.)
Johnson, Frances
Leavitt, Ollie
Logue, Eva (R.N.)

Norris, Kathleen (R.N.)
Rexroth, Emma
Saladin, Louise
Shoemaker, Esther (M.D.)
Pakistan
Blackstock, Constance
Boss, Margaret
Buyers, Anna (R.N.)
Ferris, Helen
Hart, Earline
Jordan, V Wynell
Reik, Elsie
Robe, Margaret
Weaver, Evelyn M
Winn, Mary
Wolfe, Ruth

LATIN AMERICA

Argentina
Abrams, Josephine
Knapp, Lena
Miller, Jane
Richardson, Patricia
Rothrock, Lois
Safstrom, Helen
Woodruff, Patricia
Bolivia
Bunn, Virginia
Brazil
Bennett, Sarah
Best, Louise
Betts, Joy (R.N.)
Bowden, Mary Elizabeth
Bowden, Sarah Frances
Brown, Rosalie
Burns, Frances
Carr, Hester
Chain, Beverly
Clark, Mary Helen
Conner, Ruth
Dawsey, Sarah
Denison, Alice
Denny, Helen
Farrar, Verda
Ford, Florence

Fox, Joyce
Fuhs, Doretta
Graves, Elizabeth
Harris, Anita
Hesselgesser, Irene
Jenkins, Rosalie
Little, Joy Marie
Main, Idabelle Lewis
McKinney, Ruth
McSwain, Mary
Oberlin, Gladys
Parker, Elsie
Simmons, Alberta
Stewart, Emma H
Terry, Zula
Chile
Kutz, Semeramis
Ragsdale, Gertrude Ann
Cuba
Beale, Elizabeth (R.N.)
Buck, Lorraine
Chapman, Virginia
Clay, Ione
Cook, Eulalia
Davidson, Lois
Donahue, Katherine
Earnest, Elizabeth
Elswick, Imogene
English, F Carroll
Fernández, Sara
Gaby, Frances
Hill, Joyce
Hulbert, Esther
Kelly, Juanita
Malloy, Agnes
Neal, Mattie Lou
Shackleford, Jimmie C
Shanks, Leora
Williamson, Ethel
Woodward, Mary
México
Arbogast, Gertrude (R.N.)
Baird, Mamie
Byerly, Ruth
Callahan, Ola

Campbell, Margaret W
Conner, Iva
Deavours, Anne
Dickhaut, Olivia (R.N.)
Dyck, Anna Bell
Eldridge, Emma
Foster, Lorena (R.N.)
Gibson, Clara
Givin, Olive
Hall, Pearl (R.N.)
Hodgson, Helen
Lewis, Jean
McKimmey, Orlene
Nixon, Irene
Rawls, Lula (R.N.)
Richardson, Faithe
Santillán, Mary Lou
Schmidt, Dora
Seal, May Bell
Warner, Ruth
Weber, Emilia
Willingham, Pauline (R.N.)
Perú
Evans, Janet M
Games, Mary Helen
Greve, Ella
Hackman, A Christine
Hahne, Jane
Hare, Naomi
Lorah, Mabel
Meier, Opal
Overholt, Treva
Sandfort, Dorothy
Spradling, Grace
Vanderberg, Martha
Uruguay
Alexander, Patsy Ruth
Bigelow, Frances
Cooley, Thelma
Finke, Lois A
Hoerner, Lena May
Koch, Alverna
Nelson, Dorothy
Pennington, Nathalee
Platt, Carol

HOME BASE
Billingsley, Margaret
Colony, Lucile
Derby, Marian L

French, Clara M
Lawrence, Ruth
Twinem, J Marguerite

Woman's Division 1961

INDIA

All-India Institutions
Mildred Albertson
Barbara H Beecher
Bertha May Cornfield (Ph.D.)
Naomi L Dalton (M.D.)
Marjorie Dimmitt
Mary E Dumm (Ph.D.)
Betty L Evans (R.N.)
Eunice Sluyter
Margaret Tucker (M.D.)
Lillian Wallace
Laura V Williams
Agra Conference
Elda Mae Barry (R.N.)
Lois Biddle
Mary Agnes Burchard (M.D.)
Helen Buss
Pearl Palmer
Carolyn Schaefer
Mildred Shepherd (M.D.)
Bengal Conference
Irma D Collins
Ruth Eveland
Doris I Welles
Bombay Conference
Edith J Lacy (M.D.)
Ada Nelson
Emma Stewart
Mildred Wright
Delhi Conference
Martha Coy
Colleen Gilmore
Ella Perry
Lilly Swords

Gujarat Conference
Elizabeth Fairbanks
Hannah Gallagher
Theresa Lorenz
Elizabeth Overby (R.N.)
Hyderabad Conference
Maxine Coleman
Ruth Gish
Josephine Kriz
Eunice LaRue (R.N.)
Florence Wright (R.N.)
Lucknow Conference
Janette Crawford
Frances I Major
Meriel McCall (R.N.)
Adis Robbins
Mabel Sheldon
Evelyn Strader
Mrs Emma J Thompson
Madhya Pradesh Conference
E Louise Campbell
Helen Fehr
Ida Klingeberger
Marian Warner
Moradabad Conference
Edna I Bradley
Gladys B Doyle
Martha Shelby
North India Conference
M Frances Allen (R.N.)
Ruth M Cox
Mary V Gordon (R.N.)
Maude V Nelson (R.N.)
Ann Tillou
Gladys Webb
South India Conference
Joy L Anderson (R.N.)

Virginia Baldwin
Vela Cleveland (M.D.)
Joy Comstock
Frances Johnson
Eva K Logue (R.N.)
Kathleen A Norris (R.N.)
Esther Shoemaker (M.D.)
Carol Sibert (R.N.)
Jean Cate Tarwater (M.D.)

PAKISTAN

Indus River Conference
Jean Bagnall (R.N.)
Ellen Barnette
Margaret E Boss
Dorothy Kraft
Anita Maldonado
Rose Mary Roberts (R.N.)
Wendy K Sutton
Melvina E Wilson
Greta Wiseman (R.N.)
Ruth S Wolfe
Murden Woods
Karachi Provincial Conference
Sandra Foley
Sandra Hancock
Earline Hart
Grace Honnell

NEPAL

Jo Anne Burgoyne
Winifred Sandberg

AFRICA AND EUROPE

ANGOLA
Judy Barcroft
Ada Mae Bookman (R.N.)
Violet Crandall
Shirley Himes
Karla Lee
Anne Marie Nordby (R.N.)
Rose Thomas
MOZAMBIQUE
Clara Bartling (R.N.)

Elsie Johansson
Barbara Kurtz
Victoria Lang (R.N.)
Mabel Michel
Ruth Northcott
Reva Mae Phelps
Mary Jean Tennant
SOUTHERN RHODESIA
Sylvia Aldrich
Elma Ashby (R.N.)
Marcia Ball
Marion Bayless (R.N.)
Evelyn DeVries
Marguerite Deyo
Beryl Feather
Frances Hackler
Signhild Hervold
Dorothy Hickok
Joan Hughes
Margit Johansson (R.N.)
Mrs Pearl Willis Jones (R.N.)
Jenny Larsen (R.N.)
Ruth Lind (R.N.)
Marjorie Anne Marler
Patricia Meyer
Vivian Otto
Edith Parks
Emma Lois Pfaff
Jessie Pfaff
Bernice Post
Else Roed
Esther Russell
Ila Scovill
Marjorie Smock
Mildred Taylor
Joanne Temperly
Jane Way
Alice Whitney (R.N.)

REPUBLIC OF CONGO

Central Congo Conference
Mary Elizabeth Bozeman
Sue Dunham
Anne Cary Eastman

Dorothy Gilbert (R.N.)
Barbara Hartman
Ethel Homfeldt
Lorena Kelly
Edith Martin
Margaret McDougall
Dorothy O'Neal (R.N.)
Ruth O'Toole (R.N.)
Dorothy Rees
Sonia Reid
Sarah Reinecke
Norene Robken
Annimae White
Annie Laura Winfrey
Myrtle Zicafoose
Southern Congo Conference
Marie Armenia
Dorothy Buser
V Joann Carmichael
Jane Crooks
Marlene Harmon
Hanni Landert
Ruth Muller
Carolyn Schaefer
Charlotte G Taylor

LIBERIA

Uniola Adams (R.N.)
Burnetta E Armstrong
Doretha Brown
Sallie Lewis Browne
Borghild Hoviskeland (R.N.)
Gladys Jewell Lineberger (R.N.)
Sandra Rodgers
Julia Sever
Margaret Ann Weedon
Patricia Wild
Lois Ruth Zimmerman (M.D.)

ALGERIA

Laura Chevrin (R.N.)
Emmy Gisler (R.N.)
Carolyn Langille
Liv Larsen
Earline Ledbeter

Nancy Lochhead (R.N.)
Helene Manz (R.N.)
Gwendoline Narbeth
Mary Sue Robinson
Louise Werder

TUNISIA

Marjorie Lochhead
Else Wendle

JAPAN AND KOREA

JAPAN
Iris C Allum
Mrs Marie Finger Bale
Elizabeth Bandel
Helen Barns
Bobbie Barrett
Ethel Bost
Gertrude Byler
Sallie Carroll
Elizabeth Clarke
Olive Curry
Gertrude Feely
Joyce Gillilan
Mrs Lucetta Harkness
Doris Hartman
Fern Holcombe
Elizabeth Howell
Rosemarie Kascher
Louneta Lorah
Margery Mayer
Donna McAninch
Pearle McCain
Mary McMillan
Martha Meek
Helen Moore
Geneva Morris
Joy Nowlin
Mary Belle Oldridge
Patricia Olmsted
Mildred Anne Paine
Maud Parsons
Anne Peavey
Marilee Phelps
Helen Post

Eva Saito
Mary Searcy
Marian Simons
Anne Smeland
Susan Smith
Alberta Tarr
Elizabeth Tennant
Sharon Vallance
Rose Waldron
Eleanor Warne
Marilyn Watson
Sandra Webster
Margaret Whitfield
Lois Williams

KOREA
Peggy Billings
Sylvia Bobo
Joan Carey (R.N.)
Marion Conrow
Kathleen Crane
Barbara Firl (R.N.)
Frances Fulton
Maude Goff
Clara Howard
Dorothy Hubbard
Gloria Jameson
Marian Kingsley (R.N.)
Esther Laird (R.N.)
Dorane Lowman
Thelma Maw
Sadie Maude Moore
Barbara Moss (M.D.)
Rachel Pickett
Jean Marie Powell
Barbara Reynolds
Roberta Rice (M.D.)
Marion Shaw (R.N.)
Edith Simester
Ruth Stewart (R.N.)
Elsie Stockton
Euline Weems
Faith Whitaker
Emma Wilson

LATIN AMERICA

ARGENTINA
Josephine Abrams
Josephine Laskey
Helene Reulos
Norma Lee Richardson
Patricia Richardson

BOLIVIA
Virginia Bunn
Thelma Cooley
Ernestine Harman
Janice Long
Adele Phillips
Joyce Reed
Catherine Rockey
Helen Wilson

BRAZIL
North Brazil
Lora Lee Brown
Sara Dawsey
Verda Farrar
Irene Hesselgesser
Jacqueline Skiles
Zula Terry
Willa Marie Tische
Central Brazil
Sarah Bennett
Frances Bowden
Rosalie Brown
Frances Burns
Glenda Cail
Patricia Dillon
Elizabeth DuRant
Doretta Fuhs
South Brazil
Barbara Barnstable
Joy Betts (R.N.)
Mary Helen Clark
Alice Denison
Florence Ford
Gladys Oberlin
Wilma Roberts
Mary Jacqueline Wright

CHILE
Sadie Doughton
Semeramis C Kutz
Jane Miller
COSTA RICA
Virginia Lane
Sandra Strawn
CUBA
Elizabeth Beale (R.N.)
Lorraine Buck
Virginia Chapman
Eulalia Cook
Lois Davidson
Elizabeth Earnest
Sara Fernández
Frances Gaby
Helen Hill
Joyce Hill
Esther Hulbert
Juanita Kelly
Agnes Malloy
Mattie Lou Neal
Leora Shanks
Helen Thompson
Ann Wilkinson
MÉXICO
Frontier Conference
Margaret Wade Campbell
Iva Conner
Anne Deavours
Joy DeLeon (R.N.)
Anna Belle Dick
Olivia Dickhaut (R.N.)
Charlie Ann Dunn
Lorena Foster (R.N.)
Olive Givin
Pearl Hall (R.N.)
Naomi Hare
Helen Hodgson
Evelyn Keim
Marcella Mathys
Irene Nixon
Carrie Radcliffe (R.N.)
Lula Rawls (R.N.)
Faithe Richardson

May B Seal
Mary Trewyn
Pauline Willingham (R.N.)
Central Conference
Gertrude Arbogast (R.N.)
Mamie Baird
Lottie May Bell
Carol Dean Chappell
Kathryn Edwards
Mary E Ferguson
Mary Fitzpatrick
Blanche Garrison
Treva Overholt
Mary Lou Santillán
Daphne Swartz
Ruth Warner
PERÚ
Janet Evans
Joan Goforth
Ella Greve
Christine Hackman
Jane Hahne
Mabel Lorah
Opal Meier
Patricia Riddell
Dorothy Sandfort
Martha Spilman
Kay Waddell
URUGUAY
Lois Finke
Mary F Johnson
Diane Kennedy
Frances Mitchell

SOUTHEAST ASIA AND CHINA

BURMA
Maurine Cavett
Martha Farnham
Kay Grimmesey
Rhoda Linton
Hazel Winslow
HONG KONG
Louise Avett
Ruth Hansen

Judith Hawks
Anne Herbert
Delores Miller
INDONESIA
Anne Metz
Gusta Robinett
MALAYA
Kathleen Clancy
Helen Desjardins
Betty Lou Fitch
Evelyn Gislason
Miriam Gruber
Ann Harder
Joanne Hornby
Louise Killingsworth
Mathilde Killingsworth
Helen Loomis
Evelyn Mercer
A Mabel Mitchell
Dorothy Ruth Parks
Caroline Plant
Eugenia Savage
Laura Schleman
Nancy Swan
Doris Wilson
Jessi Wolcott
PHILIPPINES
Lucy Blanton (R.N.)
Doris Hess
Grace Huck
Elizabeth Johannaber
Janice Johnson

Madaleine Klepper
Annual Conference
Marion Walker
Northwest Philippines Annual Conference
Doris Garrett
Dana Tyson
Northern Philippines Annual Conference
Barbara Leonard
Betty Rogers
Mindanao Provincial Conference
Carol Moe
Marjorie Tyson
SARAWAK
Ellen Atkinson
Edna Floy Brown (R.N.)
Barbara Chase
Fannie Dewar (R.N.)
Alma Eriksen (R.N.)
Martha Graf
Lorraine Gribbens
Marion Holmes
Susie Mayes
Sandra McCaig
Jane Sutlive
Thelma Taber (R.N.)
Judith Warren
TAIWAN
Wenda Carter
Louise Crawford
Dorothy Jones
Gloria McCurdy
Mrs Ralph A Ward

Foreign Missions Division 1964

AFRICA

ANGOLA
Andreassen, Rev and Mrs Harry Peter
Jackson, Mr and Mrs Warren G
Nordby, Rev and Mrs Jeul Magnar
Schaad, Mr and Mrs Loyd Otto
CONGO
Central Conference
Adams, Rev and Mrs Dan Gilbert

Cobb, Rev and Mrs David
Collinson, Mr and Mrs Donald
   Eugene
Crowder, Rev and Mrs Douglas Leon
Culp, Rev and Mrs Wayne Alfred
Davis, Rev and Mrs Joseph
Gaddis, Mr and Mrs Ronald Jay
Gorham, Rev and Mrs Jack Dean
Hughlett, Mr and Mrs John Packard
Hughlett, Mr and Mrs William Smith
Law, Mr and Mrs Burleigh Aubrey Jr

Lovell, Rev and Mrs Eugene Hendrix
Maclin, Mr and Mrs Harry Tracy Jr
Maughlin, Mr and Mrs C Stanley
Maw, Rev and Mrs Joseph Henry
Noris, Miss Barbara
Pleimann, Mr and Mrs Larry Gene
Reid, Rev and Mrs Alexander James
Reitz, Mr and Mrs Jack
Stevenson, Mr and Mrs James Roland
Thomas, Rev and Mrs George
    Benjamin
White, Dr and Mrs Robert Bracken
Southern Conference
Alexander, Mr John Paul
Alger, Mr and Mrs Sylvester N Jr
Allen, Rev and Mrs David Lawrence
Bartlett, Rev and Mrs Elwood Robert
Brinton, Rev and Mrs Howard
    Thomas
Brouwer, Mr and Mrs James Martin
Cooper, Rev and Mrs Lee Ronald
Corbitt, Dr and Mrs Duvon Clough Jr
Davis, Rev and William Darlington
Enright, Rev and Mrs Kenneth Donald
Eschtruth, Dr and Mrs Glen R
French, Mr and Mrs Carroll George
Freudenberger, Rev and Mrs
    Carlton D
Gaddis, Mr and Mrs Ronald Jay
Gebhard, Mr Duane
Guthrie, Mr Jon D
Hartzler, Rev and Mrs Omar Lee
Harvey, Mr William R
Henk, Rev and Mrs Wallace
Hickman, Mr and Mrs John M
Hoepner, Mr Pete Edward
Hooper, Mr and Mrs John W
Hoover, Mr Robert W
Kendall, Rev and Mrs Richard Mory
Liles, Mr and Mrs Opie Clayton Jr
Matthews, Rev and Mrs Edward G
Moore, Rev and Mrs Douglas E
Nussbaum, Mr and Mrs Loren Vaughn
Persons, Rev and Mrs Maurice Eugene

Roberts, Mr and Mrs Alfred R
Robinson, Rev and Mrs Lawrence
Starnes, Rev and Mrs Billy McDonald
Whelchel, Rev and Mrs Albert F
Wolford, Mr Marvin Stanley
Woodcock, Rev and Mrs Everett
    LeRoy
LIBERIA
Black, Miss Mildred A
Brown, Mr William Allan
Caldwell, Mr and Mrs Wendell Lee
Cason, Rev and Mrs John Walter
Cofield, Mr and Mrs Bonnie Bryant
Fadely, Mr and Mrs Darrell
Frazer, Dr and Mrs Hugh Milton
Getty, Dr and Mrs Paul Allen
Golden, Rev and Mrs Wendell L
Gray, Rev and Mrs Ulysses Samuel
Hankins, Rev and Mrs James H
Janousek, Mr and Mrs Gerald Loyd
McVeigh, Rev and Mrs Malcolm Jr
Sundar, Rev and Mrs Paul Nikolai
SOUTHEAST AFRICA
Adkins, Mrs Lilburn Edward
Adolfsson, Rev and Mrs Tage
    Erik Valter
Anderson, Mr and Mrs William
    Franklin
Bjerkerot, Rev and Mrs Ernest M
Duncan, Mr and Mrs Hall F
Flachsmeier, Dr and Mrs Horst
Greenberg, Mr and Mrs Harry
Horton, Rev and Mrs James Yeend
Kemling, Rev and Mrs Max Vernon
Knutsson, Mrs Gunborg
Korswing, Rev and Mrs David Rune
Mendes, Mr and Mrs Francisco
Perrson, Rev and Mrs Borje Alfred
Ream, Mr Carl Milton
Rodrígues, Mr and Mrs Antonio
Simpson, Dr and Mrs Robert L
Slade, Mr and Mrs Kenneth Henry
Southern Rhodesia
Alvord, Rev and Mrs Alexander Mapes

Anfinsen, Rev and Mrs Hans F
Bisby, Rev and Mrs Joseph B
Blomquist, Rev and Mrs Lennart G
Brancel, Mr and Mrs Frederick B
Carroll, Mr and Mrs Seavy Alexander
Close, Dr and Mrs Gerald A
Culver, Rev and Mrs Maurice Edwin
Curtis, Rev and Mrs Thomas L
Deale, Dr and Mrs Hugh Sisson
Dewey, Mr and Mrs Lloyd G
Eisenberg, Rev and Mrs J Lawrence
Eriksson, Rev and Mrs Kaare Emil
Finster, Mr and Mrs William C
Griffin, Rev and Mrs Hunter Dale
Hanson, Rev and Mrs Coriless V
Harmon, Rev and Mrs Roger J
Heyer, Rev and Mrs Edward Leon
Higgs, Mr and Mrs Barnie Allen Jr
Hillendahl, Mr and Mrs Louis
Hughes, Rev and Mrs Robert E
Johnson, Rev and Mrs J Morgan
Kaemmer, Mr and Mrs John E
Kalso, Rev and Mrs Milton L
Kauffman, Mr and Mrs Robert Allen
Kinyon, Mr and Mrs Wallace Virgil
Landin, Mr and Mrs Ernest J Jr
Leiknes, Rev and Mrs Asbjorn
LeMasters, Mr and Mrs Charles D Jr
Matzigkeit, Mr and Mrs Everett M
Miller, Rev and Mrs Charles Miner
Murphree, Rev and Mrs Marshall W
Noah, Rev and Mrs Raymond E
Perry, Mr and Mrs James Lane
Piburn, Dr and Mrs Marvin Frank
Plumb, Mr and Mrs William I
Roberts, Mr and Mrs Tudor Rhodes
Rudy, Dr and Mrs Donald B
Schevenius, Mr and Mrs John T
Sells, Rev and Mrs Ernest Lawrence
Shryock, Mr and Mrs John E
Simonsson, Mr and Mrs Bengt Karl
Stine, Rev and Mrs Ovid Arthur
Taylor, Mr and Mrs J Claggett Jr
Thomas, Rev and Mrs Norman E

Watson, Mr and Mrs Raymond E
Whanger, Dr and Mrs Alan Duane
NORTH AFRICA
Albricas, Rev and Mrs Lincoln Goetz
Aurbakken, Rev and Mrs Hans
　Lornets
Bres, Rev and Mrs Paul Henri Phillips
Butler, Mr and Mrs David W
Dierwechter, Dr and Mrs Ronald
Griffith, Rev and Mrs Lester Edgar Jr
Heggory, Rev and Mrs Willy
　Norman
Hook, Mr Reily
Johnson, Rev and Mrs Hugh O
Paolini, Rev and Mrs John
Schreck, Rev and Mrs Gerhard
Sink, Mr W Larry
Speight, Rev and Mrs R Marston
Teigland, Rev and Mrs Thorleif
Williams, Rev and Mrs Rolla Ward

EUROPE

Austria
Brenneman, Rev and Mrs Richard F
Gebhart, Rev and Mrs Robert
　Franklin
Hanson, Rev and Mrs Robert Martin
Belgium
Mohler, Rev and Mrs Hallock
Morrison, Rev Kermit Blancher

SOUTHEAST ASIA AND CHINA

Burma
Eddinger, Mr C Robert
Howard, Rev Robert Crawford
Manton, Rev and Mrs Frank Ernest
Shields, Mr and Mrs Edwin William
Hong Kong
Bush, Rev and Mrs Richard C Jr
Byler, Mr and Mrs Delmar R
Clements, Mr and Mrs Jesse W
Lung, Rev Thomas William
McIntosh, Rev and Mrs Kenneth B

Pope, Mr Harold C
Turnipseed, Rev and Mrs Robert L
Malaya
Abram, Rev and Mrs H Emerson
Berckman, Mrs James H
Bodeen, Mr V Duane
Brown, Mr and Mrs Thomas Markwell
Castor, Rev and Mrs Howard Paul
Dennis, Rev Louis Reece and Mrs
    (R.N.)
Foster, Mr and Mrs Robert A
Garrett, Rev and Mrs Guy Douglass
Grose, Rev and Mrs Charles William
Kesslering, Mr and Mrs Ralph Adolph
Knutsen, Rev and Mrs Kjell C
Lundy, Mr and Mrs John T
Lundy, Rev and Mrs Robert Fielden
McGraw, Rev and Mrs Eugene Oliver
Reinoehl, Rev and Mrs Waldo S
Small, Mr and Mrs Donald K
Smith, Mr and Mrs Donald Merton
Smith, Rev and Mrs Robert Lindsay
Snead, Mrs Elizabeth Betts
Stockwell, Rev and Mrs F Olin
Teilmann, Rev and Mrs Gunnar Johan
    Jr
Walls, Mr Charles B
Wingeier, Rev and Mrs Douglas E
Zimmerman, Mr and Mrs Norman
    William
Philippines
Anderson, Rev and Mrs Gerald H
Briggs, Mr R Keith
Case, Mr and Mrs Norman D
Clark, Rev and Mrs Byron Wallace
Deats, Rev and Mrs Richard Louis
Duncan, Rev and Mrs Norman
    William
Jacobson, Rev J Larry
Hinkle, Rev and Mrs John Edward
Lanham, Rev and Mrs Raymond Earl
Miller, Mr Roger E
Mosebrook, Rev and Mrs Charles
Nelson, Mr Merwyn

Pickard, Rev and Mrs William
    Marshall
Price, Mr and Mrs Lewis Own
Spottswood, Rev and Mrs Curran
    Lamar Jr
Suter, Mr and Mrs Dwayne A
Webster, Mr and Mrs Max Ray
Wehrman, Mr and Mrs Richard Leon
Williams, Rev and Mrs B David
Sarawak (Borneo)
Bain, Rev and Mrs M Stanley
Baughman, Rev and Mrs Burr
    Hastings
Blanchard, Rev and Mrs John Gilbert
Coole, Rev and Mrs Douglas Paul
Crisologo, Dr and Mrs Loreto L
Fowler, Mr and Mrs J Andrew
Funk, Mr and Mrs William J
Harris, Mr and Mrs Thomas A
Heard, Mr Ernest W
Hipkins, Rev and Mrs James R
Reid, Mr Donald Frank
Root, Rev and Mrs Charles Floyd
Schuman, Dr and Mrs Norman Dean
Sutlive, Rev and Mrs Vinson H Jr
Temple, Mr and Mrs Edwin Allan
Van Winkle, Mr Michael W
Wiant, Mr and Mrs B Leighton
Sumatra
Alm, Rev and Mrs Karl Ragnar
Armstrong, Rev and Mrs W L Jr
Babcock, Rev and Mrs Richard
    Harold
Day, Rev and Mrs Jackson Wesley
Gonia, Rev and Mrs Robert E
Lager, Rev and Mrs Per Eric
Stone, Rev and Mrs W Denver
Walker, Rev and Mrs Dale F
Taiwan
Cole, Rev and Mrs Theodore Fonda
Downie, Dr and Mrs Gerald L
Dunn, Rev and Mrs Clyde Hugh
Dyson, Mr Joseph W
Hayes, Rev and Mrs E Pearce

Knettler, Rev and Mrs Edward Karl
MacInnis, Mr and Mrs Donald Earl
Morrill, Rev and Mrs Miron A
Overbey, Mr and Mrs Joseph
    Henderson
Phillips, Rev and Mrs J Carlisle
Smith, Rev and Mrs Franklin Pierce
Ury, Rev and Mrs William Alvin

EAST ASIA

Japan
Adams, Rev and Mrs Evyn Merrill
Bascom, Mr and Mrs Gilbert
    Emmerson
Bell, Rev and Mrs Otis Wilson Jr
Benner, Mr and Mrs Patterson D
Bray, Rev and Mrs William Davenport
Camp, Mr and Mrs James Robert
Cobb, Rev and Mrs John Boswell
Cox, Rev and Mrs Samuel E
Dornon, Rev and Mrs Ivan Forest
Elder, Mr and Mrs William Milton
Flach, Rev and Mrs S Richard Jr
Follett, Mr John David
Foster, Mr and Mrs Robert Arthur
Fukada, Rev and Mrs Robert Mikio
Gamblin, Mr and Mrs Arthur Ernest
Germany, Rev and Mrs Charles Hugh
Harbin, Rev and Mrs Andrew Van
Haruyama, Rev and Mrs Justin Gilchi
Harvey, Rev and Mrs Pharis J
Hilburn, Rev and Mrs Samuel Milton
Hulslander, Mr Malcolm L
Hunter, Mr David J
Johnson, Rev and Mrs Paul E
Jones, Rev and Mrs Randolph
Joyce, Mr and Mrs James Albert
Kitchen, Rev and Mrs Theodore
    Jackson
Krider, Rev Walter W
Krummel, Mr John W
Kulhman, Rev and Mrs Franklin R
Linde, Mr and Mrs Richard
Linsell, Mr Phillip N

McWilliams, Rev and Mrs Robert
    Winter
Moss, Rev and Mrs John Adams
Palmore, Rev and Mrs P Lee
Palmore, Mr and Mrs Peyton L III
Parrott, Mr and Mrs George Wood
Parsons, Mr and Mrs Norman Walter
Rahn, Rev and Mrs Robert William
Rasmussen, Mr Eric A
Reedy, Mr Boyd
Reid, Rev and Mrs James David
Sager, Mr Gene C
Saito, Mr and Mrs Morse
Seely, Mr Donald Hubbard
Shimer, Mr and Mrs Eliot R
Skillman, Mr and Mrs John Harold
Stubbs, Rev and Mrs David C
Swain, Rev and Mrs David Lowry
Thompson, Rev and Mrs Everett
    William
Thompson, Mr Lawrence Herbert
Victoria, Mr Brian Andre
Korea
Aebersold, Rev and Mrs John Philip
Burkholder, Rev and Mrs M Olin
Ferrell, Rev and Mrs Gene B
Hale, Dr and Mrs Lyman L Jr
Harmon, Mr Thomas A
Harper, Rev and Mrs Charles Henry
Hodges, Rev and Mrs James Bartlett
Jeffrey, Rev and Mrs Finis
    Breckenridge
Jense, Mrs Maud K
Johnson, Rev and Mrs Hobert B
Judy, Rev and Mrs Carl W
Laney, Rev and Mrs James Thomas
Matthews, Mr and Mrs Gene E
Mattson, Dr and Mrs Donald
    Sheldon
Moore, Rev and Mrs James H
Ogle, Mr George Ewing
Poitras, Mr Edward Whitney
Riggs, Mr and Mrs Robert Elba
Roth, Dr and Mrs Robert Frank

Sansom, Mr and Mrs Donald Forrest
Sauer, Mr and Mrs Robert Grant
Schowengerdt, Mr and Mrs Dean
    Louis
Shaw, Mrs Juanita R
Sidwell, Rev and Mrs George
    Lincoln Jr
Soon, Rev and Mrs Kim-Yong
Spitzkeit, Rev and Mrs James W
Stokes, Rev and Mrs Charles D
Theis, Mr and Mrs Jack J
Weiss, Dr and Mrs Ernest Walter
Okinawa
Arinaga, Mr and Mrs Thomas Homio
Barberi, Mr and Mrs Mario Charles
Hambrick, Rev and Mrs Charles H
Huber, Rev and Mrs George H
Rickard, Rev and Mrs C Harold
Warner, Rev and Mrs Paul F
Williams, Mr R Bruce Jr

SOUTHERN ASIA

INDIA
Agra
Fosmire, Dr and Mrs George P
Gregg, Mr and Mrs Henry C
Pickett, Rev and Mrs Douglas R
Powell, Mr and Mrs Lyle H Jr
Rugh, Rev and Mrs Donald Emanuel
Bengal
Benedict, Mr and Mrs C Edward
Elliott, Rev and Mrs John Norris
Griffiths, Rev and Mrs Walter G
Morgan, Rev Homer LeRoy
Somers, Mr and Mrs George E
Taylor, Mr and Mrs Richard Warren
Bombay
Wagner, Rev and Mrs Paul Edward
Delhi
Allen, Rev and Mrs Daniel D
Amos, Mr and Mrs Franklin B
Hackney, Rev and Mrs Edwin Atwater
Kawata, Mr and Mrs Kazuyoshi
King, Mr and Mrs Russell H
Smuth, Rev and Mrs Richard R

Terry, Mr and Mrs George Lloyd
Townsley, Rev and Mrs Hendrix A
Welch, Rev and Mrs Carlos Alvin
Gujarat
Aldrich, Dr and Mrs Herschel C
Bauman, Rev David B
Farneth, Mr and Mrs C Ray
Finney, Rev and Mrs John Wilton
Johnson, Mr and Mrs Gerhard T
McClendon, Dr and Mrs James
    Eugene
Hyderabad
Garden, Rev and Mrs George B
Johns, Mr and Mrs H Drewer
Moon, Rev and Mrs William Rex
India General
Allison, Rev and Mrs J Richard
Burgoyne, Rev and Mrs Samuel R
Dearmun, Mr and Mrs Eric Bernard
Fleming, Mr and Mrs (M.D.) Robert L
Garst, Dr and Mrs Ronald Joseph
Hartman, Dr and Mrs Gerald V
Henry, Mr and Mrs William Jr
Lott, Mr and Mrs Guy Jr
McEldowney, Rev and Mrs J E
Smyres, Rev and Mrs Robert W
Leonard Theological College
Dail, Rev and Mrs F Roderick
Galloway, Mr and Mrs Gilbert M
Presler, Rev and Mrs Henry Hughes
Thoburn, Rev and Mrs Charles
    Stanley
Wray, Rev and Mrs Fred Crowell
Lucknow
Balis, Mr and Mrs John Steward
Bittenbender, Rev and Mrs Edwin L
Jones, Rev and Mrs William Wayne
Stringham, Dr and Mrs James Alley
Lucknow Christian College
Bauer, Mr William E
Forsgren, Mr and Mrs Robert E
Howard, Mr Arthur W and Mrs (R.N.)
Scott, Rev and Mrs David C
Madar Sanatorium
Hall, Dr and Mrs (M.D.) Sherwood H

Madhya Pradesh
Emerson, Rev and Mrs Henry Morse
Marble, Rev and Mrs Robert Vernon
Moradabad
Bunce, Rev and Mrs Ross Jr
Workman, Rev and Mrs George B
North India
Holmes, Mr and Mrs John Peter
Martin, Rev and Mrs Tunnie Jr
Nave, Mr and Mrs Robert W
Perrill, Charles V (M.D.) and Mrs
    (M.D.)
Petersen, Dr and Mrs Robert F
Riel, Dr and Mrs Eugene Moore
South India
Ginn, Mr and Mrs (M.D.) Wesley
    Dunham
Heins, Rev and Mrs Conrad P Jr
Linn, Mr and Mrs Kennie M
Moody, Dr and Mrs Jackson C
Pickard, Raleigh H (M.D.) and Mrs
Root, Mr and Mrs Stephen E
Schneck, Rev and Mrs Alfred F
Vreeland, Mr and Mrs Richard L
NEPAL
Berry, Dr and Mrs Robert Edward
Fleming, Mr and Mrs Robert Leland
Miller, Dr and Mrs Edgar Raymond
PAKISTAN
Indus River
Acton, Rev and Mrs Philip John
Bergh, Mr Gary Dennis
Bowes, Dr and Mrs Donald Earl
Brush, Mr and Mrs Stanley Elwood
Hammerlee, Rev and Mrs James D
Hill, Mr and Mrs Jarvis Harley
Keislar, Rev and Mrs Marvin
Kinder, Rev and Mrs James Lester
Lehto, Rev and Mrs Markku Kalevi
Lockman, Mr John R
Lowdermilk, Rev and Mrs Max Kearn
Price, Rev and Mrs Floyd William
Ratliff, Mr and Mrs Charles E
Seaman, Rev and Mrs Alan Monroe
Sheets, Rev Sankey L

Smith, Rev and Mrs Edgar Hoyt
Wheeless, Mr and Mrs Carl M
Young, Mr and Mrs F Leroy
Karachi
Garrigus, Rev and Mrs David Allen
Garrison, Mr S Mark
Maring, Rev and Mrs Robert Milton
Rutherford, Rev and Mrs Vincent
    Arnell
Scheuerman, Mr and Mrs Lee N
Speakman, Mr and Mrs Daniel Earl
Thomas, Mr and Mrs Franklin C
Wilmot, Mr and Mrs James B

LATIN AMERICA

Argentina
Asay, Mr and Mrs Archie Delbert
Boots, Rev and Mrs Wilson Texter
Chartier, Rev and Mrs Richard Arthur
Dawes, Rev and Mrs Gilbert H
Dehainaut, Rev and Mrs Raymond K
Grettenberger, Rev and Mrs George B
Knowlton, Mr and Mrs Roger
    Hoddinott
Knox, Rev and Mrs James Floyd
McKenna, Rev and Mrs Richard John
Norris, Rev and Mrs John M
Rankin, Rev and Mrs Victor Lee
Ream, Mr and Mrs Albert W
Sherman, Rev and Mrs Ira Edick
Stroud, Rev and Mrs Robert Allen
Trommer, Rev and Mrs Siegfried
Wilcoxon, Rev and Mrs Clair Duane
Bolivia
Adams, Rev and Mrs David Livingston
Alley, Dr and Mrs James William
Barber, Mr and Mrs Edward Earl
Caufield, Rev and Mrs Robert Leslie
Dickson, Mrs Nora B
Dilley, Rev and Mrs Russell Dean
Eppley, Mr and Mrs Ernest Dillard
Frank, Rev William Floyd
Fritz, Rev and Mrs Gary Gruber
Good, Mr Dale Warren
Hamilton, Mr and Mrs Keith E

Herschell, Miss Gladys
Jewell, Dr and Mrs Patrick
King, Rev and Mrs Charles F
Kramer, Rev and Mrs Wendell Barlow
Marshall, Dr and Mrs Bill Jack
McAden, Rev and Mrs Robinson Hicks
McCleary, Rev and Mrs Paul Frederick
McFarren, Mr and Mrs Charles F
Middleton, Rev and Mrs Loyde M
Pace, Rev and Mrs James W Jr
Palmiter, Mr and Mrs Richard Paul
Peacock, Mr and Mrs Harry Wade
Robinson, Rev and Mrs Milton
    Harvey
Robinson, Rev and Mrs William T
Smith, Rev and Mrs LeGrand B
Smith, Mr and Mrs LeGrand B II
Spencer, Mr William A
Thompson, Dr and Mrs Thoburn F
Toadvine, Mr and Mrs George K
Tuttle, Mr James D
Williams, Mr and Mrs Carl Clinton Jr
Brazil
Andrews, Rev and Mrs Wiliam E
Betts, Rev and Mrs John Nelson
Bigham, Rev and Mrs William O
Brom, Rev and Mrs Norman Paul
Burns, Mr and Mrs Keith P
Cady, Rev and Mrs Manasseh Curtis
Clay, Rev and Mrs Charles W
Cooper, Rev and Mrs Clyde L
Davis, Mr and Mrs Robert Spencer
Dawsey, Mr and Mrs Cyrus B Jr
Dinkins, Rev and Mrs Burrell David
Garrison, Rev and Mrs John William
Goodwin, Rev and Mrs James W
Gravely, Rev and Mrs James L III
Hanson, Mr Philip G
Heath, Mr and Mrs Charles R
Hinson, Rev and Mrs William
    Jefferson
Maitland, Rev and Mrs Fred B
Martin, Rev and Mrs J Robert
Megill, Rev and Mrs George Caskey
Morris, Rev and Mrs Fred B

Peterson, Rev and Mrs Arthur T
Purviance, Rev and Mrs Jay Oliver
Reily, Rev and Mrs Duncan A
Renshaw, Rev and Mrs J Parke
Santee, Rev and Mrs Derrel Homer
Schisler, Rev and Mrs William R Jr
Smith, Rev and Mrs Wilbur K
Spencer, Rev and Mrs Robert Lee
Strunk, Rev and Mrs Leon Everett
Tims, Rev and Mrs James Edwin
Traxler, Rev and Mrs Kenneth Earl
Tyson, Rev and Mrs Brady Bradford
Walter, Mr and Mrs Ned Foster
Way, Rev and Mrs Marion W Jr
Williams, Rev and Mrs Leonard Allen
Wofford, Rev and Mrs Warren
Chile
Barnes, Rev and Mrs Donald E
Bedwell, Mr and Mrs Robert L
Campbell, Mr James M
Dunstan, Mr David Allen
Garrison, Mr and Mrs L C Jr
Harms, Mr Gary D
Jackson, Mr and Mrs Larry A
James, Rev and Mrs Vincent Lee
Johansson, Mr and Mrs Robert
    Victor
Johnson, Mr and Mrs Robert James
Keller, Mr and Mrs Glenn H
Lang, Rev and Mrs Russell Clark
Lowry, Rev and Mrs David Todd
Mason, Rev and Mrs Walter F
Moore, Mr and Mrs Stanley E
Phillips, Rev and Mrs Edward P
Prouty, Miss Florence J (R.N.)
Tucker, Rev and Mrs C Clyde
Valenzuela, Rev and Mrs Raymond A
Waddell, Rev and Mrs Donald W
Yoder, Mrs Ingram Charles
Costa Rica
Bideaux, Rev and Mrs René O
Dewey, Mr Glenn H
Floyd, Rev and Mrs Hubert E
Miller, Mr and Mrs Ralph Mervin
Nesman, Mr and Mrs Edgar G

Schneider, Rev and Mrs David Reeg
Tavenner, Rev and Mrs Herbert Gale
Truitt, Mr Glenn E
Vuncannon, Mr and Mrs Jesse M
Weed, Miss Alice L
México
Chaffee, Mr and Mrs Arthur William
Conerly, Rev and Mrs Robert Howard
Groves, Rev and Mrs John L
Milk, Mr and Mrs Richard G
Panamá
Butler, Rev Charles Owen
Darg, Mr Kenneth F
Eddy, Mr and Mrs William Emra
Goodwin, Rev and Mrs E Ray
Hallett, Mr and Mrs John A
Reitz, Rev and Mrs Walter Keller
Perú
Anderson, Rev and Mrs Gordon F II
Bower, Mr and Mrs Edwin Thomas

Brown, Rev and Mrs Edward
    Covington III
Corson, Mr Richard A
Dassing, Mr and Mrs Edwin Allen
Long, Rev and Mrs James Barton
Miller, Miss Elizabeth W
Petry, Rev and Mrs Richard Allen
Russell, Mr and Mrs Raymond H
Sherman, Mr Arnold Ira
Stanford, Rev and Mrs James Carlton
Watlington, Rev and Mrs Elton A
Williams, Rev and Mrs J G
Uruguay
Bartlett, Rev and Mrs W Merle
Lee, Rev and Mrs Lawson Gerald
Pigueron, Rev and Mrs George H
Smith, Rev and Mrs Earl Matin
Snedeker, Rev and Mrs James H Jr
Warren, Mr Charles B Jr
Williams, Rev and Mrs Paul Stark

Woman's Division 1964

AFRICA

Angola Conference
Himes, Shirley
Nordby, Anne-Marie (R.N.)
Congo-Central Conference
Gilbert, Dorothy (R.N.)
Hemfeldt, Ethel
Kelly, Lorena
Lewis, Evangelyn
Martin, Edith
O'Toole, Ruth (R.N.)
Rees, Dorothy
Robken, Norene
White, Annimae
Zicafoose, Myrtle
Congo-Southern Conference
Bozeman, Mary E
Buser, Dorothy
Landert, Hanni
Reinecke, Sarah
Rothrock, Patricia

Liberia
Adams, Uniola (R.N.)
Brown, Doretha
Browne, Sallie Lewis
Dunham, Gwendolyn
Gruver, Loretta M
O'Neal, Dorothy (R.N.)
Zimmerman, Lois Ruth (M.D.)
Special Term
Cohen, Beverly
Hughlett, Vera
Mozambique
Bartling, Clara (R.N.)
Johansson, Elsie (R.N.)
Kurtz, Barbara
Lang, Victoria (R.N.)
Michel, Mabel P
Northcott, Ruth
Tennant, Mary Jean
North Africa
Chevrin, Laura
Gisler, Emmy (R.N.)
Green, Kay F

Lang, Ruth
Larsen, Liv
Manz, Helene (R.N.)
Narbeth, Gwendoline
Robinson, Mary Sue
Wendle, Else
Werder, Louise
Southern Rhodesia
Ashby, Elma (R.N.)
Ball, Marcia Mary
Bayless, Marion (R.N.)
Deyo, Marguerite
Hackler, Frances
Himes, Shirley
Johannson, Margit (R.N.)
Larsen, Jenny H
Lind, Ruth H (R.N.)
Otto, Grace
Otto, Vivian
Parks, Edith
Pfaff, Jessie
Post, Mrs Bernice
Russell, Esther
Scovill, Ila
Taylor, Mildred
Special Term
Boyd, Grace
Comstock, Marjorie
Martiny, Joanne
Short, Joan
Temperly, Joanne

LATIN AMERICA

Argentina
Abrams, Josephine
Clark, Ruth
Hill, Joyce
Laskey, Josephine
Richardson, Patricia
Special Term
Starr, Judith Charlene
Bolivia
Beale, Elizabeth (R.N.)
Harman, Ernestine

Wilson, Helen
Special Term
Beadles, Eloise
Berry, Donella
Cason, Karlene
Caufield, Barbara
Long, Janice
Love, Anne R
Robinson, Shirley L
Brazil
Bennett, Sarah
Betts, Joy (R.N.)
Bowden, Sarah Frances
Burns, Frances
Clark, Mary Helen
Dawsey, Sarah
Dillon, Patricia
DuRant, Elizabeth
Farrar, Verda
Fuhs, Doretta
Oberlin, Gladys
Roberts, Wilma
Routh, Bethany
Tische, Willa Marie
Special Term
Jahn, Lela Dawn
Roberts, Wilma
Wallace, Iva Jean
Chile
Ferguson, Mary E
Kutz, Semeramis
Miller, Margery Jane
Special Term
Barbosa, Marie
Hedgpeth, Eunice Ruth (R.N.)
Wood, Janet Louise
Costa Rica
Cook, Eulalia
Lane, Virginia
Shanks, Leora
Cuba
Fernández, Sara
Gaby, Frances
Malloy, Agnes

México
Arbogast, Gertrude (R.N.)
Baird, Mamie
Campbell, Margaret W
Deavours, Anne
DeLeon, Mrs Joy (R.N.)
Dickhaut, Olivia (R.N.)
Dyck, Anna Bell
Garrison, Blanche
Hare, Naomi
Hill, Helen
Humphreys, Ray
Keim, Evelyn
Matthews, Bobbie
Mathys, Marcella
Neal, Mattie Lou
Nixon, Irene
Overholt, Treva
Richardson, Faithe
Santillán, Mary Lou
Willingham, Pauline (R.N.)
Special Term
Bell, Mrs Lottie
Berry, Donella
Handlin, Helen
Johnson, Beverly
Stanek, Jean
Thompson, Patsy
Winterburn, Hazel
Perú
Evans, Janet M
Greve, Ella
Hackman, A Christine
Hahne, Jane
Meier, Opal
Riddell, Patricia
Sandfort, Dorothy
Thomas, Beulah
Special Term
Kennedy, Mary Cameron
Pugh, Nancy Ann
Uruguay
Chapman, Virginia
Finke, Lois A

Johnson, Mary
McClure, Georgia May
Special Term
Hohman, Sharon
Kennedy, Diane
Parker, Barbara
Rice, Judith

SOUTHERN ASIA

INDIA
Farr, Mrs Louise
Agra
Barry, Elda Mae (R.N.)
Beecher, Barbara
Burchard, Mary Agnes (M.D.)
Palmer, Pearl
Robinson, Mrs ArDelia
Schaefer, Carolyn
Shepherd, Mildred
Sorenson, Borghild (R.N.)
Bengal
Eveland, Ruth
Major, Frances
Naess, Bjorg (R.N.)
Sketchley, Beryl
Bombay
Nelson, Ada
Wright, Mildred
Delhi
Coy, Martha
Perry, Ella
Swords, Lilly
Tucker, Margaret (M.D.)
Gujarat
Fairbanks, Elizabeth
Gallagher, Hannah
Gilmore, Colleen
Lorenz, Theresa (R.N.)
Overby, Elizabeth (R.N.)
Hyderabad
Coleman, Maxine
Kriz, Josephine
Wright, Florence (R.N.)

Lucknow
Robbins, Adis
Sheldon, Mabel
Sluyter, Eunice
Strader, Evelyn
Wallace, Lillian
Madhya Pradesh
Campbell, Louise
Fehr, Helen
Landon, Louise (R.N.)
Warner, Marian
Moradabad
Allen, M Frances (R.N.)
Bradley, Edna
Doyle, Gladys
North India
Albertson, Mildred
Gordon, Mary (R.N.)
Nelson, Maude (R.N.)
Tillou, Anna
Webb, Gladys
South India
Anderson, Joy (R.N.)
Baldwin, Virginia
Cleveland, Vela H (M.D.)
Comstock, Joy
Cornfield, Bertha
Hobson, Ruby (R.N.)
Johnson, Frances
Logue, Eva (R.N.)
Nelson, Ada May
Norris, Kathleen (R.N.)
Saladin, Louise
Shoemaker, Esther (M.D.)
Sibert, D Carol (R.N.)
Wells, Irene
Special Term
Dumm, Mary
Pakistan
Boss, Margaret
Fehr, Helen
Tomlinson, Eugenia
Wilson, Mrs Melvina
Wiseman, Greta (R.N.)

Special Term
Adams, Susan Margot
Headrick, Elizabeth
Hertzler, Barbara
Johnson, Mrs Alyce
Martz, Elaine
Roberts, Rose Mary
Tomlinson, Sudie E

SOUTHEAST ASIA AND CHINA

Burma
Cavett, Maurine
Winslow, Hazel
Hong Kong
Avett, Louise
Harder, Ann L
Hawks, Judith
Herbert, Anne (R.N.)
Special Term
Green, Marilyn
Hansen, S Ruth
McAlester, Barbara
Schulze, Linda Mae
Indonesia
Robinett, Gusta A
Malaya
Fries, Roberta
Gruber, Miriam
Killingsworth, Louise
Killingsworth, Mathilde
King, Orpha
Loomis, Helen
Parks, Dorothy Ruth
Savage, Eugenia
Schleman, Laura
Special Term
Allison, Anita Louise
Bell, Linda
Cooper, Janet Marie
Philippines
Baxter, Pearle
Garret, Doris
Huck, Grace

Ingerson, Mary Helen
Johannaber, Elizabeth
Klepper, Madaleine
Mercer, Evelyn
Moe, Carol
Tyson, Dana
Walker, Marion
Special Term
Kline, Marion
Sarawak
Atkinson, Ellen
Brown, Edna Floy (R.N.)
Chase, Barbara
Constantine, Annette Marcella
Eriksen, Alma (R.N.)
Harvey, Margie L
Holmes, Marion
Mayes, Susie
Taber, Thelma (R.N.)
Special Term
Gribbens, Loraine
Teatsorth, Kay L
Thompson, Carolyn Ruth
Taiwan
Crawford, Louise
Miller, Reah Hortop
Studley, Ellen
Ward, Mrs Ralph
Special Term
Jones, Dorothy
Shogren, Glenna
Vaught, Valera Lee

EAST ASIA

Japan
Allum, Iris
Bale, Dr Marie Finger
Bandel, Myrtle Elizabeth
Barns, Helen
Bost, Ethel
Carroll, Sallie
Clarke, Elizabeth J
Curry, Olive
Dickerson, Barbara A

Feely, Gertrude
Foster, Mary C
Hartman, Doris
Hillhouse, Helen F
Howell, Elizabeth
Lorah, Louneta
Mayer, Margery
McCain, Pearle
McMillan, Mary
Meek, Martha
Moore, Helen
Morris, M Geneva
Parsons, Maud
Pearson, Sonjie E
Peavy, Anne
Post, Helen
Simons, Marian
Smeland, Anne
Tarr, Alberta
Tennant, Elizabeth
Waldron, Rose
Warne, Eleanor
Watson, Marilyn
Special Term
Beatty, Norma Judy
Brooks, Anne Page
Brooks, Olive
Childs, Mary Anne
Dodge, Judith
Grant, Mrs E Wainwright
Harkness, Lucetta
Hedlund, Sonja
Martin, Marjorie
McAninch, Dona Lee
Miles, Bess Clara
Olmsted, Patricia
Richardson, Katherine
Sparks, Dorothy
Thacher, Juliana
Thomson, Anna Mae
Vallance, Sharon
Vermeulen, Mrs Marie
Korea
Billings, Peggy

Bobo, Sylvia
Brandt, Adeline
Carey, Joan (R.N.)
Cassidy, Margaret
Crane, Kathleen
Fulton, Frances
Goff, Maude
Howard, Clara
Hubbard, Dorothy R
Johnston, Lela Mae
Kingsley, Marian E (R.N.)
Laird, Esther (R.N.)
Martin, Margaret
Maw, Thelma
Moore, Sadie Maude
Powell, Jean Marie

Rice, Roberta (M.D.)
Robinson, Lenna Belle
Shaw, Marian (R.N.)
Sievert, Anneliese
Stewart, Ruth S (R.N.)
Stockton, Elsie L
Terry, Marilyn
Weems, Euline S
Wilson, Emma
Special Term
Eichelberger, Sally Jo
Hiler, Julianne
Kraft, Elizabeth G
Reynolds, Barbara Jane
Reynolds, Ruth E (R.N.)

[Notes]

1. Union, Organization, and Philosophy

1. Frederick A. Norwood, *The Story of American Methodism* (Nashville: Abingdon Press, 1974), p. 410.
2. "The Times They Are A-Changin'," Bob Dylan. Copyright © 1963 by Warner Bros. Inc. Copyright renewed 1991 by Special Rider Music. All rights reserved. International copyright secured. Reprinted by permission. Web site www.bob-dylan.com/songs/times.html
3. Alice G. Knotts in *Fellowship of Love: Methodist Women Changing American Racial Attitudes, 1920–1968* (Nashville: Kingswood Books, 1996), p. 139.
4. Sydney Ahlstrom, *A Religious History of the American People* (New Haven: Yale University Press, 1972), p. 840.
5. This is not to say that Barclay was ahead of his time in the ways he wrote about women, only that he included their names and ministries as part of his story. This inclusion of women contrasts with many missionary histories that focus only on the men.
6. Wade C. Barclay, *The Methodist Episcopal Church, 1845–1939: Widening Horizons*, part 2, vol. 3, *History of Methodist Missions* (New York: Board of Missions of The Methodist Church, 1957), p. vii.
7. The women's organizations within the MPC originally controlled their own funds but were forced to compromise in a restructure in 1928.
8. William Hutchison, *Errand to the World* (Chicago: University of Chicago Press, 1987), p. 4.
9. For example, examination of the writing and letters of Bishop James Thoburn, noted nineteenth-century Methodist missionary, shows a frequent lament that the missionaries were not able to communicate the difference between being Western and being Christian.
10. Hutchison, *Errand to the World*, pp. 9–11. Bartolomé de Las Casas was a Spanish priest who served among indigenous people in Guatemala and Chiapas in the sixteenth century. He opposed conversion of indigenous people by force and sought to set them free. Roger Williams was banished from Massachusetts by the Puritans in the seventeenth century and began a Baptist church based on the principle of liberty — that is, the freedom of religion — in Rhode Island.
11. Hutchison, *Errand to the World*, p. 13.
12. While Hutchison's interpretation is used because of how it fits in the larger picture, credit needs to be given to R. Pierce Beaver, who first did biographical work on Anderson in the 1960s.
13. Hutchison, *Errand to the World*, pp. 77–80. This should not be surprising since

premillennialism was not yet as popular nor does it seem to have the underpinnings of theology for mission. Further study needs to be done on this issue.

14. George Tinker, *Missionary Conquest* (Minneapolis: Augsburg Fortress, 1993), p. 114.

15. Dana Robert, "From Missions to Mission to Beyond Missions: The Historiography of American Protestant Foreign Missions since World War II," *International Bulletin of Missionary Research* 83 (October 1994): 146–162.

16. Norwood, p. 307.

17. Essays in this book provide a range in both social location and theology but emphasize the vocational understandings of women in Methodism. See Rosemary Keller, *Spirituality and Social Responsibility: Vocational Vision of Women in the United Methodist Tradition* (Nashville: Abingdon Press, 1993).

18. James S. Thomas, "How Theology Emerges from Polity," in Theodore Runyon, ed., *Wesleyan Theology* (Nashville: Kingswood Books, 1984), p. 15.

19. Mott did not write it in this form, but his words imply it. Nearly every missionary who was interviewed, *unprompted*, repeated this phrase at one time or another.

20. John R. Mott, *Methodists United for Action* (New York: Department of Education and Promotion, Board of Missions, Methodist Episcopal Church, 1939), p. 54.

21. Careful evaluation of this development is covered by Russell E. Richey in *The Methodist Conference in America: A History* (Nashville: Kingswood Books, 1996).

22. Carol Marie Herb, *The Light Along the Way*, a special report to the Woman's Division, Journal Appendix O, Woman's Division, October 1994, p. xii.

23. Transcript of "Oral History of Harry C. Spencer," December 10, 1984, pp. 14–19. Transcript in possession of Spencer's daughter, Mary Grace Lyman, Northport, N.Y.

2. The War Years

1. *Journal of the First Annual Meeting of the Board of Missions* (New York: Board of Missions, 1940): 91–92.

2. Annual Conferences established by the missionaries in nineteenth-century India actually afforded greater participation for lay members and for women than was possible in the U.S. because missionaries had voice, though not vote, over matters that concerned their work.

3. W. W. Reid, "Remarks at the funeral of Ralph Diffendorfer," typescript in the Diffendorfer files, United Methodist Archives and History.

4. Alice R. Appenzeller, *The Korea Mission Field* (Seoul: YMCA Industrial School, 1940).

5. Kristian Jensen and Maud Jensen, *Methodist Union* (n.p.: 1940), p. 61.

6. Richard T. Baker, "Dark Days in Korea," *World Outlook* 36 (September 1946): 5–7; Hugh Heung-wu Cynn, "Rebuttal from Korea," *World Outlook* 37 (April 1947): 10–11.

7. J. Tremayne Copplestone, *Twentieth-Century Perspectives (The Methodist Episcopal Church, 1896–1939)*, vol. 4 of *History of Methodist Missions* (New York: Board of Global Ministries, The United Methodist Church, 1973), p. 1184; John W. Krummel, *Methodist Student Evangelism in Japan* (n.p.: Japan Wesley Study So-

ciety Report #2, 1971), pp. 17, 21, 30, 87, 91. Mizuno was a Harvard graduate, a second-generation Christian, and an art patron. He reenlisted in the Japanese military in the Second World War and was killed when his plane was shot down over the Pacific. Takahara was national director of the 4-H movement in Japan after the Second World War, worked in private business, and served as a volunteer in numerous social service projects.

8. Barbara Lewis, ed., *Methodist Overseas Missions, Gazetteer and Statistics* (New York: n.p., 1953). Information on student groups during this period may be found in Krummel, *Methodist Student Evangelism*, p. 32.

9. T. T. Brumbaugh, "The Challenge of Japan's United Church," *Christian Advocate* (October 9, 1941).

10. Press release announcing the retirement of Yoshimune Abe, May 31, 1965. "At the First General Assembly in November 1942 the bloc system was dissolved effective April 1943 at the insistence of the government. Consequently, Methodists as a distinctive group continued in Japan until April 1943." Krummel, *Methodist Student Evangelism*, p. 92.

11. Letter in board report, November 12, 1940.

12. Board report, January 1941.

13. Material for this interchange is found in the files of Ralph Diffendorfer in United Methodist Archives and History.

14. Krummel, *Methodist Student Evangelism*, p. 35.

15. Michi Kawai, *Sliding Doors* (Tokyo: Keisen-Jo-Gaku-En, 1950), pp. 7, 13–15, 18, 30–33, 40–41.

16. Gerald H. Anderson, "The Protestant Churches in the Philippines Since Independence," *World Outlook* 13 (May 1967): 12.

17. José L. Valencia, *Under God's Umbrella: An Autobiography* (Quezon City, Philippines: New Day Publishers, 1978), pp. 80–83; Nolan B. Harmon, "Valencia, Jose Labarrette, Sr.," and "Guansing, Benjamin I.," in *Encyclopedia of World Methodism*, 2 vols., gen. ed. Nolan B. Harmon with Albea Godbold and Louis L. Queen (Nash-ville: The United Methodist Publishing House, 1974), 1: 1047, 2: 2408, respectively. Guansing taught at Union Theological Seminary in Manila and also edited the *Philippine Christian Advance* beginning in 1948.

18. Report of Executive Secretary (New York: Board of Missions and Church Extension of The Methodist Church, 1946), Exhibit K, p. 355.

19. "A Brief Summary of the Factors Presented by the Evacuees on Board the SS *Mariposa*," November 25, 1940.

20. "Church and Mission in Korea," Report of Executive Secretary (New York: Board of Missions and Church Extension, January 1941), p. 2

21. "Church and Mission in Korea," Exhibit A, p. 14.

22. "Church and Mission in Korea," Exhibit A, p. 14.

23. "Church and Mission in Korea," Exhibit A, p. 14.

24. First Annual Report of the Woman's Division of Christian Service, 1940, p. 28.

25. *Journal of First Annual Meeting of Board of Missions*, 1940, p. 130.

26. Ruth M. Danner, "Li Yu Kuei — Public Health Nurse," *Methodist Woman* 9 (September 1948): 7.

27. W. W. Reid, "Kaung, Z. T.," *Encyclopedia of World Methodism*, 1: 1314.

28. Letter from Lila Templin, January 1939, in the Templin Collection, United Methodist Archives and History.

29. Unpublished manuscript by Lawrence Templin, Templin Collection, United Methodist Archives and History. *Journal of First Annual Meeting*, p. 112. The Templins continued to work for justice in the United States.

30. Letters in Templin Collection, United Methodist Archives and History.

31. First Annual Report of the Woman's Division, p. 26.

32. *Journal of First Annual Meeting*, p. 115.

33. First Annual Report of the Woman's Division, p. 33.

34. Nolan B. Harmon, "Zunguze, Escrivâo Anglaze," *Encyclopedia of World Methodism*, 2: 2632.

35. Nolan B. Harmon, "Shungu, John Wesley," *Encyclopedia of World Methodism*, 2: 2152.

36. Eunice Jones Strickland, "Dreams Unfolding," *World Outlook* 35 (January 1945): 7–8.

37. Joseph Boayue, "A Mano Tribesman's Story," *World Outlook* 41 (June 1951): 14–15.

38. Paul N. Garber, "Visits with the Polish Methodists," *World Outlook* 37 (January 1947): 8.

39. Undated newspaper clipping, Gaither Warfield files, United Methodist Archives and History. Warfield's experiences are also recounted in Robert S. Sledge, *"Five Dollars and Myself": A History of Mission of the Methodist Episcopal Church, South, 1845–1939* (New York: General Board of Global Ministries, 2005), pp. 410–411.

40. Paul N. Garber, "Bartak the Czech," *World Outlook* 36 (June 1946): 6–7.

41. W. K. Glaeser, "The Methodist Church in Austria," *World Outlook* 39 (September 1949): 5.

42. First Annual Report of the Woman's Division, pp. 95–98.

43. First Annual Report of the Woman's Division, p. 30.

44. *Journal of First Annual Meeting*, p. 58.

45. First Annual Report of the Woman's Division, p. 31.

46. *Journal of First Annual Meeting*, pp. 151–153.

47. *Journal of First Annual Meeting*, pp. 161–163.

48. *Journal of First Annual Meeting*, p. 81.

49. *Journal of First Annual Meeting*, p. 263.

50. No author, "The Church's Ministry to the Family Among the War Workers," *World Outlook* 35 (May 1945): 25.

51. "History of the Emma Norton Residence," typed photocopy, no author, no date, in files of the Norton residence, St. Paul, Minnesota.

52. The Emma Norton residence has continued in operation ever since, serving young women who came to the city, much later serving primarily deaf women in need of housing, and most recently providing homes for single women with young children. It remains a project of the (now) United Methodist Women of Minnesota.

53. *Journal of First Annual Meeting*, p. 289.

54. Mary Frances Berry, *Black Resistance/White Law: A History of Constitutional Racism in America*, rev. ed. (New York: Penguin Books, 1994), pp. 129–134; Charles H. Houston, "Charles Hamilton Houston and the War Effort among African Americans, 1944," in *Let Nobody Turn Us Around: Voices of Resistance*, ed. Manning Marable and Leith Mullings (Lanham, Md.: Rowman & Littlefield, 1999), pp. 339–340; first published in *The Nation*, October 2, 1944.

55. José M. Fernández, "A Latino Perspective," Charles E. Cole, ed., *Christian Mission in the Third Millennium* (New York: General Board of Global Ministries, 2003), pp. 228, 230. Fernández points out that Spanish-speaking people in Southern California have preferred the term "Latino" in reference to themselves, whereas "Hispanic" is preferred by those in the Southwest. This usage is followed here, except that "Hispanic" is used as the more generic term for the entire U.S.

56. Edward Drewry Jervey, *The History of Methodism in Southern California and Arizona* (Nashville: Parthenon Press for the Historical Society of Southern California-Arizona of The Methodist Church, 1960), pp. 90–99.

57. Ricardo Romo, *East Los Angeles: History of a Barrio* (Austin: University of Texas Press, 1983), p. 116.

58. Governor Earl Warren signed a bill in 1946 repealing school segregation in California, but the bill did not cover housing and other discrimination. See Romo, *East Los Angeles*, p. 168.

59. Report, Social Problems Committee, Frederick B. Trotter, chair, Journal of the Southern California–Arizona Annual Conference, 1942, pp. 161–162; and 1943, p. 209.

60. Romo, *East Los Angeles*, p. 167.

61. Alfredo Náñez, *History of the Rio Grande Conference of The United Methodist Church* (Dallas: Bridwell Library, Southern Methodist University, 1980), pp. 96–97; Walter N. Vernon, *One in the Lord: A History of Ethnic Minorities in the South Central Jurisdiction, The United Methodist Church* (n.p.: Commission on Archives and History, South Central Jurisdiction, The United Methodist Church, 1977), p. 79.

62. On Holding Institute, see Sledge, *"Five Dollars and Myself"*, pp. 272–273; on Patterson Institute, see J. W. Daniel, "El Instituto Lydia Patterson," *El Heraldo Cristiano* 2 (September 1940): 6; on Harwood Girls' School, see "Un Dia Tipico en 'Harwood Girls School'," *El Heraldo Cristiano* 2 (January 1949): 6; on WhoSoEver, see Alfredo Náñez, "Fe Como un Grano de Mostaza," *El Heraldo Cristiano* 2 (December 1942): 9.

63. Church reports and editorials in *El Heraldo Cristiano*, 1943–1945; "Encuesta Metodista de Nuestras Escuelas de Iglesia," *El Heraldo Cristiano* 2 (April 1947): 9; "Young Adult Fellowship," *El Heraldo Cristiano* 2 (March 1947): 10.

64. Náñez, *History of the Rio Grande Conference*, p. 110; Vernon, *One in the Lord*, p. 81.

65. Numerous articles in *El Heraldo Cristiano* promoted the Crusade for Christ and World Service, for example, "La Gran Cruzada por Cristo," 2 (November 1944): 8–9; editorials, 2 (December 1944): 3; 2 (April 1949): 4; and Alberto Shirkey, "Nuestra Responsiblidad in el Servicio Mundo," 2 (February 1941): 7.

66. In fleeing México for the U.S. to escape civil war, Galindo was part of a movement. From 1910 to 1930, 925,000 Mexicans entered the U.S., a large increase over previous years. From 1913 to 1915, however, the number was small because of the difficulties of travel made dangerous by the war. Romo, *East Los Angeles*, 42–44.

67. "El Rev. Manuel C. Galindo Es Llamado al Hogar Celestial," *El Heraldo Cristiano* 2 (June 1947): 6.

68. John C. Granbery, "La Mision del Protestantismo en la America Latina," *El Heraldo Cristiano* 2 (December 1941): 6; William Bernardo O'Neill, "Los

Laicos Ahora Tienen La Palabra," *El Heraldo Cristiano* 2 (April 1947): 4; no author, "América es el Jardín de la Infancia de Dios para las Naciones," *El Heraldo Cristiano* 2 (January 1947): 7, 14.

69. Pablo O. Calderon, "Democratic Experiment," *El Heraldo Cristiano* 2 (March 1949): 16–17.

70. Náñez, "Fe Como un Grano de Mostaza"; Vernon, *One in the Lord*, pp. 81, 83–84.

71. Information on Náñez from Reverend and Mrs. Conrado Soltero, El Paso, Texas. Mrs. Soltero is the niece of Náñez. On Onderdonk, see Sledge, *"Five Dollars and Myself"*, p. 326.

72. No author, *They Went Out Not Knowing: 100 Women in Mission* (New York: United Methodist General Board of Global Ministries, 1986), pp. 43, 45, 48. Warrick had another distinction in that she had been ordained a deacon in 1939. The Methodist Board of Education established a more impressive record of including African Americans on its professional staff. Matthew S. Savage served on the Board of Education staff from 1941 to 1959 and John A. Greene from 1943 to 1952. Vernon, *One in the Lord*, p. 126.

73. Sylvia M. Jacobs, "The Impact of Black American Missionaries in Africa," in *Black Americans and the Missionary Movement in Africa*, ed. Sylvia M. Jacobs (Westport, Conn.: Greenwood Press, 1982), p. 22.

74. *Central Jurisdiction Daily Christian Advocate*, June 12, 1948, p. 6. Brooks called especially for missionaries to serve in education, but he also suggested that others go as pastors and district superintendents. He seems to have meant men only.

75. Ralph A. Felton, "A Texas Farm Boy Carries the Gospel to Liberia," *Central Christian Advocate* 130 (December 1, 1955): 6–7.

76. Photo essay, *World Outlook* 44 (April 1954): 19.

77. Daniel Lyman Ridout, "Answer to Letter on Segregation in the Methodist Church," *Central Jurisdiction Daily Christian Advocate*, June 10, 1948, pp. 5–6.

78. I. B. Loud, "Methodism and the Negroes," Olin W. Nail, ed., *The History of Texas Methodism* (Austin: Capital Printing, 1961), p. 107. Brooks was at first ashamed to hear other white bishops say they had met their quota, when his conferences had not, only to learn later that they were referring to pledges, not actual paid amounts.

79. Journals of the Indian Mission of Oklahoma, 1939–1945 passim; Vernon, *One in the Lord*, pp. 36–37. The Indian Mission of Oklahoma changed its name to the Oklahoma Indian Mission Conference in 1944. The 1972 General Conference changed the name to the Oklahoma Indian Missionary Conference.

80. Muriel Day, "Times Have Changed," *Methodist Woman* 10 (July-August 1949): 8. For example, Herman Paul Tsosie went to Baldwin Wallace College in Ohio; Bernice Dailey went to nursing school; Jimmy McCabe to Iowa State College; and Wilfred Billy to Highlands University, Las Vegas, New Mexico. Photo caption, *World Outlook* 46 (June 1956): 19; "Wedding Bells Ring for Mission Graduates," *Methodist Woman* 10 (November 1949): 19.

81. M. Katharine Bennett, "The American Indian in 1944," *Methodist Woman* 5 (September 1944): 12–13, 31; Marjorie Vandevelde, "Chippewa Methodists in Minnesota," *World Outlook* 56 (March 1966): 10–11; Amy Lee, "Sioux City Center," *World Outlook* 51 (December 1961): 34–36; Homer Noley, *First White*

Frost: Native Americans and United Methodism (Nashville: Abingdon Press, 1991), pp. 222–226; Dorothy Reuter, assisted by Ronald A. Brunger, *Methodist Indian Ministries in Michigan, 1830–1990* (Grand Rapids, Mich.: Eerdmans Printing for the Michigan Area United Methodist Historical Society, 1993).

82. *Zenanas* were residences within homes in India where women were confined. No men were allowed past the door. The allusion was a powerful one because the existence of *zenanas* had been an important impetus to forming a separate women's missionary organization.

83. Herb, *The Light Along the Way*, p. ix.

84. First Annual Report of the Woman's Division, p. 112.

85. "World Work Report, Western Trip – February, 1948," mimeographed three-page document, File 7C-6; "Board of Missions," Iliff School of Theology Archives, Denver, Colorado.

86. "Upon the Circle of the Earth," Report of Executive Secretary, Second Annual Meeting, pp. 3–8.

87. Second Annual Report of the Woman's Division, p. 259.

88. Second Annual Report of the Woman's Division, pp. 273–274.

89. Third Annual Report of the Woman's Division, pp. 78–81.

90. Richard T. Baker, "Let Us not Be Ashamed," *World Outlook* 36 (April 1946): 5–7.

91. "In the Strength of the Lord," Report of Executive Secretary, 1942, p. 74.

92. Of the 126,947 Americans of Japanese descent living in the U.S., 112,353 lived on the West Coast. Quotations from Martin E. Marty, *Under God, Indivisible, 1941–1960* (Chicago: University of Chicago Press, 1996), pp. 77, 79.

93. *Journal of the Southern California–Arizona Annual Conference*, 1942, pp. 161–162; and 1944, pp. 50–51. The quote about suspending constitutional rights is from the April 1944 issue of *Fortune*.

94. "Committee on the State of the Church," *Daily Christian Advocate*, May 3, 1944, p. 108.

95. Marty, *Under God*, pp. 81–83. Thompson's work is reported here and in Betty Burleigh Scudder, "The Slant of the Heart," *World Outlook* 35 (April 1945): 5–9.

96. Scudder, "The Slant of the Heart," pp. 5–6.

97. "In the Strength of the Lord," Report of Executive Secretary, 1942, p. 22.

98. Third Annual Report of the Woman's Division, pp. 37–38.

99. Third Annual Report of the Woman's Division, p. 72.

100. Third Annual Report of the Woman's Division, p. 78.

101. The survey was reported in *The Methodist Woman* (May 1941).

102. Report on the Conference on Christian Education of the Methodist Church in the Belgian Congo, Cincinnati, Ohio, January 13–14, 1943.

103. Sledge, *"Five Dollars and Myself"*, p. 392.

104. Gustavo A. Velasco, "Avila, Sixto," *Encyclopedia of World Methodism*, 1: 190.

105. Eleazar Guerra report to the Forty-First General Conference of The Methodist Church, *Daily Proceedings* (n.p.: 1944), p. 61.

106. W. W. Reid, "Guerra Olivares, Eleazar," *Encyclopedia of World Methodism*, 1: 1047–1048.

107. Vicente Mendoza, ed., *Libro Conmemorativo de las Bodas de Diamante de la Iglesia Metodista de México, 1873–1948* (n.p.: Imprenta Nueva Educación, 1948), pp. 86–89, 98–105. Eduardo Zapata's experiences with the Methodist

Episcopal mission in Panamá and Costa Rica are detailed in Copplestone, *Twentieth-Century Perspectives*, pp. 306–312, 1094–1096, 1106–1108.

108. Mendoza, pp. 131, 145–147, 153.

109. Mendoza, pp. 196–197.

110. Nolan B. Harmon, "Zóttele, Pedro," *Encyclopedia of World Methodism*, 2: 2631.

111. Lena Knapp, "Christian Leaders in South America," *World Outlook* 35 (August 1945): 3.

112. Sterling A. Neblett, *Fifty Years of Methodism in Cuba* (n.p.: 1949), pp. 264, 272–273, 287–289, 320, 344–345; *They Went Out Not Knowing*, p. 39. The Corbitts' son, also named Duvon, became a medical missionary and served on the staff of The United Methodist mission board for many years. The son of Justo and Luisa González, also named Justo, became a respected church historian in the U.S.

113. Joseph A. Pérez, *Cuba* (New York: General Board of Global Ministries, 2003), p. 70.

3. Recovery—Creation of a New Order

1. Kristian Jensen, pamphlet, 1953, containing a report by Diffendorfer called "Now Is the Time!"

2. Garber, "Bartak the Czech," *World Outlook* 36 (June 1946): 5–8.

3. Vaclav Vancura, "Barták, Joseph Paul," *Encyclopedia of World Methodism*, 1: 228–229.

4. Paul N. Garber, "Visits with the Polish Methodists," *World Outlook* 37 (January 1947): 8.

5. No author, "The Methodist Evangelical Church of Italy," *New World Outlook* 55 (May-June 1995): 41. Methodists in Italy survived with leadership from Vicenzo Nitti, who was superintendent before and after the war and used the headquarters of a Baptist church in Rome for a counseling center for ex-priests from the Roman Catholic Church. The situation of Protestant churches in the predominantly Catholic Italy remained precarious after the war. The new constitution retained one feature of the dictator Benito Mussolini's Lateran Pact with the Vatican, which was that the Roman Catholic Church retained all the privileges of state recognition. Religious freedom as practiced in the U.S. did not exist. In those pre–Vatican II days, Methodists welcomed former Catholics because of their knowledge of the language and the culture. An Italian immigrant to the U.S., the Reverend Anthony Caliandro from Montclair, New Jersey, became head of the Ex-Priests' Association of Italy. Caliandro made his Italian base the Casa Materna in Naples, a Methodist orphanage that had survived the war. See Betty Burleigh, "Is a New Reformation Under Way in Italy?" *World Outlook* 38 (April 1948): 8–10.

6. Paul N. Garber, "A Report on Bulgarian Methodism," *World Outlook* 38 (May 1948): 7–9.

7. Walter Klaiber, "The United Methodist Church in Germany," *New World Outlook* 55 (May-June 1995): 27.

8. J. W. Ernst Sommer, "The Church in Germany," *World Outlook* 38 (January 1948): 15–16; "One Hundred Years of Methodism in Germany," *World Outlook* 40 (April 1950): 11–12.

9. Gaspar de Almeida, "To Adapt Jesus' Teachings to Africa," *Central Christian Advocate* 131 (December 1956): 21.

10. Paul N. Garber, "The Methodist Mission in North Africa," *World Outlook* 40 (April 1950): 10.

11. Adam F. Sosa, "Barbieri, Sante Uberto," *Encyclopedia of World Methodism*, 1: 222–223.

12. Dorothy Nelson, "Crandon and the *Altiplano* of Bolivia," *World Outlook* 17 (October 1956): 39–40.

13. Marion F. Woods, "Alphonse, Efraim (Ephraim) Juan," *Encyclopedia of World Methodism*, 1: 96–97.

14. Ephraim Alphonse, *Autobiography of the Rev. Dr. Ephraim John Alphonse*, ed. Adelaide Jones Alphonse (Panamá City: Imprenta Universitaria, 1994), pp. 22–23, 111–112. Alphonse's name is spelled variously as "Efraim" and "Ephraim."

15. Pérez, *Cuba*, pp. 45–49.

16. Roberto Escamilla, "The Spanish Americans," *World Outlook* 55 (May 1965): 34; "Puerto Rican Pastor Serves in New York," *World Outlook* 41 (February 1951): 47; Leonard Perryman, "Busy Methodist Preacher Puerto Rican Style," *World Outlook* 47 (June 1957): 12.

17. Sarah S. Parrott, "The Advance Helps Puerto Rico," *World Outlook* 46 (October 1956): 23–24. Some of the information on Puerto Rico was provided by the Reverend Conrado Soltero, El Paso, Texas.

18. Reid, "Guerra," *Encyclopedia of World Methodism*, 1: 1047–1048.

19. Lula Thomas Holmes, "A Service of Love: Mamie Baird," *World Outlook* 43 (November 1953): 37–38.

20. Much of the material for this section is taken from an unpublished manuscript written by Sauer. His strong opinions come through in his writing, which contains far more information than any of the written reports. In many ways he represents "the old school" of missionaries. Sauer's manuscript is at the United Methodist Archives and History in the Charles Sauer collection.

21. Letter of Maud Jensen, October 1, 1946, in the Jensen files, United Methodist Archives and History.

22. Material from Laura Jean Brooks file, Cornell College Archives, Mt.Vernon, Iowa.

23. Belle Harris Bennett (1852–1922) was president of the Woman's Parsonage and Home Mission Society and also of the Woman's Missionary Society in the Methodist Episcopal Church, South. See Sledge, *"Five Dollars and Myself"*, pp. 280, 292–294, 300, 344–347. Other exceptional women are described in Ethel W. Born, *By My Spirit: The Story of Methodist Protestant Women in Mission, 1879–1939* (New York: United Methodist Women's Division, 1990), and *They Went Out Not Knowing*.

24. Fourth Annual Report, 1944, Woman's Division of Christian Service, p. 18.

25. Thelma Stevens spoke in support of a committee report at the 1944 General Conference: "We recommend that committees arranging for general meetings of the Church seek to locate such meetings in places where entertainment can be provided without distinction on the basis of race." The committee report was amended so that the church could continue to meet in segregated hotels and restaurants. It passed on a show of hands. Not only was it ironic that this action could take place in a nation ostensibly fighting a global war for democracy,

but further irony came through the speech of John E. Stephens of the North Mississippi Conference, who claimed to be a former missionary to Cuba, and who paternalistically said, "I love the race of coal-black color. My old black mammy nursed me." The conference found his remarks amusing and apparently was also amused that a woman like Stevens would have the audacity to ask for such radical action. But Stevens proceeded to implement an inclusive policy for the Woman's Division. See *Daily Christian Advocate,* General Conference, 1944, pp. 168–169.

26. James Thoburn, later missionary bishop to India, decided early in his ministry to cross a river to minister to someone in need. The river marked the line dividing Methodist territory from that of the Presbyterians, as had been arranged by comity agreements. These boundaries were established so that Protestant churches did not duplicate efforts. Crossing the river marked a new era in mission.

27. J. Waskom Pickett, "Chakko, Sarah," *Encyclopedia of World Methodism,* 1: 444; Sarah Chakko, "The Christian Witness in the World," *Methodist Woman* 10 (January 1949): 14–15.

28. Kezia Munson, "Dr. Luke—Pioneer Physician," *Methodist Woman* 13 (July-August 1953): 5.

29. David A. Seamands, "Awakening in India," *World Outlook* 42 (February 1952): 7–8.

30. E. Pearce Hayes, "Chen Wen Yuan," *Encyclopedia of World Methodism,* 1: 462.

31. Author interview with John B. Cobb, Jr., October 2000.

32. Thoburn T. Brumbaugh, "A Tale of Two Cities," *World Outlook* 38 (May 1948): 10–11.

33. Mrs. Frank G. Brooks, "Three Marys of Japan," *Methodist Woman* 10 (May 1949): 14–15.

34. John B. Cobb, Sr., "Muto, Takeshi," *Encyclopedia of World Methodism,* 2: 1695; John W. Krummel, *Methodist Student Evangelism,* p. 88. In 1959 Muto became chair of the National Christian Council of Japan and then served as pastor emeritus of the Hongo Chuo Church.

35. Thoburn T. Brumbaugh, "The New Women of East Asia," *World Outlook* 43 (April 1953): 28.

36. Letter from Marlene Arch, *New World Outlook* 43 (November 1953): 3; John W. Krummel, "Michiko Kawai," *Letters from Japan, 1956–1997* (Kearney, Neb.: Morris Publishing, 1999), pp. 141–142.

37. Krummel, *Methodist Student Evangelism,* pp. 84–91. Those studying in the U.S. included Hogo Kimura, who studied at Candler School of Theology and was a leader in the Christian Endeavor movement; Takuo Matsumoto, the son of the first Japanese minister ordained in the Methodist Episcopal Church, who studied at Ohio Wesleyan, Drew Theological Seminary, and Pennsylvania University and was head of the Hiroshima Woman's School and the Shizuoka Eiwa Girls' School; Shigemi Kega, who was a graduate of Pacific School of Religion and became a noted Wesleyan scholar and president of Aoyama Gakuin; Saburô Imai, who studied at the University of California, Pacific School of Religion, and Harvard and became a chaplain and teacher at Aoyama Gakuin; and Isamu Omura, who was a graduate of Aoyama Gakuin and Boston University School of Theology, then became dean of the Aoyama Gakuin School of Theology and moderator of the Kyodan from 1962 to 1966. Those who studied at

schools in Japan included Yorrichi Manabe, a graduate of the Aoyama Gakuin School of Theology, who served as moderator of the Kyodan 1942–1946, head of the Japan Christian Social Work League 1950–1970, and in 1971 chair of the Aoyama Gakuin Board of Trustees.

38. Christie R. House, "The Advance at 50," *New World Outlook* 57 (July-August 1997): 4–8.

39. Spencer transcript, p. 42. Spencer asserted that from this experience came the proposal that the General Conference establish a commission on radio and film. "We did not mention TV because it had not become a household necessity at that time," he said (p. 43). Later he concluded: "But I did wish we could have started out with television" (p. 48).

40. Christie R. House, "Celebrating Fifty Years of Crusade Scholars," *New World Outlook* 55 (March-April 1995): 4–7. The first scholar was a U.S. citizen, Frances-Helen Foley, the daughter of Methodist missionaries in the Philippines, where she had been raised and where she had spent much of the Second World War in a Japanese concentration camp. Other leaders who received an education from the program included Ole E. Borgen, Emilio J. M. Carvalho, Joseph C. Humper, Arthur F. Kulah, Dinesh Agarwal, José C. Gamboa, Jr., Emerito P. Nacpil, Paul Ayres Mattos, Frederico J. Pagura, Joel Martínez, and Melvin G. Talbert—all bishops. José Míguez Bonino, a renowned theologian and ecumenical leader; and Emilio Castro, who became general secretary of the World Council of Churches, were both recipients. Graca Machal, first lady of Moazambique; Lucia Panicett, president of the Brazil Confederation of Methodist Women; and Carmel Silva de Dias, faculty member of Colegio America, Perú, were recipients. Later when the program included ethnic minorities from the U.S., Lois Neal, the first woman Native American district superintendent in the Oklahoma Indian Missionary Conference (OIMC); Homer Noley, a Native American pastor, author, and the first Native American on the staff of the mission board of The United Methodist Church; and Thomas Roughface, the first Native American conference superintendent in the OIMC, were recipients.

41. Manuscript in the Charles Sauer collection, United Methodist Archives and History.

42. Report by T. T. Brumbaugh. Personal files found in the United Methodist Archives and History.

43. Report by Kristian Jensen, October 15, 1947.

44. Report to the Board by Billingsley, June 1950.

45. Jensen pamphlet, 1953.

46. Jensen pamphlet, page 8.

47. Report to the Board, T. T. Brumbaugh, November 1952.

48. Hee-Seop Wong, "The History of Mission of the Korean Methodist Church," Ph.D. diss., Fuller Theological Seminary, 1997, pp. 274–275.

49. Thoburn T. Brumbaugh, "The New Women of East Asia," *World Outlook* (April 1953): 28.

4. Mission at Midcentury

1. "The Christian Bases of Race Relations," *Central Christian Advocate* 130 (February 1, 1955): 4–5, 22.

2. Peter C. Murray, "The Racial Crisis in The Methodist Church," *Methodist History* 26 (October 1987): 3–5. Murray later published his work as *Methodists and the Crucible of Race, 1930–1975* (Columbia, Mo.: University of Missouri Press, 2004).

3. Thurman L. Dodson, "The Central Jurisdiction—Shall We Swap It for Another Island of Segregation?" *Central Christian Advocate* 130 (June 1, 1955): 7.

4. News note, *New Christian Advocate* 1 (June 1957): 1.

5. News note, *New Christian Advocate* 1 (March 1957): 99. For example, the Reverend Paul Turner, a Baptist in Clinton, Tennessee, was beaten because he supported school desegregation. The Reverend Robert Graetz, Jr., a white Lutheran pastor of a black congregation in Montgomery, Alabama, had his home bombed and a year and a half later moved to Ohio. See Dale A. Johnson, "Revisiting the Sixties," *Religious Studies Review* 28 (April 2002): 111.

6. "Deep South Clergy Speak on Race Relations," *New Christian Advocate* 1 (December 1957): 97–98; News note, *New Christian Advocate* 1 (June 1957): 1; "Biographical Sketches of Bishops," *Daily Christian Advocate, Central Jurisdiction* (July 16, 1960): 4; Vernon, *One in the Lord*, p. 135; *Central Christian Advocate* 131 (June 11, 1956): 7; "News and Trends," *New Christian Advocate* 1 (August 1957): 99; photo caption, *New Christian Advocate* 1 (March 1957): 103; "Willa Player, Pioneering College Leader, Dies at 94," *Faith Watch* (August 29, 2003).

7. Other African Americans going to Africa as missionaries were Alberteen Ware and Rose Thomas, who went to Angola. Burnetta Armstrong served in Ganta, Liberia. Several others went to the Belgian Congo: Daisy and Douglass Moore, June Green Pembroke, and Farrell and George Thomas. Ronald Schooler went in 1960. Most of these were short-term missionaries, although the Moores served 1960–1968.

    Others going to India were Dr. Tunnie and Eloise Martin from Orangeburg, South Carolina, and Holly Pond of Alabama, who went to Clara Swain Hospital in Bareilly. Ellen Barnette served in Bardoa, India, and then later at the Lucie Harrison School in Lahore, West Pakistan.

    Also serving in Asia was Doris J. Wilson, who followed the Harrises to Malaysia. "Negro Missionaries Start for Africa," *Central Christian Advocate* 130 (April 1955): 16; Task Group on the History of the Central Jurisdiction Women's Organization, "Black Missionaries and Deaconesses of The Methodist Church," *To a Higher Glory: The Growth and Development of Black Women Organized for Mission in The Methodist Church, 1940–1968* (New York: Women's Division, The United Methodist Church, 1978), Appendix, p. 112.

8. *Central Christian Advocate* 130 (November 1, 1955): 18; "Black Missionaries and Deaconesses," p. 113.

9. George W. Carter, "My Crusade Scholarship," *Methodist Woman* 13 (February 1953): 9.

10. Marion Homer, "The Triumph of an Indian Woman," *World Outlook* 45 (April 1955): 20. Other Native Americans in Oklahoma of note were Hunting Horse, who had served as a U. S. Government scout during nineteenth-century conflicts. A Kiowa, at age 100 he delighted in presenting the saddle of the Apache leader, Geronimo, to Bishop Angie Smith. One who also seemed to enjoy such ceremonies was Lee Motah, who was called "chief of the Comanches." He "adopted" Bishop Smith as an honorary Comanche chief in 1948 and in

1968 went to Philadelphia with others to "adopt" Bishop Fred P. Corson as an honorary Comanche chief and to present him with a war bonnet. Motah served several churches and also served at one time as secretary of evangelism in his district at Anadarko, Oklahoma.

McKinley Billy was a Choctaw licensed preacher who owned several oil properties. His will provided scholarships for every Choctaw and Chickasaw person who enrolled as a full-time student at Oklahoma City University.

Harry B. Long, a Muscogee, was licensed to preach in 1949 and studied at Oklahoma City University and Southeastern State College. He served churches in the Oklahoma Indian Missionary Conference (OIMC) for thirty-three years, then pastored Fort Yuma, Arizona, United Methodist Church. He created a street ministry, the Ministry of Presence, among Native Americans in Phoenix. He also served as a board member of the General Board of Global Ministries. From articles in *World Outlook;* journals of the Oklahoma Indian Missionary Conference; Noley, *First White Frost.*

11. Noley, *First White Frost*, pp. 222–224; Vernon, *One in the Lord*, pp. 42–43; "'A Mighty Rock in a Weary Land,' History of the First United Methodist Church of Shiprock," two-page typed paper provided to the editor by the Reverend Paul N. West.

12. 1952 *Book of Discipline*, ¶ 1202.

13. The letter is signed by several members of the Official Board, but the address of the church is nowhere on any of the materials. A copy of the letter was sent to the *Mississippi Advocate*, indicating a location somewhere in the South.

14. 15th Annual Report of the Woman's Division, 1955, p. 113.

15. 15th Annual Report of the Woman's Division, p. 120.

16. 15th Annual Report of the Woman's Division, p. 141.

17. 16th Annual Report of the Woman's Division, 1956, p. 101.

18. 16th Annual Report of the Woman's Division, p. 110.

19. 1952 *Book of Discipline*, ¶ 1590, "Radio and Film Commission"; 1956 *Book of Discipline*, ¶ 1581, "Television, Radio, and Film Commission"; 1956 General Conference, *Daily Christian Advocate*, "Will Show Methodist-Produced Films at Lyceum Theatre and Auditorium," p. 22; "Methodists Will Use Film to Recruit Missionaries from College-age Group," pp. 216–218; 1964 General Conference, *Daily Christian Advocate*, "Report Number Three of the Co-ordinating Council: Recommendations Concerning Methodist Periodicals," pp. 25–26. Harry Spencer said one problem with the Radio and Film Commission was that it had very few funds and did not have the authority to require cooperation from the boards. These problems were ameliorated in the 1952 legislation for TRAFCO. The actual purpose of the new agency was not totally clear, and Spencer wrote: "Which is more important, to get help from the local church so that the board can do its world-wide job, or to help the local church use wisely its own funds and the assistance of the boards so the local church becomes stronger and more effective?" Spencer transcript, p. 67.

20. Eugene L. Smith Report to Board, July 1954. The Quessua institutions were begun by The Methodist Episcopal Church. Copplestone, *Twentieth-Century Perspectives*, p. 580.

21. Paul Ellingsworth, "All Africa Conference of Churches," *The Encyclopedia of World Methodism*, 1: 87.

22. Charles C. West, "The Church and Communism," *New Christian Advocate* 1 (October 1957): 26.
23. Helen Loomis, "A Methodist Woman of Malaya," *World Outlook* 45 (May 1955): 38.
24. Helen Loomis, "Woman Magistrate in Singapore," *World Outlook* 49 (March 1959): 37–38.
25. Brumbaugh, "The New Women of East Asia," p. 25; Dorothy McConnell, "Helen Kim," *World Outlook* (June 1954): 40.
26. Eugene Smith, Report to Board, July 1954.
27. Author interview with Dr. Edward Poitras, February 1, 2001.
28. Language skills of missionaries during this era varied greatly. Ralph Dodge had also spent time in Africa with the local people, incurring much the same response from older missionaries around him, but without acquiring facility in the language. Poitras developed his skill to an impressive degree, not only preaching in the language but later engaging in significant translation work.
29. These comments are based on the interview with Edward Poitras but reflect a more informal gathering of information over a number of years that included conversations with missionaries in India, Japan, and Angola, to name only a few. As alluded to elsewhere in this document, "the women and their money," a phrase first expressed at the 1884 General Conference of the Methodist Episcopal Church, has been an area of continual discussion and dissension.
30. The possible exceptions include missionary children. The statement about superiority is based on numerous conversations with missionaries of various ages and some missionary children.
31. Leta Belle Mills Gorham, "Attitudes of the Missionary Wife," master's thesis, Southern Methodist University, May, 1960; in the United Methodist Archives and History.
32. Krummel, *Methodist Student Evangelism*, pp. 43, 48.
33. Krummel, *Methodist Student Evangelism*, p. 51.
34. This and the following quotation are from Smith, Japan Travel Report, June 1954.
35. Quoted from an anonymous Japanese person who had attended the Student Christian Fellowship. See Krummel, *Methodist Student Evangelism*, p. 61.
36. Smith, Japan Travel Report, June 1954.
37. Interview with Charles Germany.
38. Woman's Division, 16th Annual Report, p. 116.
39. Brumbaugh, "New Women of East Asia," p. 27; Valencia, *Under God's Umbrella*, pp. 97–112.
40. Copplestone, *Twentieth-Century Perspectives*, pp. 810, 1130, 1144, 1152. Pickett was made director of a study of mass movements and became the acknowledged authority on their use in evangelism in India.
41. *Lands of Witness and Decision* was issued in 1957 by the Editorial Department of the Joint Section of Education and Cultivation. Executive Secretary Eugene Smith wrote the opening, with articles on each country written by experts from the church.
42. "Methodism's Pink Fringe" was the title of an article in *Reader's Digest* by Stanley High. An overall history of this period in the context of U.S. Protestantism may be found in Martin E. Marty, *Modern American Religion* (Chicago: Univer-

sity of Chicago Press, 1996), pp. 354–375. A detailed narrative of the events surrounding the charges against Oxnam may be found in Ralph Lord Roy, *Communism and the Churches* (New York: Harcourt, Brace, 1960), pp. 233–260.

43. George D. McClain, "Pioneering Social Gospel Radicalism: An Overview of the History of the Methodist Federation for Social Action," in *Perspectives on American Methodism: Interpretive Essays*, ed. Russell Richey, Kenneth Rowe, and Jean Schmidt (Nashville: Abingdon Press, 1993). McClain's work is important in understanding the way that the church was influenced by the politics of the time.

44. *1958 Annual Report*, p. 6.

45. Field Newsletter of the Division of World Missions, June 1958, series 1, no. 19, pp. 4–6. The missionary newsletter is in missionary correspondence files at the United Methodist Archives and History.

5. New Frontiers

1. James L. Cox, *The Impact of Christian Missions on Indigenous Cultures: The "Real People" and the Unreal Gospel* (Lewiston, N.Y.: Edwin Mellen Press, 1991), p. 62. Cox quotes from a letter to him from Gould, October 6, 1983. Gould's idea of a school was not totally original, since the superintendent of the Alaska Mission, G. Edward Knight, had previously suggested a school. Knight's idea was that indigenous Alaskan Native Americans needed education to balance the secular society developing in Alaska. See Cox, pp. 58–59.

2. Cox, *Impact of Christian Missions*, pp. 64–65. The quotation is Cox's understanding of Gould's ideas.

3. The names of the members of the first board of trustees are listed in Leonard Perryman, "College on the Frontier," *Methodist Story* 1 (May 1957): 13–14. This promotional article does not mention Native Americans. At the 1956 General Conference, however, a delegate, Walter C. Gum of Virginia, speaking in support of the college proposal, said, "Alaska will be granted statehood in the future. It will become a great empire. It is, therefore, an urgent necessity to provide for training indigenous leadership for her future." See *Daily Christian Advocate*, April 30, 1956, p. 162.

4. Cox, *Impact of Christian Missions*, pp. 115–117, 126–127, 161–171, 179. In the 1970s the university lost its accreditation but did not quite close. Glenn Olds, the former president of Kent State University in Ohio, became president in 1977. He rescued the school from its near-termination, renamed it Alaska Pacific University, and saw it become a permanent United Methodist school in the U.S. See Cox, pp. 198–203.

5. His report was dated December 10, 1959, and titled "Christian Communication in Africa," Board of Missions, 1959, United Methodist Archives and History. The report is quoted at length to illustrate the information the board received for its planning. His observations about the attitudes of the missionaries does not tally with any of the interviews conducted for the current book. What is noteworthy is that it is the information that was reported. This disjunction between missionary analysis and outside expert commentary illustrates the difficulties for the board in assessing information and making decisions.

6. The board appears to have been successful. The random sampling of persons

interviewed for this project reveals they almost unanimously felt the board had prepared them well for what lay ahead; there were few surprises.

7. An example of this was India, where early missionary efforts had succeeded in acquiring land in the central areas of towns and cities. Much of this land was strategic and valuable. But the question of whether this property was in locations that allowed for church growth and outreach was rarely addressed.

8. David Halberstam, *The Children* (New York: Random House, 1998), pp. 47–209 passim.

9. Johnson, "Revisiting the Sixties," p. 111.

10. 1960 *Discipline*, pp. 26–27; *Daily Christian Advocate*, 1960 General Conference, p. 42; *Christian Advocate* 4 (May 26, 1960): 31. The official date at which a majority of conferences approved the amendment was April 8, 1958. The conference also expanded a resolution on race that had been passed in 1956. It added one significant phrase to a paragraph on changes brought about by the 1954 Supreme Court decision: "Let these things, however, be done in love lest the cause of Christ suffer at our hands." The effect of this addition was to weaken the struggle for justice, only incidentally mentioned. The resolution also asked: "That Methodists at national and international meetings of the church make provision for equality of accommodations for all races, without discrimination or segregation." Of course, this statement had no legal or binding power. See the 1960 *Discipline*, ¶ 2026.

11. Murray, "Racial Crisis," p. 6.

12. Murray, "Racial Crisis," pp. 7–8.

13. Memo from the Interdivision Committee to the Council of Bishops, editors of Methodist Publications, and Conference Missionary Secretaries in June 1960, United Methodist Archives and History.

14. Letter from Dorothy Gilbert, July 17, 1960, in Africa missionary correspondence, United Methodist Archives and History.

15. Report to Interdivision Committee on Foreign Work—Africa from Harold N. Brewster, September, 1960, United Methodist Archives and History.

16. Author interview with Fred Brancel, January 2001.

17. Letter from Charles and Mildred Reeve, May 1961, Africa missionary correspondence, United Methodist Archives and History.

18. Letter from Rolla Swanson, December 1960, Africa missionary correspondence, United Methodist Archives and History.

19. Material on the consultation is summarized or directly quoted from the document by C. Melvin Blake, report of The Methodist Africa Consultation, presented to the Division of World Missions, October 1961, and also presented as Exhibit A in the 1962 Report of the Executive Secretary.

20. The flexibility sought by the African church was a forerunner to concessions made much later by the General Conference of The United Methodist Church, which finally began to allow greater variety in local structures.

21. No author, "Angola," *New World Outlook* 84 (May-June 1994): 31.

22. The situation illustrates that the popular view of missionaries as agents of the government or even as secret operatives was just the opposite of reality for most missionaries.

23. Material from this section is taken from interviews with Fred Brancel and materials in the Angola files at the United Methodist Archives and History.

24. Interview with Ralph Dodge.

25. Stephen Supiya, *World Outlook* 23 (June 1963): 33.

26. Correspondence for a period during April and May 1962 is found in the correspondence files of the Board of Missions, Joint Section of Education and Cultivation, United Methodist Archives and History.

27. Manuscript entitled "The Changing Pattern of Mission Today," dated September 1962 and labeled "to Motive." Elements of the materials appear in several reports, but the document from the United Methodist Archives and History is quoted at length here because of the way that it summarizes the direction to which Eugene Smith was giving leadership.

28. Ralph E. Dodge, *The Unpopular Missionary* (Westwood, N.J.: F. H. Revell Co., 1964).

29. Thelma Stevens, *Methodist Woman* 22 (February 1962): 25.

30. Although many books chronicle the work of the time, *Fellowship of Love* was written by Alice G. Knotts specifically to address the role of Methodist women and the challenge of changing racial attitudes. Details about this aspect of the work of the Woman's Division are well covered in her book.

31. Josephine Beckwith, "Capturing Cities for Christ," *Methodist Woman* 19 (January 1959).

32. Joel Ajo Fernández, "Signs of Hope in Cuba," in *Sailing in Hope: Methodist Mission in the Caribbean*, ed. Keith Rae and F. Allen Kirton (New York: General Board of Global Ministries, 1993), p. 41; Henry C. Whyman, "Spanish Methodism in New York," *World Outlook* 52 (May 1962): 32–33.

33. Sam Tamashiro, "La Huelga Round Two," *World Outlook* 57 (June 1967): 28–35.

34. "Methodist Women Aid UCM, Texas Marchers," *World Outlook* 56 (November 1966): 45; Stan Steiner, *La Raza: The Mexican Americans* (New York: Harper & Row, 1970), pp. 280–289, 368–369, 374–377.

35. Vernon, *One in the Lord*, p. 86. Later, however, the Río Grande Conference membership grew more slowly, and in 1970 the conference experienced a slight loss in membership.

36. Pérez, *Cuba*, p. 81; Amy Lee, "Refuge in Miami," *World Outlook* 53 (September 1963): 28–30.

37. *1965 Annual Report*, Board of Missions, p. 19; J. Edward Carothers, "What We Learned from MUST I," *Christian Advocate* 12 (May 2, 1968): 11–12.

38. Author interview with Joanne Russell, October 4, 2001.

39. Interview with Joanne Russell.

40. "Cubans Elect Two Bishops," *Christian Advocate* 12 (March 21, 1968): 3; Pérez, *Cuba*, pp. 71–73.

41. Marjorie Vandervelde, "Church Women of Mexico at Work," *World Outlook* 51 (June 1961): 41–43.

42. Robert H. Conerly, "Methodism in Monterrey," *World Outlook* 53 (August 1962): 17–18.

43. Report of the India consultation, April 19–29, 1963, p. 12.

44. Joseph Szczepkowski, "Methodism in Poland," *World Outlook* 51 (February 1961): 8–9.

45. *1965 Annual Report*, pp. 58–60; *1968 Annual Report*, p. 67; no author, "Methodism in the Baltic States, Central and Southern Europe Central Conference," *New World Outlook* 85 (May-June 1995): 21–24, 31–35; "Methodist Church in

Estonia Still Alive" and "Czech Methodists Pick New Superintendent," *World Outlook* 52 (July 1962): 45.

6. Unease—Growing Pressures in the U.S. and the World Beyond

1. Author interview with Marston Speight, July 2000.
2. Several missionaries interviewed indicated that they might have stayed in the country where they served if they had been allowed. While many found it natural to return to the U.S., where they had family and friends, they often felt they were leaving "home" to do so. The policy of the board, however, was that they had to return.
3. *New York Times*, November, 1966.
4. Interview with Marston Speight.
5. Tracey K. Jones, *Our Mission Today: The Beginning of a New Age* (New York: World Outlook Press, 1965), p. 91.
6. Note the accuracy of his statement.
7. "Emergency Programs Slated for Africa," *World Outlook* 57 (March 1967): 49.
8. Nolan B. Harmon, "Zunguze, Escrivâo Anglaze," *Encyclopedia of World Methodism*, 2: 2632.
9. Nolan B. Harmon, "Nagbe, Stephen Trowen, Sr.," *Encyclopedia of World Methodism*, 2: 1697.
10. No author, "Mozambique," *New World Outlook* 84 (May-June 1994): 32.
11. Nolan B. Harmon, "Shungu, John Wesley," *Encyclopedia of World Methodism*, 2: 2152.
12. No author, "Zimbabwe," *New World Outlook* 84 (May-June 1994): 33; Robert J. Harman, *From Missions to Mission: The History of Mission of The United Methodist Church, 1968–2000* (New York: United Methodist General Board of Global Ministries, 2005), pp. 128–130; *Who's Who in The Methodist Church* (Chicago: A. N. Marquis Co., 1952), p. 944.
13. Letter from Bob and Dottie Hughes, September 17, 1964. United Methodist Archives and History, Africa letters.
14. *Rhodesia*, pamphlet prepared by Education and Literature Department of the Joint Commission of Education and Cultivation, Cincinnati, 1967.
15. Board of Missions press release, November 21, 1967.
16. Roy Harrell, *World Outlook* (October 1966).
17. Hee-Seop Song, "The History of Mission of the Korean Methodist Church," Ph.D. diss., Fuller Theological Seminary, 1987, pp. 275–279.
18. Anderson, "The Protestant Churches in the Philippines Since Independence," pp. 12–14; Nolan B. Harmon, "Guansing, Benjamin I.," *Encyclopedia of World Methodism*, 1: 1047. Guansing served a scant year in the episcopacy before dying in 1968, and Valencia resumed office, effectively serving as Filipino bishop 1948–1968.
19. Ben F. Youngblood, "The Task of Christian Education in Hawaii," *World Outlook* 53 (December 1963): 14–15. Hawaii eventually became a part of the California-Nevada Conference.
20. No author, "Minister from Fiji," *World Outlook* 38 (October 1948): 36; Fred Cloud, "Strides Toward Unity in the South Pacific," *World Outlook* 53 (October 1963): 24–25.

21. Krummel, *Methodist Student Evangelism*, p. 91; Krummel, *Letters*, pp. 26, 33, 35, 36, 40, 44; Krummel, "Church Unity and Mission in Japan," *Japan Christian Quarterly* (spring 1971): 100–101.

22. Castro became the director of the WCC Commission on World and Evangelism in 1983 and served as general secretary of the WCC 1985–1992. José Míguez Bonino, *Emilio Castro: A Passion for Unity, Essays on Ecumenical Hopes and Challenges* (Geneva: World Council of Churches, 1992), p. viii; *Who's Who in The Methodist Church*, p. 220; Library and Archives Team, World Council of Churches, Geneva, e-mail to editor, February 17, 2004.

23. Mortimer Arias, "Latin American Evangelicals Explore a 'New' Theology," *Christian Century* 85 (March 13, 1968): 336–339. Another report on the same conference was given in "Latin American Encounter: Church and Society," *Christian Century* 85 (February 28, 1968): 272–273.

24. Preceding Pagura and Valenzuela and retiring at this meeting were Sante U. Barbiere of Buenos Aires, Argentina, and Pedro Zóttele of Santiago, Chile. Also elected as officers of the Directive Committee were Celia Hernández from México, vice chair, and Gerson Rodrígues, Brazil, secretary.

25. Rae and Kirton, *Sailing in Hope*, p. 7; *1968 Annual Report*, p. 72; Nolan B. Harmon, "Latin American Evangelical Methodist Churches, Council of," *Encyclopedia of World Methodism*, 2: 1391.

26. Edwin H. Maynard, "By and for Latins," *World Outlook* 56 (September 1966): 20–21.

27. "Latin America I," "Latin America II," Quadrennial Reports: Reports of the Boards, Councils, Commissions and Committees of The Methodist Church to the General Conference (Nashville: The Methodist Publishing House, 1968), pp. 85–87.

28. "México," a newsletter of the Methodist Church of México, July-December, 1966, 1967, 1968; Olga Vela and Margaret Wade Campbell, "Cinco Centros," a brochure published by the Methodist Church of México (n.p., n.d.); September 1967 mimeographed letter from Margaret Wade Campbell to supporters in the U.S.; Mendoza, *Libro Conmemorativo*, pp. 100–101. The Pérez quote is from "Mexico," 1968.

29. "México," *Christian Century* 85 (May 29, 1968): 737–738.

30. Maynard, "By and for Latins," p. 21; Edwin H. Maynard, "Hernandez, Ulises," *Encyclopedia of World Methodism*, 1: 1117.

31. *World Outlook* 56 (April 1966): 45; quoted from the National Division Report in the *1965 Annual Report* of the Board of Missions.

32. Pinezaddelby went to the 1970 General Conference and spoke about Native Americans in the first report of the Commission on Religion and Race. Native Americans were also agitating for more recognition from the denomination. The OIMC had never been granted the right to elect members to the General Conference. The 1972 General Conference approved this right, and the first two persons who went were the Reverand Thomas Roughface and Minnie Toahty, who attended the 1972 General Conference as nonvoting members. Native Americans also asked for and eventually received the appointment of a Native American, Homer Noley, on the staff of the National Division. Report of General Superintendent D. D. Etchieson, Oklahoma Indian Mission Conference Journal, 1968, p. 33; Homer Noley, *First White Frost*, p. 220; *Daily*

Christian Advocate, April 22, 1970, pp. 100–101; 1972 *Discipline* ¶ 655.3. Noley was the first Native American on the missions board staff, and he served from 1971 to 1975.

33. Adolph L. Dial and David K. Eliades, *The Only Land I Know: A History of the Lumbee Indians* (Syracuse, N.Y.: Syracuse University Press, 1996), pp. 109–110, 159–160. The origin and nature of the Lumbees is controversial, but they consider themselves Native Americans and have been in what is now North Carolina for centuries. The name apparently derives from the Lumber River of North Carolina. The Prospect United Methodist Church was reported to have had a membership of six hundred in the early 1970s.

34. Minerva N. Garza, "The Influence of Methodism on Hispanic Women Through Women's Societies," *Methodist History* 34 (January 1996): 83; *They Went Out Not Knowing*, pp. 15, 40; editor interview with Mary Lou Santillán Baert, January 15, 2004.

35. Thelma Stevens, *Legacy for the Future* (New York: General Board of Global Ministries, New York: 1978).

36. The other members besides Raines were the presidents of the administrative divisions and the joint section (Bishop Gerald Kennedy, Mrs. J. Fount Tillman, Bishop William C. Martin, Bishop W. Ralph Ward, Bishop Lloyd C. Wicke) and other board members (Dr. Dow Kirkpatrick, the Reverend Allen Mayes, J. Wesley Hole, John Sagan, Mrs. Harold Baker, Mrs. Glenn Laskey), and the general secretaries as advisory members without vote (Mrs. Porter Brown, Dr. H. Conwell Snoke, Dr. Eugene L. Smith, and Dr. Gerald Clapsaddle).

37. Elected staff members were the heads of the divisions and the board treasurer. Other staff members were simply hired by the administrators of the board.

38. Author interview with Tracy K. Jones, July 2000.

39. Stevens, *Legacy for the Future*, p. 87.

40. Author interview with Sue C. Johnson, June 2001.

41. Most of this material is culled from the "10-Year Review of the Woman's Division of Christian Service," completed in 1974. The sense of loss that is written into the review is reflected in the statements here. A better analysis of the restructure and its effects would come in evaluation of the general board, taking into account the 1968 merger. The loss felt by the women did not diminish with the years, however. For example, a presentation by Woman's Division staff at a 2001 School of Christian Mission included discussion of the "agreements of 1964" and what they had meant and continued to mean to the organization. Thirty-seven years later, the women had still not forgotten what they had lost.

42. The full statement was: "The supreme aim of missions is to make the Lord Jesus Christ known to all peoples in all lands as their divine Savior, to persuade them to become his disciples, and to gather these disciples into Christian churches; to enlist them in the building of the kingdom of God; to co-operate with these churches; to promote world Christian fellowship; and to bring to bear on all human life the spirit and principles of Christ." 1964 *Discipline* ¶ 1176. This paragraph had been in the *Discipline*, with slight editorial changes, for several quadrennia.

43. 1964 *Discipline*, ¶ ¶ 1204 and 1207.

44. Murray, "Racial Crisis," p. 9.

45. Murray, "Racial Crisis," pp. 12–14.

46. James M. Lawson, Jr., "Black Churchmen Seek Methodist Renewal," *Christian Advocate* 24 (March 7, 1968): 24.
47. *Annual Report 1965*, Board of Missions, pp. 90–93, 135–146; *1968 Annual Report*, Board of Missions, pp. 75–77, 100.
48. Krummel, *Letters*, p. 39.

7. The Church—Mirror or Beacon?

1. Mott, *The Evangelization of the World in This Generation* (New York: Student Volunteer Movement, 1905), p. 7.
2. A detailed and careful treatment of reunification can be found in Russell E. Richey in *The Methodist Conference in America: A History* (Nashville: Kingswood Books, 1996). Chapter 16 expands on themes mentioned here. Much more detailed material on the Central Jurisdiction can be found in James S. Thomas, *Methodism's Racial Dilemma* (Nashville: Abingdon Press, 1992) and Murray, *Methodists and the Crucible of Race.*
3. Word that some of the men were going to introduce legislation to limit the fund-raising possibilities led the women to active lobbying before the General Conference, so that the issue never came to the floor.
4. Off-the-cuff responses in several interviews revealed that many knew of at least one, if not several, women who had carved out what were virtually "queen-doms" in their mission work. The point is not to examine this use or abuse of power but to recognize the fact that while men had opportunities in nearly every segment of society to establish such patterns, women had few. The importance is not that a few women may have been power-hungry but that the church became a place where gifted women could exercise leadership in a far less-restrictive environment than was available elsewhere.
5. Stories of these women in the late 1950s are being gathered by Barbara Troxell at Garrett-Evangelical Theological Seminary.
6. Further discussion of this is beyond the scope of the work attempted here. But a methodology that combines theology with history and study of social developments could give the more complex analysis that could be both instructive to the church and illuminating to historians.
7. Lamin Sanneh, "University Lecture in Religion in 1998," Arizona State University.
8. Although outside the era of this work, one of the most significant examples of this attempt to change the culture was the role of missionaries in bringing information about the abuses in the selling of infant formula in many developing countries. As a boycott developed, organizing in churches was aided by the information from missionaries who could report firsthand about the situations. See Harman, *From Missions to Mission*, pp. 392–395.
9. This theological and political position was even more direct. Dorothy Mc-Connell, daughter of activist Bishop Francis McConnell, coedited *World Outlook* for many years.

[Permissions]

Used with permission of AP/WIDE WORLD PHOTOS: Photos of Pearl Harbor, December 7, 1941, p. 36; Detroit race riots, 1943, p. 62; John F. Kennedy and John Glenn, p. 196.

Used with permission of the Commission on Archives and History, The United Methodist Church: Photos of Yoshimune Abe, p. 33; Alaska Methodist University, p. 198; Joseph P. Barták, p. 312; Eliza Bowman College, p. 17; Laura Jean Brooks, p. 113; Thoburn T. Brumbaugh, p. 141; Emilio Castro, p. 271; Sarah Chakko, p. 124; Citrus workers protest, Texas, cover, p. 237; Deaconesses in Nuremberg ruins, p. 95; Ralph Diffendorfer, p. 75; Ralph Dodge, p. 165; Vivienne Gray, p. 69; Eleazar Guerra, p. 107; Sara Estelle Haskin, cover, p. 28; Ulises Hernández, p. 312; Theressa Hoover, p. 290; Hunting Horse being photographed by Toge Fujihira, cover, p. 71; Mary Johnston Hospital, p. 39; Tracey K. Jones, Jr., p. 309; Z. T. Kaung, p. 47; Michi Kawai, p. 137; Helen Kim, p. 173; James M. Lawson, Jr., p. 207; Dorothy McConnell, p. 162; Bishop Arthur J. Moore, p. 13; Arthur J. Moore, Jr., p. 193; John Z. Moore family, p. 42; Stephen T. Nagbe, p. 312; Leo Nieto, p. 279; G. Bromley Oxnam, p. 189; Lydia Patterson Institute, p. 66; Guy Quetone, p. 152; Sue Robinson, p. 101; Alejandro Ruíz, p. 276; John Wesley Shungu, cover, p. 52; Eugene Smith family, p. 168; Ernst Sommer, p. 54; Henry C. Sprinkle, 162; Thelma Stevens, p. 303; Olin Stockwell, p. 19; James S. Thomas, p. 293; Rose Thomas, cover, p. 305; Betty Thompson, p. 193; Yoshi Tokunaga, p. 312; José L. Valencia, p. 182; Ethel Watkins, p. 159; Chen Wen Yuan, p. 128; Pedro Zóttele, p. 103; Escrivâo Anglaze Zunguze, p. 263.

Maps: of Indian American Methodists, p. 9; Korea, p. 31; Town and Country Work, p. 57; Latin America, p. 86; U.S. Community Centers, p. 114; Japan, p. 179; Africa, p. 217; the Philippines, p. 268; Spanish American Methodists in U.S., p. 282; Annual Conference Boundaries, 1956, p. 300.

Used with permission of the General Board of Global Ministries and Commission on Archives and History, The United Methodist Church: Don Collinson photo of returned Korea missionaries, cover, p. 145.

Used with permission of The Image Works: Selma protest March, p. 291.

Used with permission of the Library of Congress: Ansel Adams photo of Manzanar Japanese-American internment center, cover, p. 80.

[Acknowledgments]

Thanks to those who have contributed to this history through critical readings, editing and proofreading, design assistance, suggestions on resources, assistance in locating photographs, provision of helpful information, and advice and counsel:

Linda Allen, Hermitage, Tennessee
Alford Alphonse, Miramar, Florida
Norma Kay Bates, Nashville, Tennessee
Barbara Campbell, Asheville, North Carolina
Margaret Campbell, Pineville, Louisiana
Frank DeGregorie, Jerry Joerger, Wendy Whiteside, and the Communications
    staff, General Board of Global Ministries, New York, New York
Kitty Fisher, Mark Flory, and Laura Harris, Denver, Colorado
Betsy Fletcher, Columbus, Ohio
Charles Germany, Maplewood, New Jersey
Melynn Glusman, Chapel Hill, North Carolina
John Goodwin, Demarest, New Jersey
Joyce Hill, Norwalk, Connecticut
Ben Houston, Gainesville, Florida
Tracey K. Jones, Jr., Sarasota, Florida
Rosemary Skinner Keller, New York, New York
J. Lloyd and Edith L. Knox, St. Petersburg, Florida
Mary Grace Lyman, Port Washington, New York
Homer Noley, Wilburton, Oklahoma
Dana Robert, Boston, Massachusetts
Mark Shenise, United Methodist General Commission on Archives
    and History, Madison, New Jersey
Roy I. Sano, Oakland, California
Conrado and Anna Soltero, El Paso, Texas
Liza Stolz, Hamline University, St. Paul, Minnesota
Dwight J. Strawn, Seoul, Korea
Betty Thompson, New York, New York
F. Thomas Trotter, Indian Wells, California
Jose L. Valencia, Jr., Vestal, New York
Brenda Wilkinson, New York, New York
Barbara Williams and Chris Crochetière, Durham, North Carolina
David Wilson, Oklahoma City, Oklahoma
David Yoo, Claremont, California

[Index]

Abe, Yoshimune: 32, 43. *See also* photo, 33.

Acculturation: 85, 199, 306, 311.

Advance for Christ and His Church: for Alaska Methodist University, 197; for Danish Methodists, 250; founding and development of, 138–139; in Korea, 171; promotion of and income to divisions, 294–295; and Río Grande Conference support for, 67; and special for cars in Africa, 249, 262; and specials led to uneven funding, 204, 245; mentioned, 146, 192.

Africa: 97–102; 255–259; 219–233; and Africanization of church, 249; and Africans wanted to move into leadership roles, 218; and Angola Christians hostile to departing missionaries, 211; and apartheid, 163–166; as area of first Methodist mission outside U.S., 5; and Belgian Congo mission conference, 84–85; and Brumbaugh report on needs in 1960s, 202–203; building projects continued in Second World War, 82; and churches of developed indigenous leaders unevenly, 202; and concern of Board of Missions for Christians in newly independent Republic of the Congo, 209; and consultation in, 216, 218–219, 230, 238, 313; and gaps in Board communications about, 198–200; indigenous leaders of, 51–53, 254, 261–262; and missionary wives in, 176; and need for European languages in, 202; and spread of Communism in, 195; and treasurers in annual conferences of as dispersers of funds, 219; mentioned, 25, 205, 231, 241, 243, 315. *See also* photos,

cover, 52, 69, 101, 165, 263, 305, 312; map, 217; vignettes, 164, 262.

Africa Christian Advocate: 264.

African Americans: and Beckwith as urban worker in 1959, 235; and California resolution on, 65; congregations of in Central Jurisdiction, 23; employed by Board of Missions, 119; and Hispanic awareness of discrimination against, 67; incorporation into missionary work after Second World War, 93; as missionaries, 68–70, 150–151, 151 *n7*; and number of, 118; paid price for continuing racism, 299; and response to changes of 1950s, 148–150; and Sallie Hill as Haskin coworker, 29; situation of during Second World War, 63–64; and students protesting segregation in U.S., 204–206; and Woman's Division hospital for, 116; and Woman's Division schools for, 115; mentioned, xvi, 139 *n40*. *See also* Central Jurisdiction; photos, cover, 62, 69, 159, 207, 290, 291, 293, 305; vignettes, 150, 206, 292.

African Daily News: 227.

Agarwal, Dinesh: 139 *n40*.

Agricultural missions: in Africa, 69–70, 146, 212, 255; in Cuba, 90; in the Philippines, 184; in Sarawak, 70; mentioned, 109.

Aim of missions: 288.

Alaska: as mission conference, 281; Native Americans in, 72, 73; and number of Alaskan Americans, 119; and Seward Peninsula facilities, 157; and Woman's Division hospitals in, 116; mentioned, 163, 254.

moved to, 210; and missionary lot much better in, 214; and most Americans in were missionaries, 221; and whites of bought ammunition, 212. *See also* map, 217.

Southwest Mexican Annual Conference: 65, 283.

Southwest Texas Annual Conference: 236.

Spanish American Institute: 64.

Speight, Elizabeth: 256–259.

Speight, Marston: 255–259.

Spencer, Harry: 24, 139 *n39*, 163 *n19*.

Sprinkle, Henry C.: 23. *See also* photo, 162.

Starkey, Bertha: 77.

Stauffer, Elizabeth: 274.

Steele, Emmett and Henrietta: 151.

Steger, Clara E.: 46.

Stevens, Thelma: argued for desegregation of church facilities at 1944 General Conference, 119 *n25*; and book of, 4; challenged Methodist women to work for change, 233; comment of on change in General Conference voting, 284; as leader from MECS, 28; and views on 1964 restructure discussions, 285; work of to end discrimination described by African Americans, 70. *See also* photo, 303.

Stewart, Willa: 151.

Stockwell, Olin: 130. *See also* photo, 19.

Structure: of Board of Missions at church union, 11–14; and jurisdictions, 22–23, 148–149, 299; name changes in 1952, 153; and 1964 agreements, 284–285; strengths and weaknesses of, 298–302. *See also* autonomy, central conferences, central jurisdiction; map, 300.

Sucacas, Isaias: 103.

Sudan United Mission: 295.

Sumatra: 76, 167, 190.

Sundaram, Gabriel: 265.

Suzuki, Masahisa: 270.

Swanson, Rolla: 215–216.

Swedish church: 250.

Swiss Methodists: 102, 250, 274.

Sykes, Aline: 151.

Szczepkowski, Joseph: 250.

Taiwan: 190.

Takahara, David Yoshio: 32, 37–38.

Talbert, Melvin G.: 139 *n40*.

Tamils: 266.

Tanahashi, Kei: 81.

Tarahumaras: 275.

Taylor, Clagett and Patricia: 249.

Taylor, Prince A., Jr.: 261.

Television: and Angolan missionaries appeared on, 226; and images of violent struggles on, 231; not included in commission, 139 *n39*; as part of TRAFCO, 161; and videotape production, 295.

Television, Radio and Film Commission of The Methodist Church: 161, 294.

Templin, Lila and Ralph: 48–49, 125, 224, 316.

Texas Council of Churches: 236. *See also* photo, cover, 237.

Thailand: 270.

Thoburn, James: 15 *n9*, 123 *n26*.

Thomas, Farrell and George: 151 *n7*.

Thomas, James S.: 20, 148, 291. *See also* photo, 293; vignette, 292.

Thomas, Rose: 151 *n7*. *See* also photo, cover, 305.

Thompson, Betty: photo, 193.

Thompson, Betty Jane: 118.

Thompson, Elizabeth: 57, 58–59.

Tiger, Lena Benson: 72.

Tinker, George: 16–17.

Toahty, Minnie: 281 *n32*.

Tobas: 274.

Todacheene, Vina: 72.

Together: 161, 258.

Tohdacheeny, Carl and Stella Lee: 152.

Tokunaga, Yoshi: 135. *See also* photo, 312.

Town and Country Work: 12, 115–116, 157–158, 191. *See also* map, 57.

Translations: *See* literacy.

Truman, Harry S.: 67.

Tsosie, Herman Paul: 72 *n80*.

Tsukasaki, Enjie: 183.

Tubman, William S.: 261.

Tuiloveni, Setarcki: 269–270.

Turner, Mellony: 95, 97.

Turnipseed, Robert: 243–244.

Please mail order with check payable to:
SERVICE CENTER
7820 READING ROAD CALLER NO 1800
CINCINNATI OH 45222-1800

Costs for shipping and handling for sale items:
$25 or less, add $5.35
$25.01–$60, add $6.65
$60.01–$100, add $8.05
Over $100, add 8.5%

For billed and credit card orders:
WEBSITE: www.scorders.org
E-MAIL: scorders@gbgm-umc.org
CALL TOLL FREE: 1-800-305-9857
FAX ORDERS: 1-513-761-3722
A $2.00 charge will be added for billing.

$ 14.95 PAPERBACK   STOCK #3641
$ 21.95 HARDBACK   STOCK #2877